THE DOWNFALL OF THREE DYNASTIES

TSARINA MARIE OF RUSSIA

After the portrait by Winterhalter

THE DOWNFALL OF THREE DYNASTIES

by

COUNT EGON CORTI

Translated from the German by

L. MARIE SIEVEKING

and

IAN F. D. MORROW

WITH SIXTEEN ILLUSTRATIONS

BOOKS FOR LIBRARIES PRESS
FREEPORT, NEW YORK

First Published 1934
Reprinted 1970

STANDARD BOOK NUMBER:
8369-5419-X

LIBRARY OF CONGRESS CATALOG CARD NUMBER:
79-124230

PRINTED IN THE UNITED STATES OF AMERICA

PREFACE

THE Empress Marie of Russia, the wife of the Emperor Alexander II, left instructions in her will that all her papers, and especially the letters of her brother, Prince Alexander of Hesse, should be sent to him after her death. These papers, which have been most generously placed at my disposal by Prince Alexander Erbach-Schönberg, comprise the fourteen volumes of the diary of Prince Alexander of Hesse as well as thousands of notes and letters exchanged between him and his sister the Empress Marie. Prince Alexander kept his diary with great regularity from his eighteenth year until within a week of his death. In addition to the diary and correspondence I have also made use of the diplomatic correspondence preserved in the State archives of Vienna.

Prince Alexander's career took him first to one and then to another of the great European empires. His diary therefore affords us glimpses of what was passing behind the scenes on the European stage. It is in the nature of memoirs not to include the whole of history, and therefore to give the reader only a cross-section of events. In the case of Prince Alexander's diary this cross-sectional view of European politics is rendered wider by the personal relationship between the writer and the rulers of Europe. The purpose of this book is to give its readers a picture of the lives of these rulers that will also reveal their emotions and thoughts. It is intended to show how love, gratitude, and wisdom, or again folly, envy, and jealousy determined actions, entangled the threads of high politics, and sought to unravel them again. Passing moods and outbursts of feeling throw a revealing light upon the individual temperament. I have not hesitated, therefore, to quote at times spiteful sayings, bitter words, etc., exactly as they are recorded in the correspondence and diary, although I am very well aware

v

that they were frequently not seriously meant and were simply due to a momentary impulse. Hasty words and impulsive actions, nevertheless, often have fateful results both for private lives and national destinies. In the interests of truth the historian cannot therefore pass them over in silence.

I have sought to avoid any personal bias in the narration of events. It has been my endeavour throughout to arrive at the truth.

EGON CORTI

CONTENTS

ILLUSTRATIONS

THE DOWNFALL OF THREE DYNASTIES

CHAPTER I

CHILDHOOD[1]

AT the beginning of the nineteenth century youthful princes were educated along hard-and-fast lines. Permanent impress was left not only upon their minds and characters but also upon their outlook on life itself. In the case of a scion of the ancient princely House of Hesse—sovereign rulers over the little State of Hesse—parents and teachers alike must constantly have directed the child's attention to the great figures among his ancestors. To the lovely Saint Elizabeth of Thuringia, for example, who fed the poor in disobedience to her husband's wishes and for whom, when her husband demanded to be shown what she was carrying in her basket, the miracle was performed that turned a basketful of bread into roses. Or again to those Hessian princes who—partly as a result of real love and partly owing to a Byzantine desire to flatter—were known as the Merciful, the Virtuous, the Peace-lover, the Generous, the Pious, the Faithful, and the Righteous.

Prince Alexander of Hesse was born in the grand ducal palace in Darmstadt on July 15, 1823, as the fourth son[2] of the Hereditary Grand Duke Ludwig of Hesse and by Rhine, and his wife Wilhelmina Louise, Princess of Baden. His mother's four sisters shared the thrones of Russia, Bavaria, Sweden, and Brunswick—matrimonial alliances that vastly enhanced the prestige of their family. The title of Grand Duke only dated from the year 1806, when the then Landgrave Ludwig joined the Rhenish Confederation and was in return given sovereign rank and the title of Grand Duke by the Emperor Napoleon I. Prince Alexander's mother loved a country life. Until his father succeeded to the grand ducal throne, Alexander's parents spent the greater part of the year either at Rosenhöhe, near Darmstadt, which took its name from a superb rose garden, or else at the charmingly situated Heiligenberg, near Jugenheim, on a range of hills between Darmstadt and Heidelberg. Here the children lived in a little house of their own on the edge of a forest.

B   1

On attaining the age of six Prince Alexander was considered to have outgrown feminine ministrations and was given a tutor in the person of Captain Frey, who continued to supervise his education until he left his ancestral home. Captain Frey was a clever and intelligent man and took his duties very seriously, at times, perhaps, too seriously. Prince Alexander was taught with his pretty little golden-haired sister Marie, who was a year younger than himself. From the first day Frey kept a diary in which he recorded every least event and every little trouble in the lives of his pupils. He even started what he called a "Register of Tears and Grimaces" in which he faithfully recorded day by day how often they pulled wry faces or shed tears. At the end of the month the registers of the two children were compared, and the boy was sometimes taken to task for disgracing his sex by crying more often than his sister. After Alexander's father became the reigning Grand Duke as Ludwig II on April 7, 1830, he and his wife were compelled to spend more time in their capital, and as a result the children were left in the sole charge of their instructors at Heiligenberg. Captain Frey showed himself a second father to them. He commended Alexander's intelligence and kindness of heart, but censured in him a certain apathy hardly compatible with his years, as also a tendency to laziness.

Meanwhile Princess Marie was making her first acquaintance with the serious side of life. She had been told that she must have her ears pierced to take earrings. The prospect terrified her, and her teachers thought they would allay her fears by joking about them. To the intense interest and amusement of Prince Alexander they explained to the Princess all the different methods that might be employed. For example, her ear might be laid on the table and a nail driven through it with a hammer. Or else a needle might be run in at one ear, through her head, and out at the other. Or, better still, her ears might be cut off from her body, pierced, and then joined on again. Or, as a last resort, someone might shoot holes through both her ears. These well-meant sallies entirely failed in their object. The little Princess did not take them as jokes, but spent a sleepless night from sheer terror, so that the operation had to be postponed.

Fearing lest Alexander might grow too arrogant as a consequence of his princely birth and the servility of most of those with whom he came in contact, Captain Frey composed a little homily "On Pride", which he read to his pupil. In the course of it he spoke of those who pride themselves upon riches or beauty or noble birth, all of which are due to chance or good fortune. This was just as foolish, Frey said, as if someone should be proud of winning the first prize in a lottery. At the same time Frey did his best to inculcate in Alexander respect for persons of humbler birth or in subordinate positions. He instanced the coachman, who had ideas about the treatment of horses and maintained that more was to be achieved by kindness than by severity. Frey reminded Alexander that his own life and prosperity depended upon the loyalty of that coachman and of his fellow-servants.

As was the custom in all German princely houses, Alexander on attaining his tenth birthday in 1833 was given his commission as a Second Lieutenant in the First Company of the Hesse-Darmstadt Life Guards. The boy was much surprised, showed more distress than gratification, and did not express any pleasure until he saw the fine uniform that had been made for him.

On October 10, 1835, Halley's comet became visible. Its long tail gleamed across the heavens, and Prince Alexander was seen with pencil and paper drawing a picture of it while the servants stared in mingled terror and superstition. The whisper ran through the palace that the comet portended a great misfortune, and each wondered whether he would be the victim. The superstition seemed to be justified through a terrible and unexpected misfortune which soon afterwards overtook the grand ducal family. The Grand Duchess at the early age of forty-eight suddenly fell a victim to tuberculosis. The treatment that was then adopted and the complete ignorance of the nature of the disease revealed by the bulletins issued by the physicians rendered her recovery impossible. She was bathed in ice-cold water while the fever was at its height; she was weakened by continual blood-letting, and the medical diagnosis fluctuated between pneumonia, typhus, and some intestinal disease. It was hardly surprising that the Grand Duchess speedily succumbed to her malady. Thus Prince Alexander was bereft of his mother in early childhood.

At the time of her death the Grand Duchess had been engaged in extensive plans of a dynastic nature. She cherished ambitious hopes for the future of her daughter Marie, who was growing into a very pretty and charming girl. Her relationship with the Russian imperial family awakened in the

Grand Duchess hopes of marrying her daughter—though Marie was at that time barely twelve years old—to the heir to the Russian throne, the Grand Duke Alexander, who was eighteen years old in 1836. At the time of her death the Grand Duchess had taken the first tentative steps, and her proposals had met with an encouraging reception at the Russian court. The widow of the Emperor Alexander I supported the plan, which had matured so far by 1839 that the Grand Duke Alexander was that year sent to Hesse to make the acquaintance of the fifteen-year-old Princess Marie.

The delicate state of the Princess's health was a temporary obstacle in the way of these matrimonial projects. She fell ill most inopportunely at the very time of the Grand Duke's visit, and he was obliged to go away again without fulfilling his purpose. Once more the doctors failed to recognize an obstinate cold as the beginnings of tuberculosis. But her cough grew steadily worse. It was diagnosed as whooping-cough. Nevertheless, the care with which she was treated prevented the disease from making any great progress at the time. Nor did the promoters of the marriage relax their efforts. The negotiations between the courts in Darmstadt and St. Petersburg resulted in the Russian heir-apparent making a second visit to Darmstadt in April 1840. At the time of Alexander's visit Marie was fifteen years and nine months old. A child on the threshold of womanhood, delicately made, her illness lent an added spirituality and refinement to her features. Her inherent charm and artlessness united to form a delightful picture. When Alexander saw her again he realized that the change which had taken place in her in the space of a single year held out the greatest promise for the future. He showed her every mark of attention and presented her with a magnificent diamond bracelet. Superstitious people might have seen an ill omen for the future in the Princess's loss of the bracelet on April 8, 1840, when out walking. It is easy to imagine the consternation of the Princess and the whole family. The entire police force and the grand ducal servants were sent out to try to recover it. Meanwhile Marie was kept away from the Grand Duke Alexander upon one pretext or another. Fortunately the bracelet was returned that very evening by a girl who had found it lying on the road.

The succeeding days were spent in festivities of all kinds. On April 16th an official announcement was made of the betrothal of the Grand Duke Alexander to Princess Marie.

Thereby the fate not only of the Princess but also of her brother was sealed.

Meanwhile Prince Alexander had finished a portrait of his sister which he had begun some time before, and gave it as a present to his future brother-in-law. In thanking him the Russian heir-apparent seized the opportunity to convey to him the Tsar's invitation to accompany his sister to Russia and to serve for a time in the Russian army. It was thought in St. Petersburg that a mere child like Marie would find it easier to say good-bye to her home and to settle down in completely new surroundings if she knew that her brother and playmate was to keep her company. The change from a nursery in Hesse to the State apartments of an imperial palace in a country whose civilization and even language were totally different from those of her native land was indeed so immense that such a course could only be for the best. It is true that her brother, barely seventeen years old, was perhaps hardly to be called a support for his sister in her new life. Alexander himself would also for the first time be in strange surroundings and would be entering upon a career that his ignorance of the Russian language must make very much harder for him than for any Russian aspirant to military distinction. Everything would indeed conspire to help Alexander and his sister through their difficulties—the glitter of an imperial court, the unlimited power and might of the Autocrat of all the Russias, the unbounded adoration and respect still displayed in those days by the Russian people towards every member of the imperial house. Marie of Hesse was to experience with horror the profound change that came over the relationship between rulers and ruled in Russia in the course of her life.

The Tsar and Tsarina, accompanied by their daughter, the Grand Duchess Olga, came to Darmstadt in June 1840 to take Princess Marie back to St. Petersburg with them. The Tsar conferred a captain's commission in the Chevaliers Gardes upon Prince Alexander. The farewell to home and to loved ones, to Jugenheim and to all the places invested with childhood's happy memories, must indeed have been hard. Captain Frey could not forbear telling the new Captain of the Imperial Russian Chevaliers Gardes and future brother-in-law of the heir to the imperial Russian throne to hold himself erect, to refrain from poking his chin, especially when riding and dancing, and to learn to talk Russian as quickly and as perfectly as possible. With tears in his eyes Alexander's tutor gave expression to the warmest wishes and hopes for the future of his princely charge. A long handshake, and they parted. Their paths in life which had run parallel for a decade were now destined to separate, never to come together again.

CHAPTER II

AT THE IMPERIAL COURT IN ST. PETERSBURG

THE arrival of the bride was awaited with the greatest curiosity in St. Petersburg. Tall and slender, young and handsome, and possessed of a charm that was enhanced by a certain sensitive gentleness and kindness, the Grand Duke Alexander was shy in manner but a finished man of the world. There was therefore little cause for astonishment that he should have been popular in St. Petersburg society. Nor did the fact that he culled the rosebuds along his path cause court society in Russia to believe that he was much enamoured of his future bride.

At sixteen and seventeen years of age the two young Hessians suddenly found themselves transplanted from their quiet country life in Germany to the brilliant pomp and ceremonial of the Russian court. The Tsar himself was a man of such outstanding personality that he formed a natural centre round which the entire life of the court and the capital revolved. His most prominent characteristic was his love of the army and his desire to inculcate military order and discipline in all his subjects. At the outset of his reign Nicholas I's militarism was little more than a game and an amusement, but as time went on it became the ruling passion of his life. As Count Woyna wrote to Metternich[3] in 1841, the Tsar's mind was preoccupied with a system of military organization that he desired to see introduced in all its rigour into every branch of the administration. The sight of his splendid Guards regiments intoxicated him. He never tired of inspecting them. At manœuvres he assembled hundreds of squadrons of cavalry for the pleasure of seeing their thundering ranks brought to a standstill by a single word from his mouth. An acute observer declared that Nicholas I was inspired by the ideal of transforming all his dominion, including Poland, into a vast camp where he might train and drill his millions of subjects in exactly the same fashion as he was wont to drill his Guards regiments. His subjects were to march or to halt, to manœuvre, to advance to the attack, or to take up a defensive position, after the manner of his Guards at a single command from the imperial lips. Even the clergy with their hierarchic organization resembled so many regiments. At the head of each diocese came the bishop like a colonel giving orders which were carried out by the popes as his officers. Nicholas I would have preferred to see his subjects professing only one—the Greek Orthodox—form of worship, and to have speech, customs, and habits throughout his dominions as nearly as possible uniform.

In addition to his love of military display, Nicholas I also wished to maintain a brilliant court which should symbolize to all who visited it the might and majesty of the Autocrat of all the Russias. One festivity succeeded another. Although the Tsar had been happily married since 1817 to Alexandra, the eldest daughter of King Frederick William III of Prussia and Queen Louise, he did not deny himself flirtations with society beauties and the Tsarina's ladies-in-waiting. At carnival-time there were daily balls, and all these festivities had become more frequent during the years immediately preceding the Tsarevitch Alexander's betrothal, because the three daughters of the Tsar had also reached marriageable age. The eldest was the Grand Duchess Mary, who in 1837 in her eighteenth year had been married to the Duke of Leuchtenberg,[4] a young and handsome lieutenant in a Bavarian regiment of Dragoons. Then came the two younger daughters—the Grand Duchess Olga, aged eighteen in 1840, graceful and beautiful, and the charming but rather delicate Grand Duchess Alexandra, who was then fifteen years old. Around the imperial family were grouped all who were handsome, noble, ambitious, and rich— or at all events all who wished to be considered so in Russian society.

The Tsarevitch had hardly returned from his first visit to Darmstadt before everybody began to talk about the little Princess Marie of Hesse, whom nobody knew and of whom nobody knew anything. It was rumoured at the imperial court that this Princess of Hesse was in reality the child of Baron Augustus Senarclens von Grancy, one of the chamberlains of the Grand Duke of Hesse. Count Orloff, who stood high in the favour of the Tsar, mentioned this rumour to Nicholas I, who laughed as he answered: "Goodness me, who are you and who am I?—Who on earth can ever prove such a thing? And I should not advise anyone to suggest that the heir to the Russian throne is marrying a bastard!" When, however, St. Petersburg society talked about the Hessian Princess's delicate health, gossip could not be disregarded so lightly. In the end, of course, everyone bowed to the will of the Tsar and Tsarina, and was only curious to see what this "girl from abroad" would look like and how she would comport herself in her new surroundings.

Meanwhile Princess Marie had started on the long and uncomfortable journey by coach that was to bring her from Germany to Russia in company with the Tsar and Tsarina, who were still total strangers to her. Her brother was to follow later. The Prince wrote to his sister on May 3, 1840, to tell her about a visit he had paid to a marionette theatre, and enclosed in his letter a "menagerie report" about the various animals that had belonged to them. A young fox that they were both very fond of had died and had been given a "solemn funeral, suitable to his rank"; that is to say, it was wrapped in a sheet of fine paper with gilt edges and buried in the private garden among roses. The letter and its enclosure reveal what children the brother and sister still were at the time they were transplanted to Russia.

By September 7, 1840, Alexander and Marie were again united in the Tsar's great palace at Tsarskoe Selo. The Tsar determined to reveal to them the might of a Tsar of all the Russias in the most impressive manner by means of military parades. He took advantage especially of the occasion of Marie's state entry into St. Petersburg on September 8th, when the ladies of the court drove in magnificent coaches while the brilliant suite of gentlemen followed the Tsar on horseback. When the procession approached the capital and the road began to be lined by troops drawn from the Guards regiments, the Tsar rode beside the Tsarina's eight-horse coach in which was sitting the barely sixteen-year-old Hessian Princess, dazzled by the splendid spectacle. With wide-open eyes Marie gazed upon the strange Cossacks, Circassians, and Mohammedans in their Oriental dresses mounted upon richly caparisoned horses, looking even stranger by contrast with the regiments of the Chevaliers Gardes and the Hussars in their glittering uniforms. Overwhelmed by all this magnificence, Marie looked up nervously at her future husband who rode on the left of the carriage; but he too was a stranger, and her eyes searched the Emperor's suite for her brother as though she would say: "You are the one piece of home here to give me a little help and support amidst all this splendour and strangeness."

The nearer they came to St. Petersburg the denser grew the

crowds. As soon as the imperial coach appeared it was greeted by the thunder of cannon and the cheers of thousands of troops and spectators. The cheers had at least a familiar sound; and so had the Hessian National Anthem played by all the regimental bands. Otherwise everything was new—the Greek priests with the Metropolitan at their head, the strange rites and the Te Deum in the Cathedral, everything, everything. But the sound of the immortal hymn and the indescribably magnificent scene at last effaced the feeling of terrible shyness that had at first overwhelmed this child who was the focus of all eyes. It awakened in the young Princess the proud and exultant feeling that it was for her sake that all these hundreds of thousands had assembled, and that it was she who would one day at her husband's side have rule and dominion over them all. This feeling gave her the strength to go through the long and exhausting day until the brilliant illumination of the town at nightfall brought the ceremonies to a close. It was a foretaste of the exertions that awaited her in the future.

Amid these festivities St. Petersburg forgot the famine that had broken out during July and August in several of the central Russian provinces. In a corn-growing country like Russia this famine was a glaring testimony to governmental inefficiency. At the imperial court everything went on as before, and the courtiers did their best to suppress all unpleasant news. The Prince and Princess of Hesse were still far too young to realize the crass antitheses in the conditions of the empire. They gave themselves up unreservedly to the overwhelming impressions that crowded in upon them at the Russian court. The struggle for and the consolidation of their position there, as well as palace and love intrigues, completely filled their thoughts and minds during the next few years. It was a great drawback that they spoke hardly a word of Russian and could not even read the Russian script. At first Prince Alexander was a cause of embarrassment to the military authorities. Owing to his lack of experience it was difficult to assign him any specific military duties. Hence Alexander was given as tutor and mentor a general who had formerly commanded the Corps of Pages.

The Prince soon displayed an astonishing aptitude for learning. His sister adapted herself to her new surroundings with equal ease and rapidity. She was received kindly by the Tsarina and her future sisters-in-law, and treated by the

Tsarevitch with tender consideration and love; and she showed herself as desirous as her brother of mastering the Russian language as quickly as possible. Her linguistic tuition was aided by frequent conversations with the Orthodox clergy, who endeavoured from the outset to secure influence over the future empress. Marie knew that her conversion to the Orthodox Faith was unavoidable and only a matter of time. Her change of faith caused her the less difficulty in that from the very first she was attracted by the mystical ceremonies of the Orthodox rites. Thus the popes had an easy task. When she went over to the new confession on December 5, 1840, and received the name of Maria Alexandrovna, the last hindrance to the official announcement and celebration of her betrothal to the Tsarevitch was removed.

Her health, however, still remained unsatisfactory. Marie could not stand the tremendous differences of temperature between the overheated rooms and the intense cold outside. She began to cough again. It was obvious that she would have to exercise great care if she was to be completely recovered in time for her wedding in April. She spent all January and a part of February in almost complete seclusion. This gave rise to murmurs within court circles, where the Princess was still not very popular and where her serious and thoughtful demeanour, the reserve and quiet behaviour so remarkable in one of her years, were regarded with a certain measure of disfavour. The court would have liked the Princess to have been seen about everywhere and to be praising everything ecstatically: for St. Petersburg society was intensely vain. "Russian superstition", wrote the Austrian Ambassador, Baron von Meisenburg, to Metternich[5] on February 23, 1841, "is taking advantage of these circumstances to cast a bad horoscope for a union that is beginning with such sad omens."

The Princess was forced to be absent from the Easter festivities. A rapid improvement then set in, and on April 16th the marriage of the Tsarevitch with Princess Marie of Hesse-Darmstadt was solemnized according to plan. Prince Alexander strongly objected to the use of the word "Darmstadt" in all the official accounts of the ceremony. He himself wanted to be known as "Prince of Hesse and by Rhine", and he regarded it as a diminution of his dignity that in contradistinction to other Hessian princes the name of the little capital was added to his title—and such an unpleasant name at that (Darmstadt = Intestine Town). But the magnificence of the wedding ceremonial soon caused these minor grievances to vanish from his mind.

At eight o'clock in the morning of April 16, 1841, the young couple became man and wife. The Princess was surprisingly calm and collected during the ceremony. Prince Alexander, who had been promoted to the rank of colonel, was given the Order of St. Andrew as a memento of the occasion. "Nobody has ever earned an Order more easily," he said, "unless it can be looked upon as merit to have participated at a wonderful wedding-breakfast where the horseshoe table was loaded with gold plate and the ladies all sat on the left in Russian costume and the men in their gala clothes on the right." The wedding festivities lasted for a fortnight and made severe demands upon the strength of the new Crown Princess. One ball given by the newly wedded couple was so magnificent that even diplomatists whose eyes were accustomed to such spectacles were dazzled by the superb furnishing and decoration of the rooms, by the incredible luxury of the dresses and uniforms, and by the profusion of exquisite viands and exotic flowers. This was followed by a fancy dress ball for which forty-two thousand invitations were sent out. The festivities culminated in a review in which forty thousand men of the Guards regiments took part. Many a spectator among the Tsar's guests received a shock as he stood by the marquee reserved for the Tsarina and her ladies, and suddenly beheld forty regiments of cavalry thundering towards the marquee at full gallop, to be brought to a sudden halt at a few yards' distance by a word from the Tsar. In all that array of cavalry not a single horse projected beyond another by so much as a head!

Her marriage sealed Marie's fate. It also dissipated the anxiety of her family that illness might still bring their matrimonial project to nought. Prince Alexander noted the accomplished fact with a sigh of thankfulness. Then he and his sister plunged into the mad whirl of Russian court life. Everything was new to them, everything strange, so that their experiences were doubly exciting.

It was therefore not surprising that the sudden and mysterious accidents and fires that occurred with curious frequency in the imperial palaces did not make any very great impression upon their minds. Prince Alexander, for instance, made only a short reference in a postscript to a letter to his father on August 13 (25), 1841, to the collapse of the ceiling of the George Hall in the Winter Palace just after the Emperor had held a council there. The results must nevertheless have been terrible if anyone had been in the hall at the time of its collapse. The whole ceiling fell to the ground in a single piece, and the resultant pressure of air caused the doors to burst open outwards.

The first year that Marie and Alexander spent in Russia passed swiftly amid innumerable gaieties. Diplomatists shook their heads at the overwhelming succession of brilliant social gatherings. "So many demands are made upon one here by the amusements of carnival-time," Count Woyna wrote to Metternich[6] in February 1842, "balls, dinners, dances, fancy dress balls, succeed one another with such rapidity that even the most serious-minded person can find no time to attend to politics." And even so, Woyna was only invited to the larger functions. The small and intimate gatherings at the court at which only the imperial family and a few of their closest friends were present were barred to him. Indeed, Prince Alexander's diary at this time leaves one wondering how he ever managed to find any time for his military training. He was continually with the imperial family, and very often met the beautiful twenty-year-old Grand Duchess Olga, whom he admired intensely. In the mornings there were parades, official functions, and Church ceremonies. In the afternoons there were teas and card-parties. Military duties were apt to be neglected amid all these amusements. The nineteen-year-old Prince Alexander of Hesse, Colonel in His Imperial Russian Majesty's Guards, continued for a long time to be as ignorant of military matters as a recruit, and to be incapable of mastering a horse.

At one review the Tsar and Tsarina were standing outside their marquee, and with them the beautiful Grand Duchess Olga, in whose eyes Alexander was anxious to shine. The infantry preceded the cavalry, the bands crashed into a rousing march, and at the head of his cavalry regiment there appeared Prince Alexander. As he was passing the imperial family his horse shied. He was scarcely able to bring his sword to the salute before the animal wheeled and carried Alexander backwards past the Tsar. The Tsar's eyes followed him with displeasure. He leant over towards his aide-de-camp and whispered a few words. The aide-de-camp galloped after Prince Alexander and said something to him—an imperial reproof. Alexander was so furious that he could have shot his charger "Adonis" on the spot. There followed another ride-past, first at the trot and then at the gallop; then the famous charge towards the imperial marquee. Alexander had got a fresh horse, but at the charge the curb broke; "Curassier" bolted and made straight for the imperial family. Not until he came into violent collision with one of the officers in the Tsar's suite did the horse come to a standstill. The Prince rode back to his regiment covered with confusion. The Grand Duchess Olga smiled, the Tsarina took her home, the flags were furled. The Tsar, however, remained and, as Prince Alexander records in his diary on May 6 (18), 1842, waited until the Prince's regiment again came past. Then the Tsar rode suddenly up to the Prince, and looking at him sourly called out: "See to it that you get a horse that will carry you properly! Understand? You are no ornament to your regiment! You simply throw it into confusion."

The effect of these words may be imagined. The unhappy Prince went home, dined by himself in his room for the first time, and could hardly bear to appear in public again. He did not know that the imperial explosion of wrath had been preceded by several discussions between the Tsar and his brother, the Grand Duke Michael, who disliked Alexander, in the course of which they had decided that Alexander was spending too much time with the Grand Duchess Olga, for whose future quite different and far-reaching plans had already been made. It was, however, not easy to put a stop to Alexander's increasing devotion. At the social gatherings the young couple were constantly meeting. On June 4, 1842, a medieval tournament was planned at Tsarskoe Selo. The riders procured heavy suits of old German armour. New ones were made for the Tsar and for the Tsarevitch—these alone fitted their wearers; all the others came from museums and were intolerably heavy. The modern knights buckled on their armour with difficulty. Then they went to the apartments of the Tsarina, where she awaited them in medieval costume at the head of her equally picturesquely clad ladies. It had been arranged that each knight should kneel before his lady to receive from her hands a silken scarf in her colours. The armour effectively prevented the knights from carrying out this part of the programme. Only a single one who was clad in chain mail was able to kneel down. Their next problem was to mount their horses. The horses did not understand the mummery, and shied on seeing the crested helmets and on hearing the clank of the armour and the immense swords. It

THE GRAND DUCHESS OLGA NICHOLAEVNA

was easier for the ladies, whose dresses lent colour to a brilliant scene.

Prince Alexander rode beside the Countess Sheremetieff. She also had captured his wayward fancy, and by reason of her charming, delicately featured face was known by the pet name of "Bijoutte" in court circles. Among the couples at the tournament were to be descried all those men and women who severally played important rôles at the Russian court at the time. There was that dashing cavalier and aide-de-camp to the Tsar, Prince Bariatinsky, who was also an admirer of the Grand Duchess Olga; then the handsome but furtive-looking son-in-law of the Tsar, Duke Max of Leuchtenberg, the intimate friend of the Tsar's Chamberlain, Count Orloff, who was always entrusted with delicate and difficult missions; and there was the charming Vera Stolypin.

The populace had no share in the brilliant spectacle, from which they were excluded, and only a few specially invited guests were given the opportunity of watching the tournament. The lack of an audience spoilt the colourful display. It was denuded of the lusty humanity that formed the background to medieval tournaments. The armour and the heavy costumes became unbearable to their unaccustomed wearers. Moreover, the Austrian Ambassador voiced the feelings of those present when he said that they were disappointed at having gone to so much trouble and endured so much discomfort merely to make a splendid picture for the benefit of the trees in the park. Objections were useless, since everything was done in accordance with the Tsar's wishes. A dance at the palace followed the tournament.

In July 1842 the Tsar and Tsarina celebrated their silver wedding. This was the occasion for a further succession of festivals. The members of the Holy Alliance planned to make a special effort to show their friendship for the Tsar and his consort. The King of Prussia was to be present in person. The Archduke Charles Ferdinand represented the Austrian Emperor. So exhausted was the Prussian monarch by the interminable junketings that his one wish was to escape back to his own capital. The Archduke was instructed to make every effort to please the Tsar and Tsarina. Nevertheless, his inward thoughts and feelings were in no sort of relation to his outward bearing. He was shocked at the incessant parades and at the great tattoo given in the courtyard of the palace by twelve hundred trumpeters and bandsmen. Writing to

Metternich on July 28, 1842, the Archduke said[7]: "Your Serene Highness knows that His Majesty the Tsar believes himself to be an authority upon infantry, cavalry, artillery, and even naval matters; and that whenever so much as a Company is paraded in his presence he assumes its command himself. This has even happened three times with the boys at the Cadet Schools. One may venture to say that it is degenerating into a huge game." In thanking the Emperor Ferdinand for sending the Archduke to represent him the Tsar called the Emperor his "most faithful friend and closest ally".[8] It is evident that the Archduke carried out his mission with success.

The King of Prussia shared in the Archduke's privately expressed opinions. It was obvious to the world at large that no love was lost between him and the Tsar. Alexander of Hesse noted that both monarchs, while perfectly friendly in their demeanour, soon tired of each other's company and parted with mutual relief. The absolutist Tsar was not certain as to the plans and ideas of his brother-in-law, who had only lately ascended the throne. He feared that the Prussian King contemplated innovations, and was apprehensive lest he had it in mind to confer an "abominable constitution" upon his subjects. That being so, the Tsar preferred the representative of his Austrian ally. "In your country", said the Tsar to the Archduke, "innovations are fortunately not popular, and you set an excellent example in this way." A little later the Tsar went so far as to remark that at the time when the three monarchs had come together in Münchengrätz he had still had the feeling that they were marching all three in line. Now his impression was that there were only two of them left. In spite of his close relationship to its royal house, the Tsar's feelings of friendship for Prussia were less than those he entertained for Austria.

Prince Alexander always enjoyed the festivities as long as he could be near the Grand Duchess Olga. There was a certain amount of rivalry between her and her younger sister Alexandra. Olga had the greater social success. This annoyed the Grand Duchess Alexandra, whose displeasure was further increased by Prince Alexander's persistent attentions to her sister.

Meanwhile the Crown Princess Marie gave birth to a daughter on August 30, 1842. Those members of the imperial family who disliked her, and especially the Grand Duke

Michael, rejoiced that the child was not a son, and their hostility towards Prince Alexander grew more marked during the following weeks. In these circumstances it was fortunate that the Tsar suddenly and quite unexpectedly summoned Prince Alexander on September 7, and despatched him to Darmstadt on leave until the end of the year. The Tsar thought it would be good for Alexander to be parted from the Grand Duchess Olga for a few months.

Alexander left St. Petersburg with the feeling that his only true friend there was his brother-in-law, the Tsarevitch. The feelings of the Grand Duchess Olga remained an unknown quantity. The Tsar and Tsarina were superficially friendly. Everyone else was glad to be rid if only for a time of the young foreigner of nineteen who hardly spoke Russian, and who played at being the colonel of a Russian Guard regiment.

His leave was soon spent. At New Year, 1843, Alexander was once more in St. Petersburg and caught up in the whirl of parades and amusements. Although he still adored Olga Nicholaevna, Alexander's fancy was easily caught by the married women and girls he met night after night at balls and routs. Bijoutte Sheremetieff in particular attracted him, and he always found means to circumvent the attempts made by her jealous husband to restrain the too obvious attentions paid by the young prince to his wife. All these social claims left Alexander with little time over for serious pursuits.

It is amusing to learn what importance was attached to externals at the Russian court, especially in matters of uniform. Since the Emperor took the greatest personal interest in the equipment of his soldiers, everyone did their best to think of technical improvements or new and smarter uniforms. These were then—on one occasion a shako, for instance—inspected by the Tsar in person and tried out on selected men; the Tsarevitch *en raffole*, Prince Alexander remarked with amusement in his diary. The same thing happened over a cavalry helmet for the Horse Guards, an immensely heavy, electro-plated object, but which looked very smart to the spectator who did not feel its weight on his head. This was also tested in the presence and with the personal co-operation of the Tsar.

Meanwhile carnival pursued its gay course with entertainments at which the same cavaliers invariably met with the same ladies. That this had its drawbacks is obvious. If, for example, like Prince Alexander, anyone was in love with three ladies at once—for a third youthful beauty, Orange (Eudoxia),

c

had been added to the Grand Duchess Olga and Bijoutte—he might easily come between two fires and find himself in very awkward situations. The diary mentions the names of Bijoutte and Orange on every page, and the Grand Duchess Olga, who was only playing with her admirers but who nevertheless did not like them to run after other women, began to show a certain acerbity.

Bijoutte Sheremetieff wrought havoc also among other male hearts in the imperial family. Even the Tsarevitch succumbed to her charm, with the result that his young wife became seriously jealous at one time. Marie was expecting another baby, and thus could not meet her rival on equal terms.

Every opportunity was seized to encourage the Tsar's hobby —military displays—and an exceptionally brilliant review was held on February 9 (21), 1843, to celebrate the birthday of the Grand Duke Michael. Prince Alexander still smarted under the memory of the Tsar's reproof at the time when his horses had shown themselves so refractory. At this review he had his revenge. Prince Alexander records it in his diary under this date and not without a certain malicious pleasure. "The Tsar caused his brother to be saluted and cheered," he writes, "galloped up to him and embraced him, leaning from his horse in front of the whole line of cavalry. As he did so the Emperor's helmet fell off his head and rolled down over the crupper of his saddle, with the result that his horse was startled out of its wits. His Majesty was exceedingly incommoded." Nobody dared to laugh or even to smile, but at home in his own room Alexander gloated over this piece of "poetic justice".

Soon St. Petersburg began to gossip about the large heart of the Crown Princess's brother. He was even accused of love-affairs that never really existed. When a very pretty young Mlle Rehbinder married somewhat unexpectedly a M. de Ponamaroff it was whispered in the city, and the whispers also came to the Tsar's ears, that Alexander was the cause of the hasty marriage. Alexander, who was quite innocent in this case, was amused and perhaps a little flattered. "I think it is a heavenly joke", he confided to his diary. Meanwhile Bijoutte's flirtation with him had become public property owing to carelessness on his part. It was brought up for discussion at family dinners when they were alone—occasions that the Tsar used very ungallantly to call "fools' dinners'". But Bijoutte was *too* charming, Alexander thought, "intoxicating, enough to knock you over, terribly seductive". At times she even seemed to triumph over Orange in his fickle affections. He speaks of his "two loves" in his diary. Nevertheless, if it chanced that he did not see Bijoutte or Orange for any length of time, his vanity, but also a real feeling of affection, always brought him back again to the beautiful Olga among whose most ardent admirers he was always to be counted.

CHAPTER III

THE MARRIAGE OF A TSAR'S DAUGHTER

THE attentions paid by Prince Alexander and others in court circles at St. Petersburg to the tall and blonde Grand Duchess Olga were viewed with displeasure by the Tsar. He watched her closely. After the not very brilliant match made by his eldest daughter, Nicholas I was formulating ambitious plans for Olga's future. He had no intention of consulting her wishes, and as the Grand Duchess was by nature unlikely to experience a grand passion or to fight hard to secure the object of her affections, this was not likely to cause any special difficulties. The Tsar himself said of her that she had been too strictly disciplined in obedience to her parents' wishes to entertain any notions of following the dictates of her own heart. But since she was now over twenty her father was beginning to make an attempt to find an "establishment" for her—up to the present with little success.[9] Several marriage projects had already miscarried. At one time the Tsar had sought to marry his daughter to the Bavarian Crown Prince Maximilian, who later ascended the throne as Maximilian II.

During the early months of 1840 the Archduke Albrecht, the son of the Archduke Charles, the victor of Aspern, had been sent to St. Petersburg to get to know the Grand Duchess Olga and to pay his addresses to her. Since, however, the Tsar was then still hoping for the Bavarian alliance, the Archduke was forced to leave St. Petersburg without accomplishing anything, although, as Count Grünne[10]—the Austrian Emperor's aide-de-camp—who had been made privy to the secret, wrote to Ficquelmont, the charms of the Grand Duchess had soon awakened in Albrecht "the first raptures of a dawning passion". But when Nicholas I discovered that Maximilian had decided upon Princess Marie of Prussia he, in a fury at the "Prussians' want of candour", ordered the Tsarevitch to write to the Archduke Albrecht to say that the Grand Duchess had now been liberated from a tacit understanding that had been made on her behalf with the Bavarian Crown Prince. He was to add that Olga had asked her father to inquire whether the Archduke was still of the same mind regarding herself. Albrecht replied that since at the time of his visit to St. Petersburg he had not been vouchsafed a hearing, his father had made other arrangements for him, and that a binding engagement had already been entered into. The letter concluded with various compliments intended to soften the refusal.[11]

The Grand Duchess Olga's hand had thus been rejected twice within a short space of time. The Tsar was nevertheless determined to avenge his defeat at the hands of Albrecht by securing another Austrian Archduke for his daughter. This time his choice fell upon the Archduke Stephen, son of the Palatine Joseph, who was the brother-in-law of the Tsar. Since neither Nicholas I nor his daughter had ever set eyes upon Stephen, Austrian diplomatists wondered what could have inspired this choice, and finally decided that the Tsar must be desirous of using his daughter to gain influence in Hungary.[12] At all events, Austrian statesmen were resolved to be on their guard. Such was the state of affairs at the time of the carnival season in 1843, when Prince Alexander was still largely ignorant of the true situation. At the close of carnival Prince Alexander amused himself by compiling statistics of his dancing partners. He found that Bijoutte was far ahead of all the others, while the Grand Duchess Olga came next in favour. Since Bijoutte was a married woman, Olga Nicholaevna was looked upon by everyone as the woman to whom Alexander had paid the most attention throughout the season; a fact which explains her parents' anxiety.

An unfortunate accident for which he could not be held responsible soon afterwards contributed to increase Alexander's unpopularity. He caught the measles. The doctors failed to recognize the nature of his malady, and did not at once forbid him access to his sister and the Tsarevitch. As a consequence, they both contracted the illness. This upset all the imperial arrangements for several weeks and necessitated the isolation of the sufferers. The blame was unfairly—though perhaps naturally—ascribed to Alexander's carelessness.

Meanwhile the Tsar's youngest daughter, Alexandra, had been betrothed to Prince Frederick of Hesse-Cassel. Their engagement was regarded with mixed feelings by the Grand Duchess Olga, who was now the only remaining unmarried daughter. Although the most beautiful of the three sisters, Olga had suffered several brusque refusals of her hand.

Prince Frederick did indeed ignore certain symptoms in his bride which he must have observed. Tall and slender, almost too slender for a young woman of eighteen, Alexandra had for a long time past suffered from a persistent cough. Her lungs were affected. Nevertheless, the wedding was fixed for a date early in the coming year.

There was much discussion in St. Petersburg upon religious questions. The hostility to Catholicism displayed by the imperial court was nurtured by the revolutionary activities of the Catholic Poles. Nor was the court above making jokes at the expense of their Polish subjects. Prince Gagarin told the Tsarevitch one day about a Catholic village where on Good Friday one of the peasants had been bound to a cross to represent Christ in the procession. As he was being carried out of the sacristy his head came into collision so violently with the top of the low door that the wound had to be bound up. Meanwhile the priest had ended his sermon and wanted to conclude his remarks by pointing to the symbol of the Crucifixion. He could not understand why the procession failed to appear. "What has happened to Christ?" he inquired. The sexton replied: "He's in the sacristy swearing like a Turk!" This story amused the imperial family enormously. "The Crown Prince", Alexander confided to his diary, "laughed till he was nearly ill." The story was told in the presence of two Catholics, who were deeply offended.

In September the Crown Princess was happily delivered of a son. A salute of one hundred and one guns announced the event to the capital, and the rejoicing of the imperial family was great. On the day of the christening Prince Alexander was promoted to Major-General and attached to the First Guards Division. In thus honouring the brother of the Crown Princess, Nicholas I was really honouring the mother of his grandson. He entertained no feelings of deep affection for Alexander. When the Tsarevitch and his wife went to Darmstadt in October, the Tsar granted Alexander a long leave of absence. In doing so Nicholas I hoped that before Alexander's return Olga's betrothal to the Archduke Stephen would have become an accomplished fact, and would thus put an end to Alexander's too obvious attentions to her.

On first mooting in Vienna his proposal for a marriage between Olga and Stephen, the Tsar received the answer that the Archduke was intended for a "special position" in Hungary, and that it would therefore be undesirable that he should marry a princess who was not a Catholic. In August 1843 Count Nesselrode, the Russian Foreign Minister, had told the Austrian Ambassador[13] in some embarrassment that despite that reply the Tsar was still of the same mind and anxious for the conclusion of the match. The Tsar went still further. Knowing that the destinies of Austria, and especially in matters of foreign policy, were completely in Metternich's hands by reason of the incapacity of the Emperor Ferdinand, Nicholas I invited the Austrian Chancellor to meet him in Warsaw. Metternich refused. He foresaw that the marriage project would again come up for discussion. He revealed the train of his thought in the instructions he gave to Count Ficquelmont whom he sent in his place.[14] "The Tsar", he wrote, "is moving heaven and earth in order to arrange the marriage with the Grand Duchess Olga." And then he continued by bringing forward all sorts of arguments against mixed marriages and religious controversies.[15] The real reasons for Metternich's hostile attitude are hard to find. He must have realized that the imperial court and all educated people in the Habsburg dominions could only desire to see the bonds of friendship between the two empires strengthened by means of this marriage. Nevertheless, Metternich violently opposed it and adduced all manner of religious arguments which were really meaningless in his own eyes. A more probable reason for his opposition is that Metternich did not wish to strengthen the political position of the Palatine Joseph, whom he disliked. Moreover, he feared lest Joseph and the Archdukes John and Charles should seek to undermine his own paramount voice in the Government. Once before in 1811 the Palatine had been suspected of aspiring to the Hungarian Crown with the help of his brother-in-law the Tsar.[16] For some years after 1811 Metternich had had the letters that passed between the Empress Maria Ludovica and the Archduke "intercepted", and had laid them before the Emperor with an interpretation which represented them as an attack upon the marital honour of that monarch and the peace of the realm. He had thus sown the seeds of enmity between the Emperor and the Archduke, whom he also suspected of desiring to introduce constitutional government. It was small wonder that the relations between the all-powerful Chancellor and the Palatine were frigid in the extreme.

The marriage question once more brought Metternich into conflict with his old enemy. In a communication addressed to

Ficquelmont the otherwise cautious Chancellor let fall a remark which betrayed his continued antagonism to the Palatine.[17] "Since the Treaty of Vienna," Metternich wrote, "Hungary has not been ruled as a country should be ruled; and that is mainly the fault of the man to whom the government has been entrusted. . . ." Metternich regretted that the Palatine who made such difficulties for the "highest authorities" could not be easily removed from his post—a course which he regarded as the "only effective medicine". "Princes are not as easy to get rid of as ordinary private persons", he sighed.

All Metternich's dispatches and actions at this time reveal him to have been utterly opposed to friendship with the great Slav Empire and were directed towards the frustration of the Russian marriage project. Metternich also worked upon the Archduke Stephen in this sense. The Archduke was staying in Hanover when he received a letter from the King of Prussia's brother, Prince Charles of Prussia, in which the Prince told him that the Tsar was attending the manœuvres in Berlin and would like to make his personal acquaintance. Although he had already received an invitation to the Prussian court, the Archduke excused himself from going to Berlin. In doing so he was acting in accordance not only with Metternich's wishes but also quite evidently with his own personal feelings. His action mortally offended the Tsar, whose anger was not lessened by the fact that the Archduke's excuses were obviously invented to meet the occasion.[18] Despite this affront from his daughter's intended husband, Nicholas I still saw no sufficient reason for abandoning the plans he had made for her marriage. He returned to Warsaw, where he found Ficquelmont awaiting him to carry on negotiations which Metternich hoped would come to nothing. Although Metternich's refusal to go to Warsaw was in itself another affront to his pride, Nicholas I pretended not to notice, or else deliberately closed his eyes to, this new rebuff.

Metternich was not mistaken in his surmise that the Tsar's sole desire was to discuss the marriage project. Since the Chancellor was absent, Nicholas I opened his heart to his representative. Count Ficquelmont reported to Metternich[19] that the Tsar had in three audiences laid before him the difficult nature of the situation in which he found himself as the result of the miscarriage of his previous plans for his daughter's marriage. "I am just about to get my third daughter married," the Tsar said, "and you will realize how difficult it is for me and the Empress not yet to have arranged a marriage for Olga. She is twenty-one, and there is only one man in Europe at present who is a suitable match for her. That man is the Archduke Stephen. A family tie such as this would do us both a great deal of good politically. Believe me, it is necessary that the world should be convinced that the bonds which unite us are indissoluble." A friendship between the two imperial families thus sealed before the eyes of the world would—the Tsar believed—compensate for the harm done to the opinion held in public of the alliance by the vacillating attitude of Prussia. In accordance with his instructions, Ficquelmont returned evasive replies and pleaded all manner of difficulties, including that of religion. The Tsar replied that while all this might perhaps render his proposal a little more difficult of execution, it did not in any sense render it futile. "You know my daughter," he said, as it were appraisingly, "and you know what an angel of purity and goodness she is. You also know the spirit in which I have brought up all my children, that is to say, in the spirit of the strictest obedience, and this spirit will also guide her in her relations with her future husband. Thus the question of mixed marriages is reduced to this—that the religion of the children of the marriage must be determined beforehand, and of course they will be brought up in the Catholic faith." In other cases—the Tsar continued—there had been no such difficulties; why should this controversial attitude be adopted now? Ficquelmont admitted both to himself and to Metternich that the Viennese argument lacked force in several particulars. Hence he dropped these objections and sought for others: that the imperial family alone could decide in such a matter; that the ancient Catholic supremacy of the House of Austria prescribed great circumspection, and so forth.

Ficquelmont felt uneasy in his own mind after these conversations. "It is very much in our interests", he wrote to Metternich, "to maintain the intimate political relations with the Russian court that have subsisted hitherto. Hence we must as far as possible avoid allowing this marriage question to become the cause of a nascent coolness and reserve." That was all very true; but how was it to be avoided if Vienna persisted in its refusal? Metternich's influence with the imperial family was so great that the Archduke Stephen would not have refused the marriage if the Chancellor had urged it upon him for reasons of State. Moreover, Stephen's father—the Palatine

—was in favour of the marriage. The Grand Duchess Olga was not only a very pretty girl but also the greatest match in Europe. Nicholas I was profoundly dissatisfied with his interviews with Count Ficquelmont. "After all the plans I had made," the Tsar said quite openly to the Count, "I will not conceal from you that I had hoped that you would send him [the Archduke Stephen] to me this winter. I had also hoped that our young people would at last make up their minds and that the date of their marriage might have been settled at once. If it is not to be, and if I have to forgo this project, I shall certainly meet your Emperor with the same sentiment of respect for His Majesty and his illustrious family, but I shall go to the interview with my feelings painfully hurt."

The Tsar was at last convinced that Metternich was resolutely opposed to his plan. Hence he decided to circumvent him and appeal direct to the imperial family. "The issue between myself and your Government," he said to Ficquelmont,[20] "has been settled. Prince Metternich has done his duty. It remains for me as a father to approach the family in a matter that concerns the happiness of my child." Thereupon the Tsar wrote to the Dowager Empress Augusta, and gave the letter to Ficquelmont to forward. The Count naturally informed Metternich at once. Metternich lost no time in working upon the feelings of that very pious lady by suggesting all manner of religious scruples to her. Her reply to the Tsar was couched in practically the same words as Ficquelmont had used in Warsaw. But Fate was preparing an awkward dilemma for Caroline Augusta and her advisers. The Tsar remembered that when his sister Alexandra had married the Palatine Archduke Joseph in 1799 the question of mixed marriages had been raised. He caused a search to be made in his archives which resulted in the finding of a secret agreement that had been concluded with the Emperor Francis in which the question of reciprocity in marriages between the two imperial houses found a definite solution. It had been agreed that grand duchesses marrying into the imperial Austrian house should be allowed to practise their form of religion freely for their own persons, and that archduchesses marrying into the Russian imperial house should enjoy the same freedom. Neither Metternich (who was not then in the Austrian service) nor the Dowager Empress, who had been the fourth wife of the Emperor Francis and not married to him until 1816, nor of course Ficquelmont, had the least idea of the existence of this secret agreement. Hence the

Dowager Empress was utterly taken aback by receiving a letter from the Tsar which completely annihilated her objections and those of the Austrian diplomatists.

After informing her of the secret agreement the Tsar wrote:[21] "So solemn an agreement leaves no room for doubts, Madame. It has the force of law, is binding upon both empires, so long as it is not retracted by mutual consent. I cannot suppose, Madame, that the Emperor Ferdinand wishes to break a family pact signed by the Emperor Francis; and is it not my duty to defend the rights gained by my father? So long as this document exists, Madame, I neither *can* nor *will* relinquish my just hopes. I am sending Count Orloff to bring it to the Emperor. It now rests with you and him, Madame, to decide whether the work of the Emperor, your late husband, is to come to naught, or whether his blessing shall rest upon a new bond between our two families, as we hope with all our heart. May God guide you, Madame."

Being firmly determined to have his will, the Tsar now turned to his brother-in-law, the Palatine Archduke Joseph, the father of the Archduke Stephen, and wrote to him saying that he hoped in the near future to have the pleasure of making the personal acquaintance of his son, who might at the same time meet the Grand Duchess Olga. If the young people liked one another, it would give him great pleasure to see her become a member of Joseph's family. To his great surprise, he added, Prince Metternich had raised quite unexpected difficulties over the preliminaries, and the Dowager Empress had failed to respond to his overtures, alleging the difference in religion as an insuperable objection. She had averred, moreover, that the agreement made before the first marriage of the Archduke was no longer valid, because everything had changed since then. The Empress had not, indeed, specified exactly what had changed. The Tsar then spoke of Orloff's mission and of his hope that the Emperor Ferdinand would regard the wishes of his father. In this event he requested that the Palatine would not oppose the marriage, and that the Archduke Stephen would soon come to St. Petersburg to judge for himself whether he and the Grand Duchess were suited to one another.[22]

Actually, the Archduke Joseph was in favour of the match. Moreover, in view of the Tsar's well-known determination and the great importance that he seemed to attach to the marriage, he did not think it politically wise to oppose it. At the same time he remained a loyal—one is almost tempted to say, too loyal—subject of his mentally deficient Emperor, and of his younger brother the Archduke Louis, whom Metternich had raised to power in Vienna. He wrote to the latter,[23] leaving the final decision with them, and thus delivered himself utterly into Metternich's hands, for the Emperor was a cipher and the Archduke Louis, as Metternich's creature, was absolutely subject to the Chancellor's will.

Metternich smiled sardonically over a letter written to him on the same day[24] in which the Palatine very rightly pointed out that an autocrat does not easily brook refusal, and that a rebuff might endanger the friendship and unity hitherto subsisting between the two empires. The arrival of Count Orloff was a complete surprise to Metternich. He had thought that the Tsar had been sufficiently discouraged by the previous rejections. When Orloff appeared in Vienna on February 17, 1844, Metternich realized that the struggle must still continue if he was not to see the marriage that he regarded as so undesirable realized after all. On the very same day he wrote a memorandum[25] which he addressed to the Archduke Louis and to the influential feminine members of the imperial house, saying that a struggle was in progress between the Churches to which the two imperial families belonged. The refusal of the Austrian imperial family was based upon assumptions which Metternich deemed to be of vital importance in justifying the moral attitude of the Emperor and the political attitude of his Government. Moreover, the Pope must be approached. The Archduke Louis was well coached, and when Count Orloff came to see him, he said exactly what Metternich had told him to say.[26] Count Orloff did his best to combat his excuses. The children should be brought up as Catholics, and the result of such a marriage could not but be beneficial to the position of the Catholics in Russia. A close alliance between the two empires was urgently necessary. All these arguments proved unavailing. The Count made his adieux to the Archduke in great perplexity, only to find that Metternich's refusal was even more uncompromising, though better disguised in diplomatic phraseology. During their discussions Metternich made frequent references to the Pope; and in two voluminous "Expositions",[27] which are composed in his usual didactic and condescending style, he stated that the Emperor Ferdinand— whom everyone knew to be a puppet with no mind of his own—would never consent to the marriage if the Pope were opposed to it. The transposition of the whole affair into the domain of religion produced considerable reactions in the case of the two Empresses and of the Archduchess Sophie. On February 22nd, that is to say immediately after his interview with Orloff, the Archduke Louis visited the young Empress and found her in a state of great excitement. "I do not wish to interfere in anything," she said,[28] "but if I can help toward any good end, especially if it is a matter concerning religion and the Church, I am ready to exert myself to the very utmost. This is the first I have heard of Count Orloff's mission, and I must say that I should also be opposed to the marriage. I do not think the Pope should be applied to; it will only put him and the Church into an awkward position. The Tsar is a Greek; he will promise anything, and then not fulfil his promises. It seems odd to wish to force anyone into marriage, and that a princess should apparently be proposing to a prince. If the Emperor were to give way on this point, it would be a sign of great weakness. The whole city is against the match. I know for a fact that even the Protestants are opposed to it, and would consider compliance to be beneath the dignity of our Emperor. I do not wish to mix myself up in anything, but I will do all I can to prevent this marriage."

Meanwhile Metternich had been urging upon the Palatine, both directly and through the Archduke Louis, to reply to the Tsar that in such a matter he, the Palatine, must defer to the decision of the head of the family. Although it was against his feelings and interests, the Palatine obeyed most faithfully. And thus the Tsar's double effort again failed of success. Prince Metternich proudly told the Papal Nuncio in Vienna that Count Orloff had left Vienna on March 5th with empty hands. "The Emperor, our illustrious master," wrote Metternich to Count Lützow in Rome on March 7th,[29] "has taken his stand over the religious question and subordinates political interests to it." Metternich was probably right. Nevertheless, it was he and not the Emperor who did so, and who thereby laid the foundation of the estrangement between the two imperial houses which was later to be intensified over questions of international policy by short-sighted Foreign Ministers, and finally to lead to open enmity. The women of the imperial household certainly contributed their full share towards the dissension by their sanctimonious bigotry.

Metternich communicated the whole history of the affair to Count Lützow in his long private dispatch of March 7th, in the way in which he wished it to be presented to the Pope, and which he referred to complacently as being of monumental worth. A surprise came to him from Rome. His Holiness had been interested in the matter, but, as he confessed openly, his interest had been of a "painful, oppressive" nature. "That is between you and me," Count Lützow reports the Pope as saying,[30] "but I protest against being supposed to interfere in any political concerns which might arise over the question of the marriage of an Austrian Archduke with a Russian Grand Duchess. My opinion can only affect the religious side of the affair. Above all, I must be permitted to regret . . . that my name has been adduced and that I am thus to be burdened with the odium of the refusal. . . . You have crucified the unhappy Pope," he concluded.

The latest efforts of the Tsar had ended in another mortifying defeat. It was fortunate that the subject of these negotiations, the young Grand Duchess herself, knew little of the humiliating fashion in which she was bargained for. She was having a thoroughly good time at the carnival in St. Petersburg, even though her youthful admirer Prince Alexander of Hesse was absent, and was enjoying the attentions of the Tsar's handsome A.D.C., the gallant Prince Bariatinsky, who was over head and ears in love with her. Prince Alexander, who was staying in Darmstadt, knew little of the affair, and the newspapers spoke first of one marriage project and then of another, so that it was impossible to obtain any true idea of what really was happening.

The Tsar felt the failure of Orloff's mission very acutely. He had beforehand said to the Austrian Ambassador, Count Colloredo,[31] that, whatever the issue, his sentiments towards the Austrian monarchy would never change, but that his feelings as a father might be hurt and his personal relations with the imperial family disturbed. Now the Tsar was angry and offended, and the antipathy with which he regarded the Catholic religion in his realm was, as was only to be expected, intensified. Moreover, his lack of success had become known in court circles in St. Petersburg, and this still further irritated the wound to his pride. His depression was increased by sad events within the imperial family. The Grand Duchess Alexandra, who had married Prince Frederick of Hesse-Cassel in January 1844, had developed serious lung trouble. The doctors who were treating her were utterly incapable, and professional etiquette led them always to give a unanimous opinion about any sick person of high rank, including the treatment to be adopted. In consequence they went on making the delicate, tubercular girl take ice-cold baths every day instead of sending her away to a milder climate.

In April 1844, when Alexander of Hesse returned to St. Petersburg after some months in Darmstadt, he found the widowed Grand Duchess of Mecklenburg-Schwerin and her pretty daughter Louise as guests of the Tsar. Prince Alexander had by now realized that he must abandon all hope of obtaining the hand of the Grand Duchess Olga. When he found that the Princess Louise was interested in him because he was a smart cavalry general and had a German name, and that she finally fell genuinely in love with him, he was flattered and soon grew to be so much attracted that for a time he seriously considered marrying her. As so often happens, a stupid joke on the part of an outsider spoilt everything at the critical moment. He did not declare himself, and the two ladies went away at the end of August with heavy hearts.

On July 29th the Grand Duchess Alexandra succumbed to her illness, after the premature birth of a still-born son. This tragedy affected the Tsar profoundly. "The Tsar's outbursts of grief", wrote Alexander in his diary at the time, "are truly heartrending in such a strong, powerful man."

The period of mourning which followed interrupted the whirl of gaiety at the court. The summer was spent in St. Petersburg, the autumn at the palace of Gatshina, where life was "delightfully rural". Riding and hunting were the chief occupations. Once again Prince Alexander was much in the company of the Grand Duchess Olga. She was very charming to him and, as he says in his diary, "made a complete conquest" of him. When the cold weather came and the ice-rinks were opened, skating in her society was added to other pleasures. In December the young Prince's persistent attentions to Olga began to cause the Tsar and Tsarina some anxiety again, for they were looking for a better match for their last unmarried daughter. Their eldest daughter had married beneath her rank, and her husband's life was by no means immaculate. All the more did the imperial couple hope for an especially brilliant marriage for their second daughter. Hence, when Prince Alexander was sitting beside the Grand Duchess Olga at dinner on December 18th, she told him that her mother had expressed the wish that she should not go on to the ice alone with him. "People are gossiping", she added. The fact that he was forbidden to meet her on the ice

intensified in Prince Alexander the desire to see the Grand
Duchess Olga secretly or openly on all possible occasions. He
took every opportunity of doing so. She, however, was only
playing with the young man. One day she would be charming
and gay, another time cold and "prickly". Prince Alexander
stayed away from the skating-rink for a full month because he
found that the Grand Duchess treated him so brusquely. But
he liked to fancy that she was playing this part against her will,
and therefore took a sort of perverse pleasure in the situation.
His belief in this theory was strengthened because the Grand
Duchess Olga would at some soirée suddenly be charming to
him again. And so he fell deeper and deeper in love with her.
He dreamed that he was engaged to her and overflowing with
happiness, and that the Tsarina had divined his secret thoughts
and was inquiring if he had not something to ask of her. The
awakening was all the more painful, and drew the Prince to
linger under Olga Nicholaevna's window in the hope of catching
a glimpse of her. But the more Prince Alexander was attracted
to Olga, the more reserved did the Tsar become. He had not
shaken hands with the Prince for a very long time. A sarcastic
"Good morning, Highness", or "charming lancer", or a stiff,
low bow in silence was generally all that the Tsar vouchsafed
him. At soirées and dinners he was no longer permitted to sit
beside Olga. Nevertheless, he did not cease his attentions to
her. At a party on February 28, 1845, the Prince produced
the manuscript of a gallop he had composed for the Grand
Duchess Olga's Regiment of Hussars. He had had the score
decorated with a delightful miniature representing an officer
in Olga's regiment on horseback. As he was presenting it to
her, the Grand Duchess gave orders for it to be taken to her
room. The Prince had hoped to be allowed to play his march
to her, and felt badly snubbed. On the evening of the same
day she suddenly asked him directly: "Tell me, have you
heard about the new campaign in the Caucasus? Have you
never had any idea of going there?" He could not immediately
find an answer. He stammered: "Yes, of course." But it gave
him a great shock that it should be Olga who put this question
to him.

Her suggestion remained in the Prince's mind. When he
mentioned it to his brother-in-law, the Tsarevitch said that he
thought it was very natural that a young officer should wish
to encounter the enemy, and that he rather envied him the
chance. The Tsar, he was sure, would have nothing against it,

and had in fact asked him not long ago whether he did not think that Alexander would like to go to the Caucasus. Prince Alexander took the hint. He was not the only young man who, ostensibly for the sake of coming under fire but actually on Olga's account, was going out to take part in the distant campaign. Bariatinsky was being sent there too. Things had been so manœuvred in each case that they themselves asked to be permitted to go in order that the real reason should remain secret from outsiders. Olga now markedly avoided the Prince. If Alexander made a movement to sit by her side, there was always a lady-in-waiting or someone else who sat down beside her first. She refused flatly to go for walks with him. In a word, everything was done to prevent the possibility of any declaration before his departure.

The birth on March 26th of a second son to his sister, to whom the name of Alexander was given, improved the relations between the Prince and the imperial family. The newly born infant was immediately appointed Colonel-in-Chief of the Carbineer Regiment Astrachan, and entered as an ensign in the Preobrajensky and Pauloffsky Regiments and the Hussars of the Guard. It seemed a good deal for an infant that had only just come into the world. Meanwhile Alexander's father assented to his going to the Caucasus. He told the Tsar, who replied: "Then I am entirely at your service."

Before his departure Prince Alexander attended the baptism of his sister's second son. At the festivities the Grand Duchess Olga flirted with other men and absolutely neglected him. This put him into a furious temper. Various little happenings show how attached Prince Alexander was to Olga in spite of his apparent fickleness. At an auction for some charitable purpose to which everybody had contributed something, Alexander paid four hundred and twenty silver roubles for a slip of paper on which Olga had done a little water-colour drawing. At dinner someone told the Tsarina that Olga's picture had fetched a very high price. The Tsar's inquiry as to who had bought it elicited the embarrassed reply that they had not caught the name. Olga, who knew, blushed furiously.

Just before Alexander's departure help came to him from an unexpected quarter in his love-affair with Olga. A court lady named Maria Stolypin professed herself anxious to further his cause. She was obviously not altogether sure of the Grand Duchess's feelings. Hence shortly before Alexander was due to leave she invited Prince Emil von Wittgenstein, a friend of

D

Prince Alexander's and who was accompanying him on the
campaign, to come and see her and talk the affair over. Maria
Stolypin told Prince Emil that the Tsarina had recently said
to her that both she and the Tsar had noticed that there
appeared to be some sort of understanding between Olga and
Alexander. "I am not sorry", the Tsarina had said, "that
Alexander is going away. He is beginning to pay too much
attention to Olly. At the same time," she had added reflectively,
"I don't know but that I would have done the same in Olga's
place—or even more."

Maria Stolypin, who was half in love with the Prince herself,
spoke to Alexander on the subject, and without being asked
promised to sound Olga and find out whether she really liked
him—a point, as he wrote in his diary on April 6, 1845, upon
which he was very doubtful. Alexander replied that he had
never dared to speak of love to the Grand Duchess, that he
had no illusions, and that he realized that with her great
beauty Olga might expect to marry a better man. Maria,
however, found an answer to every objection. The only man
left for the Grand Duchess to marry was the Archduke Stephen;
and this match was opposed not only by the policy of Austria
but also by the Archduke himself, whose heart was given
elsewhere. They parted after exchanging vows of absolute
secrecy. The next two days were taken up in paying farewell
visits. The Tsar and Tsarina were particularly friendly and
kind, and the Tsarina gave Alexander a little gold ring for
luck. The Grand Duchess Olga, less affected than her parents
by the parting, asked the Prince to read the ninetieth psalm
every morning as a talisman, as she did herself. The Prince
handed her her mantilla for the last time and kissed her hand
with deep emotion. She remained unmoved. Much more tender
and cordial was his farewell from his sister and the Tsarevitch,
who was genuinely attached to him. "Sacha was very much
affected," Alexander noted in his diary; "dear, good fellow."
On the following day, April 20th, the young Prince left for
the distant Caucasus via Nijni-Novgorod.

The Caucasus was a continual source of trouble to the
Russian monarchy. The Tsar was anxious to extend the
Russian frontier southwards in order to establish himself firmly
upon the western shore of the Caspian Sea. The warlike
mountaineers, however, resisted stubbornly the advance of the
infidel foreigner. It had already happened on several occasions
that Russian expeditions had met with disaster in that land of

rugged and inhospitable mountains, and generals of excellent repute had lost fame and honour over it. Now Count Vorontsoff, an exceptionally energetic and personally brave man, had been sent out as general in command of an expedition from Tiflis to northern Daghestan to demonstrate the might of the Tsar. The leader of the enemy was a fanatically religious man, brilliantly clever in military matters, named Shamyl. Prince Alexander was attached to Vorontsoff's staff; and since the intention of the Tsar was merely to keep him away from the court for a time but not to allow him to incur any particular danger, the Count was instructed to keep him at headquarters and only occasionally to send him up to the fighting-line when conditions rendered it safe. People in St. Petersburg had very little idea of what a campaign was like in those parts. So the twenty-two-year-old Prince—a general without a command— brought with him a suite consisting of twenty-seven persons, including a doctor, a valet and a scullion, as well as two non-commissioned officers, twelve Cossack orderlies, and thirty-seven horses. The sensations of Count Vorontsoff—who was in addition responsible for the Prince's life—may be imagined. Nevertheless, Alexander's military ardour and pleasing personality soon gained him the friendship of the Commander-in-Chief. The campaign did not proceed as smoothly as had been hoped. On the contrary, despite early successes, the expeditionary force escaped annihilation only with the greatest difficulty. Shamyl maintained iron discipline among his troops, and allowed them neither to smoke nor drink. Following the example of the Sultans and Tsars of the seventeenth century, he had a pipe driven through the noses of smokers, and had the nose cut off any man who got drunk. Prisoners who fell into his hands were often subjected to the most appalling tortures, to a lingering death, and to mutilation of all descriptions. But these enemies of Russia fought with almost fanatical bravery.

At first all had gone well for the Russians. As the result of an offensive movement in northern Daghestan, Shamyl's troops were forced to retreat towards Dargo, the capital of Circassia. Shamyl evacuated Dargo, occupied the heights above the city, and inflicted heavy losses upon the Russians as they pressed along the valley. For days on end Count Vorontsoff and his suite were continuously under heavy fire. When the Russians came into Dargo they found only one house intact. This was the house in which the Russian officers had been kept prisoner.

Seventeen unfortunate Russians had been incarcerated here, and had been slaughtered at the approach of the enemy. It was a little shed consisting of a single low room, which was so damp that fungi grew in it. Here the prisoners had lain upon dirty straw with chains round their necks; and since no light penetrated they had been obliged to grope for the wooden spoon wherewith to eat the mess of maize porridge that constituted their only food. Otherwise, Dargo lay in ruins. On the hills round about, however, blazed the enemy's bivouac fires. The Russians encamped in the city, but were unceasingly harassed by the Circassians' fire. The capture of this low-lying town soon showed itself to be only a Pyrrhic victory. The commanding positions remained in the hands of the rebels. On July 6th Shamyl recaptured Dargo. On the 9th the position of the Russians who were still encamped in the valley was critical. Food and ammunition were running short, reinforcements were attacked and annihilated. Nevertheless, Count Vorontsoff did not lose heart, but tried to evolve some plan whereby he might extricate his men from their perilous situation. Now Prince Alexander really came to understand what war meant; and in the next few days proved himself to be personally brave and gifted with military qualities.

There could now be no further question of the Russians remaining near Dargo. "We are all", wrote Prince Alexander, who kept his diary as carefully as ever even while he was at the front, "terribly depressed. Ours is certainly not an enviable position. It is impossible to stay here. We cannot return by the way we came, and before us lie only forests and unknown paths." Count Vorontsoff remained calm and resolute. He announced that they would march out into the plain, seek fresh provisions, and then return to Dargo. It was thus hoped to disguise the inevitable retreat. In order to lighten the baggage, the Commander-in-Chief, most of the generals, and Prince Alexander had their tents burned so that they might afterwards order the men to follow their example. It rained in torrents. The whole column moved down the valley ankle-deep in mud and "in very low spirits", as Alexander admits. Scarcely had the enemy observed that they were leaving the camp than they began to fire on them from every direction. It was with difficulty that the reduced rearguard maintained its position. The transport of the wounded, of whom several were in a dying condition, was almost impossible. The further retreat on July 14th was only made possible by a series of bayonet charges.

"Soon", says Prince Alexander, "we found ourselves surrounded on all sides and our few infantrymen were hard put to it to prevent an attack. Men, horses, guns, baggage animals, and wounded were crowded together in a close column. All at once panic seized upon this mass, and they all rushed forwards with wild shouts in terrible confusion. The Count [Vorontsoff] was almost run down. . . . I had drawn my *shashke* [sword] at the first moment, but we soon found that the enemy had only attacked the end of the column." After this attack had been successfully repulsed, the retreat continued. Then the vanguard came upon strong stockades occupied by the enemy, and was unable to storm them. Count Gurko, who was in command of the main column, rode back and forth, tried everything he could think of, and finally lost his head completely. Nothing remained but to make a desperate attempt to break through. This was done. Prince Alexander took part in the assault with a drawn sword in one hand and a pistol in the other. Although undertaken with great bravery and much cheering, the attack nevertheless failed under the murderous fire of the enemy. Numerous officers of Vorontsoff's personal staff fell; the casualties totalled two hundred wounded and killed. Since it was impossible to proceed, they had no choice but to await a relieving force. They were obliged to encamp under enemy fire. Shells and bullets fell in the immediate neighbourhood of the Commander-in-Chief and the Prince, who were preserved as by a miracle, while fresh casualties occurred every minute. "It is an uncomfortable feeling," wrote the Prince, "and this has been the longest day of my life. . . . If relief does not come soon, the whole detachment will be wiped out. The enemy grows ever more numerous, and I am writing under shell-fire." A postscript added at half-past seven that evening says: "The gunfire of our rescuers has just made itself heard. Their files can be seen through a telescope. The good news has spread like wild-fire, and all our men have begun to sing. We immediately hurled two of our precious shells at the enemy, but they replied with six, one of which fell on the legs of a sapper who had lain down to rest and tore the poor devil's body to bits. His pleasure was short-lived. Apart from that it is universal throughout the camp. Only someone who has been in a similar position—the most critical that can be imagined— can understand the joy caused by such opportune succour. Vorontsoff would have been lost without it. Hardly a man could have escaped."

Shamyl was now obliged to cease his attacks. He had already had visions of the utter destruction of the enemy columns and of the capture of the Commander-in-Chief, and had said to his second-in-command: "Take that Russian detachment and you may keep all the booty." According to an escaped prisoner, Shamyl's wife had asked to be given the prince who was with the Russians. Fortunately, Shamyl's hopes proved illusory. The retreat continued more or less unmolested under the protection of the fresh troops until the fort was reached from which the expedition had set out. Indescribable joy reigned when the men saw the red roofs of the fort in the distance and heard the salutes being fired to greet them on their return. Everyone congratulated everyone else on having survived the dangers. The last two months had seemed like two years to most of them. Hardly had he got back to the fort than Alexander of Hesse wrote to his sister:[32] "I can tell you this much—that three days ago I hardly dared to hope that I should see you again, my dear Marie. Now that it is all over I am glad to have been through it. It is worth a great deal to a soldier to have looked death in the face so often. You feel that you have more right to wear the uniform."

The result of the campaign was actually very slight. The conquered places had had to be evacuated again, and a good 20 per cent of the whole expeditionary force, including three generals, had been lost. On the other hand, the enemy capital had gone up in flames, and the whole undertaking could therefore be represented as a sort of punitive expedition. The young Prince was given the highest military distinction, the Cross of St. George, which delighted him beyond words. A few days after his return to the fort he left the expeditionary force and went first to a Caucasian spa, where everyone received him with open arms. The Tsarevitch's handsome young brother-in-law, surrounded as he was with a sort of halo of military glory, and decorated with the St. George's Cross, was fêted with balls and other entertainments, and his diary speaks of many charming dancing-partners. "Emil [Wittgenstein] and I are the lions of the hour here [at Kisslovodok]; the ladies positively run after us. This is a part that I should not care to play for very long, but for a few days it is quite amusing, and makes a pleasant change after the life of the camp."

He had heard little of the Grand Duchess Olga all this time. She never gave a thought to Prince Alexander, while he still dreamt of her. He was looking forward to appearing before her as a warrior who had proved himself in the face of the enemy, and who had been decorated with the Cross of St. George. Then he heard that the Tsarina and Olga were going to Italy together and were to spend the winter in Palermo. It was quite clear that he and Olga were to be kept apart at all costs. In Nikolaeff, Prince Alexander met the Tsar and his brother-in-law. They took him with them to Sebastopol, where a splendid review of the Black Sea Fleet took place. Then there were even more brilliant cavalry manœuvres in which no less than a hundred and eighty-nine squadrons of cavalry and twenty-two thousand horses took part. Although Prince Alexander had come straight from the front and must have regarded the Tsar's playing at soldiers with a somewhat sceptical eye, the sight of this vast body of cavalry made an indelible impression on him.

The Tsar departed to Italy after granting Prince Alexander leave of absence for six months. The Tsar went by way of Prague, where the general in command, the Archduke Stephen, greeted him as he changed coaches. The Archduke's manner was constrained, merely formally polite; he avoided any reference to the marriage project. Their short interview was therefore extremely disagreeable to the Tsar.

The Tsar might have kept clear of Prague just as he kept clear of Vienna. His passage through Prague where, as he knew, the Archduke Stephen was bound to receive him, was therefore in some sense a new attempt to see whether the Archduke would not take the opportunity to rebel against Metternich's tutelage. He did not do so. The interview was a fresh disappointment to the Tsar, and his temper suffered noticeably under it. None the less, he was determined to go to Rome to see the Pope and find out whether the stumbling-block really lay there. Various reports indicated that this was not the case and that only Vienna was to blame. Count Ficquelmont had been instructed to smooth the way for the Tsar while he remained within Austrian territory, but also to watch him and if possible to interrogate him. At a dinner in Pavia the Count had a long conversation with the Tsar. Ficquelmont found him testy and irritable.

"Do you remember", the Tsar said, alluding to the vacillating policy of Prussia under the new king, Frederick William, "my saying that of the three who were once allied only two remained? Now I am afraid I may be left alone. You know how attached I have always been to the Emperor Francis with all my heart and soul, as well as on principle. My principles have not changed; I remain the same in spite of everything."

"It is natural", Ficquelmont interjected, "that differences of opinion should sometimes arise between two great countries; but that should not affect the great political system upon which the future of Europe depends."

"That is just what I feel," replied the Tsar. "But I receive fresh proofs every day that there is no particular desire for understanding; that is to say that *I* am no longer wanted. I am obliged against my own wishes to prepare to be left alone."

"In moments of crisis, Your Majesty will always find us at your side," Ficquelmont endeavoured to pacify him, "for we have not changed."

"God grant that it may be so," replied the Tsar somewhat doubtfully. Ficquelmont knew what alarm his report of this conversation would occasion in Vienna. In consequence, he did his best to tone down the effect to suit Metternich's views in the dispatch that he sent to the Austrian Chancellor from Cremona on October 19, 1845, by saying that he believed it was not necessary to lay too great weight upon the Tsar's words. The Tsar, he thought, having just come back from the great manœuvres where he had paraded six army corps, including the Guards and the Grenadiers, almost the whole of his cavalry, and later on also the Black Sea Fleet, was still intoxicated with the sense of power, and therefore felt every divergence from his will as a grave insult. Matters would settle down. Every endeavour must be m⌐Je to dissuade him from his projected visit to Rome. Evidently the Austrian diplomatists' consciences were beginning to prick them for having said too much in the Pope's name.

Their attempt to persuade the Tsar failed. Nicholas simply ignored them. He was firmly resolved to go to Rome. Nevertheless, he was quite ready to have a second iron in the fire in case the Austrian scheme should after all prove abortive; for he was himself beginning to feel that the Grand Duchess Olga would be made to look foolish if the Austrian marriage project came to nought. Prince Alexander Gortchakoff, the Russian Minister at Stuttgart, laid the foundations of his future great career by suggesting the union of the Crown Prince of Württemberg with the Grand Duchess Olga. The Tsar went to Palermo to join his wife and daughter, and this latest plan was discussed between them. The Grand Duchess Olga was ready to agree to anything. She left the matter of her marriage entirely to her parents. The Tsar would still have greatly preferred the Archduke Stephen; and in the autocratic consciousness of his power and position as ruler of so mighty an empire could not believe that Vienna could be so blind as flatly to refuse the Tsar of All the Russias after he had made so many advances. On December 13, 1845, he went to Rome to try to remove the objections—if any—that the Pope entertained to the Austrian marriage. Some time previously the Tsar had sent a special envoy to the Pope,[33] to ask that the Holy Father should calm the consciences of the two Austrian empresses by spontaneously giving his blessing to the projected union, in the assurance that the children of the marriage should be brought up as Catholics. Rome immediately decided to turn the opportunity to account to obtain better conditions for the Catholics in Russia. Cardinal Lambruschini also communicated this intention to the Papal Nuncio in Vienna. Metternich, whose chief source of information lay in intercepting and copying the correspondence of others, discovered the contents of this letter. He at once impressed upon the Austrian Ambassador in Rome, in guarded but sufficiently clear language, that since the Tsar was not to be dissuaded from going to Rome he must so work upon the Pope and his advisers that they would not respond to the Tsar's advances but would make all sorts of demands of him. These instructions were drawn up in his own hand, and show the immense importance which Metternich attached to not having his diplomatic game spoilt by Rome.

In his overweening self-esteem, Metternich rated his influence with the Vatican too highly. The Pope was determined to seize the opportunity to extract as many and great concessions as possible from the Tsar. Gregory XVI was a reactionary Conservative,[34] who regarded the network of railways that was beginning to cover Europe as a "mighty vehicle of revolution", and objected to the invention of machinery for a reason which has grown fashionable again to-day—that the saving of human labour would be destructive to the well-being of the people. On December 13th he received in private audience the Tsar, who kissed his hand respectfully. The only information about what passed at the interview is contained in a report handed by Cardinal Acton to the Austrian Ambassador. According to this statement, the Tsar and the Pope had not discussed the marriage. It is, however, probable that the Pope gave the Tsar to understand that no further obstacles would be put in the way of the marriage if the Tsar kept his promises. The Tsar thought that it had at one time been indicated that if he made his peace with Rome no further difficulties would be made in Vienna. He now felt that he had done all that could be expected of him by his visit, by kissing the Pope's hand, and by his promises about the Catholics in Russia, and that he had only to go to Vienna to have the matter settled. What he had heard in Rome, however, awakened in him such distrust of the Austrian policy that he realized that in Austria and in Austria alone was to be found the opposition to the marriage. Hence he determined to be very cautious and reserved and not to declare himself until he saw that the path was at last being made smooth for the project that he had pursued so obstinately.

When he arrived in Vienna on the evening of December 30th he was received by Prince Liechtenstein, who had been appointed to be his equerry and who was an old friend. As a general rule the Tsar greeted him with an embrace, but this time he omitted to do so. Liechtenstein saw a pale, stricken man, whose features had taken on an expression of grave severity that was rare in him. The Tsar stepped into the imperial coach that awaited him. His mien grew even more gloomy when he heard that the Archduke Stephen, on whose presence he had reckoned with certainty, was not in Vienna.

During the drive the Tsar remarked that he was anxious about the health of the Tsarina, who had remained in Italy; and that he himself had been feeling out of sorts for some days and needed rest.

Meanwhile the carriage had reached the city. The Tsar took his companion's hand, and said: "My dear Liechtenstein, do you remember our being here together ten years ago? Everything was different then. I was very happy and contented in those days." Liechtenstein replied: "My wish, and I am convinced also that of all our people, is the happiness and welfare of Your Majesty." To which the Tsar answered gravely and decidedly: "God knows that I have always remained the same. My sentiments are unalterable, but I am no longer wanted." At that moment he noticed that the outriders were turning across the St. Michael's Square into the palace, and inquired: "Where are you taking me?" "To the palace, Your Majesty, by the command of my Emperor." The Tsar immediately had the carriage halted, and declared that on no consideration would he go there. Liechtenstein adduced the earnest desire of the Emperor and did his best to persuade the Tsar, but in vain. "To the embassy," he cried. "I am not feeling well enough to go to the palace. I order it."

The outriders turned again, nor had Liechtenstein's representations that the Emperor and all the court were expecting them the slightest effect. The Tsar simply asked the Prince to go immediately to the palace and make his excuses, and request that this evening should be granted him to collect his strength for the next few days. Arrived at the embassy, the Tsar retired at once and gave orders that he was not to be disturbed. Nevertheless, Liechtenstein entered unannounced in order once more to suggest his going to the palace. The Tsar returned a decided negative.

On the same evening the Tsar sent Count Orloff to Prince Metternich to tell the Chancellor that everything had been done that had been desired, that the Tsar had been in Rome, had shaken hands with the Pope, had even kissed his hand, and made promises to him. If Vienna was satisfied, the marriage could proceed. But if further difficulties were made, Orloff had instructions to terminate the interview abruptly and declare the matter at an end. And in that case the Württemberg project was to be carried out. Orloff soon saw from Metternich's attitude that he wished to spin out the proceedings still further, and when, after hearing about the Tsar's meeting with the Pope, the Chancellor said: "Well, well, so the affair has made a good beginning . . ." Count Orloff answered brusquely: "No, my dear Prince, the affair has not begun. It has come to an end—but not in the way you think."[35]

This completed the breach, and the Württemberg marriage was decided upon. The failure of his plans determined the Tsar's attitude during the remainder of his visit, which was much shorter than had originally been intended. He took no pains to disguise his anger and annoyance. Wherever he appeared he was cold and reserved, ostentatiously ceremonious in his behaviour to the members of the imperial family. It was obvious that the Tsar purposed that his manner rather than his words should declare his state of mind. Whenever possible, the Tsar avoided all conversation with the ladies of the imperial family. At a review he was as reserved as at court. While the troops were forming up for the march-past, and the Emperor Ferdinand took up his stand beside the carriage containing the imperial ladies, Nicholas rode right away from them into the middle of the parade-ground, so that the Archduke Albrecht who was in command did not know what the Tsar intended doing and was obliged to fetch him away when the troops began the march-past. On the other hand, Nicholas spoke much and often with the sentries posted outside the embassy, and inquired whether they were sufficiently provided with food and drink. The embassy was so lavish in this respect that Liechtenstein was obliged to protest lest there should be too much of a good thing. The men were actually served on silver dishes, which struck Liechtenstein as very amusing. He saw one old hussar with a silver bowl in his hand, and after he had eaten everything he carefully passed his fingers round the dish and licked them. It seemed as if the Tsar wanted to show how highly he rated such decent, honest fellows by comparison with intriguing officials and members of the imperial family.

The Countess Melanie Zichy,[36] who had now become Prince Metternich's third wife, and was an old acquaintance of the Tsar's, was the only person to whom Nicholas spoke at all freely. The Tsar said that he would never have believed that people on whom he thought he could rely would have mortified him as they had done. He complained of the ridiculous slanders that had been spread about his "tyranny", especially in religious matters, and inquired whether he really looked such a tyrant. He could hardly expect the wife of the Chancellor to enter into a discussion of Metternich's views. The Tsar continued to show his displeasure to everybody in Vienna in every possible way. At a military dinner given in his honour by the General Staff he was icily reserved and never unbent for a moment. Afterwards, when he should have conversed with his hosts, the Tsar entrenched himself in a "militarily impregnable" position in a mullioned window and hardly spoke to anyone of those present. At the theatre the Tsar appeared in Cossack uniform instead of Austrian, and remained grave and aloof. When they went back to the palace for tea with the Emperor, he quitted the soirée at nine o'clock on the plea of fatigue. A great programme of festivities had been planned for the following day, but the Tsar asked the Emperor and Empress to excuse him from all save the informal dinner that had been arranged, after which he would take his leave in order to have the afternoon to himself. He had some work to do, he said, and also would like to take a stroll in the town, which would be good for his health. The court was dumbfounded at the imperial guest's demeanour. On the third day the Tsar received Metternich in a long audience. When the Chancellor introduced the subject of the marriage project, the Tsar said shortly: "It is not worth while discussing it. There is no longer any question of it." On the following day the Tsar waited only until his courier arrived, and left Vienna as soon afterwards as possible. He maintained his attitude of brusqueness and disdain towards the imperial court until the very end.

A fortnight after the Tsar had returned home, deeply offended and furious with the Vienna Cabinet,[37] a special edition of the St. Petersburg newspapers published the following laconic notice: "His Majesty has received the joyful news by the hand of a courier who arrived during the night of January 22nd from Her Majesty the Tsarina in Palermo that on the sixth of this month Her Imperial Highness the Grand Duchess Olga and His Royal Highness the Crown Prince of Württemberg, following the dictates of their own hearts, have contracted an engagement of marriage."

The Grand Duchess Marie immediately wrote and told her brother Alexander, who was then on leave in Darmstadt. "She is not yet in love with him," Marie wrote, "but he is so frank and honest that she feels drawn to him." Prince Alexander replied on February 1 (13), 1846, that the news had come as the greatest surprise of his life, and that in view of the conflicting reports he had heard about the Crown Prince of Württemberg he really did not know whether to be pleased about the engagement or not. ". . . . You know my great esteem for the Grand Duchess," he wrote, "and you know how much her happiness concerns me. I really do not know anyone who is worthy to possess such an angel. May Heaven bless her choice, and may Olly be as happy as she deserves to be."

Soon after the receipt of the news Prince Alexander met the Crown Prince of Württemberg, who had just returned from Palermo. "The Crown Prince," he reports in his diary on February 9 (21), 1846, "whom I was most anxious to meet, came in and looked me up and down, remarking that he was glad to make my acquaintance, as he had heard so much about me at Palermo. His manner is to my way of thinking most unattractive. He seems cold and reserved, speaks little and very slowly. He is rather shorter than I am, a little stiff, but a good figure and well dressed."

In consequence of the engagement, everyone at the royal court at Stuttgart seemed to Prince Alexander to be filled with rejoicing. This initial promise of happiness was not fulfilled in the event. The marriage turned out an unhappy one and was a martyrdom to the Grand Duchess Olga. She had not shown herself to be possessed of any will of her own in this most important decision of her life.

The fury and indignation of the Tsar Nicholas at the Austrian refusal now affected his whole outlook upon the situation in that country. He took no trouble to avoid showing the Austrian diplomats his disdain at the conditions he had discovered during his journey through the Austrian Empire. He designated the Commander-in-Chief in Galicia as a perfect fool who would obviously be incapable of dealing with the smouldering Polish insurrection. For Metternich himself he had now only the most contemptuous expressions. "He is", said the Tsar once,[38] "not only an old windbag, but also an arrant scoundrel if ever there was one." "The things that go on in your country", he said to Count Colloredo, "are inexcusable."

The seeds that had been sown in Vienna, or rather that Metternich had sown, were beginning to sprout, but even within the imperial family they comforted one another by saying that the bad temper of the autocratic Tsar, who was unaccustomed to opposition in his own country, would work itself off in time and through the necessity for the three Powers to hold together.[39] "In any case," wrote the Archduke Louis cheerfully to Metternich, "you had already said very truly some years ago that he [the Tsar] was an awkward friend to have."

The subject of all these negotiations, the Archduke Stephen, had remained throughout in the background. It was his own person that was at stake, and he might have determined not to marry the Grand Duchess if he had put his own interests before those of his country. Others, however, should in the most urgent interests of the monarchy not have stopped the marriage. Metternich and the ladies of the imperial family who meddled in politics under the guise of religion prevented the match. And this was a misfortune for Austria and the cause of a steadily increasing hostility between Austria and Russia that was eventually to lead to the downfall of both empires.

After the engagement of the Grand Duchess Olga to the Crown Prince of Württemberg the Russian imperial family

KING CHARLES OF WÜRTTEMBERG

suffered from something like a bad conscience in regard to young Alexander of Hesse. The Tsarina prompted her daughter-in-law to suggest to Alexander that he might also get married, and indicated Princess Louise, the daughter of the Grand Duchess of Mecklenburgh, who was staying as her guest in Palermo at that time. Marie wrote to her brother that she was continually hearing from Palermo in what affectionate memory Louise Mecklenburgh held him. Olga herself had told Alexander's sister that Louise thought only of him; that she had altered very much for the better; and that they were to be sure and let the Prince know. Marie also mentioned that a Prince Windischgrätz was very much in love with Louise and had followed her to Palermo, but that she thought of one person alone. Marie urged her brother to visit the Tsarina in Italy, where he might possibly also find the Grand Duchess of Mecklenburgh. The result, however, was the exact opposite of what had been intended. Prince Alexander had been meaning to go to Italy, but altered his plans and decided to go by Vienna to Constantinople and Athens. "It seems to me", he wrote to his sister from Vienna on March 10, 1846, "that one marries to please oneself and not to please other people. I am not at all disposed to tie myself down at twenty-three and either to stay in Darmstadt with the prospect of doing nothing all the rest of my life or in St. Petersburg where I cannot live a married life at all without money. So you will not be surprised if I avoid a trap that is set so very openly."

In his diary Alexander reveals his thoughts even more frankly. "If I go to Italy now," he writes, "I walk straight into the trap and must inevitably marry Vivi (Louise). . . . Anyway, I think the whole affair has been managed rather clumsily. To try to marry me off without so much as consulting me is a little too much." Thus he repulsed the attack upon his freedom and devoted himself to making the acquaintance of the Austrian imperial family and of the beautiful city of Vienna. An informal dinner with the Emperor and Empress gave Alexander the opportunity to get a close-up view of Ferdinand I. "The Emperor", he wrote in his diary on March 26, 1846, "is a pathetic object; not to put too fine a point on it, he is an idiot. He was very polite to me, but quite unintelligible. He wore our Order of St. Louis on the clip of his watch, the cross hanging down to his knees. The Empress, who speaks no German, appeared to me very insignificant. Nobody pays the slightest attention to the Emperor."

Alexander was quite nonplussed by the sight of such a monarch. He was particularly interested to meet the much-discussed Archduke Stephen, and found him a very pleasant and intelligent man, "who might be considered rather handsome for an archduke, with his immense whiskers".

From Vienna, Alexander continued his journey as far as Constantinople. Not until long after the Tsarina had left Palermo and had returned to St. Petersburg did Alexander of Hesse—now that there was no longer any threat of matrimony —venture to go to Italy, where he visited in turn all the glorious centres of art. In Rome he arrived just at the time of the death of Pope Gregory XVI, and attended the funeral service which was celebrated by no fewer than twenty-six cardinals and forty archbishops and bishops. He thought the singing beautiful and stirring, but the ceremonies—or, as he expressed it in his diary, the "hocus-pocus"—not very edifying. In consequence of the conclave which followed, which was to elect Pius IX to the papal throne, Rome was seething with excitement. After a short visit to the Bourbon royal family in Naples, Alexander turned homewards once more in the summer of 1846, and reappeared in St. Petersburg in the early part of September.

The Prince, still only twenty-three years of age, now began to lead an extravagant life in company with many of the young men of the highest nobility in St. Petersburg. The disappointment he had had with regard to the Grand Duchess Olga had roused in him a certain spirit of defiance, and made him forget a good deal of the restraint which he otherwise practised. He drank too freely, gambled a great deal and for high stakes, and in addition to the flirtations he carried on among the ladies of society he also indulged in numerous adventures incognito. At the court balls which began again in October it was now the young and pretty Countess Sophie Shuvaloff who excited Alexander's particular admiration. At one of the tournaments she was his lady. Nevertheless he missed Olga Nicholaevna at every turn. "Sophie is a poor substitute for her", he remarks in his diary. The round of festivities, of parades, and carnival balls was even more exhausting than in the previous years. Alexander threw himself into the whirl in order to forget the pain that was still gnawing at his heart.

The news of the death of the Palatine Archduke Joseph made no particular impression in St. Petersburg since the marriage project had collapsed. Metternich could barely disguise his satisfaction at the event.[40] He much preferred Joseph's son, the Archduke Stephen. For although the father had not opposed Metternich during the last few years, he was never as certain of him as he was of the Archduke Stephen, who was ready to do anything he was told.

In April 1847 Alexander's sister gave birth to her third son, Vladimir. The happy event is noted in Alexander's diary with the remark that the little creature who had just come into the world yelled and squawked like a rook, but was at once appointed Colonel-in-Chief of the Dragoons of the Guard, and entered in the Preobrajensky Regiment and the Sappers of the Guard.

At that time financial circles in the Russian capital were in a state of great perturbation. The richest and most powerful bank was the Stieglitz Bank, whose largest clients moved in the highest circles in society. This bank had a hold over many influential people through the loans it had made to them. After the fashion of the Rothschilds in other great cities of Europe, the Stieglitz Bank had practically a monopoly of important business and financial transactions that required for their undertaking large capital and extensive connections with the chief markets of the world. The Rothschilds had already established themselves successfully in London, Paris, Vienna, and Naples. They were now anxious to set up a branch in Russia, and sent an agent named Davidsohn to St. Petersburg. Accustomed as they were to being received with the greatest friendliness everywhere, the Rothschilds thought that the prestige of their name would suffice, and thus showed themselves to be lacking in knowledge of Russian conditions. It was their very cosmopolitanism—the basis of their power elsewhere —that was against them in Russia, where the Tsar was anxious to keep his land as far as possible untouched by foreign influence. The Tsar and those surrounding him had no intention whatever of allowing a capitalist power whose centre lay outside Russia, which received its instructions from abroad, and worked in its own interests independently of the plans and wishes of the Russian Government, to gain an overwhelming influence in their chief city. Remembering their former associations with the Elector of Hesse, the Rothschilds tried to approach Alexander of Hesse. But Davidsohn displayed a want of tact and discretion in his task. All his manœuvres were watched, and the Stieglitz Bank used all its influential connections in court circles in order to frustrate Davidsohn's plans. He was told that Jews were forbidden by law to start under-

E

takings or to settle in the capital, and that his intentions could
not be reconciled with this law. Thus the Rothschilds failed in
their attempt.[41] St. Petersburg remained the only capital of a
Great Power where this otherwise omnipotent family was never
able directly or indirectly to gain a foothold.

Meanwhile the Tsar had sent word to Alexander by Count
Orloff that he was not to consort on terms of such intimacy
with the very young officers, not to behave as if he were simply
one of themselves, and not to play for such high stakes with
them. Moreover, he intimated that it would be better not to
be seen at supper quite so frequently with the best-known
actresses in the city. It was hoped that another period of leave
at home would have a beneficial effect by interrupting all
these associations and affording Alexander an opportunity of
leading a quieter life. In the course of his travels Prince
Alexander came to Stuttgart and, at a soirée, found himself
seated beside Olga. He thought she had grown very thin, but
seemed well, and looked more beautiful than ever. On the
other hand, he disliked her husband much more than before.
The Russian imperial family was still trying—though this time
without the Tsar's knowledge—to secure the Archduke Stephen
for another of the imperial princesses. The Tsar's brother, the
Grand Duke Michael, wanted to get his daughter, the Grand
Duchess Katherine, married. His wife, the Grand Duchess
Helen, tried by circuitous methods—wherein a certain Wal-
burga, Countess de Révay, played a part—to sound the
Archduke Stephen as to his views upon marriage with the
Grand Duchess Katherine. It was a foolish and inexplicable
undertaking. Since the Archduke had already refused the
Tsar's daughter, he was not likely to marry the Tsar's niece.
Countess Révay was commissioned to break the refusal gently
to the Grand Duchess Helen, and to explain that the whole
Austrian family was opposed to a marriage with a Russian.
The ladies of the Habsburg family were really fanatical about
it. Moreover, the consent of the Tsar was not to be expected.
"Quite rightly", the Archduke Stephen wrote to the Countess
de Révay.[42] "However much the Tsar might say that he had
nothing against the marriage of his niece, it must and would
rankle that in 1845 his pet scheme for the Grand Duchess Olga
failed, and in 1847 the Grand Duchess Helen brought off the
same thing for her own daughter. . . . I beg of you to write
to Her Serene Highness in my stead, my dear Révay, to explain
my reasons . . ." After this refusal no further proffers of

marriage reached the Archduke Stephen from the Russian imperial family. He never married, but remained a bachelor all his life.

When Prince Alexander returned to St. Petersburg in December, where the Tsar had been lying ill for the last three weeks, his brother-in-law "Sacha" took him to task and made him promise not to resume his fast life of the previous year. The Tsar and the Grand Duke Michael complained that he had absolutely demoralized the imperial A.D.C.s. Full of good resolutions, Alexander entered upon the year 1848, which was to bring in its train such terrible upheavals throughout the whole world.

CHAPTER IV

REVOLUTION TO REACTION

The New Year's carnival of 1848 brought in its train the usual love-affairs and intrigues. Prince Alexander paid his court to the young Countess Sophie Shuvaloff. She took the matter more seriously than Alexander intended it to be taken, and fell in love with the handsome prince, who was now twenty-five years old. The Shuvaloff family, who realized that his intentions were not serious, began to express their annoyance. When at a ball early in January the Prince asked the Countess Sophie to dance the mazurka with him, he noticed that, although she accepted, she was suddenly overcome with confusion. A few minutes later the Countess Julia Hauke, a lady-in-waiting to the Princess Marie, came upon the scene and told him that the girl's mother had threatened to take her daughter home at once if she danced the mazurka with him.

The lady to whom the unpleasant task of delivering this message was entrusted was the daughter of a Polish general, Count Maurice Hauke (alternatively spelt Hauck), whose father—at that time still untitled—had come to Warsaw with Count Alois von Brühl before the French Revolution. The son entered the army and during the Napoleonic Wars he fought in the Polish Legion. His mother was Salome Schweppenhäuser, daughter of the pastor of Sesenheim, who was brought up in the same house as Goethe's love, Frederika Brion. After the establishment of the Polish kingdom under Russian suzerainty he was appointed Polish Minister for War, although he had not a drop of Polish blood in his veins. Not until 1829 was he raised to the hereditary Russian nobility, and then he married the daughter of a French doctor named de la Fontaine. At the outbreak of the Polish Revolution of November 29, 1830, mutinous cadets pushed their way in to the palace of the Governor-General, the Grand Duke Constantine, the brother of the Tsar Nicholas. General Hauke faced them and exhorted them to loyalty, but was murdered by them. His youngest daughter Julia was later appointed lady-in-waiting to the

Princess Marie in memory of the heroic bearing of her father, and of his death in the service of Russia. She conceived an affection for the Princess Marie's brother from the very beginning, and thanks to her position and the opportunities afforded by the carnival season they met very often.

The imperial family was more and more anxious that Prince Alexander should make a suitable marriage and settle down, and they now had another candidate in view. This was the Grand Duchess Katherine, the Tsar's niece, who had been secretly suggested for the Archduke Stephen in the previous year. The balls and other festivities continued, while the first faint rumours came from France of the subterranean rumblings that heralded a revolution. On March 5, 1848, after a parade of the Horse Guards, a *déjeuner dansant* took place at the Tsarevitch's palace. While the mazurka was in progress, the Tsar appeared carrying a telegram in his hand: "A republic has been proclaimed in France, the royal family has been driven out, the Tuileries have been plundered, the royal palace is in flames, and a provisional government has been formed by the leaders of the opposition." In addition, the Tsar had received a special edition of a Prussian newspaper, the *Allgemeine Zeitung*, which he now handed to Alexander of Hesse to translate. The whole gay company gathered round to hear the startling news, while the orchestra continued playing in the ballroom as though nothing had happened. When the Prince had finished reading the newspaper, the Tsar said: "I shall certainly not shed a drop of Russian blood to put Louis Philippe back on to his throne. But you may as well see to your equipment, gentlemen." Then he let the dance go on again as if to show that not even the greatest shocks in other countries could disturb the equanimity of Russia or at all events of its rulers. This evening Alexander again danced the mazurka with Sophie Shuvaloff, who showed him by every means in her power how much he meant to her.

The next few days brought news of the repercussions of the French Revolution in the smaller German States, in many of which Liberal and Nationalist claims were put forward. A National Assembly elected from all German States was demanded. At the outset the Tsar was minded to march in and set things to right again. Then he decided to hold his hand awhile. In Hesse, too, a revolution took place, though a bloodless one, on March 5th and March 6th, with the result that the freedom of the Press, a Citizens' Guard, and so forth, were conceded. But the Opposition demanded more. The Grand Duke was obliged to yield; his life was probably at stake. Finally nothing remained to Alexander's father but to appoint his eldest son Louis co-regent and to transfer all affairs to him. The old man agreed to everything and signed the edict with the words: "There—that is how a Grand Duke abdicates!" He embraced his son Louis with tears in his eyes, and thanked him for taking the difficulties of life off his shoulders at such a time. Nor was Louis unable to restrain his tears, and he exclaimed despondently: "Here am I, a child of the revolution. What will the world say of me!" The news caused Alexander the liveliest concern. But for the time being he remained in Russia awaiting events. The soirées and other court entertainments continued. On March 19th the news reached St. Petersburg that revolution had broken out in Vienna too, that Metternich had been overthrown, and a constitution demanded. Even the royal palace had been handed over to the National Guard. "How disgraceful— how cowardly!" exclaimed Prince Alexander.

The news of the events in Vienna on March 12th to March 14th created a tremendous sensation in St. Petersburg court circles. Although the Emperor did not at all approve of Metternich, he was shocked at the manner of his downfall and was horrified at all the subsequent happenings that went so utterly against his absolutist ideas. The reports of the Russian chargé d'affaires at Vienna sounded very gloomy and expressed the greatest anxiety for the future of the Austrian monarchy. The Tsar sent for the Austrian Ambassador, Count Thun, to discuss affairs with him. "Austria has always been my most faithful ally," Count Franz Thun reports him as saying[43]; "I counted upon this country as my surest support. . . . I was the sincerest and most devoted friend to the Emperor Francis, and swore to him never to abandon Austria. God is my witness that I have kept my promise up to the present and shall always continue to do so. He commended it to me on his deathbed, so to speak, and almost left his sons in my care. Now they are talking of proclaiming a constitution there and all sorts of things. . . . I shall not be the one to desert Austria or to put difficulties in its way. I could never bring myself to believe that the policies of Austria and Russia could be divorced and take different directions. But it is a matter of life and death for me. I could never in any circumstances permit a centre of revolution to exist at my very gates where it might infect my Poles. If a revolution should break out in Galicia, and the greatest severity were not used to suppress it, I should be forced sorely against my wish to intervene." And Baron von Lebzeltern[44] reports his saying: "If Galicia should try to secede, I shall invade it without hesitation, and shall occupy it in the name of the Emperor Ferdinand, without any personal motives, however much ado may be caused by it!"

When finally news came to St. Petersburg of revolution in Berlin, of the incidents at the palace and of the withdrawal of the troops by the King, the Tsar was filled with utter disgust at the whole of "Europe gone mad".

"What I wish with all my heart", said the Tsar most significantly, "is that we could build a real Chinese Wall against the rest of Europe, so as to cut off every kind of connection with it." The Tsar feared lest the fire should spread to his own realm, would have preferred to put a ban on all foreigners entering Russia, and regretted that St. Petersburg was a port which made it practically impossible to prevent or regulate the entry of strangers.[45]

The Tsar used to tell the latest news of the various revolutions to the members of his immediate family. He was not surprised at what happened in Prussia. The king being what he was, the Tsar had foreseen something of the sort for a long time. The origin of his resentment against King Frederick William IV was his knowledge that the late King Frederick William III had at his—the Tsar's—instigation left a will forbidding his successors to make any alteration in the structure of the State. When the Tsar mentioned this to the new king with reference to certain reforms in Prussia, King Frederick William IV averred that the testament had not been signed and was therefore invalid—a remark that seriously displeased the Tsar. Prince Alexander's opinion of these events naturally took its colour from the Tsar's.

While all over Europe peoples and governments were at variance with one another, an historical tournament by the court took place in St. Petersburg, and the populace was shown the imperial power in an almost challenging manner in reviews and ceremonies with a great parade of troops. War was rumoured now in one place, now in another. The Tsar Nicholas, who received daily reports that his intervention in Germany was feared, said to this and to rumours which actually spoke of an alliance between France and Russia: "I can only think of one case in which I should frankly make common cause with France against Germany, and that is if Germany were mad enough to declare war on me. And even then it would depend on France's having a legitimist government."

It certainly was a troublous age for monarchs. Every day the Tsar thought he must expect to hear of another serious collapse somewhere. Russia had 390,000 men under arms, that is, 120,000 more than before the various revolutions took place. It was a formidable army according to the ideas of the time. In addition to the shadow of war the terrible spectre of cholera now appeared and claimed its first victims in Moscow.

Love ignores even world-shattering events. Countess Sophie Shuvaloff had taken a friend, Antonia Hendrikoff, into her confidence, who contrived meetings for her with Prince Alexander by the little so-called Chinese garden. She spoke quite frankly to the Prince of Sophie's love for him and told him that Sophie was refusing all other suitors for his sake. Alexander received the news with mixed feelings. He was fond of Sophie, but he did not really want to get married and therefore saw the development of the situation with some anxiety.

The month of June in the year 1848 brought sad news for the Prince. His father, the Grand Duke, died, and the government of Hesse-Darmstadt was therefore permanently in the hands of his brother Louis. Meanwhile the cholera outbreak had reached St. Petersburg. It was a disease which there was no means of combating at that time. Every day there were over a thousand fresh victims and five to six hundred deaths. The imperial family, however, had the good fortune to escape. On July 15th Alexander celebrated his 26th birthday. Amongst other things he received flowers with mottoes or verses attached from no less than five ladies, among whom was the Countess Julia Hauke.

The Tsar's anxiety lest he should be involved in a great war had diminished during the last few months. Nor did the attempts to unite Germany cause him as much apprehension as formerly. He watched with interest the course of the revolution which had broken out in Northern Italy, and the war which Radetzky was carrying on against King Charles Albert, "the sword of Italy", and the rebels. His success and clever strategy increased the Tsar's admiration for the aged Field-Marshal. The Tsar still regarded Prince Alexander with disfavour. Once more the Grand Duke Michael asked the

Tsarevitch to urge his brother-in-law to behave sensibly. This time, however, Alexander's conscience was clear. He had hardly gambled at all nor drunk too much recently, and had indulged in comparatively few love-affairs. Hence he sought a reason for this new attack. "I wonder", he writes in his diary, "if he is really annoyed with me for not paying addresses to his daughter?" And then he went at 5.30 to take his daily walk beneath Sophie Shuvaloff's window. On the following day— August 21st (September 2), 1848—the Tsar said to his daughter-in-law: "I am not fond of match-making, but I should like to give your brother a hint. It would be much more sensible of him to marry the Grand Duchess Katherine than to carry on this flirtation with Sophie Shuvaloff, which I want to see brought to an end." Whatever may have been the cause, the Grand Duke Michael took every opportunity at manœuvres and parades to fulminate, sometimes positively foaming at the mouth, against Prince Alexander and his regiment. Moreover, Sophie's parents were now determined to put an end to the affair.

The girl confided in Julia Hauke, who was herself in love with Alexander. Julia found Sophie greatly overwrought and terribly unhappy. To crown all, Sophie's father and mother discovered a correspondence between her and the Prince, which consisted in their lending each other books in which love passages were underlined. The parents considered referring the matter directly to the Tsar, but finally decided to send Sophie away from St. Petersburg. The poor girl was desperate. The whole atmosphere was electric and everyone was expecting a social scandal of the first water. Then the Prince's sister intervened, and had a long and serious talk with her brother, as a result of which he promised to make a final breach with Sophie.

"It was the saddest evening of my life", Alexander wrote in his diary. At a ball which took place that same evening he told Sophie himself when they were dancing a quadrille together that he had decided in her own interests not to see her any more. With an expression of indescribable sadness she replied that she would not stand in the way of his happiness. Then he pressed her hand for the last time and they parted with tears in their eyes. If the imperial court was under the impression that the way had now been made clear for the Grand Duchess Katherine, it was completely mistaken. Prince Alexander was not going to be forced into marrying a woman he did not love.

The Grand Duke Michael continued to make the most of every opportunity of being unpleasant to Prince Alexander. He positively persecuted the men in the two regiments of Alexander's brigade, and once when he caught three men from the Chevaliers Gardes, who had overstayed their leave, Alexander as Brigadier was given a sharp reprimand in the order of the day. Thus the Prince did not have too easy a life at the Russian court.

Besides his love-affairs the young Prince grew more and more interested in the exciting political events of the world which changed kaleidoscopically, especially in Austria, and the final outcome of which was at that time quite impossible to foresee. The news of the storming of the arsenal in Berlin on June 14, 1848, was received in St. Petersburg with real indignation, as was also that of the discussion of a draft Constitution in the Prussian National Assembly. The Tsar followed the debate with exasperation and could hardly restrain himself in March and again in May from invading Prussia and restoring order. Prince Alexander records in his diary on October 7 (19), 1848, that the Tsar made him compose a letter in German which Count Benkendorff handed to Count Dohna, the General in command at Königsberg, on October 19, 1848.[46] In this letter the Tsar recommended Dohna to be the Jellačič of Prussia, to save Berlin and the King, as Jellačič had saved Vienna and the Emperor. Democracy in Berlin must be destroyed and the King rescued whether he liked it or not. The Russian army would act as a reserve force if necessary. An attempt on the part of the King of Württemberg, the father-in-law of the Grand Duchess Olga, to win over the Tsar to the idea of the unification of Germany by means of a plan according to which the kings alone were not to be mediatized, failed completely. The Tsar Nicholas said that by suggesting such an injustice the King was putting himself on a level with Gagern and other "cretins". Prince Alexander observes in his diary on February 9 (21), 1849, that it was obvious that the idea of a united Germany would be stubbornly opposed by the Tsar.

Within the Austrian monarchy, rebellions had broken out simultaneously in the autumn of 1848 in Hungary, Bohemia, and Italy. The insurrection in Hungary especially was a most serious menace to the empire. Then there was a rising in Vienna itself in October, which obliged the court to flee to Olmütz, and made a formal military expedition necessary for the recapture of the capital. It now became impossible for a

COUNTESS SOPHIE SHUVALOFF

mere figurehead like the Emperor Ferdinand to remain on the throne, and Prince Schwarzenberg effected the abdication of the Emperor in favour of his nephew Francis Joseph, who ascended the throne on December 2, 1848. The change was hailed with joy in Russia. The man who had absolutely ruled Ferdinand, and who had for the past few years worked against the Tsar's policy, had already fallen, and now he was followed into oblivion by the nominal ruler who had been no more than a screen for his autocratic chancellor.

Now, the Tsar thought, an eighteen-year-old youth was coming to the throne who was not responsible for all the mistakes and spite with which Metternich during the last years of his Chancellorship disturbed the relations with the Tsar and hence with Russia. He would not, the Tsar hoped, refuse to listen to the experienced counsel of his older friend and ally; and thus the old intimate understanding would be re-established that had obtained between the two dynasties and their realms in the days of the Emperor Francis.

The expression of these feelings which were at that time shared by the young Emperor and his paladins was found in the correspondence between the two emperors after Francis Joseph's accession to the throne. Pressed on all sides, the advisers of the young monarch were obliged to value the more highly the support that the Tsar represented, and hence a letter written by the Emperor Francis Joseph[47] on December 28, 1848, reminds the Tsar that he promised his grandfather the Emperor Francis at Münchengrätz that his successors might invariably count upon his friendship and help in times of need, and that they should jointly defend the principles of justice and order in Europe. The Tsar caused Count Buol to write to Schwarzenberg[48] to tell the Emperor that his feelings for the Emperor were those of paternal affection, that he did not wish to influence him or to force his advice upon him, but that he would always remain the friend of his family, and that in time of need he would always be found ready to help. True, the Tsar regarded the Frankfurt Assembly simply as a "lunatic asylum", from which nothing good could be expected to emerge, and considered that Austria paid too little regard to German affairs. But he hoped that the Emperor Francis Joseph would soon see eye to eye with him on this point and then act in a manner which could be more easily reconciled with the feelings and desires of the Autocrat of all the Russias.

Only too soon was the Tsar to find that he was expected to

redeem his recently confirmed promise to give help in case of necessity. Since a great part of the Austrian army together with its best commander, Radetzky, was occupied by the revolt in Milan and the campaign against the King of Sardinia, it was found impossible to quell the revolution in Hungary. In fact, it took on an increasingly threatening form. Windischgrätz was defeated and Hungary's independence proclaimed. On April 23rd Pest had to be evacuated by the Austrian troops, and the Hungarian revolutionary hordes were already threatening Vienna. In Italy, it is true, the victories of Mortara and Novara eased the military situation to some extent. But of what avail was this in view of the disquieting successes of the Hungarian revolutionaries? Now was the moment to turn to the Tsar for aid. Francis Joseph implored the Tsar urgently to help him suppress the Hungarian revolt, which, as the young Emperor said, "might shortly assume the dimensions of a European calamity". The Tsar's feelings were cleverly played upon when the young Emperor was induced to write from Olmütz[49] on May 1, 1849: "The Magyar camp . . . has become the meeting-place of the stragglers from every lost cause. Sectarians of the most various origins, persistent conspirators, especially Poles, have gathered under Kossuth's banner. Every success won by the insurgents is hailed by the revolutionaries of all countries as the forerunner of the imminent triumph of their abominable practices. . . . I am firmly convinced that with God's help our glorious comradeship in arms is destined once again to preserve modern society from the certain destruction with which it is threatened by these men, who under the high-sounding name of progress are only preparing a return to new and terrible barbarism."

This was the diplomatic and formal wording of the urgent cry for help which Major-General Prince Lobkowitz presented in St. Petersburg. Psychologically it was cleverly framed. The reference to the Poles especially, whom the Tsar always regarded with the utmost suspicion, did not fail of its effect. The answer of the Tsar,[50] written from St. Petersburg on April 28 (May 10), 1849, to this "urgent letter" was to the effect that the Emperor Francis Joseph had not counted in vain upon the old and sincere friendship of the Tsar. He was glad, he said, that his troops—who were already under way— should find Polish exiles among the armies of their opponents— armies composed of those eternal enemies of the two empires, the soldiers of anarchy, recruited from every country in the world. There followed a campaign in which the Russo-Austrian troops broke the hitherto more or less successful Hungarian revolution by their superior numbers. Görgey, the Hungarian Commander-in-Chief, surrendered to the Russians. The same letter, dated August 4 (16), 1849, in which the Tsar informed Francis Joseph of the capitulation, contained a prayer that the Emperor should exercise that fairest prerogative of a sovereign —mercy. "Mercy for those who have erred," the Tsar begged; "it is your friend who asks it of you. Let a just punishment be meted out to the instigators as the cause of the evil which has befallen the country." In his reply Francis Joseph speaks of his intense pleasure—a pleasure to which he also gave expression in Vienna in speaking to the Tsarevitch upon his return from the campaign: "I cannot sufficiently thank you, my friend, for having given me the pleasure of embracing Alexander and telling him the extent of my gratitude for all that you have done for me." Then he agreed to the Tsar's plea for mercy to the insurgents, assented to the remark about punishing the ringleaders, and ended by saying that he hoped the steps which he proposed to take in this matter would meet with the Tsar's approval. In further letters to Francis Joseph the Tsar advocated that mercy should be extended wherever possible.

Meanwhile the Tsarevitch wrote from Warsaw on August 15th (27th), to tell his brother-in-law Prince Alexander about his visit to Vienna. He was surprised at the composure and discretion shown by the Emperor Francis Joseph—a composure all the more remarkable on account of his youth. He remarked that Francis Joseph had been most friendly with him, and had appointed him to the Fifth Curassier regiment, which was recruited in Italy and had distinguished itself particularly in Hungary, in place of his Colonelcy of a regiment of Hungarian Hussars that had gone over to the rebels. The Tsarevitch was boyishly pleased at the attention: "The uniform is a blue tunic with rose-coloured collar and facings, and silver lace. (My favourite colours.) I must admit that I am delighted, for I love and honour the splendid army that has proved itself so worthy of its traditions not only by its bravery but also in its political principles." Thus the Tsarevitch, too, was animated by friendship and esteem for Austria, and did not change his sentiments until he was forced to do so.

Despite all his protestations of gratitude, the friendly act of assistance had wounded the vanity of the youthful monarch; and this proved the starting-point of that unfortunate policy

during the next few years, which caused the young Emperor of
Austria to become the greatest disappointment ever experienced
by the Tsar. Even during the campaign there was a certain
amount of friction between the allied armies. Now the question
of the punishment of the rebels became the cause of a serious
difference of opinion between the two monarchs. True, the
Emperor Francis Joseph wrote to the Tsar on August 23rd
assuring him that next to God it was due solely to the friendship
of the Tsar that an end had been put to the civil war and that
gratitude was indelibly graven upon his heart. He added that
the Tsar's desire that mercy should be shown to Görgey and
the remaining insurgents should be complied with. Then,
however, Haynau's tribunal seized upon the conquered, and
men like Count Louis Batthyány and numbers of other prominent persons expiated their opinions on the scaffold or facing a
firing party. In view of his previous petition for mercy, the Tsar
was furiously indignant; nor was his anger lessened when
several individuals were executed for whom Russia had made
a special plea. Subsequent letters from the Emperor Francis
Joseph, the phraseology of which was intended to tone down
the impression left by the executions, did not fulfil their object.
Paskievitch returned to St. Petersburg raging against the
Austrian Government and against certain individual Austrian
generals. And Prince Alexander of Hesse, who had remained
in St. Petersburg, heard on all sides that now that the campaign
was over and they had seen the way in which the Austrians
behaved to the conquered enemy, the Russian corps of officers
felt much more in sympathy with the Hungarians than with
those on whose side they had fought.

The Grand Duke Constantine, who had been through the
Hungarian campaign at the Russian headquarters, was
according to Prince Alexander delighted with the personality
of Görgey whose acquaintance he had made after his surrender
at Grosswardein, and equally indignant with the Austrians.
The Tsarevitch during his visit to Vienna with difficulty
managed at least to effect the pardon of Görgey.

The letters which the young Emperor Francis Joseph was
induced to write were full of fine phrases about unity and
friendship, but his actions showed the true ideas and sympathies of the advisers to the too youthful ruler. It was obvious
that the Tsar's intervention in Hungary was undertaken
mainly in his own interests, just as were also his plans to lend
the King of Prussia his army to help him re-establish his absolute

power. He feared for his own position. Everything that went on in the neighbouring countries ran counter to his deepest convictions regarding the rights of princes, order, and the forms of government. Hence it was natural that he should wish to prevent the kindling of the flame on his own hearth. At the same time he took the opportunity of appearing as the benefactor of those whom he had helped. The curious thing was that both monarchs, the Prussian as well as more especially the Emperor Francis Joseph, had, as the subsequent period of reaction was to show, at the bottom of their hearts exactly the same absolutist tendencies and theories as the Tsar Nicholas.

While Germany and the Austrian monarchy as well as most other European countries were passing through such critical times, Russia alone remained more or less untouched by all these happenings. During the carnival of 1849 the whirl of court life continued as of old. As usual, Prince Alexander took the liveliest share in it, and indulged the more freely in gaieties and light adventure because he wanted to drive out the memory of Sophie Shuvaloff. Except for the Grand Duchess Olga, she had meant more to him than any other woman. It was very easy for him, for society ladies as well as the stars of the theatrical firmament met the young cavalry officer, the Tsarevitch's brother-in-law, with open arms. At a great ball of the nobility, for instance, the Princess O. D. passed him a little note containing fervent protestations of love. At supper she made ardent advances to him, and when Alexander saw her home afterwards he had hardly got into the carriage beside her before she fell upon his neck and assured him that she had fallen in love with him at the first glance. She continued that she was honest enough to tell him at once that it would not last long, since she was a person whose moods varied from day to day. She had chosen an inauspicious moment. Alexander was thinking about Sophie Shuvaloff, who had nearly died of pneumonia the week before, and so he said good-bye to the Princess at the door of her house. "She must think I am very cold", remarked the Prince in his diary. However, Alexander did not remain permanently unresponsive.

In addition there were lively bachelor suppers with theatrical beauties. Most of these were Frenchwomen, who had come to the far north to make their fortunes, attracted by the glitter of the imperial court. Prince Alexander, however, did not really enjoy this life; his true disposition was a steady one. Since the summer of 1849 he had grown more and more interested in his sister's clever and goodlooking lady-in-waiting, the Countess Julia Hauke, whom he saw daily, and who was now filled with a consuming passion for him, which he gradually came to return. When the Prince came back to St. Petersburg after the manœuvres, the flirtation developed into a serious affair. "Julia Hauke is looking lovely", he wrote in his diary, when he met her again. He fell more and more in love with Julia and she could hardly bear to wait for the day when Sophie Shuvaloff should go to the altar with another man.[51]

Gradually those immediately surrounding the Emperor began to realize who was Prince Alexander's latest love. The Tsar once accidentally went into the Countess Julia's rooms, which were next door to those of the Princess Marie, and found Alexander of Hesse with her. Although his neglect to become a suitor for the hand of the Grand Duchess Katherine aroused some exasperation, as did also his refusal to agree to any of the other marriage projects that had been planned for him by the imperial family, nobody really believed that the affair with Julia Hauke would seriously come to a head. The idea of marrying him to Katherine was still uppermost in their minds, and as late as January 3, 1850, the Tsarina spoke to the Prince and once more advised him to apply for the hand of Katherine. Meanwhile, even in the short intervals between their meetings, Alexander received passionate love-letters from Julia. The Tsar was anxious to see Alexander married to the Grand Duchess, although her mother had long since been considering other candidates. The Tsar, however, would have none of these, and when the hereditary Prince of Altenburg, who had been encouraged by the Grand Duchess Helen, came to St. Petersburg on January 13, 1850, in order to introduce himself to the Tsar, the latter suddenly said to him: "I am very glad to see you. But remember this—if I had any reason to think that you had come to marry my niece behind my back, I should send you off within twenty-four hours!" Another German Prince was refused by Katherine herself, and finally the approaching visit of Duke George of Mecklenburg-Strelitz was announced. "That will complete the collection of aspirants", said Alexander in his diary. "It is a very good thing that I am not intending to join the throng."

On January 30, 1850, Alexander received the unexpected news of Sophie Shuvaloff's engagement to Prince Alexander Bobrinsky. Julia Hauke had known of it two days earlier, but had not dared to tell Alexander. Now she could hardly conceal her joy. "Although I thank heaven for it", remarked Alexander in his diary, "I can hardly bear the idea of Sophie's belonging to anyone else." Sophie, however, appeared to be much in love with her new Alexander and declared that she would confess all her past to him. Alexander's disinclination to marry the Grand Duchess Katherine had still further increased the imperial family's vexation with him. The intimacy of the Prince with his daughter Mary Leuchtenberg also irritated the Tsar, and he admonished Mary not to permit the familiarity with which Alexander treated her: "His manners", said the Tsar, "are the result of his principles, so-called modern principles, which I suppose he brought with him from Germany in 1848." Mary Leuchtenberg lost no time in repeating the Tsar's words to Alexander of Hesse. She may have embroidered them a little, for she liked to see everyone at her feet and had often been annoyed at Alexander's paying attentions to other women.

Alexander sardonically watched the train of princes who continued to be paraded in St. Petersburg for Katherine's benefit. On May 31, 1850, he writes: "Prince Frederick Charles of Prussia, the thousandth aspirant to the hand of the Grand Duchess, is expected." Her engagement in July to Duke George of Mecklenburg-Strelitz put an end to the game. The Prince was safe from this side at least. In August he was granted a very long leave of absence, in the hope that he might be detached from the various undesirable connections that he had formed in St. Petersburg. At first he went home to Darmstadt, later he spent some time in visiting Paris and London. In London he was particularly interested in *The Times* offices and the Bank of England. In November 1850 *The Times* used to publish two editions, one at 5 a.m. and one at 12 noon. The steampress, which had only been invented in 1848, delivered sixteen thousand copies an hour. Fifty to sixty thousand copies were published every day, figures that roused the greatest wonder in the Prince.

According to Alexander's statement, *The Times* brought in £60,000 a year to its owner, Mr. Walter. At the Bank of England the Prince was shown the workshops where the banknotes were printed, and the regulations for the supervision of the workmen were explained to him. He was also taken down into the vaults where £2,000,000 lay in gold bars. Finally, he was shown a safe containing £14,000,000 in banknotes, a packet of a million

F

was taken out and the Prince was allowed to hold this vast sum in his hands.

Alexander visited Warwick Castle, where he saw glorious family portraits painted by Rembrandt, Van Dyck, and Titian. The last-named artist had actually painted one of the portraits in question on the spot. The conversation turned on heraldry, and the origin of the unicorn in the British coat of arms, and Prince Alexander said to the caretaker who was showing him round that he supposed that the horn of the fabulous monster must have been derived from that of the narwhal. The caretaker replied most indignantly, "Certainly not. The unicorn is a real live animal. You don't think that we should have a fabulous monster in our English coat of arms!"—"Quite right," replied Prince Alexander, "your unicorn is just as true to life as our Russian double eagle."

At the beginning of 1851 Prince Alexander returned to the Russian court, where he resumed his friendship with the Countess Julia Hauke, and found her more and more attractive. The Tsarevitch, who did not believe that he was serious, was less severe with his brother-in-law, because he had a bad conscience himself. He was already beginning to neglect his young wife, and to make love to a girl named Eugenie Macoff, to whose charms he had succumbed. Prince Alexander tranquillized himself and his sister on this score by remarking that it seemed to be a very depressing, apparently innocent, and rather tedious love-affair.

Meanwhile the Prince's relations with his sister's lady-in-waiting had progressed to the point at which the Tsar's official sanction to their engagement must be sought. That, of course, came as a bombshell to the whole court and at first roused apparently insuperable difficulties. Marriage with one of his sister's ladies-in-waiting was bound to make Prince Alexander's situation awkward in view of the strictly exclusive ideas of the day that made it essential to live and obviously also to marry within one's own caste. When after manifold struggles and efforts on the part of his sister and brother-in-law to dissuade him he still insisted upon making the Countess Julia Hauke his wife, he was obliged to reckon with the fact that there could no longer be any question of his remaining at the Russian court. It had been far too much of an open secret that he had been expected to marry the Grand Duchess Katherine, and that he had flatly refused to do so. Moreover, how was the rank of his wife to be determined, and how were the innumerable difficulties to be met that were bound to crop up in her relations with the other ladies of the court? The decision to make a marriage out of his own rank formed a turning-point in the life of the Prince. It seemed to rob him of all his future prospects and to put an abrupt end to his career.

The Tsar, the court, and society were inexorable if anyone broke through the rigid laws made by themselves and upon which alone rested their pre-eminence and their favoured position in the world. The very rumour of such a marriage set the whole of court society by the ears. The handsome, much-courted Prince was grudged by everyone to the poor lady-in-waiting with her newly created title, and coming of a non-Russian upstart family. Many ladies who had given him their favours, or who had vainly wished to do so, felt his choice as a personal insult. His Hessian relatives, led by Alexander's brother, the Grand Duke, who had always hoped for an influential Russian marriage for Alexander, were most disappointed. In a word, there was no one who was even partially satisfied with this step. The ambassadors of the Powers in St. Petersburg reported to their chiefs how angry the Tsar was with Prince Alexander, and how inexplicable it seemed to everyone that the Prince should sacrifice his position at court, his brilliant career, his whole future, for the sake of marrying this particular woman.

On October 4, 1851, Prince Alexander of Hesse left St. Petersburg heavy at heart, after spending over ten adventurous years there. What hurt him particularly was that the Tsar with every mark of disfavour struck him off the strength of the army. Three weeks later, on October 28, 1851, Alexander, then aged twenty-eight, led the Countess Julia Hauke, who was two years younger, to the altar. His young wife, however, was not allowed to bear the name of Hesse, since the Grand Duke had only consented to a morganatic marriage. For the time being she kept the title of Countess.

The feelings of the Tsarevitch and his wife concerning this affair were very mixed. Marie was very fond of her lady-in-waiting, and could not find it in her heart to blame her for falling in love with the brother to whom she herself was so greatly attached. But that she should marry him was too much. The Tsarevitch, again, though he was as conservative as his father, was very fond of Alexander of Hesse personally, and it grieved him that he should be treated with such scant ceremony. But the Tsar's will was law. The Tsarevitch's thoughts and feelings were much too nearly allied to those of the Tsar for him ever to have opposed his father. Hence he and his wife did not attempt to stay the decree of banishment. But they determined to remember Alexander and his wife, and when a little time had passed to do what they could to help them. Prince Alexander had in the fullest sense of the word won a friend in the future Tsar of Russia, and one who was to remain true to him in spite of everything all through his life.

In the world of politics the years 1850 and 1851 showed signs of improvement in the relations between Russia and Austria. This was due to the fact that the Tsar soon realized that Schwarzenberg and the young Emperor were proceeding on Conservative lines in matters of internal policy. The Austrian Prime Minister, moreover, had told the Tsar that the Austrian Constitution which had recently been granted could if necessary be rescinded. Since the Tsar believed that the Prussians were less disposed to break with the revolution, he felt more drawn to the young Emperor Francis Joseph again. His anger at the execution of the Hungarian rebels retreated into the background, and therefore in the conflict that was now developing between Prussia and Austria for the pre-eminence in Germany the Tsar took the side of Austria. Since it was now obvious to Prussia that in case of war there would, in addition to uncertainty regarding France, be three foes to reckon with—Austria, Southern Germany, and Russia—it was decided to compromise and to agree at Olmütz to a reorganization of the German Federation that led to the restoration of the old Federal Diet. Thus Russia had once again done the Emperor Francis Joseph a great service, and the Tsar had every reason to hope that in the future the much younger Austrian Emperor would reveal himself a willing pupil in political affairs especially as—in the Tsar's view—it was to be expected not only out of gratitude but also from their common conservative interests. As time went on, too, Francis Joseph's Government carried out further reactionary measures which tranquillized the Tsar's mind. Moreover, an excellent impression was made upon the Tsar by Francis Joseph's cultured and agreeable manner, assured despite his youth, which the Tsar observed on various occasions, such as at their meetings at Olmütz and Warsaw. Although it is to be assumed that diplomats such as Baron von Lebzeltern, when he wrote to Prince Schwarzenberg on June 9 (21), 1852, and said that the Tsar considered Francis Joseph to be a marvel were deliberately

PRINCE ALEXANDER OF HESSE AND HIS WIFE

exaggerating, it is none the less indubitable that Nicholas felt true affection and friendship for the younger man. Now that Metternich had been removed the Tsar attributed to him all the misadventures regarding the Grand Duchess Olga's marriage, and hoped that the happy days of intimate concord that he had enjoyed with the old Emperor Francis would be restored. Only now the rôles would be reversed. At that time the Emperor Francis had helped the youthful Tsar, whereas now the Tsar acted as fatherly adviser to the young Emperor. All ill-humour was forgotten, the Tsar enjoyed reviewing the splendid Austrian troops and was convinced that if necessary they would fight beside his own.

The cordial relationship between the two men was also shown in their correspondence. The letters of the Tsar especially breathe warm friendliness: "My dear, faithful friend," he addresses Francis Joseph on October 11 (23), 1851,[52] "How glad I was, how delighted, at the strong and excellent resolutions that you made for the good of your native land in accordance with the desires and wisdom of your noble soul! I congratulate you with all my heart and pray God to bless your efforts. . . ." "I envy my son for coming to see you, and should be delighted if I were able to do you some service. I shall hope to have the opportunity some day."

The Emperor Francis Joseph's replies were also couched in warm words, but they bear the imprint of professional diplomacy in their well-turned phrases. For instance, when the Tsar writes to the Emperor on April 7 (19), 1852, his words sound quite simple and natural: "I feel I must tell you how fond I am of you, and how glad I am that you are being more admired and honoured every day." He requested that there should be no ceremonial at the forthcoming visit: "Your friend Nicholas is simply coming to embrace his dear friend Francis Joseph and nothing more."[53]

The Tsar was utterly delighted when on December 31st Francis Joseph suspended the imperial Constitution. He still found almost daily exhilaration in watching his splendid regiments of Guards from whose ranks Prince Alexander of Hesse was now absent. In view of the friendly attitude of the government in Vienna, the Tsar was extremely distressed by the death of Schwarzenberg, who was struck down unexpectedly on April 5, 1852, by an apoplectic fit. He hoped, however, that this would not entail any change in the tendency of Austrian policy. He did not guess that from now onwards the autocracy of the young Francis Joseph in addition to the maladroitness of Buol, the newly appointed Minister for Foreign Affairs, who disliked the Tsar personally, would bring with it a very radical alteration in Austria's policy towards Russia.

Count Buol may have felt that he was badly used in St. Petersburg as Austrian Ambassador, but that is not the only reason for his later attitude. He was simply incapable of making clear and logical suggestions to his young sovereign, and thereby encouraged the self-reliance of the Emperor, who from now on thought he could do everything himself. In the summer of the year 1852 the change was not yet noticeable. When Baron von Hess, an Austrian infantry general, was sent on a mission to the Russian court, the Tsar paraded his splendid Guards' Corps before him and said to the Austrian: "These are your reserves, which are always prepared to come to the help of my friends. A second and a third are at the disposal of yourselves and of all who share my views. Prussia has not got so far yet. And as far as those are concerned who do not agree with my principles, I shall stay at home."[54]

Not until King Frederick William IV began to show increasingly reactionary tendencies did the relations between the Tsar and Prussia improve, and the Tsar cherished hopes of re-establishing within the framework of his unchanging convictions the concord of the three Great Powers who had once been allies. Nevertheless, even though the outward form seemed to have returned, inwardly the relations between the three States had altered.

Meanwhile Prince Alexander of Hesse was obliged to set to work to carve out a new career for himself. In October 1852, while the Tsarevitch and his wife were staying in Darmstadt, the Tsarevitch asked the reigning Grand Duke, the brother of Prince Alexander, to give his brother-in-law the supreme command of the grand ducal forces. He was, however, given an evasive answer, for even at the Hessian court the Prince's morganatic wife was looked upon as a terrible embarrassment. Entry into the Austrian service was a second idea that presented itself. The Tsarevitch had sounded the Emperor at the October manœuvres in Austria as to his willingness to appoint Prince Alexander to the post of Major-General in his army. Despite the fact, however, that an obvious and easy favour could thus have been done to the Russian court, he only had a very provisional "contingent" assent. When he met his brother-in-law in Vienna in November 1852 nothing had been decided definitely, and the Emperor Francis Joseph simply said to the Tsarevitch that he would be glad if the Tsar would first restore the Prince of Hesse to his rank in the Russian army, so that if he joined the Austrian army malicious tongues might not say that a general who had been thrown out of the Russian army was immediately taken over into the Austrian army. Prince Alexander wrote to his sister in desperation to say that by his harsh procedure the Tsar had at one blow destroyed not only his prospects in Russia but everywhere else as well. The Emperor Francis Joseph insisted that the Prince must be completely rehabilitated in the army, and wrote saying so to the Tsar, who replied on January 13, 1853, that the Prince had not forfeited his charge, but had been allowed to retire at his own request, since it was impossible for a lady-in-waiting to become the sister-in-law of the Crown Princess. There was no question of anything dishonourable.[55] Francis Joseph's reply was delayed for a long time. On February 18, 1853, on the bastion in Vienna, he received a dagger-wound in the throat from the hand of a tailor's assistant named Lebenyi, a former mutineer from a Hussar regiment, which gave him a further excuse for not replying immediately. At the Tsarevitch's unremitting importunity the Tsar finally gave way and granted Prince Alexander the right to wear Russian uniform again. Nevertheless it was feared in St. Petersburg that Francis Joseph would still not make up his mind definitely. In July 1853, however, the Emperor of Austria at last sent word to Prince Alexander that there was no reason against his entering the Austrian army as brigadier. A new sphere of activity was thus assured him. When he arrived in Vienna the Hessian Prince was well received, although the Emperor's attitude remained somewhat reserved. The Archduchess Sophie, however, the Emperor's mother, whose power at court was very considerable, greeted him by saying: "I am very glad indeed that you belong to us now." He was now to have opportunity of seeing how the efforts of the Tsar and the Tsarevitch for the preservation of the friendship between the two empires were viewed and treated in Vienna.

CHAPTER V

FRANCIS JOSEPH AND THE TSAR AT THE PARTING OF THE WAYS

MEANWHILE the international political situation in Europe had taken on a threatening aspect. At the beginning of the year 1853 the position of the Tsar and of his empire was still very satisfactory. Russia had been untouched by revolution, its position as a Great Power had been completely maintained, and hence it had as it were a dominant standing in Central Europe. This was demonstrated in the arrogance with which the Tsar treated the newly crowned Napoleon III, addressing him in a letter not with the appellation customary between monarchs of *mon frère* but simply as *mon ami*. The Tsar, nevertheless, regarded himself as safe for the time being on that side, and believed that he might therefore revive the policy of Catherine II in the Balkans and in the Turkish dominions in general.

"The sick man" in Constantinople was asked to give his assent to a number of demands. The Russian Ambassador in Constantinople used threatening language, and since the Sultan, spurred on by France and England, did not adopt a conciliatory attitude, a Russo-Turkish war impended as early as January of 1853. The Eastern complications were a subject of daily conversation at the court in St. Petersburg, where it was the custom not to conceal even the most important State secrets from the ladies of the imperial family. It sometimes happened that they were carelessly passed on by these ladies in conversation and in letters to their relatives. Hence during the whole of the Crimean War a correspondence was carried on between the Crown Princess Marie and her brother Prince Alexander of Hesse that was most dangerous to the State. For Alexander was now in the Austrian camp—which, as was soon to be seen, was practically on the enemy's side—although his heart was still with Russia.

"Napoleon III", wrote Marie to her brother at Darmstadt towards the end of January 1853, and Alexander copied her letter into his diary on the 25th, "swallowed our *ami* instead of *frère* quite quietly, although he did not care for it. Regarding Turkey we are not so sure; it may yet come to a war . . . some of the reserves have been called up. The people are in a great ferment about it, and the country is buzzing with rumours of war."

The Tsar's conviction that owing to the services rendered to Austria during the revolution Francis Joseph would be on his side played a great part in determining his policy. When a dispute with Montenegro for a time brought an Austro-Turkish war within the bounds of possibility, Nicholas wrote to his friend in Vienna: "If a war with Turkey should result, you may rest assured that it will be the same as if they had declared war on me."

If the cases should be reversed the Tsar counted on the same attitude on the part of Francis Joseph. But he was mistaken. The Austrian Emperor regarded the Tsar's plans and his autocratic behaviour in Constantinople with mistrust. Hence friction arose in the diplomatic relations between Vienna and St. Petersburg, and eventually also between the two rulers. The Emperor Francis Joseph emphasized this by cancelling a visit that he had been planning to pay the Tsar in the summer. The Tsar still persisted in his friendly feelings towards Francis Joseph and refused to believe that the threatening indications from Vienna could really be the harbingers of serious differences of opinion. The Tsar finally decided to demand the protective jurisdiction over all Greek Christians on Turkish soil in the form of an ultimatum. Confidently Marie wrote to her brother on June 17th: "We expect a definite answer from Constantinople to-day or to-morrow. I am still hoping that it will not come to war, at most an occupation of the Danubian provinces."

When the Turks, encouraged by England and France, rejected the ultimatum the Tsar, to the great displeasure of Francis Joseph, marched his armies into Moldavia and Wallachia, and proposed to occupy these principalities as security for the satisfaction of his demands. The letters exchanged by the two monarchs still apparently breathed the greatest cordiality. True, Francis Joseph wrote very cautiously to Nicholas on June 16th, saying that he would "try his best to give" the Tsar the help he asked,[56] but even so he refused to indulge in open hostilities with the Porte, and in further letters he showed that he did not agree with the Tsar's plans for partitioning Turkey. One way and another he was becoming more and more

opposed to the Tsar's policy. Nicholas, however, still would
not abandon his hopes of Austrian co-operation, and decided
to visit Francis Joseph in Olmütz in order to win him over to
his point of view. Thus the interview of September 24, 1853, was
arranged. Prince Alexander of Hesse was in the suite of the
Emperor Francis Joseph, and looked forward with very mixed
feelings to the arrival of the Tsar. He was in doubt as to how he
would be received by him.

On the evening of September 25th the two Emperors and
Count Buol, the Austrian Minister for Foreign Affairs, talked
together for hours. The Tsar realized that Francis Joseph,
instead of falling in with his plans was demanding guarantees
that Russia would respect the integrity of Turkey. These
guarantees included a demand that the Danube should not be
crossed by the Russian armies. It was the beginning of the
vacillating policy that was subsequently to be pursued by
Austria. Nor was the change in Francis Joseph's attitude
towards Russia wholly veiled by the military pomp and
circumstance displayed in honour of the Emperor of Russia.
The Tsar, however, was still unable to believe in the defection
of Francis Joseph. He was indeed quite justified in his disbelief,
for Viennese policy changed from day to day.

In the course of the visit Prince Alexander found an opportunity to point out to the Tsar that he could not have acted
otherwise than he did in the matter of his marriage, and that
therefore the Tsar should not show displeasure with him
permanently. He was to some extent taken back into the Tsar's
good graces, but there was no talk of his re-entering the
Russian service. So the Prince had to resign himself to making
a career in a new country and another army. Here again matters
were not simplified for him by his morganatic marriage. It
was thought that if he were sent to the place where the aged
Archduke John was living—who also had a morganatic wife,
the Countess of Meran, the daughter of the postmaster of
Aussee—he and his wife might find life easier. So he was sent
to Graz, where he immediately called upon the Archduke and
his wife, finding the Countess a "very pleasant woman, but
rather common", as he noted in his diary on October 9, 1853.

Prince Alexander took his duties as newly appointed brigadier
very seriously. It was not long before he also took a prominent
place in society. There was at that time a perfect epidemic of
table-rapping and spirit-raising. The cult had been introduced
by the Empress Eugénie and had spread all over Europe. It

is ludicrous to read in Alexander's diary how at one of the séances the spirit of a butcher, who had died one hundred and forty years earlier, was conjured up, and favoured the company with a farrago of the most arrant nonsense concerning the future of all those present, not without showing a remarkable familiarity with the ambitions of the Prince of Hesse. The visitant was not always the butcher. On another occasion when the séance lasted for three hours, Alexander the Great's repose was broken in upon, and he was requested to foretell the future careers of all the men present, but he also made some very awkward revelations about the faithfulness or otherwise of certain officers' ladies in Graz. The passion for table-rapping increased to such an extent that, especially after Turkey had declared war on Russia on October 23rd for not evacuating the Danubian principalities, and everyone was therefore the more anxious to look into the future, counsel was sought of spirits in Graz almost every evening.

The Tsar accompanied the outbreak of war with a message to the Emperor Francis Joseph in which he designated the prospective war as a crusade in which Russia would defend Christendom, while the Western Great Powers were committing the infamy of fighting for the Crescent. Writing to Francis Joseph on November 14th (26th), the Tsar asks: "Do you want France and England ruling in Constantinople? No, a thousand times no. It would be better for us two to remain united, so as to counteract such an infamous combination."[57] The Tsar, however, did not find Francis Joseph responsive. Far from joining Russia, the Viennese court feared a dangerous increase of power in Russia at the expense of Austria. The Emperor Francis Joseph decided upon a step which, especially from so youthful a man to the older ruler in St. Petersburg, was regarded not merely as a disappointment but as an offensive mockery. On January 7, 1854, Francis Joseph personally wrote in German the most important parts of the draft of a letter to the Tsar, which was then translated into French.[58] In this letter he demanded the positive and solemn assurances of the Tsar that he would not deviate in any way from his earlier promises. The reply of the Tsar,[59] who immediately expressed his painful surprise that he should be treated with such insulting distrust, showed the deep breach which Buol not only did not prevent but actually promoted. Even the unconditional neutrality demanded by the Tsar as the least possible concession was refused, and thus the alliance that had existed between the two Empires for forty years was broken. Nicholas could hardly believe it. "Are you really intending", he wrote to Francis Joseph on January 4th (16th), "to make common cause with the Turks? Does your conscience allow you, the Apostolic Emperor, to do so? If it is really the case, then Russia must march alone on its sacred mission under the sacred symbol of the Cross. But if you were to join forces with the Crescent *against me*, it would be a parricidal war, I do not hesitate to say so. Not thus did your grandfather of venerable and glorious memory look upon the world!"

"The possibility of hostilities between us", he wrote a few weeks later on February 17th (29th), [60] "appears to me a *monstrous absurdity*, when I think that you might come to attack Russia, which only a few years ago came of its own accord to sacrifice its blood in order to reduce your errant subjects to order."

The Emperor Francis Joseph found this reminder of past services galling to his pride. He negotiated with Russia's enemies, France and England, who feeling their power in the East threatened, declared war on Russia on March 27, 1854. Nevertheless Buol did not sincerely desire an alliance with them. He vacillated, first lost Russia's friendship, and finally also that of the Western Powers, when they found out that he was only temporizing with them.

Prince Alexander followed these changes in the relationship between the two empires with growing anxiety, since in a certain sense he belonged to both. His position in the event of an outbreak of a war between Russia and Austria would be invidious. He expressed himself eloquently on the point to his uncle, Emil of Hesse, [61] in a letter written from Graz on April 13th: "The first shots of a European war have been fired, and we are on the eve of the day when the members of the Holy Alliance, which has now gone the way of all flesh, will mutually rend one another and open the door to revolution by purposely destroying the last bulwarks that guard the divinely appointed monarchies. . . . All this threatens to put me in a very difficult position. . . ." Alexander confessed to his uncle that he could not disguise his sympathy for Russia and its army. "This at least is certain," he said in the same letter, "that I shall *never* draw my sword against our erstwhile brothers in arms."

The Emperor Francis Joseph was married at this time to the Princess Elisabeth of Bavaria, who was described by Prince Alexander as "perfectly delicious". He particularly noted the unnecessarily loud "Yes" of the Emperor at the wedding ceremony.

His honeymoon did not prevent the continuance of the Emperor's calamitous Russian policy. "God grant", wrote the Tsarevitch[62] to Alexander of Hesse on May 12th (24th), "that the deplorable policy which Austria has been pursuing lately, and which I am convinced will lead to its own downfall, does not put you into an untenable position."

Meanwhile, on May 24th, a son was born to Prince Alexander, and received the name of Louis. This was Prince Louis of Battenberg, who later became an Admiral in the British navy, and who was at the time of the outbreak of war in 1914 First Lord of the Admiralty. He married Princess Victoria of Hesse, the sister of the Grand Duke Ernest Ludwig of Hesse and of Alexandra, the wife of Tsar Nicholas II.

The young father read the threatening notes which Count Buol sent to Russia on the subject of the evacuation of the Danubian principalities, and wrote letter after letter to his sister and brother-in-law to assure himself that both felt towards him as they had always done. The draft of a letter written on June 4th (16th) reads: "The unfortunate turns of an incomprehensible policy may place me in a camp hostile to Russia, but they will never succeed in altering my convictions and my sacred feelings of loyalty."

Meanwhile the war between Russia on the one side and England, France, and Turkey on the other, continued. The Franco-British fleet lay before Cronstadt, the key to St. Petersburg. An attack was daily expected, and the imperial family was constantly on the alert. A declaration of war by Francis Joseph was also feared at every moment. "The Emperor of Austria is mad", wrote Marie from St. Petersburg as Alexander notes in his diary on July 8th, "to think that the welfare of his empire lies in what I believe will lead to its downfall. . . . It grieves me deeply to know you in the service of an ungrateful and perfidious country like Austria. But what can one do? One must just make the best of things." According to what the Tsar's daughter Olga told Alexander, the Tsar was very much aged and changed by his anxiety over recent events: "I find myself not only lacking in moral courage; but I fear that my physical strength is waning", sighed the Tsar. The Tsarevitch, who was distressed at the effects of the war upon his father, utterly failed to understand Austria and its Emperor. As he wrote to Alexander of Hesse[63] on July 10th (22nd): "I say nothing of gratitude, to which I should have thought we had some right, but I fail to see how Austria's interests are served by conducting her policy in a way that will make war with us inevitable. What can she expect to gain? I foresee only the most unhappy results for her future. I am really sorry to see the young Emperor whom I genuinely liked choosing so mistaken a course. May God forgive him the evils that he is bringing not only on us but also on his own country."

Since the Western Powers did not succeed in achieving any success before Cronstadt and St. Petersburg, they determined to concentrate their efforts on the campaign in the Crimea, which was so far away from the centre of Russia that owing to the lack of railways it was impossible to send down reinforcements quickly. Soon the fortress of Sebastopol became the focus of events. Prince Alexander reported to his brother-in-law from Graz that the Austrian army and its generals were entirely in sympathy with Russia, and did not at all agree with the new course that was being pursued.

"Your remarks about Austria's infamous policy", replied the Tsarevitch[64] on September 11th (23rd), "seemed to me so right that I submitted them to the Tsar. The feelings which you say animate the brave Austrian army pleased him; you know his affection for our late brothers-in-arms. How sad it is to see them helplessly exposed to so great a strain upon their discipline."

A totally unfounded report that Sebastopol had fallen only a day or two after the landing of the English and French was circulated after the French victory on the Alma. It was said to have been brought from the theatre of war by a Tartar. Besides his arrogance at such mare's nests which he did not at all believe in, Alexander of Hesse also expressed his indignation that Francis Joseph should take such an opportunity—the whole of Europe had accepted the report as true—to direct his Ambassador in Paris to congratulate the French on their victory. "I am not the only one here", wrote Prince Alexander to the Tsarevitch on September 29th (October 11th), "to condemn openly this unfair way of treating a Power with which we are not yet at war. That is Buol's latest atrocity, and is a worthy successor to his past actions. . . ." Prince Alexander shows once again in this letter how very strongly he had taken root in Russia during the years he spent in St. Petersburg: "The deep respect that I bear to His Majesty", he continues, "and my love for Russia (which I still regard as my true home), must of course make me look at things from exactly the same standpoint as you do. My feelings are being subjected to severe ordeals. I am condemned to live in a hostile camp, and forced to display a half-hearted sympathy."

In Vienna the real sympathies of Major-General the Prince of Hesse were known. His transfer on November 3rd to the Italian army at Verona might therefore be said to give a hint of the nature of the plans which Francis Joseph was making to govern his future relations with Russia. Alexander dismisses the news in his diary with the remark: "A proof that the Emperor realizes my exceptional position; and, secondly, that war on Russia has been decided upon." The Prince went to Vienna to thank the Emperor for making allowance for his anomalous situation. Francis Joseph said that he was still hoping that war with Russia would not eventuate. Although she was expecting a baby, the Prince thought the Empress very beautiful; but as she made only stereotyped remarks such as: "Have you been here long? How long are you going to stay in Vienna?" he seems to have found her a little insipid. As soon as the Prince took up his new post, he paid a visit to the aged Radetzky in Verona. The old Field-Marshal, who thought well of anything that came from Russia, and to whom the Tsar had several times given presents and high honours, was particularly friendly to the young man. "Old Radetzky", Alexander wrote to the Tsarevitch[65] on December 20th (January 1st), "overwhelms me with marks of friendship. He is most charming, too, with Julia, and is Russian to the finger-tips, as are most of the officers and generals in the army in Italy, who are in any case pretty free in their expressions of opinion. With the exception of Lieutenant-General Count Lichnowsky, who is moderately Western in his views, the other generals refer habitually to Buol as a 'rascal' or a 'brute', to use their own expressions."

The bad omen of the transfer of the Tsarevitch's brother-in-law was followed immediately by a most hostile step. On December 2, 1854, Count Buol had concluded a closer treaty of alliance with the Western Powers, and from then onwards—a mistake which could never be rectified—confronted the Tsar, Austria's neighbour, as the confederate of those who were ranged in war against him. It made no difference to the effect of this action upon the ruler of Russia that the Emperor Francis Joseph did not actually carry out the terms of the treaty with the Western Powers, but always managed to postpone taking action at the cost of his reputation for dependability. The effect upon the Tsar in St. Petersburg—according to well-authenticated reports he is said to have had the portrait and the equestrian statue of the Emperor Francis Joseph that stood in his study removed and to have made his valet a present of them—as well as that upon Russia in general, was immense. In every palace and every cottage throughout the country Austria's behaviour so soon after Russian blood had been shed in saving it from a revolution was most adversely criticized. Prince Alexander of Hesse observed the policy of Count Buol with the greatest indignation, and attributed the blame for the change in the young Emperor to his influence particularly, calling him (Buol) the "most eminent blunderer" in his diary on January 23 and 26, 1855.

The disappointment over Austria, the unsatisfactory progress of the war, and tragic events within his own family very greatly affected the health of the Tsar, who was now fifty-nine years old. The course of the Crimean War put the finishing touch to his condition both physical and mental. In addition, Nicholas caught a cold at a parade during the early part of February, which turned to pneumonia and confined him to his bed. On February 17th his condition grew so much worse that Mandt, the German doctor who was treating him, feared the worst. According to old tradition Nicholas lay on a plain iron camp bed covered with two blankets and an old grey military overcoat. He was very weak and his breathing was laboured. An icy blast howled in the chimneys and big snowflakes were driven against the windows. The sickroom was dimly lighted by a single wax candle burning before the inexorably ticking clock. The doctor examined the Tsar, and realized from the rattling breath that the lung was beginning to collapse. Many years earlier the Tsar had made Mandt promise that he would tell him the absolute truth if death were approaching. Now— fearing that if the sacraments for the dying were not administered in time the Russian doctors, who hated him as a foreigner, might expose him to abuse—Mandt fulfilled his promise with cruel exactitude. "Tell me, Mandt," asked the Tsar anxiously after the examination,[66] "am I going to die?" The doctor took the Tsar's left hand as it lay on the coverlet, pressed it, and said steadily: "Yes, Your Majesty."

"What is wrong?"

"The lung is beginning to collapse, Your Majesty."

The effect of this answer upon the dying man was shattering. There is hardly a man who would wish to be told the truth so baldly at such a time.

"How do you dare to tell me such an opinion so definitely?" the Tsar asked the doctor. Then he set about putting his affairs in order.

A courier had just come from the Crimea with letters and dispatches. "That has nothing more to do with me", said the Tsar, and had them handed over to the Tsarevitch. "Henceforward I belong wholly to God."

The Tsarina, herself very ill, took a heart-rending farewell of her husband. The priest fulfilled his office with tears coursing down his cheeks. The Grand Duchess Mary, the Tsarevitch, and Alexander of Hesse's sister followed each other into the death chamber. "I have done my best", said the Tsar to his son. "I am sorry not to have made a better job of it."[67]

Then the Tsar bade farewell to his whole family and also to his household and all his servants in a voice that grew ever weaker and with breath that became more and more laboured. Only an hour before his death he asked the doctor: "When, oh when will it end?"

The Tsar was conscious to the very last, then his lung would hardly function any more, the grey overcoat rose and sank more and more slowly and feebly under the failing breath, and at noon on February 18th a new Tsar stood beside the deathbed of his father.

With Nicholas's death a monarch passed who was not altogether guiltless of the difficult condition in which he bequeathed the kingdom to his successor. He had all his life paid too much attention to the army, and even then had been too greatly occupied with old rigid dispositions and parade-ground drill. Other mistakes, such as the neglect of road and railway construction, which in a gigantic country like Russia made the rapid concentration and shifting not only of troops and munitions but also of food for the population impossible, wholly deprived the army of its effectiveness, as was shown especially during the Crimean War. Nevertheless, although he was not altogether capable of carrying out his difficult task of governing a country like Russia, Nicholas I was a man whose intentions were of the best; he had a strong sense of duty and of love to his native land, was a good father and altogether an honourable and upright character.

The unexpected news of his death called forth the liveliest dismay all over Europe, and not the least in Prince Alexander at Verona. The Prince's brother-in-law and sister were now Tsar and Tsarina of all the Russias. This fact might be of incalculable consequence to him. He went at once to old

G

Radetzky, who had all his life been most attached and grateful to Nicholas, and found him alone in his study, with his hands before his face, weeping bitterly. Both were taken utterly unawares by the news, for they had heard nothing of the Tsar's illness. Radetzky could hardly speak for emotion: "It is terrible for an old man like me to be obliged to see yet another loved prince die before me. I no longer understand the century in which we are living; and less than ever can I interpret the irresponsible policy of my young Emperor. He is completely lost in illusions as to the real goal towards which Austria has been blindly aiming for the past year." From Albert of Saxony, who often conversed with the Emperor, the Prince of Hesse heard that Francis Joseph was anxious to preserve peace, but that "this fool of a Buol" and General Hess, who sided with Russia, were on such bad terms with one another that one or other of them would very soon have to resign. Albert of Saxony asserted that Hess had fearlessly told the Emperor that war between Austria and Russia would mean the downfall of Austria, even if it were supported by a million bayonets. Prince Alexander wrote and told all this to his sister the Tsarina and added that his last hope was that the recent sad event would make a permanent impression upon the young Emperor. "Possibly", he wrote on February 23 (March 7), 1855, from Verona, "his heart may not at this moment be altogether free from remorse at having met such great trust with such base ingratitude. I wish he might be convinced that the intentions of his counsellors are not honest, either towards him or towards Austria."

For a moment one might almost have believed that the Tsar's death had indeed had such an effect upon the Emperor Francis Joseph. Prince Alexander of Hesse copied in his diary on March 18, 1855, a letter from the court Chamberlain, Count von Adlerberg, telling him that the Emperor with his condolences had sent word to St. Petersburg to say that he was particularly grieved that the misfortune should have occurred just at the moment when he had hoped to express his gratitude actively. He begged the new Tsar to believe that he would give him the opportunity of seeing that he had come back into the right path again.

In reality this letter was no more than an expression of one of the continual vacillations in which Austrian foreign policy indulged during the Crimean War. At the very same time the Emperor Francis Joseph refused the offer of a closer alliance with France, which Napoleon sent by the French Foreign

Minister. Francis Joseph's letter of February 24th contained no more than the customary expressions of condolence. The prophetic reply of the Tsar Alexander II,[68] written on March 5th (17th), reads much more seriously: "You will readily understand what effect the political events of the past year must have produced upon my father's feelings. He was *deeply wounded*, for instead of finding in you the *friend and faithful ally* upon whom he counted and whom he loved like his own son, he saw you pursuing a political course which brought you into ever closer touch with our enemies, and which if it is not altered *must inevitably lead to a fratricidal war, for which you will be answerable before God.* . . . As long as we remain united, I am absolutely convinced that the whole of Europe will be preserved from a general collapse; if we do not—it will be unfortunate for Europe, for then the last bar will go down before the revolutionary hydra."

Alexander II sent a request to Vienna that his brother-in-law might be given leave to go to Russia, and this was granted. Prince Alexander was received by the Emperor Francis Joseph on April 1st, but not a word was spoken about politics. Hardly had the Prince arrived in St. Petersburg than the new Tsar asked him whether the Emperor Francis Joseph had not given him any message. Alexander II was the more unpleasantly surprised by the negative answer since the Russian difficulties in Sebastopol and the Crimea were increasing. The message of condolence had given the Tsar some reason to hope for an Austrian move in his favour, and now nothing of the kind was happening after all. An attempt at the Emperor Napoleon's life in the Champs Elysées on April 30th had—"unfortunately", thought Prince Alexander—failed of success, and from the side of England no change of opinion was to be expected. Nevertheless Russia's young ruler longed to put an end to the war, so as to have leisure to familiarize himself with the duties of the high position that had fallen to him so unexpectedly soon. There was, however, small prospect of his obtaining this leisure.

The new Tsar overwhelmed his brother-in-law with marks of friendship during his visit. When they parted he said to him: "I hope that your return to Russia may one day be arranged." Loaded with presents, but somewhat disappointed none the less, Prince Alexander returned to Verona. On his way through Vienna Francis Joseph questioned him very closely as to the opinions of the new Tsar, whether he really desired peace, and whether everything would now be changed in St. Petersburg. "Yes; but national honour must not be affronted", was the answer.

"Thank goodness", remarked Francis Joseph in reply, "there is no likelihood of a war between ourselves and Russia now. But I am doubtful whether we shall be able to extricate ourselves from the present complications without a war of some sort."

"The Tsar Alexander", replied the Prince, "commissioned me to tell Your Majesty that he counts upon you to find an honourable means of retreat from the awkward state of affairs that prevailed at his accession to the throne. The decision lies in Your Majesty's hands."

"I hope with all my heart that I may be able to prove myself useful to the Tsar and to procure peace."

In spite of his encouraging words the promised deeds fell very far short of the expectations of the Tsar and of his brother-in-law, and Alexander returned to his military duties in Italy.

It was terribly hot there during that summer. The dust was fearful, and thus everything conduced to the spread of the cholera epidemic that swept across Northern Italy and led to a panic among the population. The people fled in tens of thousands from the cities into the higher Alps. Alexander of Hesse lived in the greatest disquiet. He saw with horror that the skill of the doctors failed utterly, and that in the "hotbed of cholera", Verona, four patients out of five died. He discovered with amazement that the doctors did not dare to go to the bedside of the sufferers, but contented themselves with looking at them from the doorway. Often they had to be fetched by the police and forced to do their duty.

While threatened by these immediate dangers, Prince Alexander observed the happenings around Sebastopol with growing misgivings. The war was turning out badly for the Russians during that summer. On the other hand the hostile fleets before Cronstadt and Sveaborg had been unable to batter down the fortifications. On August 9th and 10th the Allies bombarded the fortress of Sveaborg uninterruptedly for forty hours. Over twenty thousand large calibre shells were used in the bombardment without doing any appreciable damage. Since the bombardment occurred in the immediate neighbourhood of St. Petersburg, it affected the nerves of the Tsar and Tsarina considerably. But they soon realized with joy that the enemy was doing no particular harm. "The only damage", the Tsarina reported to her brother on August 4 (16), 1855, "is to the navy's store of fuel for the winter, which has been burnt.

Costy [the Grand Duke Constantine] wants to know whether it costs him more to renew his stock of wood or them to supply the thousands and thousands of shells to which they treated Sveaborg. He said it reminded him of the story of Louis XIV's having Algiers bombarded and the town set on fire. After the capitulation the Dey took aside the Admiral in command of the French fleet and asked him how much the undertaking had cost the King. When the Admiral replied by naming a very large sum, the Dey exclaimed: 'Why did he not give me the money—I would have set the town on fire myself!' "

The news from the Crimea was less satisfactory. A vain attempt was made to relieve the garrison in Sebastopol, the Malakoff fort was stormed by the enemy, and this sealed the fate of the fortress. Prince Alexander assured his brother-in-law of his sympathy, and again regretted the fact that a recently planned attempt upon the life of Napoleon III had been frustrated. "Clumsy fools", Alexander calls the would-be assassins in his letter. The Tsar's longing for peace was increased by the fall of the fortress. By making reasonably favourable suggestions for peace Austria might now have won back a large part of the sympathy it had lost in Russia. Buol liked the idea of being an arbiter between the belligerents, but only managed to embroil Austria with both sides.

Eventually peace was concluded on terms which undoubtedly involved a deep humiliation for the Tsar Alexander and his mighty empire. The Russians blamed "faithless" Austria almost more than their actual enemies. Nevertheless peace had been signed and they had to make the best of it. This was the feeling at the Russian court, and it is reflected in a letter written by the Tsarina to her brother on March 26 (April 7), 1856: "I shall say no more about the peace treaty. You know what I think of it. We are resigned but not pleased." Count Peter Shuvaloff, of whom the Tsarina thought a great deal because he was interesting and amusing, described his experiences at the French court after his return from Paris. The only person who impressed him at all was the Emperor himself. He considered those about him to be "less than nothing". There was great luxury everywhere, but not always good taste. He found Plon-Plon, "the cousin of the nephew of the uncle"—one of the numerous nicknames given to the son of King Jerome Napoleon—on very bad terms with everybody; and he thought the Empress beautiful, "especially at a distance". On the whole Shuvaloff brought away not too bad an impression of France, and was of opinion that in future it would be well for Russia to be on better terms with this country.

From that time onwards the policy of Prince Alexander Gortchakoff, who had been appointed Russian Foreign Minister in place of Nesselrode in April 1856, was on the whole directed towards the achievement of a Franco-Russian *rapprochement*. His appointment was a result of the Crimean War. In view of Austria's attitude Gortchakoff, then ambassador in Vienna, had been so filled with burning hatred of the country and of the inspirer of its foreign policy that he found it easier to forgive France, the open enemy, than "secretive" Austria. The story goes that when Buol spoke to him at their farewell meeting, the fifty-eight year old ambassador said in reply to Buol's hope of an early reconciliation: "We are separated by an abyss. If you wish to bring about a reconciliation you must hurl yourself into the abyss like Curtius." Even if he did not really make this remark, it represents Gortchakoff's views; and he left Vienna firmly resolved that Austria should yet pay dearly for her attitude during the Crimean War.

Prince Alexander disliked the new Russian Foreign Minister personally and disapproved of his political views.

Whenever he had been in Vienna he had felt himself treated as of little account by the Russian Ambassador, and had heard Gortchakoff remark that for a German prince his sympathies were too Russophil.

Alexander II, who was good-natured and easily swayed emotionally, regarded affairs rather from the emotional than the judicial standpoint, and therefore preferred to make compromises instead of taking clean-cut decisions. He was very glad indeed of peace despite the undeniable humiliation. He would at last be free to begin on the reconstitution of Russia, according to his own ideas—a task that had hitherto been impossible on account of the war. His reforms were to be introduced by a magnificent coronation in Moscow, which was to benefit all his subjects and to show the world that in spite of what had happened all classes of the Russian population still congregated about their ruler. The aristocracy gathered in Moscow from near and far for the festivities. Among the guests was the Emperor's brother-in-law, Prince Alexander of Hesse.

On Friday August 29, 1856, the coronation ceremonies began with the brilliant entry of the Tsar and Tsarina into Moscow. Thirty golden coaches with six horses apiece followed the imperial gala-carriage that was drawn by splendid white horses, and a glittering escort of cavalry and guardsmen completed the procession. Accompanied by the sound of glorious singing, by the thunder of artillery, and by the pealing of the eight thousand bells of Moscow's sixteen hundred churches, Alexander II and his wife, who looked pale and exhausted with her exertions, entered the cathedral which contained the miraculous Madonna of Vladimir—the most revered picture in all Russia. At the coronation ceremonial in the cathedral there were several awkward incidents. When four court ladies tried to fix the crown, which did not fit, more firmly onto the Tsarina's head, it fell, to the general dismay, into the folds of her cloak, and was only just saved from falling onto the ground. The ceremonial had been imperfectly rehearsed and badly organized. Since there were continual delays it went on for four hours. Count Ploudoff and Prince Shahoffskoy let fall the cushion on which lay the collar of the Order of St. Andrew at the very moment when they were about to hand it to the Emperor. Everyone was glad when the interminable ceremony was over and they could go on to the banquet, where the Tsar and Tsarina were served on golden platters by staff officers. According to ancient custom, Prince Dolgoruki, the chief cup-bearer, presented the Tsar with a golden goblet of mead. This brought the official part of the banquet to an end.

Next came a military review at which the Tsar personally paraded eighty thousand men before his wife. The populace was given a vast banquet. Innumerable tables to seat the three hundred thousand guests, who were served by several regiments of infantry, covered something like five and a half square miles of ground. At intervals fountains had been erected which flowed with wine, beer, and liqueurs instead of water. By night Moscow looked like a magnificent sea of light. Every free male subject of the Tsar received a commemoration medal. Although Prince Alexander was now no longer a Russian subject, the Tsar presented him with one, saying: "I wish at least that you could have worn it on our uniform, for I know that in these sad times you have never ceased to be one of us."

This brought the coronation festivities to an end. After Moscow in its holiday season, Prince Alexander's little garrison at Verona seemed even meaner and more lonely. But military service did not permit of lengthy brooding. Only the memory remained to Prince Alexander, accompanied by a secret regret that he had been but a visitor in Moscow when he really belonged there in his heart.

CHAPTER VI

CARNIVAL TO CARNAGE

THE Emperor Francis Joseph was mistaken in believing that Austria was bound to benefit by the Crimean War inasmuch as its future lay in the East, where Russia's influence and power would be circumscribed as a result of the war. "It is hard", he wrote to his mother[69] on October 8, 1854, "to be obliged to proceed against former friends, but in politics it cannot always be avoided. . . . One must be an Austrian first of all, and therefore, apart from the Tsar Nicholas personally, I am glad that Russia is now so weak."

Actually, however, the Tsar personally could not so easily be left out of account. He was absolute ruler of his dominions, and anyone who was opposed to the policy of Russia became the personal enemy of the Tsar of all the Russias. The outcome of the Crimean War was quite different from what Francis Joseph had hoped for. He had managed to offend all belligerents, while little Piedmont had far-sightedly fought beside the two Western Powers.

In their post-war policy these two Western States simply acted in accordance with the logical conclusion to be drawn from this attitude of Austria's. Napoleon III caused confidential inquiries to be made of Cavour as to what he, Napoleon, could do for Piedmont and Italy. But he kept carefully aloof from Austria. This change in the situation had an immediate repercussion in the Italian provinces of Austria to which Prince Alexander had been transferred, and where hope began once more to spring up of liberation from the hated foreign yoke by the help of France. Hitherto revolutionaries in Lombardy and Venice had been very harshly treated. After the collapse of an attempted rebellion organized by Mazzini in February 1853 at Milan, the Emperor had confiscated the property of all who had left Lombardy and Venice for political reasons. This affected some of the most noted aristocratic families, whose sons had offered their services to Piedmont. In the name of the Kingdom of Piedmont, which made the affairs of the Italian-speaking provinces its own, Cavour, at the Congress of Paris in 1856, accused Austria before all the world of oppressing those parts of Italy which were under its dominion. Many Italian families in Lombardy and in Venetia avoided all intercourse with the Austrian officers. Hence the imperial army in Italy became more and more socially isolated. This was the state of affairs when Alexander of Hesse, who was very sociably inclined, was transferred to Italy with his young wife. His garrison town was at first Verona, where Radetzky's headquarters were. Owing to the friendly feelings with which the old Field-Marshal, who in 1854 was eighty-seven years of age, had always regarded Russia and its Tsar, very amicable relations soon sprang up between Radetzky and the new Tsar's brother-in-law. Both anxiously watched the outcome of the Congress in Paris in April 1856. The Emperor Francis Joseph, becoming aware of his isolation in Paris, determined to visit the Italian provinces in company with his charming young wife, who aroused the liveliest admiration wherever she appeared, and to repeal certain harsh laws that had been promulgated in former times, in the hope that he might thus effect a reconciliation. The Emperor was tending increasingly to act on his own initiative in these days. As early as the spring of 1852, after the sudden death of Schwarzenberg, he had said in a letter to his mother,[70] dated April 14, 1852, that he would be obliged more and more to attend to things himself, because he could trust nobody else as he could trust himself—which had, he felt, its good side too.

Towards the end of November 1856 the Emperor and Empress appeared in Venice, where they met with a lukewarm reception. An amnesty and the revocation of the sequestration of the property of exiles was announced. Unfortunately it only looked as if the Emperor were trying to curry favour. Prince Alexander of Hesse went from Verona to Venice to greet the Emperor, whom he thought looking well and very sunburnt, but much thinner. He was rather offended that the Empress, as "pretty as a picture", and leading her little daughter by the hand, passed by him without saying a word, although "with infinite grace". The Prince observed how well the Emperor talked Italian to the people, but smiled over the little Italian phrases that the Empress had obviously learnt by rote. Incidentally, the Prince was also amused at her very imperfect French.

The reception accorded to the imperial couple lacked

enthusiasm both on their arrival and at the various festivities, and on their appearance at the Teatre Fenice. The tremendous difference was noted at public functions between the appearance presented by the Commander-in-Chief, Field-Marshal Radetzky, who was looking particularly worn and tired at this time, and the slender form of the young Emperor. Francis Joseph himself was much struck by the senility of his aged champion. "The Field-Marshal", he wrote to his mother[71] on December 4, 1856, "has become terribly altered and childish." He decided to place Radetzky on the retired list and to set new men at the head of the military and civil administration of the Italian provinces. At a short visit which the Emperor paid to the Field-Marshal on December 18th he gave him clearly to understand that he was to offer his resignation. "It is high time", the Emperor wrote to his mother soon after this, "to settle things in Verona."—"Dear old Radetzky", Prince Alexander told his sister the Tsarina at about the same time in a letter dated December 23, 1856, "is going to retire, and not of his own free will, although he has often suggested doing so."

Early in January the Emperor and Empress left Venice and went on a short visit to Verona. At every place they stopped there were great receptions, and the garrisons were turned out. At the court dinner parties there were continual difficulties with the Italian ladies, some of whom refused invitations altogether, while others came only under compulsion, spoke only Italian, and declared that they understood no other language. Prince Alexander complained that the Emperor and Empress treated his wife badly. They did indeed invite her to dinner with her husband, but did not admit her to their private apartments. At dinner the Empress addressed only a few curt phrases to her, the Emperor merely inquired: "Were you at the review this morning?" Afterwards the Emperor passed by the Countess Julia, who stood at the head of the ladies waiting to speak to him, without saying a word, and began to talk to a lady-in-waiting standing next to her, the Countess Orti. "Such rudeness", writes Prince Alexander indignantly in his diary, "naturally mortified poor Julia terribly, especially since she was accustomed to the friendly gallantry with which the Tsar treated ladies." A gala performance at the theatre that evening proved a miserable failure. The applause and cheering were very meagre and gave the impression of having been carefully rehearsed. On January

PRINCESS JULIA OF BATTENBERG

9th the national festival, the *bacchanale dei gnocchi*, was celebrated after having been prohibited since 1847.

This festival consisted of a great procession in fancy dress. On thirty-five colossal cars each drawn by four to six oxen, whole scenes, ships, and gigantic symbolic figures were set up. Between the cars rode men in various costumes on horses and donkeys. Twenty musicians accompanied the procession at the end of which came the *re dei gnocchi* with his suite, and finally Jordis, the governor of the province, in his coach surrounded by horsemen in quaint costumes. The procession marched past the Emperor, and the king of the *gnocchi* entered a marquee which had been erected immediately opposite the imperial grandstand, where the unhappy Jordis was made to take a seat at a table. After making a speech the king of the festivities raised the lid of a steaming dish, and fed the governor with *gnocchi*. Poor Jordis cut a pitiable figure. It was too severe a contrast to his usual haughty reserve, and the Emperor held his sides with laughing. The Mayor of Verona also brought the Emperor a plate of it, and he had willy-nilly to taste it. At this sight the twenty thousand spectators broke into a storm of applause. The high officers of State and of the army, however, went home with very mixed feelings. They felt that an otherwise harmless national festival had, on this occasion, been made into a sort of mockery of the highest officials of Verona and of the Emperor himself.

A great circus in the arena on the following day gave the Emperor an opportunity of seeing this vast Roman amphitheatre with ten thousand people in it. It would easily have held a great many more. The spectacle was amazingly impressive; but the Emperor's reception was again very lukewarm. Soon afterwards the Emperor and Empress went on to Brescia, where, according to Prince Alexander, their reception "was cordial on the part of the workmen and countryfolk, but very cold on the part of the aristocracy". Not a single lady of the nobility had herself presented. Nor were things much different in Milan. Count Wallmoden, who accompanied the Emperor, tells that sixty per cent. of the aristocracy stayed away from the court and visited neither the Scala nor the Corso. A court ball which had been planned in Milan had to be cancelled, because no more than twenty ladies from the whole of Milan society would appear at it. None the less Prince Alexander found the Emperor and his wife in good spirits, and the Empress actually much more talkative than before. A far worse reception even had been anticipated, and many Austrian generals considered that the court went too far in trying to conciliate the Italians. "The Countess Litta, *née* Bolognini," writes Prince Alexander in his diary, "who instead of going to the drawing-room at the palace drove up and down the Corso at the same hour in a four-horse coach, was in spite of this piece of insolence invited to a court dinner and treated most courteously. By way of thanks she left Milan on the following day, so as not to expose herself to a second invitation to the imperial court!"

Prince Alexander further relates in a letter to Baron von Drachenfels[72] on February 6th that Count Litta appeared at an audience only after the Emperor had told his brother the Duke to advise him very seriously not to stay away. He obeyed the imperial command and immediately after the above-mentioned dinner he accompanied his wife into the country.

Various young people had to be sent out of Milan as quickly as possible because they were taking lists from house to house containing a demand that people should bind themselves by signature not to appear at court. Showers of anonymous letters had been coming from Turin during the past months, telling the ladies that if they were seen at court all the newspapers in Piedmont would publish their past and present secrets, liaisons, etc., if necessary inventing them.

Although Prince Alexander's impression was that the attitude of the people towards the Austrian Emperor was for the moment at all events friendly, and that there was a certain want of confidence between the populace and the leaders of the aristocracy, he was nevertheless convinced that no gratitude was to be expected in return for the far-reaching indulgence that was now being shown to the Italian provinces. "The Emperor's journey has gone off far better than anyone had dared to hope in Vienna," wrote Prince Alexander to his sister on February 13th, "but it is not going to make much difference to the mental attitude of the people."

On March 1st special editions of the papers gave the news of Radetzky's retirement, of the appointment of the Archduke Ferdinand Max, the Emperor's brother, as Governor-General of Venice and Lombardy, and of General Count Gyulai, a protégé of the Adjutant-General Count Grünne, as Commander-in-Chief of the Austrian army in Italy. The newly appointed Commander-in-Chief wanted to have Count Wallmoden as his second-in-command, but he refused for a long time to agree to it. According to an entry in Prince Alexander's diary on March 3rd, Count Wallmoden confided to him that in a long conversation between himself and Count Gyulai, he had said amongst other things that Radetzky's retirement was regretted throughout the army in Italy. Gyulai had utterly lost his temper and had replied furiously: "I know that I am hated and that people say, 'There goes Gyulai the policeman,' and all that sort of thing, but the army's opinion does not concern me at all. I demand only blind obedience, and I intend to have it. I don't care a damn about popularity, and as for the idiotic sentimentality that goes on about the Field-Marshal, it is high time it stopped, and I shall see to it that it does."

After a day's hunting, which was really a massacre at which no less than nine hundred and fifty-seven ducks were shot, the Emperor and Empress started on their homeward journey. First, however, an embarrassing farewell call had to be paid on Radetzky in Verona. On the way through Cremona, there were great festivities. At dinner in a palace which the Marquis Alaponzoni had bequeathed to the Emperor together with some valuable art treasures, Prince Alexander sat next to the Empress Elisabeth, who appeared dressed in a crinoline according to the latest Paris fashion. "The size of her dress", he wrote to his sister in St. Petersburg, with much amusement, "was so immense that I was half covered by it!"

The journey was then continued to Verona, where the Emperor and Empress went to the house of the aged Field-Marshal. The farewell was touching. Radetzky broke down utterly, and the Emperor too was in tears as he left the Field-Marshal's room. The old man was terribly unstrung, and on the following day yielded to the extraordinary whim of shaving off the moustache that he had worn since the Battle of Novara as a sign that he was no longer on the active list.

Prince Alexander visited the Field-Marshal on the same day and found him still very depressed. When the Prince saluted him, Radetzky held out his hand: "My dear good sir, I no longer have the right to accept salutes, I am nothing now." Nevertheless, despite his years, the aged Field-Marshal could not grow accustomed to being inactive. He put it even more bluntly to his immediate circle: "They are throwing me away like a squeezed lemon", he said.[73]

Prince Alexander was glad when the Emperor's stay in Italy was over. "I must own", he wrote to his sister, "that I am not sorry that all this commotion is coming to an end." The Emperor Francis Joseph left Italy with mixed feelings. He hoped very much that the presence of his brother, who was gifted with great charm, and the establishment of a real court, would please the Italians and put them into a more amicable frame of mind. "On the whole we quite enjoyed being here," he wrote to his mother[74] from Milan on March 2, 1857, " . . . and I feel rather more satisfied, if not altogether at ease. This country must be one of the most difficult in the world. . . . God will help us; and time, together with Max's tact, will do much."

Prince Alexander was distressed that the Emperor had refused to transfer him from Verona to Milan on account of his wife. He felt the slight the more keenly because his marriage was a very happy one. On April 5, 1857, another boy, the third child, was born to them. The Prince asked the Tsar and Radetzky to be the baby's godfathers and it was therefore called Alexander Joseph. Filled with emotion, the ninety-year-old Field-Marshal attempted to say a few words at the christening. All those present were touched at the spectacle of the contrast between the old man and his godchild, which made them involuntarily think of the cradle and the grave, the beginning and the end.

Meanwhile the relations between Austria and Piedmont had grown noticeably worse. Austria's Italian provinces not only regarded Piedmont as a State of the same nationality, but also envied it the system of government which Cavour had introduced there. The Archduke Ferdinand Max's gallant ways and his well-meant efforts at conciliation were unavailing. Moreover, his conciliatory régime soon brought him into sharp opposition to the Commander-in-Chief of the army as well as to his brother the Emperor. Francis Joseph was very anxious to make friends with the Italians, but he was given to understand that his brother's efforts were going rather too far.

The continuous friction between Piedmont and Austria finally led to the rupture of diplomatic relations. Cavour was using every means to provoke war, and to secure that Piedmont should enter into it with powerful allies, and as well equipped as possible. Austria's attitude during the past years was not forgotten in Russia. When the Tsarina heard of the diplomatic breach on March 21 (April 2), 1857, she remarked: "Our sympathies are neither with the one side nor with the other."

On June 8th of this year Prince Alexander received a letter

from his brother, the Grand Duke of Hesse, containing the news that on July 5th "the Russians would invade them and would roll along to Wildbad on the 7th". This was his way of announcing a visit from the Russian imperial family, whom Prince Alexander did not on any account want to miss.

Napoleon III, who was staying near by at Plombières, tried to obtain an interview with the Tsar. He first invited the Grand Duke of Hesse and Prince Alexander to visit him. The Emperor had sent for his wife to be present at this interview. "To pass the time of day", as Alexander remarked. He thought the Empress Eugénie beautiful and graceful, especially when after dinner she taught the guests the latest dance—the lancers. Napoleon took advantage of a suitable moment to ask Prince Alexander to request his brother-in-law the Tsar to suggest a meeting.

The Prince fulfilled the commission at Kissingen, where the Tsar was staying at the time, and whither he had secretly sent for the Burmese general, d'Orgoni, in order to discuss the situation in India with him. Although Gortchakoff tried to dissuade the Tsar from receiving d'Orgoni, he had him presented on the promenade of the Kurhaus in full view of the public. The general handed the Tsar a memorandum containing a detailed plan of attack upon British India by a Russian army.

After this incident the Tsar replied to his brother-in-law that he wished to make the personal acquaintance of Napoleon, and suggested that the middle of September would be a good time for the meeting. Then he told him jokingly that Prince Alexander Cantacuzene wanted to make him (Alexander of Hesse) king of Roumania.

The rumours of an imminent meeting between the Tsar and Napoleon roused anxiety in Vienna. The complete isolation of Austria after the Crimean War would be emphasized even more sharply by a newly arising friendship between France and Russia. Hence Vienna also planned to use Prince Alexander's services as go-between. Count Rechberg, the Austrian representative to the Federal Diet in Frankfurt, an opponent of Buol's anti-Russian policy, urged upon Prince Alexander to use his peculiar position as regards the two emperors to prepare the way for a reconciliation. "Evidently", wrote Prince Alexander on August 19, 1857, to his brother-in-law, who had returned to St. Petersburg, "I am designed by all the emperors, your august colleagues, to act the flattering part of the Genius of Reconciliation. Here I am once again with an olive branch in my hand, and this time I am speaking in the name of the Emperor of Austria, who also requests a personal interview with you."

The Tsar Alexander replied that he would not care to agree to a meeting except at Warsaw, where he would be on Russian soil.

"If he [Francis Joseph] is really anxious to make friends with us," wrote the Tsar[75] to Prince Alexander on August 13 (25), 1857, "let him show it before the whole of Europe. I do not need his friendship, but neither do I reject it, and I should be really glad to receive him in Warsaw, where he came barely eight years ago to *beg for my father's help. He may have forgotten, but we have not, that Russia shed its blood to preserve his crown.*

"His former guest in Pest and Vienna, whom he treated with so much friendliness in those days, has long since forgotten any personal affronts. But the Emperor of Russia dare not be oblivious to all the misfortune that his [the Emperor Francis Joseph's] infamous policy has brought upon Russia."

Prince Alexander said to himself that Warsaw would be quite impossible. "It would be a sort of trip to Canossa, and would therefore be absolutely refused in Vienna."

He suggested some neutral ground such as Darmstadt, but this was declined by Alexander II. Finally, Weimar was agreed upon since both Emperors were anxious for a meeting.

Prince Alexander first accompanied his brother-in-law to Stuttgart on September 24, 1857, to meet Napoleon III. The two monarchs felt more in sympathy with one another after a series of short interviews, and talked about the "changes in the map of Europe", as Napoleon expressed it.

"Sooner or later it will be necessary", he declared, according to Prince Alexander's notes of the meetings, "because the stipulations of 1814 will always be humiliating." When the Tsar asked Napoleon about his plans regarding Italy, he replied that he thought "a confederacy of Italian States under the presidency of the Pope, and with the exclusion of Austria would probably be best".

When they parted, Napoleon III shook hands with Prince Alexander and said: "*Adieu, mon prince*, and many thanks, for you brought about this meeting."[76]

Soon afterwards the Tsar and his wife went with Prince Alexander to Weimar to meet the Emperor of Austria. The Tsar was fairly certain that Francis Joseph was seeking the meeting only in order to soften the impression made upon the world by the Stuttgart interview. Nevertheless the present interview might be productive of fruitful results. The Emperor of Austria consented to pay the first visit to the Tsar, and was taken to him by the Grand Duke of Weimar in a coach drawn by six splendid cream-coloured horses. To all outward appearance the greetings and embraces that passed between the two emperors were most cordial. Actually Francis Joseph was desperately embarrassed. Not a word was said about the Crimean War or the Tsar Nicholas, the political gain of the meeting was slight, and the cordiality was all on the surface. The Tsarina Marie received Francis Joseph coldly though courteously. And when he sent word by Prince Alexander asking the Tsar whether, since they both went the same way, he would care to share his carriage to Dresden, Gortchakoff whose sympathies were with France, dissuaded him from accepting, not wishing that the meeting with Napoleon III should be put in the shade by too great an appearance of intimacy with Francis Joseph. Prince Alexander was given the unpleasant task of conveying the negative reply to the Emperor.

As a reward for his services as intermediary Prince Alexander was given the right by the Tsar to wear Russian uniform again, and by Francis Joseph the Grand Cross of the Order of St. Leopold as well as the transfer to Milan that he had asked for some months earlier.

When Prince Alexander returned to Italy, Count Radetzky thanked him cordially for his services in the attempted reconciliation between the two monarchs, which the old Field-Marshal regarded as the only safeguard for the future welfare, and indeed the continued existence of the two empires and their dynasties. "The poor old man is terribly weary of having nothing to do", Prince Alexander wrote of the Field-Marshal. "But he insists on going to watch parades and manœuvres, for which occasions he has had a special carriage built, into which he can be helped from the back."

In Milan Prince Alexander was received in a very friendly manner by the Governor-General, the Archduke Max. The Archduke introduced him to his seventeen-year-old wife Charlotte who talked to the Prince in German, and whom he thought "delightful, very charming, courteous, and really pretty. . . . She looks like an Italian," he continued, "not at all an Orléans like her brothers, and she speaks all languages. The only thing I find irksome in her is that she speaks too

H

slowly." The Archduke's court was arranged "on grand, but somewhat too original lines". Anyone to whom he sent a gold button with the initials F.M. and a coronet on it was thereby invited to every function throughout the season. Every evening at six o'clock there was a large dinner party of twenty-five to thirty people, with an orchestra and a crowd of servants dressed in Louis XV style, with powdered hair and wearing posies in their buttonholes. At every door were stationed halberdiers, ushers, grooms, priests, gamekeepers, lackeys, fierce Dalmatians armed to the teeth, and even negroes, who were employed about the house. At his castle at Monza the Archduke introduced an English country-house mode of life.

Meanwhile the aged Count Radetzky fell ill with a serious attack of influenza that brought pneumonia in its train. The old Field-Marshal's iron constitution, however, staved off dissolution for six whole days. His death was expected hourly. No officer went to any theatre or public place of entertainment. On the morning of New Year's Day, 1858, Prince Alexander was admitted to the Field-Marshal's room. He was sitting up in an armchair that was continuously wheeled about the room so that breathing should be easier for him. The Field-Marshal recognized the Prince, but he could no longer speak and only managed weakly to wave good-bye to him. The old man lived for several more days, and it was not until the morning of January 5th that he died after a terrible struggle, at the age of ninety-one years and two months. The funeral service was held with tremendous pomp at the cathedral, to the twenty-six pillars of which were affixed shields bearing the names of the battles in which the Field-Marshal had fought, from Belgrade in 1788 until Novara in 1849.

On January 17th the sensation caused by Radetzky's death was effaced by the news of Orsini's attempt upon the life of the French Emperor and Empress, by throwing a bomb at them in front of the Grand Opera House in Paris. The episode roused the more attention since the three ringleaders among the assassins were Italians, and it soon turned out that the attack was to have been a punishment for the fact that Louis Napoleon, who had once been a member of the Carbonari in Italy, had as Emperor done nothing as yet to help the cause of Italian unity. The bomb injured innocent persons and missed the Emperor and his wife. It was none the less an effective threat to Napoleon III, and one which had no small bearing on the events of the two following years.

To outward appearances little was to be seen in Milan of all the unrest simmering beneath the surface, nor of all the hopeful expectancy of some event that should bring the land to freedom. The carnival season of the year 1858, at which the ladies appeared in the immense crinolines then in fashion, was a particularly gay one.

The court set the standard, but Alexander of Hesse did not altogether agree with the way in which the Archduke Max "truckled to the Italians".[77] "I can hardly think", he wrote, "that this system would meet with the Emperor's approbation, if he were to discover the true state of affairs; especially if he knew that the Governor-General seems positively ashamed of the imperial uniform at his receptions, and that he sends his aide-de-camp to request the few officers who are invited to the balls not to have themselves introduced to the Italian ladies! Count Gyulai of course takes the army's part against the exclusively Italian court camarilla. The most regrettable discord already prevails, and the Governor-General as well as the Commander-in-Chief embrace every opportunity of being rude to one another."

It was in the social sphere especially that the political opposition of the native elements to the foreign army of occupation was continually coming to the fore. It happened from time to time that members of the high Italian nobility who appeared at the Archducal court were insulted by masked men of good standing at the *vegliones*—the masked balls at the Scala—which frequently led to duels ending tragically. None the less the populace would not forgo two days of the coriandoli-battles that had been prohibited since 1848, and only reintroduced since the Emperor's visit. "This Carnavalone", wrote Prince Alexander to his sister on February 14 (26), 1858, "is the maddest business you can possibly imagine. The two hundred thousand inhabitants of Milan throng the Corso San Francesco [now the Corso Vittorio Emanuele], the Cathedral Square, and the neighbouring streets. From noon until six o'clock in the evening hundreds of carriages, in some cases real monsters with six or eight horses, and filled with people in fancy dress, drive three or four abreast through the closely packed crowds, some of whom are also in costume, and throw little plaster of Paris balls, called coriandoli, at anyone they can get at. Big baskets of these missiles stand on the cars, and are thrown by means of wooden spoons. Every window, balcony, and roof is closely packed with ladies and gentlemen, who in their turn rain down coriandoli upon cars and foot passengers. Thus amid wild shouting, tremendous battles take place, especially when as often happens the lines of cars get jammed. It is worst of all when two monster waggons meet, with fifteen or twenty pierrots or clowns to each. The amount of coriandoli used up in these two days is fantastic. At every street corner piles of sacks weighing a hundred pounds apiece are offered for sale and are bought by the combatants. In the end the ground is covered to a depth of several inches with gypsum, and for days afterwards the white dust has to be taken out of the city in carts. On Saturday we fitted out a carriage and spent four hours down amongst it all. We all wore dominoes and wire masks to protect our eyes and had immense baskets of coriandoli between us, and big wooden spoons. At our first appearance in the narrowest part of the Corso San Francesco we were literally smothered. Julia was choked, and was so terrified that at first she nearly insisted on going home again. But one gets used to the bustle, and finally we bombarded everybody furiously. The Archduke was on the balcony of the Palazzo Busca with his Charlotte and the Modenas. They were well pelted as they drove home too, till the ladies hardly knew which way to turn. I really admired the behaviour of the Milan populace at this time. . . . The carnavalone, days of the most unbridled freedom, passed without the slightest disorder. There were no fights, no molestation of women, and I never saw a drunken man. It cannot be denied that the Italians have tact and culture. On the part of the military authorities the greatest precautions had secretly been taken. . . . The men in all the barracks stood to arms, with loaded rifles and cannons, and with their horses saddled." But they were never required to intervene.

In contrast to the merry bustle in Milan was the trial of the men concerned in the bomb outrage in Paris. Aware that death would be his penalty, Orsini declared before the court that he had wished to kill the Emperor simply because he regarded him as an obstacle on his country's road to freedom. A letter, purporting to be written by Orsini to Napoleon from prison, made a great sensation. In it Orsini prayed as one on the steps of the scaffold for the liberation of his native land. Tens of thousands of copies of it were sold openly in Piedmont, and smuggled over to Lombardy and Venice by every possible means.

The name Orsini and the dramatic nature of his trial put

all Italy into a fever of excitement. After the execution of Orsini, who died at the hangman's hands on March 13th with the words: "Long live Italy!" on his lips, the students of the University of Padua had a requiem mass sung for him. In consequence the term was brought to a premature close and eight students were sent down. Similar episodes occurred in every town in Italy. In Venice a Countess Strozzi, the daughter of Field-Marshal Count Nugent, was insulted at the Teatre Fenice, because she wore a dress in the Austrian colours—black and gold—and all that could be done was to arrest a number of young men who were sitting near her and whistling continuously. Nor did their friendliness to the Italians help the Archduke and his wife. Once when they appeared in St. Mark's Square the crowd disappeared into the back streets as if at the word of command.

"The excitement", Prince Alexander described the situation, "roused by the Orsini trial in Italy is very great, although there has been no actual demonstration in Milan. The new course followed by our friend from Plombières [Napoleon III], since the attack on him is *most* noticeable."

The situation of the Austrian officers in Lombardy and Venice now became most difficult. In the university towns in particular there were continual riots. There were rough doings in hot-blooded Pavia. A certain Count Moltke, a Captain in the 12th Regiment of Lancers, twice asked a waiter who was blocking his view to stand aside. As the man took no notice, Moltke pushed him aside, whereupon the waiter turned round in a flash and dashed his fist in the Count's face before he could draw his sword. A riotous mob of students and populace gathered immediately, stones were thrown at the officers, the military were called out, and the café was closed.

Meanwhile Napoleon III had had his momentous meeting with Cavour at Plombières, on July 20th, at which war with Austria was decided upon, and Sardinia was promised military assistance by France. The object of the Allies was to drive Austria out of Italy, and to form a confederation of States under the presidency of the Pope. In return, Sardinia was to cede Savoy and Nice to Napoleon III, and the daughter of King Victor Emanuel was to marry the Emperor's nephew, Jerome Napoleon, though the young man's reputation was none of the best.

Although nothing was known of this interview, the storm that was gathering over Austria nevertheless gave numerous warnings of its advent. The main difficulty confronting Napoleon III and Cavour was to find a plausible reason for war. The conspiracy found Austria in a position of diplomatic isolation. The Weimar interview did little to change the existing discord between Austria and Russia. Prince Alexander quite realized this, but felt that he himself could for the moment do nothing to help. "Much as I long for a permanent improvement in this unhappy state of affairs," he wrote to Baron von Drachenfels from Vergiate on August 15, 1858, "I shall not stir a finger so long as G. [ortchakoff] and B. [uol] are at the head of things. I have, I am sorry to say, been forced to see that the blind hatred of the servants makes every advance on the part of their masters fruitless."

Gortchakoff, on the contrary, observed with pleasure the continually increasing difficulties in the south of the Austrian empire; and Prince Napoleon, who had been sent to Warsaw, brought back encouraging assurances of Russia's neutrality in case of a conflict with Austria.[78] In Milan Italian patriots were urged as in 1848 not to smoke, in order to decrease the revenues of the Austrian treasury.[79]

"All this", wrote Prince Alexander of Hesse to Baron von Drachenfels from Milan on November 27th, "is so cleverly used by democracy for its own ends, that for some weeks we have been living in a very uncomfortable atmosphere. In various cities, including Milan, placards are continually being posted, urging people not to smoke and not to subscribe to the State lottery. Three students were arrested in Pavia recently for threatening anyone smoking in the street and shouting: 'Throw away your cigars; only Austrian spies smoke.'" Only soldiers were now to be seen smoking in the streets, and the cigar factory was obliged to dismiss hundreds of its employees. The Opposition smoked Piedmontese tobacco in clay pipes, which frequently bore a portrait of Orsini. "The political air", Prince Alexander continued, "grows more and more sultry in Lombardy and Venice, and our neighbour Piedmont is becoming increasingly arrogant as it feels itself backed up not only by France, but in some sense also by Russia's resentment against Austria."—"This unfortunate state of affairs between us and our neighbours", he wrote to his sister the Tsarina a few days later, on December 3rd, "is very uncomfortable for me. Especially since your family makes pilgrimages alternately to Turin and Nice, and since we should be committing high treason against Russia if we went to Milan!"

The Tsarina Marie wholly shared in the views and feelings of her husband. "The condition of Lombardy", she wrote to her brother on December 4th (16th), "would leave me quite cold if it were not that you are there with your wife and children. . . . I care as little for Sardinia as for Austria." There was indeed no sympathy for the Sardinian court in St. Petersburg. On the contrary, members of the imperial family, and among them the Grand Duchess Mary, now the widow of the Duke of Leuchtenberg, made fun of the king. She had met him in Turin, and even when she was quite close to him she still refused to believe that the "rustic in shooting gaiters, a dirty Eton collar, no gloves, etc.", could be the king and kept on asking : "But which is he?", as Prince Alexander told his sister in the letter of December 3rd.

Russian indifference to events in Italy was the more comprehensible since the Tsar was already fully engaged in combating the resistance called forth by his ideas on reform which culminated in the abolition of the serfdom of the peasantry. "The business of liberation", the Tsarina said, "goes on very slowly on account of the passive resistance of those in high places, and of the great prevailing ignorance. There has been a good deal of dispute in various local governments about it, and the majority is against it everywhere. The situation is serious, and the Tsar's position very difficult, since people show little or no sympathy with him. But thank God he is not losing courage."

A campaign waged by discontented exiles by word and pen was already beginning against the régime in Russia. One of the most eminent leaders of the anti-Tsarist movement was a Jew, Alexander Herzen, who had originally been in the Russian State service, but who had been obliged to emigrate to England on account of his views. There he published a periodical called *Kolokol* (The Bell), chiefly concerned with Russian affairs, and which despite its being prohibited in Russia was secretly read there by high and low, including the Tsar himself, though with great aversion. "Herzen", wrote the Tsarina Marie, "is doing us as much harm as he possibly can with his *Kolokol*. He has published the memoirs of the Tsarina Katherine, and says in so many words in the introduction that the Russian dynasty is descended not from the Tsar Peter I, but from Sergius Soltikoff, her lover !"

On New Year's Day of the year 1859, the Emperor Napoleon expressed his regret to the Austrian Ambassador Hübner that his relations with the Austrian Government were not as friendly as they had been. This was the somewhat prematurely revealed outward sign of the secret treaty concluded between France and Piedmont on December 10, 1858, in which the Emperor bound himself to come to the help of Piedmont against Austria with two hundred thousand men, and to drive the Austrians out of Italy. He did this because he apprehended no interference on the part of Russia and hoped that the country would also restrain Prussia.

Prince Alexander spent Christmas at his home in Darmstadt, and as a Christmas present his brother, the reigning Grand Duke, raised his morganatic wife and children to the rank of Princes and Princesses of Battenberg, a small place in Hesse.

Alexander was greatly affected by the news from Paris, and wrote at once to his brother-in-law: "God grant that the peace which Russia needs so badly at this time of internal crisis may not be disturbed by our friend Napoleon. I am always afraid that he may be tempted to undertake an Italian Odyssey with the twofold aim of re-establishing his popularity which has sunk so low in France, and of saving himself from the daggers of republican Italy by professing to work in its interest."

Since the news from Italy grew increasingly serious, the Prince cut short his leave in Hesse and went back to Milan. On his way he visited the Emperor Francis Joseph in Vienna and called on the most important members of the court and Government. He found everybody in a state of considerable depression. Even Buol seems to have admitted in a very frank discussion that he "had made a bad muddle of things", that he was not blameless in the matter of Russia, and that he had not succeeded in safeguarding the Italian provinces from French influence.

Echoes of the speech of King Victor Emanuel of Sardinia were just coming through to Vienna. He had said on January 10th that he was "not deaf to Italy's cry of agony, and was waiting, fully prepared, for the dispensations of Providence". Prince Alexander was perfectly right when he wrote in his diary on January 12th: "The situation in Austria remains . . . very serious. Count Buol has isolated it completely; even Prussia will not express itself in favour of Austria."

The Emperor Francis Joseph elucidated this still further: "We hope for Prussia's support if we are attacked in Italy. But we have unfortunately obtained no promise from them yet. Probably Prussia is intending to dictate its terms to us at the last moment."

Alexander also discovered interesting things from the Arch-duchess Sophie. As, for instance, that Count Gyulai had once been promised that he should not only follow Radetzky as Commander-in-Chief of the army, but also as Governor-General, for which reason he had been "ill-disposed" towards the Archduke Max from the very beginning.

The tidings from Italy and France made it necessary to strengthen considerably the Austrian army in Italy. For safety's sake the Archduke Ferdinand Max sent his wife Charlotte to Trieste upon some pretext.

On January 30th Cavour's arrangements were carried out by the marriage of Prince Jerome Napoleon Bonaparte, the cousin of the Emperor of the French, to the fifteen-year-old Princess Clothilde of Sardinia. "Poor little political victim", was Prince Alexander's comment, as he wrote to the Tsarina on January 18th (30th), full of indignation against Victor Emanuel for sacrificing his pretty, fifteen-year-old daughter to a "dis-solute man like Prince Napoleon, who is despised by all decent people, and ridiculed by the whole of France, merely in the hope that he may thereby, with French help, conquer a few square miles of land".

He also recorded in the same letter the information, which he declared authentic, that Victor Emanuel, before the advent of "*Craint-plomb*", as the Parisians had spitefully nicknamed Jerome Napoleon since the Crimean War, had spent hours with his daughter weeping over her sad fate.

To the manifestations from abroad were soon added demon-strations in Milan of which the purport was unmistakable. One evening at the Scala, the opera "Norma" was being given in which occurs the famous chorus beginning with the words "War, war!" The *Italianissimi* present at the performance suddenly burst into frenzied applause and insisted upon an encore. On January 30th, Prince Napoleon's wedding-day, the opera was given again, and this time the Austrian officers who had occupied the whole of the first four rows of stalls made a counter-demonstration. They, in their turn, greeted the chorus "War, war!" with furious applause and shouts of "Bravo", and encored it, which finally led to an indescribable uproar. The Archduke Ferdinand Max, who had led a very retired life since his wife's absence in Trieste, grew more and more depressed at the development of the situation. He had taken up his office with the greatest enthusiasm and filled with many hopes, and had honestly believed himself capable of winning over the country to its rulers by gentleness and a spirit of conciliation. But it was made clear to him in Italy that although his personal attitude and his good will were appreciated, he was the representative of a régime whose gentleness only meant weakness, and that nothing could change the universal enmity to it. Prince Alexander's view was that nothing but the most rigorous severity could avail. He might have reasoned from Metternich's experience that it was this that had first sown the seeds of the terrible hatred, for under the Empress Maria Theresa and her excellent government, for example, there were hardly any malcontents in Northern Italy.

Then the famous pamphlet *Napoléon III et l'Italie* appeared in Paris at the inspiration of Napoleon himself, who intended that it should unofficially disseminate the ideas held in high quarters. The culminating sentiment of the booklet was that Italy should unite in a confederacy of States under the presidency of the Pope, and that Austria must be driven out of Italy. Despite the French Foreign Minister's—altogether untruthful—assurance that Napoleon knew nothing of the pamphlet, it was clear to everybody that it had come into being at the initiative of the highest authority. As he read it, Prince Alexander remembered the remarks that the Emperor of the French had made to the Tsar at Stuttgart, and which corresponded strikingly with the statements in this little work. Although at that time no treaty had been signed, it was clear to the Prince that Russia would not interfere with Napoleon if he undertook any venture in Italy. Indeed Prince Alexander foresaw the future even more prophetically. "And it will not be so very long," he wrote to his sister, "after Russia has successfully weathered her emancipation crises and has completed her network of railways, before she will in any case join with France if it is a case of fighting Austria."

The danger of war came ever nearer. None the less balls and other entertainments succeeded one another in Milan. Although Prince Alexander participated in them, he was secretly sending home box after box of silver and other valuables to Darmstadt.

The most was made of every opportunity for political demonstration. When the young Count Emilio Dandolo, who had distinguished himself in 1849 at the defence of Rome, died unexpectedly towards the end of February, all the boxes at the theatres belonging to the "distinguished opposition", as Prince Alexander called the nationalist members of the

NAPOLEON III AND THE EMPRESS EUGÉNIE

aristocracy, remained empty. At his interment all the *Italianissimi* of the highest rank were represented. All the "lionesses"— that is, the wives and daughters of those members of the aristocracy who belonged to the nationalist club *dei leoni*—joined on foot in the funeral procession wearing deep mourning with flowing veils. The whole Corso along which the train passed was black with people, and since disturbances were feared the garrison stood to arms in its barracks.

At the burial service a professor delivered the funeral oration, and referred almost in so many words to the revolution that was soon to break out, and to the imminent proclamation of a republic. Three days' national mourning were announced, and it was decided to permit no masked balls. On February 23rd when one was due to take place at the Scala, all the streets leading to the theatre were filled with demonstrators. In the new square in front of the Scala where demolition works were in progress, young men collected beside the heaps of stones. Every time a carriage arrived at the steps of the Scala, the Marquis Trivulzio or Count Trotti or some other one of the nobles who sat in the corner café on the Square gave a word of command, whereupon the windows of the carriages were broken. Any who came on foot in fancy dress were thrashed and forced to flee. When the police at last restored order, all inclination to go to the masked ball had vanished. On the following day balls had been announced at four theatres, but nobody appeared for fear of molestation.

The Archduke Max had not been in Milan since February 18th. He had actually only intended to visit his wife for a few days, but this was interpreted as flight. For weeks past thousands of people had collected in the Cathedral Square every morning to see whether the imperial standard were still flying over the royal palace. When it was struck for a short time at the Archduke's departure, a great sensation was created all over the city. Gradually other Austrian officers' families also left the town, and Prince Alexander's was also prepared to move. The Archduke Ferdinand Max, however, hearing of the effect produced by his absence, returned with his wife early in March, and settled at Monza. He found that the situation had changed very much for the worse during the few days that he had been away and was greatly vexed with his brother whose wish to govern Lombardy from Vienna made the proposed independence of the Italian administration impossible.

In other countries, including Russia, this development was

hailed with undisguised malicious pleasure by the enemies of
Austria. The letters of the Tsarina Marie mirror clearly the
feelings of the Tsar. Alexander II was delighted that Count
Buol had successfully isolated Austria. The hopes that the
Emperor Francis Joseph and his Ministers cherished of Prussia
were soon to prove abortive. "Buol", runs a letter of the Tsarina's
which Prince Alexander copied into his diary on March 9th,
"is very much wondering where he stands with Louis Napoleon,
and would love to make use of us again to pull the chestnuts out
of the fire for him. Too naïve !" The Tsarina and her husband
got on excellently with the new Prussian Ambassador, Otto von
Bismarck, who had arrived in St. Petersburg towards the end
of March, and who also cherished hostile feelings towards
Austria. He shared the conservative views of the Tsar and
Tsarina, and thought as they did that democracy under the
mask of patriotism added fuel to the fires of militarist unrest
in the world, and was only an excuse for fishing in troubled
waters. "Bismarck said the same thing to me", wrote the
Tsarina from St. Petersburg on March 26th (April 7th).
"So far as one can judge after one meeting, I like him."

The Prince of Hesse regretted the adverse circumstances that
in addition to his physical separation from Russia now also
caused a political abyss to yawn between it and Austria.

The general political situation had taken another turn for
the worse. France and Sardinia were making ready for war
and the tension between the two parties in northern Italy was
growing appreciably. The sons of the foremost families in
Milan, among them Duke Visconti and most of the young men
of the "distinguished opposition", entered the army of Piedmont
as volunteers. In Austrian circles the story went the round that
the beautiful Countess Litta had threatened several men never
to speak to them again if they did not take part in the impending war. Actually such threats from the fair were hardly
necessary any longer. National enthusiasm permitted of no
hesitation.

If Austria wanted to clear up this intolerable situation by force
of arms, the war must be short and sharp, and the French and
Piedmontese must be prevented from joining their forces. The
situation in Austria, however, was in every respect inauspicious
for such procedure. The Austrians wanted war, but they were
totally isolated and rapidity and vigour of action were paralysed
because they were trying to assure themselves of the co-
operation of Prussia and of the German Confederation. On

April 11th, at the eleventh hour, the Archduke Albrecht was sent to Berlin on a special mission, but the negotiations led to no positive result. Then the Emperor Francis Joseph's patience gave out. He brushed aside the doubts which must have beset him in view of his isolated position, and ordered an ultimatum to be sent to Piedmont. Although he had not yet found allies, the Emperor hoped that he might find them before the ultimatum expired. This was, however, only a vague hope, and therefore the dispatch of the ultimatum was most rash. Moreover, military preparations were carried out indecisively and half-heartedly. After time had been wasted in negotiations, General Gyulai was ordered, even in case of a negative reply to the ultimatum at the expiry of the three days' grace, "*not* to proceed to an offensive immediately, but to await telegraphic instructions from His Majesty". Gyulai regarded this as unsatisfactory in every respect and declared that he could not see his way clear in face of the unexampled levity and superficiality of the leading diplomats. In a letter to Alexander of Hesse, which the Prince copied into his diary on April 27th, Gyulai said: "You or I would be cashiered if we did our work in such a way." News from Berlin remained unfavourable. The Archduke Albrecht felt that the ground was cut from under his feet by the ultimatum and showed his annoyance at the sudden action of the Government in Vienna. Gyulai was now convinced that Prussia was about to leave Austria to her fate. "It is beyond me", remarked Prince Alexander. "We seem to be recklessly challenging the whole world." On the morning of the 28th, after an unsatisfactory answer had been sent to the ultimatum, Gyulai at last received orders to take the offensive. On the 30th, the first Austrian troops, with Prince Alexander's brigade as advance guard, crossed the Ticino. The Austrian army in Italy silently awaited the orders of its Emperor. "The army", wrote the Prince to Russia, "permits itself no criticism of the actions of its sovereign who is the sole arbiter of his country's honour." The curt note sent by the Emperor to the Archduke Ferdinand Max ordering him to take command of the fleet as soon as the army crossed the frontier was also received in silence. The Archduke was thus relegated to inactivity in the most humiliating manner.

The highest ranks in the army had little hope for the outcome. "Our generals", wrote Prince Alexander in his diary on May 1st, "have not the smallest confidence in a successful issue to the campaign. They all regard our venture as foolhardy both in a military and a political sense." It might at least have been supposed that Gyulai would now do all he could to prevent the French from joining up with the Piedmontese, and to defeat the latter while they were isolated. On the contrary. He hesitated, wasted time, and missed every opportunity that still presented itself.[80] "We cannot understand", the Prince remarked in his diary on May 6th, "why Gyulai remains inactive for so long and gives the French more time to advance into Piedmont." The truth was that every action which he proposed was vetoed by orders from Vienna. The Commander-in-Chief was thus rendered powerless. In any case Gyulai was not a man who really knew his own mind. The Austrian army did indeed, though very late, advance across the River Sesia, but only to retire behind it again at once. The corps commanders fumed with rage. Gyulai heard of it and complained to the Prince of Hesse on May 11th that his situation was growing daily more difficult; that as he was about to make a general advance he had received the following telegram from Vienna: "In present circumstances our most advantageous battlefield is on the Mincio." The general did not say who had despatched this telegram. The orders and counter-orders that he received and their consequences undoubtedly relieve him of some of the responsibility. Prince Alexander saw the future in the darkest colours: "We have", he wrote on May 12th, "taken the whole odium of the breach of peace upon our shoulders, have given the French the pretext that they needed, have put the most dangerous weapon into the hands of Austria's enemies, and all for nothing. Louis Napoleon is sending his whole army into Italy, and unless a strong diversion occurs on the Rhine at a very early date we shall without any doubt be defeated." Meanwhile the French and the Piedmontese joined up at their leisure, and Gyulai now left the initiative entirely to them. The reconnaissance and skirmish at Montebello, in which Prince Alexander's brigade took part, was unsuccessful, although they bore themselves well. Immediately after the fight the Prince of Hesse received the gratifying news that he had been promoted general of a division, and that he was to relinquish his brigade. Hence the Prince took leave from his corps commander and also called on Lieutenant-General Benedek, who abused the High Command furiously. Then he went to the army headquarters at Mortara to report himself to Gyulai. He found the General in the lowest depths of depression. Gyulai could talk of nothing but the failure of various corps and of adverse conditions. The general situation he regarded as most unsatisfactory; in short, he was already out-manœuvred and had given the order to retire back across the Ticino. He also made a remark about lost military reputation. His self-confidence had vanished utterly, and to all the importunities of Prince Alexander that he should take the offensive he would only repeat: "I must keep the army intact!"

"He was", the Prince summed up, "in a pitiable state"; and this at a time when only small skirmishes and no pitched battle had taken place. The Prince found his Chief of Staff, Colonel Kuhn, also in a great state of excitement, but chiefly of rage with Gyulai. "Our situation is not so serious", the Colonel said, "as the General makes out. This is the moment for falling upon the French flank. But the General cannot make up his mind to do it. I have refused to agree to the retirement over the Ticino and have appealed to His Majesty the Emperor. He must decide between us."

This was the situation at the headquarters of the Austrian army when the Emperor Francis Joseph in person set out for Verona to investigate the state of affairs for himself. Prince Alexander requested an audience as soon as the Emperor arrived and spent two hours telling him how things stood at the front. Francis Joseph remarked that he could not understand why Gyulai had not fallen in with Kuhn's suggestions, and that he had been greatly taken aback to receive the news of the retreat over the Ticino instead of the report of a battle; he trusted, however, that General Hess, whom he had attached to Gyulai as "adviser", would attempt an offensive. The Emperor was still hoping that Prussia would decide shortly to propose to the Federal Diet that the Federation should take part in the war. After the Battle of Magenta on June 4th it was only Gyulai's weakness of will and tendency to panic that led him to give the order to retreat and to retire behind the Adda, sacrificing Milan.

General Benedek's troops covered this retreat and fierce hand-to-hand fighting took place in the streets of Melegnano. The General told Prince Alexander immediately after the battle that the Transylvanian Saxons of the XIth Infantry regiment had encountered Zouaves frenzied with excitement in the houses. The fighting that ensued was so violent that the stronger threw the weaker out of the windows. In Benedek's words, from every floor "there rained alternately Saxons and Zouaves for several minutes on end".

Russia stood aside and looked on. The Tsar nevertheless watched the course of events with mixed feelings. For although he detested Francis Joseph and Buol for their attitude during the last few years, he felt kindly towards the Austrian army. "The Tsar's heart", wrote the Tsarina to Prince Alexander on May 28th (June 9th), "beats as always for the Austrian army. The troops of all nations are brothers so long as they prove themselves worthy; and it would be as impossible for him to enjoy doing what Francis Joseph did a few years ago in being the first to congratulate Napoleon upon his success at Sebastopol, as for so noble a nature as his to indulge in any other baseness."

But the Tsar did not stir a finger to help Austria. On June 7th General Hess approached Prince Alexander and urged him to use all his influence to persuade his brother-in-law no longer to countenance Napoleon's "revolutionary" proceedings. That was the lure to which every Tsar had hitherto succumbed. Hess wanted the Prince to represent to Russia that it was committing suicide by continuing to pursue its present policy. He was to urge the Tsar not to let the whole of Europe perish by supporting the common danger—Napoleon. For he, Napoleon, though an emperor himself, had determined upon the overthrow of all existing monarchies and all conservative principles. Prince Alexander, however, was very sceptical and of opinion that "the political hostility of Russia would cause it to remain deaf to all common-sense arguments until Austria was brought to her very knees". This view was perfectly correct. Bismarck, who was then ambassador in St. Petersburg, reported in a private letter to Schleinitz[81] on June 11th that the news of the continual disasters to the Austrians on the field of battle was greeted with as much rejoicing in St. Petersburg as if they had been victories won by the Russian army.

On June 10th Prince Alexander once more visited General Gyulai, whom he found somewhat less despondent than the week before. But he was once again given an opportunity of seeing the serious disputes and lack of unity at headquarters. Confidence in the High Command had received a deadly blow after Magenta even among the men themselves. Now they were already retiring towards the Mincio line. At last, on June 17th, General Gyulai resigned and his successor, Count Schlick, ended his first order to the army with the words: "We belong to the brave Austrian army, we love our Emperor— everything else will settle itself."

Francis Joseph wrote to his mother from Verona on June 16th

saying that he was feeling thoroughly dejected.[82] He admitted that great mistakes had been made and opportunities missed, but he still hoped that the real justification for his venturesome policy in sending the ultimatum would prove to exist and that Prussia would come to his aid. "I am looking into the future calmly," he therefore wrote optimistically, "am resolved to carry on the fight to a finish, and hope that perhaps Germany and this wretched scum, Prussia, will after all stand by us in the end."

Prince Alexander reported all these events and changes in his letters to his sister in St. Petersburg, in one of which, written on June 23rd from Mozzecane, he remarked that everyone was much disheartened by the "terrible way in which Gyulai had jeopardized his army". The army had whispered of treason, he continued, and everyone was so indignant that since his retirement Gyulai did not know where to turn to be safe from insult. The letter closed with a violent philippic against the "crowned carbonaro", who had been so successful up to the present, and who threatened to destroy all the foundations upon which the peace of Europe rested.

It is a matter of old experience and a fact that in times of difficulty during a war each party is apt to think that the enemy is in much better condition than he is himself. So it was before Solferino. The Allies had kept the upper hand until then, and owing to Gyulai's irresoluteness had conquered almost the whole of Lombardy. But they were getting further and further from their base and neither the Piedmontese army nor the French could hope for reinforcements within a short space of time, since the latter dared not denude its own country entirely of troops in view of the still doubtful attitude of Prussia. The Empress Eugénie, who in spite of victories regarded the Italian venture with increasing anxiety on account of the other Powers, telegraphed to her husband on June 22nd, full of fear, to say that if he crossed the Mincio a coalition would be formed against him; that Prussia was already mobilizing and that France was too weak on the Rhine as a result of the Italian war. She feared an invasion of France itself and was therefore longing for peace and for the return home of the army. Napoleon showed the telegram to King Victor Emanuel and both found in it much food for thought. On the following day, however, June 24th, owing to the general advance of the Austrian army, whose commander had at last made up his mind to attempt an offensive, the Battle of Sol-

I

ferino was fought. Prince Alexander's division was marched off somewhat later at the express order of his corps commander because of the necessity to give the troops time to have a meal. But as the day went on, the Prince, having given the order for a bayonet attack, personally led a battalion of the Imperial Infantry several hundred yards to the attack and kept the enemy in check for a long time. The Prince's horse was wounded, a bullet struck his water-bottle, but he himself was unhurt. Towards evening both Alexander's division and that commanded by Benedek, which was stationed at San Martino opposite the Sardinians, were obliged to join in the general retreat. At Volta the Prince saw the sad spectacle of a disorderly mass of guns, baggage waggons and men who had been wounded or got separated from their units, barring all the streets leading to the pontoon bridges at Valeggio and Verri. For some reason the French did not pursue them and the troops were able to retreat behind the Mincio without further losses. Nevertheless the new Commander-in-Chief had not been able to bring any change in the fortunes of war, and a second great battle had been lost. By July 1st the army had retreated still further. In Verona Prince Alexander met the Emperor Francis Joseph, who was greatly disappointed, but who none the less thanked him for the brave endurance with which he had defended Cavriana. Alexander discussed the situation with Francis Joseph, and the Emperor asked him anxiously: "The army has not lost courage, has it?"

Subsequently the French advanced as far as Villafranca. Despite their victory matters were not going too well on the enemy's side either. Serious news was coming from the Rhine, and the Tsar, although he had no wish to reverse the Austrian defeat, was nevertheless beginning to be afraid lest the "revolutionary sovereign of France" should win too sweeping a victory. The principle of nationality might perhaps raise its head again in Hungary and Poland. The French, and especially the Piedmontese, army had suffered very heavily at Solferino, and it was far harder for them to make good their losses than for the Austrians. Prussia's preparations were disquieting, and hence a letter brought by an aide-de-camp of the Tsar's to Napoleon III at Valeggio on July 4th containing the advice to make peace met with a favourable reception. Whatever his allies thought about it, the dangers which were rising up before Napoleon's mental vision were too great, and he determined to make an end of his military adventure.

Prince Alexander was now treated with the greatest friendliness by the Emperor and was daily summoned to dine at the royal table in the imperial headquarters. The Emperor invited him to apply for the Cross of the Maria Theresa order, the highest military Order in Austria, and discussed both the military and the political situation with him. As the Prince was strolling homewards with Count Rechberg on the evening of July 6th, suddenly a singular procession crossed their path. A berline appeared bearing the French imperial coat of arms on its door. On the box sat a non-commissioned officer of Napoleon's bodyguard, and a bugler with a white flag of truce. Inside the carriage was Count Fleury, the aide-de-camp of the Emperor Napoleon. A squadron of Austrian lancers escorted it. The Prince and Rechberg hurried back to the Emperor's quarters at top speed, and found him already in bed. He was wakened and dressed himself rapidly in order to receive the Frenchman at once. The letter[83] that the General brought was most oddly worded: "*Monsieur mon frère,*" it ran, "information has reached me from Paris that a Great Power is about to suggest a truce to the belligerents. If Your Majesty would be inclined to accept this proposal, I should be glad to know, because then I would order the Fleet—which would otherwise attack Venice—not to do so, since it is our duty to prevent unnecessary bloodshed."

The Emperor Francis Joseph knew nothing of any such suggestion. He told Napoleon so in his reply, but at the same time expressed his readiness to negotiate directly with him about an armistice. On the same day Prince Murat appeared with a fresh letter from Napoleon in which the Emperor motivated his initial move towards obtaining an armistice by declaring that he regarded it as the prelude to a direct understanding between the two monarchs, which might perhaps lead to a mutual agreement. He only wished to be assured that hostilities would not be recommenced. It would be painful if strife were to break out anew between him and the Emperor after he had just come to know and like him. After this letter the Emperor Francis Joseph sent for Prince Alexander on the morning of July 9th, and requested him to undertake a mission to the French headquarters and to sound the Emperor Napoleon as to the conditions of peace that he intended suggesting at their meeting. Francis Joseph was at pains to give the Prince a thorough insight into the general situation. He spoke long and very frankly of the critical position in which he found himself,

stated that Prussia had continually put him off with false
promises, and that having been led astray by them he had been
obliged to attack before a sufficient army had been collected
in Italy. He explained that Russia was proving daily more
hostile and that England too was in sympathy with Louis
Napoleon. He, the Emperor, stood alone, and had to choose
between either carrying on the war to the bitter end—which
in the completely exhausted state of Austria's finances could
be not more than a few months off—or else of concluding a
disadvantageous peace. At home, especially in Hungary, he
continued, there was much discontent, the army in Italy was
considerably demoralized after the unfortunate campaign, and
afforded little hope of the satisfactory development of future
hostilities. Hence it would be very desirable to come to a direct
understanding with the Emperor Napoleon, so long as he made
no impossible demands. Further, the Emperor told the Prince
of a telegram that had just arrived from London, and that
contained a programme upon which France, England, Russia,
and Prussia were said to have agreed. According to this telegram the main point was that Austria should cede Lombardy
to Piedmont, should make Venice an independent Archduchy,
and that the Pope should be president of the Italian Federation.
The telegram, which was sent from London by Count Apponyi[84]
on July 7th, was based upon information from Count Persigny,
the French Ambassador in London, which had been passed on
to Lord John Russell to be repeated in confidence, and thus—
though Francis Joseph did not know this—came originally
from a French source. The Emperor then told the Prince what
concessions he was prepared to make if the worst came to the
worst. He would cede Lombardy, since "in the course of the
next—probably imminent—European war it could be re-
conquered", would give up Parma and co-operate in the
reforms in the Papal States. As points to which he would not
agree, the Emperor indicated the creation of Venice into an
independent Archduchy, and the sacrifice of provinces which
did not directly belong to him, such as Modena and Tuscany;
further, the enforcement of a liberal constitution in the provinces that remained to the Emperor, or in fact any alteration
in the existing (absolutist) system of government. Finally, the
Emperor charged the Prince to ensure that King Victor
Emanuel did not "force himself in" at the meeting. Thereupon
Francis Joseph gave Alexander a letter to Napoleon in which he
acceded to the interview and suggested as a means of preventing

any renewal of hostilities that before they met they should have a frank exchange of views upon the possibilities of an agreement. "The Prince of Hesse," the letter runs, "who has the honour of bringing these lines to Your Majesty, has my entire confidence. If you would also grant him yours, I hope and believe that a meeting in Villafranca would be much more easily productive of a satisfactory result."

At about midday on July 9th Alexander went with young Prince Joachim Murat to Valeggio, where, without any ceremony, they passed the French sentries into the camp of the Imperial Guards. Napoleon's headquarters were situated in the same villa which a fortnight earlier had housed the Emperor Francis Joseph. Prince Alexander was at once taken into the Emperor's very simply furnished room. Napoleon came several steps to meet him, but took the letter without offering his hand. He then asked Prince Alexander to sit down, and requested permission to read the Emperor's letter before entering into any conversation. Meanwhile the Prince had a good look at the Emperor. He found him looking ten years older than he had done at their last meeting two years before. His beard was quite grey, his face sallow and tired. In the forty-five minutes' discussion that followed upon the reading of the letter, Prince Alexander soon realized that he would have to take back bad news to his Emperor. Louis Napoleon read to him the same London project of which Francis Joseph had already told him. He introduced it by saying: "Well, here are some suggestions that have reached me from London recently." The Prince replied that it was a perfectly impossible programme, and that there was no prospect of Austria's agreeing to it. Thereupon the Emperor Napoleon took a sheet of paper and wrote the following note[85] on it to indicate the basis for the peace negotiations:

> "Italian confederation of all Italian sovereigns.
> Union of Lombardy and Piedmont.
> Venice under an Archduke."

The Prince protested against these conditions. The Emperor repeated several times that the cession of Lombardy was the main point upon which he must insist and that everything else was a matter of detail upon which he was confident he would be able to agree with Francis Joseph. He requested the Prince to take with him the note that he had written, and added,

"I shall be glad of an answer." Then Napoleon spoke of the Battle of Solferino. He inquired what forces had been opposed to the army of Piedmont. When Alexander replied: "General Benedek with 22,000 men", Napoleon smiled in a manner hardly flattering to the Piedmontese as though he would say: "After all, we French did all the hard work." The Prince then told him that he had been charged with the defence of Cavriana. To which Napoleon said: "You made a fine defence." Finally, the Emperor dismissed Alexander, and held out his hand, saying: "After having fought bravely, I think one may shake hands."

Although it was dinner-time, the Prince was not invited to dine. Before his return he had a brief conversation with Count Paul Shuvaloff, the Tsar's aide-de-camp, who had brought Napoleon the letter which had caused him so much anxiety. The streets of Valeggio presented a gay and picturesque appearance. All the uniforms of the French army were to be seen, and officers and men of all branches of the service thronged the town.

On his arrival in Verona the Prince went straight to the Emperor, to whom Count Rechberg was also summoned. The basic conditions of the peace were regarded as very hard, and the Emperor repeatedly said that he had not imagined that the situation was so desperate. After a lengthy discussion it was decided to agree to the interview, on the definite assumption that it would still be possible to bargain with Louis Napoleon. Therefore Prince Alexander announced in writing to the Emperor* that though the conditions laid down did not appear acceptable to his imperial master, he would nevertheless be happy to come to an interview at Villafranca at nine o'clock on the morning of July 11th, in the hope that it might be productive of some good. The Emperor Napoleon replied that he would be equally happy to come to Villafranca at the time suggested, and would be very glad to meet the Emperor Francis Joseph.

At three o'clock in the afternoon of July 10th a French orderly officer drove up to Prince Alexander's quarters in Verona and brought him the following letter from Napoleon:

"I have agreed to the interview suggested by Your Royal Highness at the command of the Emperor, despite the description 'unacceptable' which he applied to my proposals, because

* See Appendix.

I hope that at this decisive moment the Emperor's judgment will prove to be equal to his courage. I will tell you my views quite frankly.

"Without entering into a discussion upon the origins of the war, I wish to assure you that I never felt either hatred or animosity against Austria or her sovereign. I believed myself to be obliged in the interests of my country, and indeed of the peace of Europe, to defend the cause which I had embraced; but that is all.

"I entered into the war with the sole desire of seeing it ended as speedily and as favourably as possible for both sides. In choosing the present moment to make direct overtures to the Emperor, I am actuated by the feeling that circumstances are propitious for all concerned. Indeed, matters have so fallen out that although fortune has not been auspicious, yet the military honour of Austria remains untarnished. I am near Verona, it is true, but the Emperor is within reach of all his supplies. The fortunes of war have gone in my favour, but the enemy army remains intact. There has been no opportunity for me to follow in pursuit, and conditions are therefore most suitable for honourable negotiation. As yet there is neither victor nor vanquished. Two sovereigns and two great countries are facing one another, both armed to the teeth and with equal prospects for the future. In these circumstances it is surely possible to debate the matter coolly and to seek some means of coming to an understanding.

"The fundamental idea is one which is shared by nearly every Cabinet in Europe—that in the interests of world peace, and of Austria herself, Italy must in one form or another be constituted an independent State. If the Emperor admits this principle, everything else can be arranged easily enough.

"And now permit me with the same frankness to show you that it is to the interest of the Emperor to agree to peace proposals now. If by any chance our interview to-morrow should not lead to a satisfactory result, I shall, of course, ensure that the moderation and disinterestedness of my propositions receive recognition, and shall not fail to do all I can to make certain that Prussia shall remain in her state of neutrality.

"Given security on the Rhine, I shall concentrate my army upon Italy.

"At present I have on the Mincio—apart from the 65,000 Sardinians—150,000 fighting men, and a siege train of two hundred guns of the latest model. In France I have 450,000 more men, though as every soldier will know, that represents only 250,000 actual combatants.

"Having nothing to fear from the German side, I can therefore bring another 250,000 men from France within a few days, which with the force that is already in the North yields the enormous total of 400,000 men. A part of them will operate near Venice to attack the positions on the Adige; the remainder will be directed upon the coast of Dalmatia. Thus the war will take on immense proportions. The Emperor, for his part, will no doubt receive large reinforcements and German contingents. Nevertheless, I have no hesitation in saying that I believe my chances to be at least equal to those of the Emperor.

"Finally, after long and bloody fighting had gone on, Europe would probably intervene and dictate conditions to which we might just as well agree to-day of our own free wills. Thus there is every advantage in our coming to a direct agreement. Austria, moreover, will gain the firm and faithful friendship of a great people; for, as I said to Your Royal Highness yesterday, if we dispose of the unhappy Italian question, there is nothing over which we need quarrel with Austria.

"I have spoken my mind to you quite freely, bluntly, and plainly. I beg you to inform the Emperor of all I have said, and thus to prepare the way for an interview which cannot but be fruitful for the peace of the world and for the re-establishment of international relations.

"I have much pleasure in renewing to Your Royal Highness the assurance of my esteem and regard.

"NAPOLÉON."

The Prince read the letter to the Emperor Francis Joseph and to Count Rechberg. It is in many respects a highly interesting document. Future plans were described with boastful exaggeration, and were intended to frighten Francis Joseph into abandoning the war. An unprejudiced person might indeed ask himself why, if the future looked so rosy, Napoleon should suddenly take the initiative in seeking to put an end to the war. Nevertheless, the letter did not fail in its object, owing to the temper that prevailed at the Austrian headquarters. Stress was laid on those parts only which permitted of the assumption that Napoleon might be inclined not to hold absolutely to the conditions which he first propounded.

The French orderly officer was kept to dinner, and sent back at six o'clock with a reply to the Emperor Napoleon.

Prince Alexander said in this letter that he had conveyed the sense of the letter to the Emperor with certain reservations, and that Francis Joseph was quite decided to go to the interview at Villafranca.

On the morning of July 11th Francis Joseph rode over to Villafranca without taking Prince Alexander with him. The Emperor of the French had arrived there somewhat earlier than Francis Joseph, and came out more than half a mile to meet him. The two sovereigns then repaired to the Casa Gaudini, where they remained for three-quarters of an hour. Louis Napoleon, with some embarrassment, once again brought forward the three points of which Prince Alexander had already been informed, and demanded, moreover, the deposition of the rulers of Tuscany and Modena, to which Francis Joseph refused absolutely to agree. On the other hand, he declared himself ready as ruler of Venice to join a Federation of Italian States under the presidency of the Pope. It was further agreed, according to an entry in Prince Alexander's diary on July 12, 1859, that King Victor Emanuel must break with the revolution and *dismiss Cavour*, to which Napoleon assented. Finally, after a long discussion, Francis Joseph said:

"Sire, this is my last word. I will give up Lombardy as far as the Mincio, for the fortunes of war have decided in your favour. But I will concede nothing further. I shall keep Venice, and it is essential that the Grand Duke of Tuscany and the Duke of Modena shall be reinstated on their thrones. If Your Majesty cannot agree to these conditions, we shall recommence hostilities."

"I must have time to think, Sire", replied Napoleon.

Thereupon the two emperors reviewed each other's escorts, exchanged a few words with the gentlemen in their suites, and remounted their horses. Napoleon had made a better impression upon Francis Joseph than the Austrian had expected. He found him perfectly natural and courteous, grave and dignified in demeanour as befitted the seriousness of the occasion. He accompanied Napoleon a part of the way towards Valeggio as a return for his politeness in coming to meet him in the morning, and then went back to Verona. The Emperor of the French took counsel in Villafranca with the King of Sardinia and Prince Napoleon. The latter was far more strongly opposed than his father-in-law to the conclusion of peace at a time when the programme of Italy's liberation had not been fully carried out. The Emperor Napoleon, however, was no longer concerned with Italy. He saw himself threatened by Germany, and was anxious to bring the war to an end. "The situation", he protested, "in which I am at present is no longer tenable. I must get out of it, and I shall write to the Emperor." As bearer of the letter of acquiescence, which, however, contained a few changes in detail, the Emperor of the French chose his cousin, who in view of his personal opinions urgently requested him to select someone else for the mission. The Emperor, however, insisted, and so Prince Napoleon went to Verona to the headquarters of the Emperor Francis Joseph. The latter, who had sat down to dinner with his suite immediately upon his return from the interview, was lingering over dessert when Prince Napoleon was suddenly and quite unexpectedly announced. According to an entry in Prince Alexander's diary, the company broke up in dismay. The Duke of Modena changed colour in fury at Plon-Plon's impudence in showing himself here, and dashed home in such haste that he left his sword behind. The two young Tuscan princes, for whom it would have been particularly unpleasant to meet the gentleman who had been instrumental in turning them out of house and home, vanished rapidly through side doors. "As it chanced", Prince Alexander remarks, "I was not in Verona that day. I was exceedingly glad to have so fortunately missed making the undesired acquaintance of that fat scoundrel." Prince Napoleon was immediately conducted to the Emperor, and the famous interview took place of which the only full description emanates from Prince Napoleon himself.[86]

The essence of the conditions agreed upon in Villafranca was preserved, but details were passionately debated. The Emperor Francis Joseph insisted that he did not wish to hear the word "Constitution" mentioned, and laid stress on the greatness of his sacrifice in being obliged to relinquish his fairest province. Throughout the conference Francis Joseph avoided mentioning the name of Cavour. Napoleon III, whom Prince Alexander had informed at the Emperor's command that Francis Joseph did not wish to negotiate with Victor Emanuel direct, sent a copy of the draft to Victor Emanuel, who signed it with the reservation: "I ratify all that concerns myself." The Emperor sent back the papers to Francis Joseph the same evening.

On meeting Prince Alexander shortly after the arrival of the draft treaty, Count Rechberg exclaimed: "Peace has been signed to-day."

The Prince went straight to the Emperor, who said as he came into the room: "Have you come to condole with me?" Alexander of Hesse replied: "No, Your Majesty. It is only the army that needs condolence. We had secretly been hoping to have another chance of trying conclusions with the French."—"Let us call things by their right names", answered the Emperor. "It is a deplorable peace that I have concluded, but I have no choice. The decision has been made now, and I do not think that in the interests of the monarchy I can act otherwise."

At the news of a truce Cavour had instantly left Turin for Victor Emanuel's headquarters at Monzambano. On July 10th —nothing conclusive had happened yet—he had a quiet discussion with his king. But on the 11th, after the convention had been signed, the famous stormy interview between the king and his Prime Minister took place round about midnight, in the course of which Cavour absolutely forgot the respect due to the Emperor of the French and also to his own king. The interview took place partly between the two alone, and partly while the draft of the treaty was read—in the presence of Nigra.[87]

Victor Emanuel caused Nigra to read to Cavour the conditions of the treaty, which left Venice under Austrian rule. It is, however, very questionable whether he also told him that his dismissal was necessary. If this was the case it can only have been expressed by Victor Emanuel with the indication that if the step demanded by Francis Joseph through the Emperor of the French were not complied with, then France would withdraw her troops and leave Piedmont to face Austria alone. Possibly, however, indignation at the condition of the treaty was enough to make Cavour, foaming with rage, hand in his own resignation, so that neither Napoleon nor the King was obliged to require it of him. Cavour saw his life's work attended with only partial success, and was confronted by the impossibility of continuing it. He went so far in his anger as to tell the king that he would have to abdicate. When Victor Emanuel answered that, after all, he was the King, and it was his own affair to consider such a matter, Cavour, forgetting himself absolutely, is said to have replied: "The king? I am the real king." Whereupon Victor Emanuel called Nigra, who was waiting in an anteroom, and said to him: "Take him away to bed, Nigra." This makes it easier to understand what Cavour meant when a few days later, on July 15th, in the presence of Kossuth he said to Senator Pietri, the confidant of the Emperor of the French: "True enough, one is often obliged to compromise in politics. But there is one thing with which an honest man does not compromise, and that is honour. Your Emperor has dishonoured me. Yes, Sir, dishonoured. He gave me his word and vowed solemnly that he would not rest until he had driven the Austrians out of Italy altogether, and stipulated for Savoy and Nice in return. I persuaded my king to accept the bargain and to make this sacrifice for Italy's sake. My good, honourable king agreed to it, relying upon my word. And now the Emperor takes his fee, but leaves us in the lurch half-way. . . . I stand dishonoured before my king. Terrible, terrible! . . . The peace shall not come about. . . . I shall become a conspirator! A revolutionary! But this peace treaty shall not be put into effect. No! A thousand times, no! Never! Never!"[88]

The terms of the Peace of Villafranca, which upset all Cavour's plans, were made still more unpalatable by the fact that Napoleon had agreed to abandon the man with whom, at Plombières, he had devised and subsequently carried out the whole plan. The man who had brought about the war and won Lombardy for Italy left his king's headquarters a fallen star, a dismissed servant, a private person.

On July 12th the Emperor Francis Joseph sent Count Rechberg to Valeggio to put the finishing touches to the work of peace. When he was taken to Napoleon's room he met him not yet fully dressed in the ante-chamber, thought at first he was an aide-de-camp, and was just about to ask him brusquely where the Emperor was when he realized his mistake. Napoleon, however, did not wait for him to speak, but exclaimed at once: "Just to show you that I can keep promises, read this!" and handed Rechberg the written communication of the King of Sardinia that he had appointed as Prime Minister Count Revel, the head of the Conservative Party, which implied the dismissal of Cavour. It has up to the present not been discovered whether the Emperor Napoleon really demanded his dismissal by threatening Victor Emanuel. It seems probable that Cavour's resignation, handed in in the heat of his indignation over the Convention, was taken advantage of by Napoleon, who represented the matter to Austria as being due to his efforts and took the credit for having fulfilled his promise to the Emperor Francis Joseph so promptly.

Napoleon had used every possible means. The alleged London Draft Convention was really worked out in Paris by Persigny, and was officially accepted neither by England, Russia, nor Prussia. It is true that utterances by the Foreign Ministers of these States in the sense of the terms of the Convention are extant.[89] But the Emperor would have waited in vain for any active help. Now the treaty was signed and the war was over, and the fact had to be accepted. Louis Napoleon left Italy and returned to Paris by way of Milan. On the evening of July 12th the Emperor Francis Joseph sent for all the Corps Commanders present in Verona, told them of his determination to make peace, and commanded them to ensure that the officers refrained from abuse and recrimination which had become very prevalent since the conclusion of the armistice.

The cessation of hostilities was also welcomed by the Russian Government. It now became anxious to know what Napoleon's next move was likely to be. The Tsarina Marie tried in her answer to refute a letter of her brother's written just before Solferino and containing a veiled reproach that Russia had stood too much on the side of the revolutionary Napoleon.

"Thank God", she wrote on June 27th (July 9th), "the armistice gives one a little rest and breathing-space. We heard of it with so much pleasure." The Tsarina understood her brother's sentiments very well, but she rejected the idea that her husband could have acted from so base a feeling as revenge or hatred of Francis Joseph. "If we consider our diplomatic relations now," she said, "we have since the Peace of Paris always found France favourably inclined, especially in the East (where all our interests are concentrated). On the other hand, we have always and everywhere found Austria hostile. . . . And then, in a war which did not concern the interests of our country at all, would it not have been madness to have got on to bad terms with France, with whose standpoint we sympathized, for the sake of Austria which has treated us badly?"

Prince Alexander answered on July 13th with the impression of the great events he had lived through still fresh in his mind, and remarked that he had felt very uncomfortable at meeting Louis Napoleon: "I had a long conversation with this representative of modern civilization, and experienced a real sense of disgust at the cynicism with which he quite unashamedly utters the most immoral theories now that he has thrown off the mask: 'I am not a revolutionary myself, but I do not shrink from using revolutionary means to achieve my ends.' I replied somewhat brusquely: 'Sire, it is a two-edged sword that you are using, and it will bring you ill-fortune.' I assure you that if the Tsar had been present at this conversation too, he would have been just as unpleasantly affected as I was to hear him boast: 'The Tsar of Russia thinks in these matters just as I do (meaning the right of European peoples to throw off any sovereignty for the sake of national independence), and I am certain of his support.'"

Prince Alexander, who took the whole intrigue of the Anglo-Russian armistice proposals at its face value, related also how much Napoleon had compromised the Prince Regent of Prussia by producing evidence of his unwillingness to help Austria.[90]

As regards his own political convictions, which were Conservative, the issue of the war must have seemed very unsatisfactory to Prince Alexander. "As a thoughtful man", he wrote to his sister from San Bonifacio on July 6th (18th) "the future looks very black to me. The monarchical principle received another severe blow at the Mincio. . . . How is it that all the Great Powers are letting themselves be intimidated by the French adventurer to such an extent that they calmly watch him knocking down stone by stone the edifice upon which the peace of the world and the whole political organization of Europe have rested for the last forty-four years. . . . The French suggestion of an armistice occurred at the time when it was least expected, and the whole behaviour of Louis Napoleon recently proves conclusively that he cares just as little for the welfare of the Italianissimi as he cared for the fate of the Turks during the war with Russia. He spoke with the deepest contempt of his noble ally, Victor Emanuel, and treated him like a lackey; while the French generals quite openly made mock of the Piedmontese army, which numbered 65,000 men, for having been repulsed with 9,000 casualties by Benedek and his corps of 22,000 men on June 24th."

The numerous letters which Prince Alexander wrote to his sister, and thus indirectly to his brother-in-law, were all couched in similar terms, and did not fail of their intended effect. The Tsar and Tsarina would naturally be concerned to preserve their sovereignty. Although the Tsar, to avoid offending Napoleon, at first hesitated to give his brother-in-law—an imperial Austrian general—a higher class of the St. George's Cross for the campaign in which he had just been engaged, he now did so with the most cordial expressions and the assurance that he hoped always to be reckoned as the Prince's first and warmest friend. The Tsar was especially indignant at Louis Napoleon's having used Russia's name in the alleged London peace project.

"The generally accepted assertion", the Tsar wrote to Prince Alexander* on July 19th (31st), "that the three Great Powers, including Russia, had proposed conditions of peace agreed to among themselves, and which were less advantageous than those offered by France, *is a scandal*, at least as far as we are concerned, *for we knew absolutely nothing about it.* We have made a protest on the subject, following the example of Prussia. Prussia is now—and in my opinion most unjustly—being made the object of all manner of accusations by the rest of Germany in general and Austria in particular. Its position was very difficult, though I admit that there might have been greater steadiness in the conduct of its affairs. None the less, I do feel that it has rendered a real service to Europe at large by preventing the war from becoming general, which would inevitably have brought about the collapse of our whole social order; for then revolution, which was at Napoleon's heels and before which he seems himself to have flinched, would have had no further bar, and must have broken out everywhere.

"I have no illusions, I may say, about this lame peace which has just been concluded in a manner so unexpected by everyone. I regard the future as more than ever pregnant with trouble, and my confidence in our friend Nap. is seriously shaken. It remains to be seen what this strange but fortunate individual will think of next to occupy the ardent imaginations of the French. I can quite understand how disagreeable you must have found your mission to him; and I also realize as a soldier how this unexpected peace must have come as a cruel disappointment to the brave Austrian army, whose one desire was to have its revenge, and for which, I repeat, I have kept all my old affection. And now, amen to politics."

The Tsar's letter reveals above all else that owing to Gortchakoff's too lively coquetting with Napoleon he had grown suspicious. The emphasis so often laid by Prince Alexander

* See Appendix.

upon the connection between the Emperor of the French and revolution began to have its effect on the Russian monarch.

The Tsarina also sought to set her brother's mind at rest on the score of Russian policy with regard to Napoleon: "We shall not let ourselves be led by the nose by him," she wrote on July 20th (August 1st), "and are in no way bound, but are quite free to choose whatever course is best in our own interests. It is true that hatred of Austria is very strong here, but it neither must nor will influence our policy as soon as we consider reconciliation to be possible and desirable. To believe that Gortchakoff is prepossessed in Napoleon's favour would be a mistake. He is in favour of our keeping on good terms with France, but has no personal confidence in Napoleon and no lust to be revenged on Austria. He is much too ingenuous for a diplomatist, and would never be able to conceal such feelings from me if they existed. He speaks of Austria quite coolly. The Tsar, on the other hand, has not forgotten how disgracefully the Emperor F. [rancis] J. [oseph] behaved towards his father. But these are his feelings as a son and not as a monarch, and will never influence his policy." Prince Alexander, whose custom it was to enter the most important letters that he received in his diary verbatim, was not convinced by his sister's representations concerning Gortchakoff. He put significant queries and exclamation marks beside the words "mistake" and "ingenuous". In Alexander II's letter the part that made the most impression upon him was that in which the Tsar spoke of the shattering of his confidence in Napoleon. Two expressive exclamation marks indicate this.

Prince Alexander missed the next events in Italy as he went home on leave. The war was over. Despite its unsatisfactory outcome for Austria, the Danubian monarchy's renown was none the less increased, though perhaps not from the military standpoint. After the defeat which he had sustained, the Emperor Francis Joseph, now totally isolated, felt a great desire for the support of Russia, which he had hitherto treated with such scant courtesy. And in order to achieve this he proposed to make use of Prince Alexander of Hesse in the weeks following immediately upon the end of the war.

CHAPTER VII

REVOLUTIONARY BEACONS

COUNT RECHBERG assumed the conduct of foreign affairs in Vienna in succession to Buol, and endeavoured to bring order out of the chaos left by his predecessor. His first step was to make an attempt at reconciliation with Russia. On hearing that Prince Alexander of Hesse had been invited to stay with the Tsar, Rechberg suggested to the Emperor Francis Joseph to ask him to come to Vienna on his way. The Prince expected that he was to be entrusted with an important mission, but the Emperor simply desired him to ascertain the Tsar's views.

Deeds rather than words had been expected in St. Petersburg. Indeed, Gortchakoff told Prince Alexander that Russia would no longer be satisfied with mere words. Concrete proposals must be made. While, as far as the conservative principles were concerned which Austria was always holding out as a lure to Russia, he considered that Russia had always come off badly when it had gone to war solely for the sake of principles. Prince Alexander realized that it was going to be difficult for Rechberg to regain the ground lost in St. Petersburg by his predecessor. The Prince also obtained a clear insight into Napoleon's scheme, for the Tsar showed him the letters he had received from him at the time of the Italian campaign. In one, written two days before the Battle of Solferino, Napoleon observed that he had fought at Magenta with an Austrian corps that had come straight from the Galician frontier; a remark which sounded like a thinly veiled remonstrance with Russia for failing to keep its promise to compel Austria to be on her guard on the Austro-Russian frontier. The Tsar regarded this as gross impertinence.

Alexander II merely echoed Francis Joseph's polite words in the answer conveyed to the Austrian Emperor by Prince Alexander. But he mentioned casually that he had tried on his Austrian uniform in case of eventualities, and had had it sent to Warsaw. From which the Prince concluded that he would

K

not go out of his way to avoid meeting Francis Joseph if the occasion should present itself.

Very soon after this Prince Alexander returned to Vienna, where he discovered that he had been advanced to the rank of Corps-Commander and that he had been awarded the Cross of the Maria Theresa Order. He told the Emperor what he had gathered during his visit to St. Petersburg, and advised him to go to Warsaw in person. Nevertheless the Archduke Albrecht was sent, and he failed to achieve anything positive. When Prince Alexander was staying in Vienna again in November, the Emperor Francis Joseph told him that the Tsar had complained to the Archduke Albrecht that at the Weimar interview in 1857 not a word had been said about the late Tsar Nicholas. The Emperor requested the Prince to write and remind the Tsar that a mutual agreement had been made at the time not to mention the past. The Tsar, however, replied to Prince Alexander's letter indignantly denying that he had ever heard of or entered upon such an agreement.

The value of Prince Alexander of Hesse as a go-between and as a link with the Tsar's family was beginning to be recognized in Vienna. During their Italian tour the Emperor and Empress had treated the Prince's wife in a cold and distant, indeed almost insulting, manner. Although she had made no move in the matter, she was now invited to dine at Schönbrunn, and was seated beside Francis Joseph at table. Nor did this change of demeanour fail of its intended effect upon Prince Alexander. The Emperor ordered Count Rechberg from now on to keep the Prince fully informed of the state of foreign affairs, especially in regard to the relations between Austria and Russia. This remarkable change in the manner of his treatment is to be attributed to the representations of Rechberg, who was doing all that lay in his power to repair the mistakes of his predecessor in throwing away the friendship of Russia.

Gortchakoff, however, remained far more reserved than his sovereign, who was already very much inclined to take his brother-in-law's advice and to come to a better understanding with Austria. Prince Alexander redoubled his efforts to induce the Tsar to take the Austrian side against Napoleon, but came involuntarily into ever greater opposition to Gortchakoff, who had for a long time been jealous of his influence. In a political New Year's commentary which Prince Alexander sent to his sister from Venice on January 5 (17), 1860, he had some sharp words to say about the "political madman in Paris". "God grant that red Republicanism may not keep the upper hand. It looks very serious in every country to-day. The spectre of democracy is raising its head everywhere, and is actually being conjured up by monarchs and their ministers, as though they had been smitten with blindness. I hear from Paris that the calm and placid way in which Louis Napoleon moves amid the chaos he has created is nothing short of uncanny. He makes Metternich play waltzes, and then he and the Empress dance to them; he designs and sketches uniforms, builds palaces, etc. He came . . . into the world as an emissary of God, or rather of the Devil's, to tread under foot the established princely houses; and the Great Powers of Europe are hopelessly deluded and are helping him to give the death-blow to Divine Right and all sacred principles.

"In our miserable spite and jealousy we have now sunk so low that there is no longer any solidarity between the Great Powers. Each one is pleased if the others are in a bad way, and refuses to move so long as its own skin is not affected. This is also due to the fact that the gentleman [Napoleon] is so clever in basely twisting the truth . . . that even the Tsar is taken in by his insinuations." All this was put with calculated bluntness, and did not fail of its effect upon the imperial couple.

Rechberg began increasingly to make use of Prince Alexander. In February 1860 he was again summoned to Vienna, where great anxiety reigned. The Peace of Zurich had indeed been signed on November 10, 1859, but in putting it into effect insuperable difficulties, especially in Central Italy, had been encountered, and it was still feared that Napoleon would break the treaties to which he had subscribed only a few months earlier. Prince Alexander urged the Tsar not to be associated with Napoleon: "The whole responsibility would be attributed to your counsellor", he wrote on February 3 (15), 1860, "if Russia—which God forfend—should ever be involved in this revolutionary avalanche, which will grow from day to day if Napoleon thinks he is being backed up by you; and which will inevitably turn the whole of Europe into a series of democratic republics." The Russian Chancellor had just recovered from a serious illness, which caused the Prince to remark acidly that the wicked always did flourish.

The Prince's numerous letters had the desired effect upon the Tsar. Alexander II was beginning to describe everything

that happened in Italy as "revolutionary". Only as regards
France he was still a little reserved. "One must admit", he
wrote to Prince Alexander[91] on May 6th (18th), "that we are
living at a time when government is very difficult; revolutionary
principles are gaining ground, and finding more and more
following among the masses. Nevertheless I shall certainly not
be the one to abandon the principles to which I have always
adhered. I set my trust in God to keep me on the right path,
and believe that He will sustain me."

Prince Alexander was not pleased with this answer. He
thought it was too vague and indefinite in view of the much
more concrete appeals that he had directed to the Tsar and
his wife during the last few months. None the less an under-
current of anxiety is to be heard in all communications from
the Tsar at this period, and for the time he was seriously afraid
that the triumph of the revolution in Italy would have fatal
consequences all over Europe.[92]

Meanwhile summer had come, the heat was quite exceptional, and Prince Alexander celebrated his thirty-seventh
birthday.

"Soon", he said, "I shall not need to worry about my bald
patch any more. And once I have got into the forties I may
even allow myself a little corporation. Who knows!"

His indignation with Napoleon III had if anything increased.
He was of the same mind in this matter as his brother the
Grand Duke of Hesse, who after meeting Napoleon III at
Baden-Baden during the summer of 1860 wrote to Alexander:
"When I had had a good look at the fellow and thought how
much misery he has brought on Europe and will continue to
bring, I shuddered. I would not have his conscience—if he
possesses one at all—for millions. The man from Plombières
with his feline eyes and his famous languor said all manner of
pleasant things about you." Prince Alexander, however, was
not moved by the amiability of the Emperor of the French.
"I pray God", he wrote to his sister on July 16th, "mercifully
to preserve me from ever meeting the man again—unless it
were on a battlefield."

What Prince Alexander really wished was to see a return of
the time-honoured Holy Alliance, by which alone he believed
that the peace of Europe might be assured. Austro-Prussian
relations had recently improved, as was shown by a meeting
between the Prince Regent and Francis Joseph which took
place on July 26th.

PRINCE ALEXANDER OF HESSE

"A piece of good news", remarked the Prince to his sister in a letter written from Padua on July 22nd, "is the meeting at Töplitz. It is only a pity that a Nordic Trio will not come into being there. Surely this combination must in the end be formed again. *It should never have been given up. For that was the beginning of all our ills. From the day when this abominable beast of a Buol helped the Emperor Napoleon to dissolve the alliance of the Three Powers of Leipzig, from that day date the misfortunes that have overwhelmed the whole of Europe. That was the day for which the revolution had been waiting for so many years, and, God knows, it succeeded in making the most of it.*"

In Vienna, too, it was felt to be desirable that a meeting with the Tsar should follow that with the Prince Regent. A hint had, however, meanwhile come from St. Petersburg to the effect that the many letters and frequent interventions of Prince Alexander were not looked upon with favour by Gortchakoff. The Prince's attacks on the minister glanced harmlessly off because Gortchakoff was clever enough to suggest to his master that Alexander was influenced by the surroundings in which he lived, and was being used by Austria to exercise improper influence upon Russia. Hence Prince Alexander himself preferred to remain in the background this time, and advised that the initiative for a meeting should come from the Emperor Francis Joseph himself. To which the Emperor replied: "Yes, yes. Prince Gortchakoff has always thought that you wanted to overthrow him." Prince Alexander longed with all his heart for the reconciliation of the three sovereigns, and regarded his imperial brother-in-law as the person who could determine the welfare of the continent. "The future of the whole of Europe", he wrote from Padua on September 11th, "lies in the hands of the ruler of Russia. If he—which God forbid—were obliged to abandon the good cause, then we should all have to become republicans, every single one of us!"

The Tsar's feelings were mixed. Actually, at the bottom of his heart, he disliked Napoleon III, the upstart with whom Gortchakoff was always so anxious to be on good terms and who had, after all, begun his reign by undertaking a campaign against his father the late Tsar. He gave sincere expression to his feelings when he wrote to Prince Alexander from Tsarskoe Selo on September 28th describing Napoleon's behaviour as baser than ever. In this respect he agreed with Francis Joseph, who had written to his mother from Laxenburg on September 1, 1859, briefly and to the point: "The Emperor Napoleon is and in spite of everything remains a scoundrel."[93]

Shortly afterwards, and to the great joy of Prince Alexander, the Emperor of Austria announced that he would visit Warsaw in October. The Prince Regent of Prussia was also invited. The meeting was delayed a little because on October 3rd the Tsarina became the mother of another son. Prince Alexander, whom Francis Joseph invited to accompany him to Warsaw, already had visions of the restoration of the Holy Alliance; and in a letter written to his brother-in-law on October 9th expressed the hope that a coalition would come into being similar to that which had in its day assured the peace of Europe for so many decades. Thus the triumphal march of the revolution would at last be stopped. However, the Prince's hopes were destined to prove illusory. After a family dinner on October 22nd the Prince had a long private talk on politics with his brother-in-law, which he reports in his diary under that date. The Tsar said plainly that Russia would never again mobilize for the benefit of the Germanic powers, and another attempt must be made to win the Emperor Napoleon for the Conservative cause. He went on to say that he had made suggestions to him on this head, and that he was hourly expecting to receive an answer, which might then serve as the basis of negotiations. Prince Alexander protested passionately, but to no avail. "All my arguments", he writes, "were shattered by Gortchakoff's theories, by which the Tsar is unfortunately absolutely permeated."

The Emperor Napoleon's expected answer arrived. But nothing definite was said in it that could make any appreciable difference to the existing state of affairs. The Prince noted in his diary very ill-humouredly on October 24th: "*Nothing is likely to be settled here.* Gortchakoff has taken good care of that. And the exhausting programme [of entertainments] makes it absolutely impossible to carry on any serious conversation." The Emperor Francis Joseph was also most dissatisfied with the course of events. On October 25th a conference lasting an hour and a half took place between the three monarchs and their ministers. "Napoleon III", remarked Prince Alexander in his diary, "must be regarded as having made a sinister and invisible fourth, represented by his creature Gortchakoff." On the afternoon of the same day the Prince visited Gortchakoff, and had a long talk that afforded him very little satisfaction.

Ultimately, both spoke to each other with great frankness, one might almost say rudeness.

Another factor mitigating against the success of the Warsaw conference was that the Tsar Alexander had had disquieting news of the state of his mother's health and was himself suffering from a feverish cold. In consequence the cavalry manœuvres, the great banquet, and a projected day's hunting were cancelled, and everyone left Warsaw on October 26th, after Prince Alexander had frustrated Count Rechberg's suggestion of giving Prince Gortchakoff the Saint Stephen's Order in diamonds. An unrehearsed incident in the programme was a Polish Nationalist demonstration in Warsaw. Prince Gortchakoff sought to explain this to the Tsar by saying that the disturbances were to be ascribed solely to the presence of the Emperor of Austria.

"The very stars in their courses fought against this unfortunate interview", complained Prince Alexander, whose political dreams had dissolved before his eyes. The condition of the dowager Tsarina had meanwhile become very grave. When she was receiving the last rites of the Church she replied to the question whether she had forgiven all those who had offended her by saying, as Prince Alexander reports in his diary on October 28th, "Yes, everyone; with the exception of the Emperor of Austria." Soon afterwards she breathed her last.

Towards the end of the month of November Prince Alexander left Russia and went back to his garrison in Italy, where General Benedek had been appointed Commander-in-Chief of all Austria's remaining Italian provinces. Benedek felt himself to have been the sole victor in the campaign of 1859, and he assumed the gruff, bluff manner which he thought appropriate to a soldierly and martial bearing. He vented his disapprobation upon the numerous sprigs of the nobility who occupied all the high positions in the army but who had not specially distinguished themselves in the recent campaign. There was a certain amount of friction from the very beginning, and Prince Alexander was vexed at Benedek's tactlessness. If anyone had any little weakness, it was certain that Benedek would remark on it.

The Venetian problem still remained the centre of unrest. As the unification of Italy progressed, attempts were made by the Italians to obtain Venice by purchase. The suggestion was regarded in Vienna as most ignominious, and was therefore rejected on several occasions.

Meanwhile, on the morning of January 2, 1861, King Frederick William IV had died in Berlin. The new king adopted the name of William I, which surprised Prince Alexander. "I suppose Frederick William V", he remarked in a letter to Baron von Drachenfels on January 12th, "was thought to be too ordinary and Frederick III too pretentious, as recalling the name of the Great King. And then William I has the advantage that it need not be changed in case a democratic German Reich should be brought into existence by Schleinitz [the Prussian Foreign Minister]."

Prince Alexander was unhappy in Italy in these days. The tenseness of the situation in the country and differences of opinion with Benedek made life very unpleasant. In addition, General Ramming wrote an essay on the Battle of Solferino which accused the Prince—who had, after all, been awarded the Maria Theresa Cross for his conduct—of having moved off his division two hours too late in order to allow his men time to prepare and eat a meal.

The Prince successfully defended himself against the attack, but the whole affair fed his growing desire to leave the service. Moreover, he became the butt of newspaper criticism. On June 6th Cavour, to the grief of all those who sympathized with the Italians, had died. Requiem masses were said everywhere for the great statesman. The police took down the names of any ladies or students who went to the services in mourning. On June 10th, a few days after Cavour's death, the officers of the Sixty-second Infantry Regiment in Strà gave a garden party in honour of Prince Alexander, which was represented by the newspapers as being a sort of feast of thanksgiving for the minister's death. This imputation again increased the growing uneasiness of the Prince. Furthermore, he had news from home that made him anxious as to the future of the Grand Duchy of Hesse. Duke William of Brunswick visited him in Venice and told him that Germany was in an abominable state. "He also abused the brainlessness of the authorities in Baden," Prince Alexander reported to his sister on July 6th, "where our poor miserable cousin is said to be on the point of concluding a military convention with Prussia as the Coburg Democrat has done. They say that Fritz of Baden, fearing that the last hour of the small States is approaching, is ready to demean himself by becoming a sort of Prussian satrap, in the hope that he may still be able to play a part when the general mediatization and annexation takes place!! Poor fool!"

The Prince was tired of the nomadic life of a soldier. He had just become the father of a fourth son, who was named Francis Joseph, and was anxious to make a home for his family in Darmstadt. About this time the Prince's nephew, Louis of Hesse, the hereditary Grand Duke, was betrothed to the Princess Alice, daughter of the Queen of England.[94]

Friction with Benedek in official matters continued. Prince Alexander complained to the Emperor, and suggested resigning his commission. At the end of the year 1861 he heard that the Tsar would give him financial assistance if he bought a palace in Darmstadt. This confirmed the Prince in his resolution to quit the Austrian service. Once again he attended the Emperor and Empress on their visit to Venice, on which occasion General Benedek after a great review made a fiery speech in which amid the immense enthusiasm of all the troops he assured the Emperor of their loyalty until death. After this scene it was clear to the Prince that Benedek's position was unassailable. He told the Tsarina of the episode, and she replied in a letter written on January 24 (February 5), 1862, that it must have been very moving, though not indeed for the Emperor Francis Joseph, who did "not feel much and was cold by nature". Prince Alexander admitted this, but thought that on this occasion Francis Joseph, although grim reality had hitherto robbed him of every illusion, had none the less been deeply affected. The temper of the Italian patriots in Italy remained the same during and after the Emperor's visit. The equestrian club of Padua ostentatiously dismissed the groom who had been outrider to the imperial carriage when the Emperor arrived, and sold the chestnut horse that he had ridden. The subsequent measures taken by the police only increased the bitter feeling. Prince Alexander's sole desire was to get away from surroundings that were so uncomfortable in every way and from a land that was so hostile. On May 7th he induced his private physician to certify him to be suffering from an obscure complaint that demanded long leave of absence, and went home to Darmstadt.

The first part of his time in Darmstadt was very depressing, nor did he have good news from his sister in St. Petersburg. On March 3rd, the anniversary of the Tsar's accession, a decree had been issued abolishing serfdom in Russia. But the difficulties arising from an edict intended to bring Russia into conformity with the new spirit of the age were soon very apparent. Added to this was the continual unrest in Poland.

On February 15th (27th) the Tsarina wrote to her brother:
"Altogether I am very heavy at heart. Gaeta;[95] Warsaw, where
the first bloodshed took place yesterday; the peasant question;
. . . and so much else."

Alexander Herzen hailed the emancipation of the peasants
with warm words of praise and named Alexander II "Tsar-
Liberator"; nevertheless, from that time on Liberals in Russia
began a more intensified form of agitation, the trend of which
grew increasingly revolutionary. Having been given an inch,
they now demanded an ell. Leaflets were distributed among
the populace: "What the nation wants", "The new generation",
"Young Russia", "Estate owners and peasants". Extremist
demands were made, and soon it was no longer merely a case
of harmless agitation by the spoken or written word, but
mysterious fires broke out suddenly in the towns and spread
disquiet and anxiety among the people. Especially during the
last days of May and the early part of June in 1862 there was
a long series of fires in St. Petersburg, and a similar criminal
project was discovered and prevented in Moscow.

"I want to give you a sign of life", the Tsarina Marie wrote
to her brother from Tsarskoe Selo on June 6th (18th), "after the
sad time we have been through, with St. Petersburg bursting
into flames at every corner. It appears that this was to be the
beginning of a series of revolutionary acts that had been planned
in London and that were to have been carried out simultaneously here and in Moscow, but which they refused to
execute down there. A number of people have been arrested,
and if sufficient proof can be found, the ringleaders will be
hanged, although we have neither gallows nor hangman nor
even the death penalty. But we are getting out of the difficulty
by declaring martial law, which has been done, among other
places, in the Caucasus. Public opinion is very strongly in
favour of making an example that will really frighten them off
doing anything of the sort again, for everyone feels that his life
and his belongings are threatened. What was most painful to
Sacha was the arrest of five officers. One for inciting to rioting,
three because they destroyed the pamphlets which a man was
carrying who was being taken prisoner by some non-commissioned officers . . ."

The Tsarina intended to convey that fortunately these were
only exceptions, and that apart from them, men and non-
commissioned officers were loyal, as was the nation from which
they derived.

"On the whole, the excesses of evildoers have called forth a reaction of good among sensible folk, and have reawakened all the love of the people for their Tsar. That is the comforting aspect of the situation, which indeed is very critical and difficult, but, thank God, by no means desperate. Sacha is bearing this heavy burden without losing courage, but his heart is terribly torn. May God help him!"

Bismarck, who had been Prussian Ambassador in St. Petersburg until April 1862, observed the internal situation of Russia during the last part of his sojourn with some concern. In consequence of his conservative tendency he had on the whole been *persona grata* at the Russian court, and his departure was regretted. "Our new Prussian Ambassador [Von der Goltz]", wrote the Tsarina to Prince Alexander on April 4th from St. Petersburg, "is extraordinarily ugly, seems to be a man of intellect, and less of a 'National Unionist' [*Nationalverein*] than Bismarck (whose departure I regret none the less), and has moreover the unusual accomplishment of speaking French perfectly. Bismarck knew it reasonably well, and had such a consummate knowledge of German as I have never met before in anyone, especially in a Prussian."

The revolutionary machinations in the interior of Russia were not the only troubles that weighed upon the Tsar. The situation in Poland became increasingly grave. Prince Alexander seemed to have been right in telling the Tsar when he met him in Warsaw that the events in Italy would find their imitators in Poland.

Now Alexander of Hesse saw his views confirmed in the event, and observed somewhat sceptically the Tsar's latest measure in appointing his brother the Grand Duke Constantine as Governor of Warsaw, with the Marquis Alexander Wielopolski, as chief of the civil administration, preaching forgiveness.

"I do not think", the Tsarina wrote to her brother from Tsarskoe Selo on May 13th (25th), "that anything else can be done at the moment. The Poles want a grand duke, a court, representation, even court intrigues, in order to checkmate other intrigues!"

The Tsarina was in a very short time to learn by bitter experience that, on the contrary, the Poles attached no importance to and expected no good of a grand duke. Hardly had Constantine arrived in Warsaw when, on July 4th, as he was leaving the theatre, a Polish Nationalist fired a revolver at him. The bullet only just grazed the Governor's collar-bone, but the attack gave a terrible shock to the Grand Duke, who had come to Warsaw only the day before with his wife, who was expecting a baby very shortly. From that day onward neither he nor his wife ever went out except under a strong escort, and felt as though the castle were a beleaguered fortress, to leave which spelt danger and death.

Prince Alexander followed these events with anxiety. He who had lived outside his own country for so long, and had been imbued with the spirit of conservatism at the courts of Russia and Austria, now realized the changes that had taken place even in his own home. The two tendencies, the "Pan-Germans" who wished to insist upon keeping Austria attached to Germany, and the "Little Germans" who wanted a unified German state centred about a Prusso-Hohenzollern Empire from which Austria was excluded, came into bitter opposition to one another.

Princes such as Duke Ernest II of Coburg and the Grand Duke of Baden, who were willing for Prussia to take the lead, stood in fierce opposition to the princes, who were all closely allied by blood, to whom Prussia was like a red rag to a bull, and who sought alliance with Austria. Among these Prince Alexander of Hesse took a prominent position. His hatred of Prussia was particularly outspoken, and he enjoyed sending his sister anecdotes that were often quite unauthenticated. Thus he told her once that Baron Heckeren, the Dutch Ambassador in Vienna, who happened to be staying at Baden-Baden in September 1861 at the same time as the Queen of Prussia, had conveyed his good wishes to her shortly before the coronation. Queen Augusta had pulled a wry face and answered: "Congratulations would only be appropriate if I were going to be crowned German Empress!" The surprised diplomat had told this to King William when they were walking together on the following day. To which the monarch had replied that he was firmly resolved to oppose any aggrandizement by the appropriation of the territory of friendly German princes. Should, however, circumstances prove to be stronger than his desire, and should he prove no longer able to resist the annexationist movement, he would renounce the throne and leave the matter in his son's hands. . . . "How nice it will be for us", said Prince Alexander to his sister, writing from Padua on October 1, 1861, "to wake up one fine day, you and I, and find that we belong to a mediatized Prussian family! And the *Nord* and the

Indépendance will have the pleasure of referring to 'the ex-Grand Duke of Hesse' !"

It was natural that, holding these views, Prince Alexander should not think highly of the Grand Duke of Baden, who was married to the daughter of the King of Prussia and was well known for his profession of liberal politics and his constitutional reforms, any more than he did of the Grand Duke's brother-in-law, the restless Duke of Coburg.

On July 13, 1862, Prince Alexander went incognito to the opening of the rifle-shooting competition at Frankfurt. From the balcony of the Hesse palace he watched the imposing procession of ten thousand riflemen from all parts of Germany. "In the middle of them", said Alexander in his description, "was that clown from Coburg marching at the head of all the five hundred club flags."

In Frankfurt he met the newly married Princess Alice, the daughter of Queen Victoria, to whom the whole Hesse family took a great fancy from the very beginning. The Prince thought her clever, friendly, and much better looking than her photographs had led him to expect. He observed that for so young a woman she was astonishingly self-possessed and that nothing put her out of countenance. Nevertheless her romantic disposition alarmed him somewhat. After having been in Darmstadt only a few weeks she began to be very bored, which was hardly flattering to her husband. Princess Alice was, according to Prince Alexander, "a bit of a blue-stocking"; she liked to indulge in discussions upon art and science and the great questions of the day. Her somewhat prosaic and very down-right husband Prince Louis, on the other hand, preferred hunting, horses, and good food. It was feared at the Hessian court that the Princess Alice would soon begin to look down on him and possibly to play the misunderstood wife. At all events, she was a stimulating element in the little city of Darmstadt.

The political future seemed dark indeed in those days. Bismarck, who had been so violently attacked by Alexander of Hesse, was appointed Prime Minister of Prussia on September 23rd, and soon afterwards Prussian Foreign Minister. On January 8, 1863, Alexander wrote on the subject to his sister, who unlike himself thought a great deal of Bismarck, largely because he agreed with the Tsar upon the Polish question:

"Your protégé Bismarck is holding Germany very dangerously in the balance. It almost seems as if he intended (for no one now mentions the weak King) to induce civil war in Germany, in order to prevent a revolution in Prussia. Bismarck's political machinations keep a happy mean between lunacy and treason. With Baden and Coburg as his *sole* allies, he is demanding that the four kingdoms and the remaining German States shall throw Austria out of the federation. I never heard such an impudent idea. Unfortunately, Bismarck seems to be reckoning on two more allies besides *Baden* (which in any case is only partly in sympathy with the Grand Duke's policy) and *Coburg* (where the Duke is hated by everyone, as Alice told me). And these allies are the Emperor Napoleon and the German democrats, who have been coming up like mushrooms since 1859 in all the States in the confederacy. Therein lies the real danger for Germany, unless King William decides at the eleventh hour to dismiss Herr von Bismarck."

"I must admit", answered the Tsarina to her brother's outburst, on January 5th (17th), "that my friend Bismarck is more fitted to be a diplomatist in St. Petersburg than Prime Minister in Berlin. But according to the latest news it appears that he is settling down and becoming a little more reasonable. Bismarck amused me, and Redern [who had just been appointed Prussian Ambassador in place of Goltz] bores me dreadfully. He is dull and very common."

After his sick leave in 1862 Prince Alexander had only returned for a short time to the land where "Orsini bombs bloom instead of lemon-trees", as he expressed it. He applied almost at once for another period of leave, but was told that he had better ask to be put on the retired list.

Meanwhile revolution had broken out in Greece against the supine King Otto the Bavarian, and the King fled on an English ship which brought him to Trieste. The result was a great search through Europe for a candidate for the vacant throne. Prince Alexander was suggested. To Rechberg's direct question whether he would agree to it if England and Austria put him forward, the Prince laughed and gave an evasive answer, as he reports in his diary on December 15th.

When Alexander left Italy, Francis Joseph promised, if the occasion arose and he wished it, to give him a post somewhere outside Venice, and in case of war to make him the commander of an army corps. This was a promise given in the Emperor's own interest, for obviously the Tsar's brother-in-law might still prove useful, and in consequence there was every reason for parting on good terms with him.

Meanwhile Prince Alexander was getting more bad news from Russia. Discontent was taking dangerous forms in Poland. Since Alexander II's accession there had never been a levy of recruits in Poland. This was now decreed, and was the occasion of the rising in 1863, which broke out in full strength in February and March. Prince Alexander was particularly displeased that among the young people who gathered enthusiastically under the revolutionary flag was a nephew of his wife's, Alexander Hauke, whom the Prince designated as a "young pup of a red republican". This young man's republican views had been considerably strengthened by the disdain with which his family had been treated by the court and society of St. Petersburg at the time of Prince Alexander's marriage. Hence he joined the Polish rebels with ardour, although he was only nineteen years old and had just begun his studies at the University of Heidelberg. Hardly had he joined up before the unfortunate youth fell in a skirmish with the Russian troops near Warsaw. This occurrence was most particularly painful to the Prince on the Tsar and Tsarina's account.

The Polish revolt did not fail to influence foreign opinion. Prussia and Austria were the first to be affected, since they both had Polish provinces, one in Posen and the other in Galicia. It would therefore have been wise for these two States to declare their solidarity with the Russian Government over the Polish question, so as not only to assure themselves against a Polish rising in their own States but also to get on to better terms with Russia. This was, thanks to the genius of Bismarck, realized in Prussia, and on February 8, 1865, a convention for mutual support in the question was signed. Although there was not much love lost between the Austrians and the Poles, Austria was again shortsighted enough—although Napoleon's offer of alliance was rejected—to admit the intervention of the Western Powers in the Polish question as expressed in diplomatic notes and demands, and thus once again, as in the Crimean War, to be looked upon as an uncertain quantity by Russia. The Polish problem created grave difficulties for Napoleon III, who was anxious to consolidate and not endanger the friendly relations with Russia for which the way had been paved by Gortchakoff. But public opinion forced him to abandon his passive attitude towards the Poles. Napoleon was obliged willy-nilly to do something for them. England, however, regarded the Polish events with satisfaction as an opportunity of disturbing the friendly relations between France and Russia which she had for long looked upon with mistrust.

At about this time a daughter was born to Louis of Hesse and his wife Princess Alice of England, and Queen Victoria asked Prince Alexander to represent his brother at the christening. Alexander was full of curiosity to get to know the Queen, for the totally unfounded rumour had been spread abroad among the ruling families that since the death of her beloved husband the Prince Consort she had been affected mentally. Prince Alexander promised his sister to find out whether she was "all there or not". On April 25th, after a stormy crossing during which "the Lord made a hotchpotch of the sea and the travellers' stomachs", he arrived at Windsor, and was allotted rooms in the castle. What chiefly disturbed the Prince, who liked his cigar, was the Queen's prohibition of smoking within the castle, which had been renovated shortly before his arrival. Victoria received him immediately upon his arrival, before he had even had time to change out of his travelling clothes, and was most friendly. The Prince did not think her handsome, being spoilt by "pendulous cheeks" and also by the remarkable dress worn by English widows. But he liked her personally, and he verified that the rumours as to her mental condition were utterly groundless.

The Prince's rooms were in the Great Tower, a mighty pile built upon a rock and over which the Royal Standard flew. The tower is connected with the rest of the castle by a long passage and some stairs. This had the advantage that Prince Alexander was able to smoke surreptitiously. Late in the evenings he was often joined by the Prince of Wales (afterwards Edward VII) and his brother Prince Alfred,[96] who came for the same purpose, although "the death penalty was attached to the weed", as Prince Alexander told his sister. He felt very strange "being so suddenly conjured into an entirely new part of the world", and failed utterly to preserve his gravity when he was solemnly preceded through the long passage by an aged chamberlain dressed in deep mourning and conducted to breakfast (nine o'clock), lunch (two o'clock), and dinner (eight o'clock) in the dining-room every day. "The Princess of Wales, whom they call Alex," Prince Alexander said to his sister in describing the royal family on May 22nd, "is perfectly lovely, and at the same time very natural and charming. But her husband is a funny little man. His features are not bad (he is a male edition of Alice), but he is so broad for his height

that he looks shorter than his wife. He is exceedingly friendly
and cordial with me, as is also Prince Alfred, whom I like
very much, and who is a clever, frank, jovial fellow, a typical
English naval officer. . . . The Princesses Helena and Louise
are pretty, especially the former, and look very intelligent.
The baby Beatrice is a dear little soul with flying golden curls
down to her waist, and seems to be on the way to being
thoroughly spoilt. Arthur and Leopold are two lank little Scots
with blue knees, but they look intelligent.

"Louis [of Hesse, the husband of Princess Alice] has become
quite an Englishman. He wears a Norfolk jacket, short breeches,
and multi-coloured garters, is very fond of sherry and horses,
reads as little as possible, and never writes at all. He is the
Queen's confidant, is popular in England, and despite his
usual liveliness, coolly and phlegmatically murders the Queen's
English in official addresses, and preaches the political ideas
of the Duke of Coburg, if indeed he can be said to have
any."

Prince Alexander passed his days, apart from the christening
festivities, in seeing the sights of London and at entertainments
of every description. There were also some talks on politics.
The Queen gave Prince Alexander to understand that he
would be doing her a great favour if he were to try to reassure
her Ministers and to recommend moderation to them. In his
conversations with Lord Palmerston and Lord John Russell,
both Ministers expressed the fear that Napoleon might declare
war on Russia and attempt a landing at Riga. They were so
bellicose in their speech that Prince Alexander, who did not
altogether perceive that the aim of the English statesmen was
to blacken Napoleon thoroughly in the Tsar's eyes, implored
them to prevent a European war. Actually, however, war was
only talked about in England, nobody really believed in it,
and certainly none of them had any intention of letting themselves in for hostilities on account of the Polish question.

Prince Alexander left England very pleased with his reception, but in some anxiety regarding the general political
situation of the world. He returned home by way of Paris,
where he had an audience of Napoleon. The Emperor of the
French spoke about the Poles and mentioned that public
opinion in France demanded peremptorily that something
should be done for them. "Would it not be possible", he
suggested, "to make an independent kingdom of the former
Grand Duchy of Warsaw? The Great Powers would at the

L

same time guarantee that the new State should not be allowed to make any claim to the old Russian-Polish provinces, and still less to Galicia or Posen." Nevertheless, Napoleon knew in his own mind that this would follow automatically.

Prince Alexander gave detailed accounts of his experiences and discoveries in the capitals of the two Western Powers not only to his sister but also to his brother-in-law in a letter written on May 18, 1863.* The Tsar remarked in this connection that what was most surprising was the ignorance of foreigners about all things concerning the Poles, and the blandness with which they raised questions of which they did not understand a word. In the Tsar's opinion the crux of the situation was in Vienna, but he was not clear what they really wanted there. He had conceded that the Polish question had "a European side" to it, but that was not to say that he would agree to any interference in the affairs of his country. Such interference would be an attack upon the honour of Russia, and he would never traffic in that. Now that the Tsar saw himself left more and more in the lurch by Gortchakoff's protégé, the Emperor Napoleon, he was seeking a means of re-entry into the old Holy Alliance. "The treaties that put an end to Poland's independence were signed by these three courts", he wrote. "Their interests in it are direct, immediate, and similar. . . . An agreement between them would be the best guarantee of that world peace in the name of which the other Powers justify their intervention."

Prince Alexander realized from this letter that the Tsar wanted to return to the programme which he had refused to consider at Warsaw in the year 1860, when he was hoping for support from France and lusting for revenge on Austria.

"The Tsar", remarked Prince Alexander in his diary, "now —but I fear it is too late—uses the same languageas I did vainly at Warsaw in October of 1860." But between then and now lay the Polish revolution and the dubious attitude of Russia's new friend, Napoleon.

Russia had hitherto politely but firmly refused all foreign intervention. She was determined before all else to quell the Polish rising with the greatest severity. The other Powers, however, would not yet admit defeat. England, France, and in spite of Rechberg also Austria,[97] sent written demands towards the middle of July, which required in six points amnesty, national representation, autonomous administration,

* See Appendix.

etc., for Poland, and which were to form the basis of discussion at a conference of the Powers.

The Austrian note, in deference to Galicia and to the relations with Russia, was the least severe, but it was once again an example of the Viennese habit of doing things by halves. It was foreign to Austrian policy to decide for one party or the other fully and without reservation in the Polish as in all other questions.

The procedure of the Powers was very ill-received in St. Petersburg. "The Tsar had to make the greatest possible efforts at self-control", wrote the Tsarina to her brother on July 6th (18th), "in order to reply moderately and politely to those impudent notes, especially the English one. But I fear that this restraint will not be acceptable to our feelings of wounded national pride, which demand war even if it means the greatest sacrifice. Whole villages are volunteering as soldiers, the reserves are mobilizing joyfully, and not a day passes without peasants coming from all corners of Russia with money, with loyal addresses or with the offer to give up their lives and their goods in the defence of their country." Nevertheless the Tsarina hoped that war might still be averted. "I hope it is a good omen for peace", she wrote to her brother, "that negotiations are going on with English bankers for a railway to be built from Moscow to Sebastopol, in which a large amount of capital . . . has already been sunk. God grant that it may be realized. Rothschild, who is jealous, has also sent his agent. He is anxious for peace, for he has subscribed fifty millions to our loan. . . . If war does not break out, Poland must be settled once and for all. Perhaps in August. The arrangements have all been made for it."

Prince Alexander was a sort of central bureau for the collection of all the information that was to be brought indirectly to the knowledge of the Tsar. When the Prince received Alexander II's detailed answer to his reports of the negotiations in London and Paris, he found them so interesting and of such importance for the realization of his dearest wish—the reconstitution of the former Holy Alliance—that he sent the letter itself to the Emperor Francis Joseph, hoping thereby to win him over to his views. The Emperor, however, did not agree with him. Writing from Laxenburg on July 14th, he said: "We must make up our minds to face the present situation; and I cannot see any peaceful way out of it unless Russia is prepared to make great concessions. Anyone, therefore, who wishes the Tsar Alexander well should advise him very seriously to agree while there is yet time to the stated conditions, which touch neither Russia's title in Poland nor her honour; and thus to preserve his realm from devastating wars and Europe from incalculable upheavals."*

Prince Alexander was greatly concerned at this warlike tone. "How can I", he asks in his diary, "convey this answer to the poor Tsar!"

Thus the Emperor Francis Joseph persisted in his anti-Russian course in foreign policy, which was eventually not only to lead to his own downfall but also to drag Germany and Russia down into the same abyss.

To talk of war and to wage it are two different things. Prince Alexander did not allow himself to be bluffed. He had now heard the views of all parties, and was able to form an accurate picture of the general situation. "I have not much faith in a war for Poland's sake," he wrote to his sister from Heiligenberg on July 22nd, "not even in a blockade, though one is prepared for any atrocity on the part of the nephew of the uncle [Napoleon III]. But he is the only one who wants war. In England they are coming more and more to the opinion that to be towed into another war in the wake of Napoleon (as in 1854) would be the greatest possible calamity for their own country."

As time went on the Russian Government increasingly won the upper hand over the Polish insurgents, and it was soon found that the paper notes of the other Powers did not really cover any serious intention of war. In Austria, Rechberg, by hedging and procrastination, and not least in overcoming his own ruler, managed at last to defeat the war party. Although they had already gone to considerable lengths, England and Austria withdrew and abandoned the Emperor Napoleon, who was personally averse to war but whose hand had been forced by public opinion in France. Napoleon sought to disguise his defeat by proposing a congress of the European Powers, but only succeeded in emphasizing it, because the new proposal also met with no acceptance. It was a diplomatic victory for Russia. The Tsar completely suppressed the Polish insurrection at his leisure and without any further interference from the other Powers.

* See Appendix.

CHAPTER VIII

THE TSAR AMID THE CRISES OF THE YEAR 1866

BISMARCK's appointment as Prime Minister and his determination to realize the "little German" idea made it essential for Austria to find some means of strengthening its own defences for Pan-Germanism. Hence the Emperor Francis Joseph drew up plans of reform for the Federation which he proposed to submit to a Congress of German princes whom he invited to Frankfurt on August 16th, 1863. Bismarck did his best to dissuade his king from taking part in it, which made the Grand Duke of Hesse simply "furious", according to Prince Alexander, who, of course, was equally angry. The Emperor Francis Joseph said to him at Frankfurt on August 15th: "Please stay here with me. I will keep you informed as to the course of the negotiations."

In consequence Prince Alexander appeared at the Emperor's side as he made his entry into Frankfurt. Twenty-five reigning princes and four burgomasters, that is to say, the great majority, had accepted the Austrian invitation. Only the kings of Prussia and Denmark were absent and four of the lesser princes. The Emperor presented his draft of the proposed reforms to the assembly and expressed his dissatisfaction at the King of Prussia's non-appearance. At the first meeting of the princes, it was resolved to send a deputation to the King of Prussia to request his attendance. Although the Emperor Francis Joseph disliked the idea of sending another invitation to William after his refusal, the King of Saxony was eventually entrusted with the mission. In the time that elapsed during his absence, the various dissensions and rivalries between the different princes came glaringly to the fore.

On August 21st the King of Saxony returned without the King of Prussia. The Emperor Francis Joseph had expected nothing else. The Frankfurt Congress of Princes was a failure and Germany was no nearer to a solution of its internal problems. The rivalry between Austria and Prussia continued, and was indeed made more pronounced by the Congress.

"So much is certain", wrote Prince Alexander to his sister from Heiligenberg on September 11th, "that the Emperor Francis Joseph has taken on a task of considerable difficulty, if he is hoping to reconcile the conflicting opinions of some twenty kings and kinglets."

The letter found the Tsarina in poor health. She had been ailing since May and, as the doctors did not recognize that she was suffering from tuberculosis, all kinds of treatments were tried without benefit to her health. The Tsar was very anxious about her, but her lengthy illness and his frequent absences made him more inclined than hitherto to unfaithfulness. True, he continued to show affection and esteem for his wife, was fond of her family and maintained very friendly relations with her, but his unfaithfulness gave him qualms of conscience and impaired the complete intimacy of former days. The Tsar excused himself by alleging the illness of his wife, who forgave him and suffered in silence. Although the Tsar's infidelities were a matter of common knowledge, they were tacitly ignored in public. Stirring political events, especially the Schleswig-Holstein question that had once again come to the fore, diverted public attention from his love-affairs. The crux of the Schleswig-Holstein problem was to be found in Bismarck's desire to add Schleswig-Holstein to Prussia, while Denmark wished to see it absorbed into its own monarchy. Prince Alexander shared the views of all Germans that the Elbian Duchies should be permanently attached to Germany.

None the less, Prince Alexander had sufficient insight to hope that a great war involving all Europe for the sake of Schleswig-Holstein might be avoided, as he said in a letter to his sister at the beginning of the year 1864:

"I am not at all anxious to see the various peoples of Europe throttling one another, to see railways and telegraphs destroyed, historical monuments shelled, and the nations ruining themselves for fifty years to come, all in order to have an Augustenburg prince on the throne of Schleswig-Holstein instead of a Glücksburg. I admit that I am too simple to get any pleasure out of the 'salutary war' that is desired by a number of blackguards who will go and hide in the nearest funk-hole once the shooting begins."

On January 14th the momentous meeting of the Federal Diet took place at which Austria and Prussia stated that they intended to settle the Schleswig-Holstein affair by themselves. The complications of the question gave many a headache to those in every Cabinet who were concerned with it. Nor were the Tsar and his wife able to make head or tail of the matter. "Your comments upon the question of the day", replied the Tsarina to her brother, "came very à propos, for on that very day I had for the first time summoned up courage to ask our former representative in Copenhagen to explain it to me. After half an hour's very lucid explanation I had to confess myself beaten. That is to say, I had to own that I understood no more than I had done at the beginning. Whereupon Ewers—who teaches Nixa[98] international law—answered that I had got as far as most of the statesmen in Europe, since the problem as a legal question remained unsolved. . . . In my opinion, South Germany is backing up Napoleon's game by setting itself in opposition to the two Great Powers. . . ."

Meanwhile the situation in Schleswig-Holstein had developed into war, and Prince Alexander followed tensely the operations of the Austrian and Prussian troops as they fought side by side.

All these anxieties left the ladies of the court at Darmstadt cold. For them there was at this time a much more burning problem. The daughter of Prince Charles had just been betrothed to the Duke of Mecklenburg-Schwerin, and the question was whether the ladies were to appear at the wedding with trains or without. The Schleswig-Holstein question was entirely overshadowed by this court dispute. The Grand Duke disapproved of trains; the bride's mother favoured them. Naturally the latter had her way, which caused wailing and gnashing of teeth among the ladies of Darmstadt, for a train was a costly article of attire. Prince Alexander evidently thought so, for he asked his sister the Tsarina whether she had not a spare one she could let his wife have. And, in fact, the Tsarina sent one, the only one, she said, that she could part with.

Meanwhile, in the Schleswig-Holstein question, Austria was anxious that all the German States should support the Austro-Prussian action in Schleswig-Holstein. Prince Alexander wanted to make an attempt to repair the "hopeless cleavage" between the German Great Powers and the Central States of Germany, and drafted a proposal for a compromise.

"In order to soothe King Max of Bavaria," he wrote sardonically to the Tsarina on March 12th, "who was convinced that Austria and Prussia had concluded a secret treaty the aim of which was the division of Germany [along the line of the Main], the Archduke Albrecht was sent to Munich. But since my revered friend the Archduke has not too light a hand with diplomatic missions, he was unlucky enough to kill off the King within twenty-four hours. [King Maximilian died on March 10th]. Since the King of Württemberg is also at the point of death, it is impossible to foresee whether my idea of engaging the whole of Germany in the war with Denmark—the only means of avoiding a civil war and the intervention of Badinguet*—will succeed or not."

In the event, Prince Alexander's proposal fell completely flat owing to the attitude of Bavaria and Saxony. He had recently been much in the company of his nephew Louis and his niece-in-law Alice of England, and had warmly debated the "Schleswig-Holstein problem" with them. Princess Alice was anxious to get to know the Tsarina and was always hoping that she would come and stay in Germany for her health's sake. "I think you would like Alice," wrote Prince Alexander to his sister on April 3rd; "she is a funny little woman, full of charm and full of perversities. Very cultured, very talented, and, while fully equipped to take up serious employment, she will drop everything if she has the chance of a three-hours' ride on a half-broken horse, or if she can accompany her husband on a hunting expedition, even if the snow is lying a foot deep or rain is pouring in torrents. And she has an unbelievable dread of meeting boring people."

Naturally, if only an account of her close relationship with the Coburgs, Princess Alice often advocated the views of Duke Ernest II, which were as a red rag to a bull where the Grand Duke and Prince Alexander were concerned.

The Tsarina Marie, having now made up her mind to come and take a cure in Germany, whither the Tsar proposed to accompany her, had not quite decided whether to go to Schwalbach or to Kissingen. "The Empress of Austria", she wrote to Prince Alexander on April 24 (May 6), 1864, "would be a frightful nuisance to me in the latter place. Crowned heads should never drink at the same Wells. I am reckoning on Elisabeth's shyness and that she will be just as little anxious to see me as I her. Of the Emperor [Francis Joseph] I say nothing, I hope his visit will be a very short one. . . ."

When the Tsar and Tsarina arrived in Darmstadt on June 11th with a suite of no less than eighty-three persons, Alexander thought his sister looking very tired and strained, and her

* A nickname given to Napoleon III; the name of the mason in whose clothes he escaped from the fortress of Ham in 1846.

husband quite unchanged. The Tsarina drove out to Heiligen-berg to visit the grave of an old friend of her childhood, Baroness Marianne von Grancy, who had just died, and to whom she put up a splendid memorial. Very much against her will she had to meet the Emperor and Empress of Austria at Kissingen. Mutual "gala visits" followed. The Emperor Francis Joseph thought the Tsar much more friendly and forthcoming and even Prince Gortchakoff seemed "a different person". Another arrival was the young King Louis II of Bavaria, whom Prince Alexander thought really attractive and gifted with a "delightful physiognomy". The King had intended only spending a few days at Kissingen, but took such a fancy to the Empress Elisabeth and the Tsarina—who thought "her young king" beautiful and a most engaging conversationalist—that he stayed a full month.[99] Although some people suspected a budding romance, the Tsar's daughter Marie, then aged eleven, had nothing to do with it. In the correspondence between the Tsarina and her brother no word or hint was ever given of any project of marriage between King Louis and the Grand Duchess Marie. Too much was known about the King in St. Petersburg.

The two emperors then met at an informal dinner. Gort-chakoff afterwards said to Count Rechberg as they were parting: "Now that each of us has had experience of Napoleon III's friendship, there is no reason for us to fight each other again." But the Tsar refused to admit that it had been Austria that had prevented a general conflagration over the Polish question.

Prince Alexander realized afresh the difficulties attendant upon a really genuine reconciliation and a return to the former intimate alliance between the two empires.

Some time later, on September 11th, a number of sovereigns and princes were Prince Alexander's guests at Heiligenberg. The Tsar, the King of Prussia, five Grand Dukes, and several other princes with large suites, some hundred persons in all, met together there. Prince Alexander felt that his place was being used as a sort of hotel, at which visits were paid to the Russian sovereigns without the slightest consideration for the master of the house. Fortunately the Tsar and Tsarina soon moved on to Nice, where the Tsarina intended spending the winter to continue her cure. Later the Tsarevitch Nicholas, (called Nixa,) whose health also caused anxiety, came from Florence to Nice, having just become engaged to Princess

Dagmar of Denmark. He was suffering from tubercular trouble which the doctors failed to diagnose, and as late as December the Tsarina was telling her brother that Nixa had some rheumatic affection.

The winter passed uneventfully in the beautiful city of Nice. But on Easter Monday the Tsarevitch suddenly had a cerebral hæmorrhage which paralysed his left side. Since the doctors regarded his case as very serious, the Tsar was at once telegraphed for and the Tsarevitch was given the last sacraments. A consultation of six doctors and a Professor Zdekauer who had been sent for in haste from St. Petersburg, resulted in the diagnosis of a very grave attack of meningitis. "Hence", remarked Prince Alexander in his dairy on April 18, 1865, "his whole treatment has been absolutely wrong for months past." On receipt of the terrible news, the Queen of Denmark immediately left for Nice with her daughter Dagmar and the Crown Prince, and they arrived at the same time as the Tsar. Until then the Tsarevitch had not been conscious of the gravity of his illness. On April 23rd, however, after a night of delirium, he was suddenly overwhelmed with the realization of the hopelessness of his condition. When, after he had again been given the sacraments, his fiancée Dagmar came to his bedside, the dying boy received her with the most touching demonstrations of affection. Twice the end was thought to be approaching, but each time a temporary improvement set in. The youthful body was resisting the destroying illness with all its might. The invalid took, with disgust, the musk and champagne with which he was continuously dosed. Dagmar knelt for hours beside the bed with his parents. At eight o'clock in the evening Dr. Oppolzer arrived from Vienna. He was only able to make a superficial examination of the patient, but said at once that he was suffering from tubercular meningitis, which was subsequently confirmed by the post-mortem examination. Yet all the imperial physicians-in-ordinary, the professors of the University of St. Petersburg, and many others had failed to recognize it and had treated the Tsarevitch for rheumatism. Late that evening he died, to the terrible grief of the Tsarina and Dagmar.

On the following day brilliant sunshine gilded the calm deep blue sea. The coffin, hidden in masses of flowers, was lifted by means of a crane on to the deck of a Russian warship and placed in an improvised chapel. The imperial couple returned, utterly broken, to Heiligenberg. As the Princess Dagmar said good-bye before leaving for Denmark, the Tsar watched her sadly and murmured: "Poor child!" To which Alexander said consolingly: "Who knows, she may yet become a member of your family."—"She would certainly be welcome", replied the Tsar.

Early in June the imperial family went back to St. Petersburg in order to attend the funeral of the Tsarevitch. Life in the little court at Darmstadt resumed its accustomed ways.

Soon afterwards Prince Alexander received an invitation to take his family to visit Battenberg, the townlet from which was derived the title that the Grand Duke had bestowed upon Alexander's wife and children. As he could not very well refuse the invitation, the visit was paid early in July with the Princess and the three eldest children. Prince Alexander— as he wrote to the Tsarina—had to earn his popularity with the Battenbergers by the sweat of his brow and with the thermo- meter at 80° in the shade. The Prince and his wife were received at the boundary of Battenberg by mounted burgesses. The postmaster of Battenberg drove the princely coach in person. There were some ticklish moments during the state entry. Triumphal arches had been erected everywhere, the houses were decorated, the whole population was afoot in its picturesque costumes. White-clad maidens, addresses, bouquets; pealing of bells, and salutes with guns and rifles made the horses shy. The most exciting scenes took place in the little age-old town of Battenberg itself. It had never occurred to the good people that unless some means were contrived of stopping the wheels, it would be impossible to halt a coach for any length of time on a steep cobbled street—the upper town lies 800 feet above the lower. One gate of honour where the town councillors, the school-children, etc., were drawn up, was situated on the slope of the hill. As soon as the Mayor began his speech of welcome, the horses began to slide backwards down the hill, dragged by the weight of the coach. Members of the Gymnastic Society rushed forward and held the wheels. But the horses were so terrified by the noise that they suddenly plunged onward at full gallop in the middle of a poem that was being recited by a young lady in white. The second coach which contained the suite was even unluckier. The horses suddenly began to dance madly on their hind legs where the crowd was thickest, and those inside the carriage could only save themselves by taking a flying leap into the arms of the bystanders. Hager, the tutor of Alexander's second and most troublesome son, whose name was also Alexander and who was called Sandro for short, shot out like a grasshopper, with his coat tails flapping, when the glass coach was only balanced on a single wheel. To crown all, one of the Guard of Honour who had never before sat a horse and who was using the reins as if they were a block and pulley, overbalanced with his steed in the midst of a cluster of shrieking peasant girls.

Luckily not much damage was done, but the Prince's family raised heartfelt prayers of thanksgiving when they finally set foot in the grand-ducal palace that had been raised upon the ruins of the ancient castle of the old-time Counts of Battenberg, now extinct. After a march-past of school-children, songs by the local Choral Society, etc., there followed a great banquet at an hotel "with the district councillors, the head forester, the priest, the postmaster, and all the rest of them", at which mine host did the honours with a face swollen and discoloured owing to his having fallen off his horse at the rehearsal for the reception. In addition to a "gargantuan repast" the visitors were treated to high-flown speeches by the priest and the district councillors.

Nevertheless, comic though the occasion was, the Prince was really deeply affected by the truly touching cordiality with which he "was received by the unspoilt people, from whom modern education had not yet stripped their best qualities".

The great political questions agitating Europe had meanwhile not been settled. The Treaty of Vienna in October 1864 did, indeed, take the duchies from the King of Denmark, but left the Schleswig-Holstein question open owing to the joint sovereignty conferred upon the two great German Powers over the conquered territory. Bismarck was already working deliberately to eliminate Austria from German affairs, and thus—since it could not be done in any other way—towards war with the Habsburg Empire. He was staying at Gastein with his king that summer and was seeking allies. He had no fear of Russia, for he had made himself popular with the Tsar by his attitude in the Polish question during the year 1863, while Austria had neglected the opportunity. At all events, it was certain that Russia would not give military help to Austria. It was, however, essential to know what standpoint Italy would adopt in the event of war between Austria and Prussia. Bismarck was so incautious as to use the new public system of telegraphy in his communications with Count Usedom, the Prussian Ambassador at Florence, and also with the Foreign Office in Berlin. Austria was in possession of the key to Prussia's diplomatic cipher, and was thus able to read Bismarck's most secret messages from the copies that remained at the post office. Interesting things came to light. For example, a telegram of Bismarck's to the Crown Prince on July 23, 1865, stating that the cost of a complete mobilization and a campaign lasting about a year would be sixty million Marks. This warned the Austrians of Bismarck's preparations for war, and a few days later the telegraph office sent up the text of further extremely interesting code telegrams revealing the Prussian Prime Minister's intrigues with Italy. Bismarck urged Count Usedom to tell him exactly how far he might rely on Italy's support against Austria. Usedom sent his secretary, Count Dönhoff, with a detailed report, but even this did not satisfy Bismarck.[100]

"In the report presented by Count Dönhoff", he telegraphed to Florence on July 26th, "I find nothing upon what is at present the most important question: What will Italy do in case of war? Is the Italian Government definitely decided and prepared, or will it wait and see? Has it been discussed by the Ministers? His Majesty requires a telegraphic answer, since negotiations with Austria are taking a serious turn, and developments may be rapid after the—as yet uncertain—arrival of the Emperor in Gastein."

Upon receipt of Bismarck's telegram, Usedom went straight to Marquis Lamarmora, who was at that time Victor Emanuel's Prime Minister, and put the question to him definitely. Napoleon's swift conclusion of peace with Austria at Villafranca in 1859, which had for the time being prevented Italy from achieving her dearest wish in the acquisition of Venice and Lombardy, still rankled in Lamarmora's mind. And his reply was worded accordingly. Thereupon Usedom reported to Bismarck on July 27th: "Lamarmora answered that at present he could only say this for certain: that Italy would not allow a good opportunity of seizing Venice to pass, but would in such a case proceed immediately to war."

This correspondence between Bismarck and the Prussian Ambassador in Florence was followed with tense interest in Vienna. It was feared that too brusque a demeanour might provoke an immediate war on two fronts, which would have been particularly awkward at that moment. The army had not been sufficiently reorganized since the unfortunate campaign of 1859, the internal political situation as well as the financial was unfavourable and Napoleon was known to be unreliable. Hence Count Blome was sent to Gastein with very conciliatory proposals. This mission alarmed Usedom. He thought that the question of war would be decided one way or the other within a few days and asked Bismarck for instructions. Bismarck replied on August 8th: "It is urgently necessary to know what is to be expected of Italy *before* the question of war is decided, since this is a material factor in our decision." Here the intercepted messages cease. By this time, however, the Austrians had learnt all that was needful and their policy at Bad Gastein was formulated accordingly. Bismarck regarded Italy's assurances as not sufficiently definite; nor was Napoleon's attitude altogether clear. Hence conditions seemed to him still too uncertain to admit of his picking a quarrel with Austria, though he was firmly resolved in his own mind to detach Austria from Germany. He proposed first to assure himself of security—of which he was already fairly sure in the east—in the west by exerting his personal influence on Napoleon, and to attach Italy to himself unconditionally.

On August 14th came the conference with Austria at Gastein, which assigned the administration of Schleswig to Prussia and that of Holstein to Austria. The other Powers were not pleased with this solution, which was really no solution and which did not do away with the bone of contention. Out of the Schleswig-Holstein problem now arose the infinitely more important German problem. The Tsarina inquired what was thought of the Gastein Convention at Darmstadt.

"The majority of people," replied Alexander on September 5th, "are furious and call this convention the abdication of Austria in favour of Prussian pre-eminence in Germany —a first partition of Germany—and all sorts of other things. Sensible people, on the other hand, are of the opinion that a definitive temporary arrangement in Schleswig-Holstein is at all events better than civil war throughout Germany. . . . But Bismarck is the man to plunge Europe into fire and blood just in order to win a few provinces for Prussia. The internal complications that have grown up in Austria since the events in 1859 and the faint-heartedness of the smaller States in Germany have made the task Bismarck has set himself easier; but I hope to God that he will not succeed in it."

At all events the Tsarina was right when she wrote to her brother from Illinskoe on September 12th (24th) in answer to his letter saying that the small States would have to be careful of Bismarck. His insight into their ways was only too good. And he realized that the system was due to be eliminated from the political life of the German people.

As an example of the harm done by it, there had for a long time been a serious rift between the Grand Duchy of Hesse-Darmstadt and the Electorate of Hesse, because the Grand Duke had not paid sufficient attention to the children of the Elector Frederick William I by his marriage with the divorced wife of a Prussian, Lieutenant Lehmann, whom he raised first to the rank of Countess Schaumberg and then Princess of Hanau. Prince Alexander tells, most entertainingly, of his brother's attempts to effect a reconciliation for the sake of his country, the interests of which were threatened by the quarrel. "Louis", he wrote to the Tsarina on October 24 (November 5), 1865, "took the heroic decision to beard the lion in his den for the sake of the country. The one-tailed lion (as you know, the Darmstadt lion has two tails, while the electoral lion makes do with one) has been growling for years because we do not wish to recognize his Barchfeld grandson[101] as a Hessian prince. In revenge he now refuses his assent to all the railway schemes made by our Government. Since the two territories adjoin in all sorts of places . . . we are completely paralysed here, and the Odenwald and Upper Hesse are waiting vainly for the railways that they need so badly."

The Grand Duke Louis finally made up his mind to enter into relations again with the Elector, and took the first step by visiting him at Hanau. The Elector was visibly flattered, regaled him with everything of the best and most expensive (with *les petits pots dans les grands*), and collected all and sundry at the Castle of Hanau for a gargantuan dinner. Thereby the Elector's family was, as it were, honoured and recognized. Not until this had taken place was unimpeded development possible of the very necessary railroad connections.

Although they were in their own country, Prince Alexander and his wife felt life to be constricted in Darmstadt by comparison with the much more brilliant social round at St. Petersburg, and longed for the Grand Duke, who had no regard for social functions, to do a little more in the way of entertaining. On this point they were in agreement with Alice of Hesse, who was hungry for life, had just come back from England, and, as Alexander said in a letter to the Tsarina on November 29th, "was more than ever impatient of all that was not English". Whenever she returned from a visit to

England she had first to grow acclimatized again to the little court of Hesse and felt that everything was "beneath her notice", as Alexander wrote to his sister on December 26th.

While the little courts continued their idyllic life, both private and public, events were preparing in the world which threatened their position and their future. Bismarck carried out his plan for safeguarding himself for his projected war on Austria by bringing pressure to bear on Napoleon. He sought out the Emperor of the French in beautiful, sea-washed Biarritz on October 4th. Without binding himself in any way, he opened up indefinite vistas of possible territorial advantages for France in, say, Belgium or Luxembourg or French Switzerland.

As a result of his conversations with Napoleon in Biarritz, Bismarck achieved his aim of ensuring French neutrality in the war that was preparing—without being obliged subsequently to bring into effect a single one of the tempting prospects that he had laid as bait before Napoleon.

Thanks to Bismarck's dynamic genius, events in Germany were tending more and more to a violent issue. He did not rest at allying himself with Italy and making himself secure from Russia and France. He sought by every means in his power to drive in a wedge between Austria and the central and southern German States which lay nearest to it. Bavaria, where the Prime Minister, von der Pfordten, was an Austrophobe, seemed to be particularly susceptible to Bismarck's cajoleries.

If von der Pfordten did not or could not go so far as to lead his king and country into the Prussian camp, his activities nevertheless contributed towards the fact that Bavaria did not go heart and soul with Austria. For the remaining Central States, however, the struggle between Austria and Prussia seemed to be a question of the continuance of their existence, as Prince Alexander said of the Grand Duchy of Hesse.

As he saw the situation, Austria would have to renounce its position within the comity of German States entirely if it did not take up the challenge in case Bismarck were really mad enough to conjure up the spectre of war. Prince Alexander was convinced that right was all on the side of Austria. "Now God's will be done", he wrote to the Tsarina on March 17, 1866. "Except it were against France, there could be no war for Austria and Southern Germany that would be more popular." Prince Alexander was wrong here, for one could hardly speak of popularity in the true sense of the word. Everything was attributed to Bismarck, against whom a wave of hatred and fury arose that dimmed the judgment even of sober men who saw a threat to their own existence and that of their country. Even Prince Alexander's pen ran away with him: "War is unavoidable," he wrote to his sister on March 29th, "but it is also impossible, as I heard someone very truly describe the situation recently. The decision still lies in the hands of the old King, and no one who knows him will even think it *conceivable* that he should permit his mad, hare-brained Minister to hazard the Prussian Crown for the sake of Schleswig-Holstein, and to ruin the flourishing land of Germany for decades to come."

If Bismarck considered it necessary to the accomplishment of his plan of uniting Germany to make war on Austria, he was in opposition to his peace-loving King, who hated the idea of a fratricidal war, as did also the Crown Prince, who was working hand in hand with his father to keep the peace. The Crown Prince, as son-in-law to Queen Victoria, sought to make use of his family connections, and with his father's concurrence wrote to Queen Victoria[102] on March 17, 1866, to say that the idea of England's mediation which had been mooted was very agreeable to the King, and that he was ready to accept such an offer. Hence it was the King's wish that England should turn to Austria and urge it to forget its jealousy and to abandon the intrigues against Prussia to which this gave rise. Although it had been intended to be kept secret from him, Bismarck heard of this letter, and feared the possible ruin of his political plans. On March 20th he telegraphed to Count Bernstorff[103] in London to say that the Crown Prince's letter had been written without his knowledge and contained expressions that "were not consonant with the state of affairs, but rather sprang from the personal desire of the Crown Prince for the maintenance of peace". Hence the ambassador was, until further notice, to regard any suggestions which reached him as a result of this letter as "lying outside the diplomatic sphere". Bismarck was especially sensitive to anything that emanated from the Crown Prince's relationship with the British royal house, and that might therefore be clearing the way for the exercise of foreign influence upon Prussian policy.

The situation became more and more critical, and the decisive breach approached ever nearer. Austria, however,

M

hoped to prevent it, and the Emperor Francis Joseph instructed his ambassador, Count Revertera, to ask the Tsar to make an attempt at reconciliation in Berlin. The Tsar took the opportunity presented him by the anniversary of the King's birthday to write a letter on March 7th (19th),[104] deploring the existing tension between the courts of Vienna and Berlin, and reminding him that the peace of Europe was continually threatened by sparks of revolutionary passion that smouldered beneath the ashes. King William's answer,[105] which shows unmistakable traces of Bismarck's influence, speaks of the gravity of the situation, and says that he could not give way over the question of the Duchies of Schleswig and Holstein without compromising the dignity of the Crown. And, he points out, war had not been declared. "We simply regard our intimacy as a thing of the past." The letter then goes on to speak of the unfriendly demeanour of an Austria that was allowing hatred of Prussia to dominate all its utterances, and did not scorn to seek allies in the camp of red Democracy. (That was intended specially to appeal to the Tsar.) The King says further that Austria is mobilizing, that bodies of troops are being massed threateningly on the Silesian frontiers, and therefore Prussia, too, must prepare in order to avoid having another such unpleasant surprise as it had had in 1850.

Thereupon the Tsar decided to appeal to the Emperor Francis Joseph. Writing from St. Petersburg on March 21st (April 2nd), he said that the idea of a fratricidal war between the two Powers made him anxious as to the fate of the Conservative principle, and was bound to hurl Germany—among whose princes both the Tsar and the Tsarina had near relatives—into immeasurable confusion.[106] He turns to the Emperor Francis Joseph with "disquiet in his heart", tells him that King William denies that he wishes to conjure up war, but that he is complaining of the massing of considerable forces in Upper Silesia, which must oblige him to take countermeasures, though up to the present he has made no move. The Tsar was appealing to the Emperor Francis Joseph just as he had done to King William: "I pray God", his letter concludes, "to inspire your decisions, for the peace of the world may depend upon them, and that is a heavy responsibility." The Tsarina was also opposed to any war, for she was considering the welfare of her native Grand Duchy, and was moreover anxious for the fate of Württemberg, where the Grand Duchess Olga, the Tsar's sister, had been Queen since 1863.

"Now", the Tsarina said, writing to Prince Alexander from St. Petersburg on April 1st (13th), "everyone's thoughts are occupied by the vital question for Germany—fratricidal war or democratic parliament. And I suppose the ultimate aim is the gradual mediatization of the small and medium-sized States. Olly [Olga of Württemberg] is very worried, and is what she calls 'shuddering inwardly'. . . . The crux of the situation is, of course, Bismarck. Some people say that if he were to retire there would be no war. Others fear that if he goes there will be a completely democratic Ministry. As regards Germany, it appears to me that even a very progressive Ministry could not be more democratic than Bismarck is at present, though he is supposed to advocate the Conservative principles. I have defended him to the best of my ability so long as I could keep a single illusion about him, but now I am tired of it. Redern is tearing out his hair in handfuls, like all reasonable people in Prussia. But he more than most because two of his daughters are married in Austria."

On April 16th, not very many days after this letter had been despatched, a man belonging to a secret society called Karakasoff—which at that time had only a small membership—fired a revolver at the Tsar at point-blank, intending to stir up unrest among the people. The attempt, however, was unsuccessful, and the Tsar was unhurt. This proved the beginning of an embittered campaign on the part of a number of half-educated people against the régime of the Tsar. While he had hitherto striven—often against the advice of those nearest the Crown—to introduce liberal reforms into his realm, this unsuccessful attack on him resulted in driving him back into the arms of reaction and its champions. In this he was supported by his wife, who had become so absorbed in her new Orthodox religion that she was the most zealous of all the ladies of the court in religious observances. The Church and its representatives were, of course, very much opposed to innovations, and thus from that side, too, a strong reactionary influence was brought to bear on the Tsar.

These changes met with the full approval of Prince Alexander, who saw in them a salutary interruption in the all too liberal course taken by public affairs in Russia. He proved his powers of observation in writing to the Tsarina on June 5th, "I am not such a hidebound Conservative and Legitimist that I would oppose wise and moderate progress, but I fear the democratic element more among the Slavs than among any other people, because they are given to exaggeration."

King William hastened to congratulate the Tsar on his escape,[107] and took the occasion to remark in the same letter that without adopting the definitely unfriendly tone of the last Austrian dispatch, he had given Vienna to understand that he was ready to disarm if the first step in this direction were taken by Vienna.

Meanwhile the Emperor Francis Joseph had also, on April 7th, replied to the Tsar's appeal[108] and had declared that he had no intention whatsoever of attacking or threatening Prussia. Alluding to the correspondence between Bismarck and Usedom which had been intercepted, he said, "I discovered in the most positive manner that the Berlin Cabinet was taking steps in Florence to conclude an alliance against me there. Feeling that a frank discussion might clear the air, I instructed my ambassador in Berlin to inquire whether the Prussian Government intended to repudiate (especially) the [Gastein] agreement by force. It is true that the Minister denied any such intention," continued the Emperor, "but his answer was couched in such sharp and insulting terms and accompanied by so little in the way of reassurance that it could only increase my original anxiety. In consideration of all this, common sense dictates my taking some slight precautions against the sudden action that is to be expected from one's knowledge of the words and character of King William's chief adviser."

Francis Joseph then endeavoured to point out how insignificant were the military precautions that had been taken, and referred to the internal and financial difficulties with which the monarchy was then contending.

"They are", wrote the Emperor, "only too well known, and it is clear that there is not a single country that needs peace more than Austria does. Surely you will not think me so blind—I had almost said criminal—as to take upon myself so tremendous a responsibility as to pick a quarrel with Germany that might lead to war, a fratricidal war. Supported by the unanimous opinion of the country, I shall not flinch, any more than will my people, before the necessity of defending Austria's honour and her interests. But, I repeat, only the need to defend these shall make me take up arms. It never has and never will cross my mind to attack a monarch to whom I am bound by so many ties of affection and esteem. I greatly

regret that biased representations should have misled King
William as to my true feelings for him." This last remark,
as well as that about the character of King William's chief
adviser, was obviously directed against Bismarck.

The Emperor Francis Joseph's letter impressed the Tsar
very deeply. He read it to General Schweinitz, pausing at
intervals to say: "That is true . . . quite right . . . that is
true, too." When Schweinitz endeavoured to defend Bismarck's last proposals for the reorganization of the Federation
and the summoning of a parliament, the Tsar replied:[109] "In
spite of all that you say, I cannot help feeling that the convocation of a parliament is dangerous. If you knew all I hear
from various parts of Germany!" (This in veiled allusion to
the letters of his brother-in-law.) "There is a general outcry
against Bismarck. He is believed to be capable of anything—
they all have visions of themselves being mediatized!"

Francis Joseph's letter was certainly not written for King
William's eyes. Nevertheless the Tsar sent him an exact
transcription with a covering letter expressing his pleasure at
the Austrian Government's agreeing to take the initiative in
disarming on a particular date, on condition of reciprocity.
The Tsar regarded it as the dawn of peace, but at the same time
gave the King to understand that the last proposals of the
Prussian Cabinet at the meeting of the German Federation
aroused in him the gravest misgivings. The letter shows how
greatly the Tsar had been influenced by his wife, his brother-
in-law, and his sister during his frequent visits to Hesse. In
his view the proposals of the Prussian Government were bound
to be regarded by the majority of the sovereigns of Germany
as the first step towards the weakening of their power, and even
of their eventual mediatization. The Tsar used almost the same
words as those that were so often in Prince Alexander's mouth:
"The Prussian suggestions", he wrote, "only serve to increase
the distrust of Prussia that I found so deeply rooted during
my last visit to Germany." Just as the letter and enclosure
were about to be sent off, a second missive arrived from Francis
Joseph, and the Tsar added an important paragraph to his
letter to the King of Prussia: "The maintenance of peace is not
only my most ardent desire, but is a necessity of which I feel
the irresistible force. In order to attain this goal I shall do all
that is consonant with the honour and dignity of Austria."

When the letter arrived in Berlin, King William as usual
handed it to Bismarck, who did not fail to note the sting con-

tained in the passages directed at him in the Emperor Francis
Joseph's letter. The criticisms of the German Federal reforms
were his first concern. In his reply the King protested that
they were absolutely essential, and that he had wished to
redress matters jointly with Austria, but that the necessary
loyal co-operation had not been forthcoming. "I had no
intention", the King averred in writing to the Tsar[110] on April
26th, "of giving Germany a parliamentary régime; but I did
intend to carry out reforms lest they should be first undertaken
by revolutionaries."

The Chancellor made the King say that he had hoped for
the happiest results from the intimacy between the two great
German Powers, and that his ideal had been a concerted policy
along Conservative lines. In any case there was no more than
a coolness between the two States, which was far from being
a breach; and hence the precautionary measures, the significance of which the Emperor Francis Joseph sought to mini-
mize, were not justified. But concerning the negotiations for
an alliance with Italy he said not a word.

What is most interesting is to see how characteristically and
with what delicate psychology Bismarck reacted to those of
Francis Joseph's remarks which were directed against him
personally. In his own handwriting he put the following
addition to the draft of the King's letter[111] dated April 26th:
"You know, my dear nephew, that I, like yourself, am in the
habit of sifting facts for myself, of reading dispatches and
newspapers, in a word, of attending to the work which God
has given me to do. I do all I can to guard against being
influenced by bad advice—which, incidentally, is not lacking
to the Emperor Francis Joseph."

Probably no one now questions the fact that neither the
Emperor Francis Joseph himself nor his new Foreign Minister,
Count Mensdorff, wanted war at that time. But Mensdorff,
who was inexperienced in diplomacy, allowed Baron von
Biegeleben, who came originally from the Grand Duchy of
Hesse and hated Prussia with all his soul, and Count Maurice
Esterházy, his two chief advisers, to interfere too much in the
formulation of policy. Nevertheless war would probably not
have broken out but for the fact that Bismarck was absolutely
determined on it.

During this time of crisis, Baron Henry von Gagern, the
Hessian Minister in Vienna,[112] reported that Mensdorff was
most depressed, and had said casually: "Whatever course is

adopted at the Federal Assembly, everything points to war, and that is bound to turn out badly for Austria." Mensdorff was no match for a man of Bismarck's force of character; for despite the fact that he gauged the situation correctly, he was too weak both in will and in deed to stand up to Bismarck. This was the state of affairs when Prince Alexander of Hesse went to Vienna towards the end of April 1866, in order to find out on the spot how the land lay. There were rumours that in case of war with Prussia the Prince was to take command of the Eighth Federal Army Corps, which was to be raised from Württemberg, Baden, and Hesse-Darmstadt. According to an entry in Prince Alexander's diary on April 28th, the Emperor Francis Joseph received him very cordially, and told him that he thought he had done everything possible to preserve peace, but now that Prussia was setting up as the champion of Italy, it was perfectly obvious that war was intended. In the Emperor's opinion, neither Schleswig-Holstein nor the rest of Northern Germany would be able to avoid becoming Prussian, and he was therefore surprised that Bismarck should not have the patience to wait for this to happen, but should be entering upon a war that could only benefit foreign countries.

Prince Alexander was not at all pleased at Bismarck's succeeding—like Cavour—in representing Austria as the attacker because it was mobilizing its army in Italy.

The Emperor replied that he had received absolutely certain reports of Italy's making preparations, and that he could not therefore expose himself to the danger of a surprise attack. Then the conversation turned upon the leadership of the Eighth Army Corps. Prince Alexander made his acceptance of it conditional upon Austrian troops joining the Federal Corps. "Yes," replied the Emperor, "if it can be done, for we shall need every man against Prussia and Italy. The rulers of Württemberg, Baden, and Hesse must remember that at the beginning of the war we shall be able to do nothing to protect them, for we cannot split up our forces when confronted with the superior forces of Prussia. We have been obliged to promise to send a few battalions to the Saxons, who are most exposed. The idea of being thrown out [of the Federation] at the same time as ourselves", said the Emperor smiling, "seems to be a comfort to them." Prince Alexander suggested the probability that Bavaria, which furnished the Seventh Federal Corps, would demand to be united with the Eighth, and to have the supreme command of both. He did not think, as Baron Henry von Gagern reported to his Government on May 2nd,[113] that it would be a good plan to assign this subordinate position to the Seventh, and in his opinion there would be a stronger guarantee of satisfactory military co-operation if both corps were directly attached to the main Austrian army. The entry of the Empress Elisabeth put an end to the conversation. Taken all in all the Prince did not carry away with him a good impression of the leading personalities in Vienna. Mensdorff, he thought, was overborne on every occasion. The Emperor's general aide-de-camp, Count Crenneville, who had been brought to the fore at the time of Grünne's omnipotence, mixed himself up too much in politics, of which he understood nothing. And the Archduke Albrecht, who was always afraid that he might have to lead the army against Prussia, had expressed childish pleasure when he was told that he was to go to Italy. "We are going to war! I am to have the army in Italy!" he had said jubilantly when he returned to the ladies after an interview with the Emperor. With this sole exception, Alexander found that all parties were unanimous that Prussia was seeking war, and that the Emperor had done all that was humanly possible to avoid it. Since, however, it appeared to be impossible to do so, they must simply fight to the last man.

From Vienna Prince Alexander went to Stuttgart to see the King of Württemberg. The news there was not altogether satisfactory. Prince Frederick of Württemberg, despite the fact that he had serious eye trouble, was offended at not having been offered the command of the Eighth Army Corps. Baden was most unreliable, which is not surprising when it is remembered that the Grand Duke Frederick I was the son-in-law of King William of Prussia. Hardly any preparations were being made for war. In Darmstadt there was considerably more disquiet. "The hatred of Prussia", reported Prince Alexander to the Tsarina on May 7th, with some exaggeration of expression as was his wont, "and of its infamous policy, the like of which I suppose has never been seen in history, is boundless. There can seldom have been a name that has been so universally anathematized in all classes of society as the name of Bismarck! Many people rather pity the weak-minded old King because of the unhappy part that his conscienceless Minister makes him play, and the fearful load of responsibility which he is taking upon his shoulders in his seventieth year. But King William does not really deserve such leniency, and history will one day make him responsible for the civil war which he is kindling in Germany." Prince Alexander told his sister about the proposal to put him in command of the Eighth Federal Army Corps. "My potential task", he wrote, "is no easy one. But the war will be popular, for the burning hatred of Prussia animating the whole population of Central and Southern Germany passes all imagination. Unfortunately the men of the Eighth Army Corps have no experience of active service, are led by old generals, and only scantily equipped. In addition, there is the unreliability of the Baden Government. The Grand Duke vacillates between all parties without coming to any fixed decision. William of Baden has recently proved to be a sort of Jacobin, and stands quite shamelessly at the head of the revolutionary party. So there you have a sad Prince and a bad jester. I shall do my best. But I must admit that I should have preferred an Austrian Corps."

The news of the general mobilization of Prussia came like a thunderbolt to the Grand Duchy of Hesse, and led to the decision to put the army on a war footing there too. The grand ducal family that was so closely related to Prussia was particularly painfully affected by the imminence of a breach with this State. For Prince Alexander's nephew Louis, the son of a Prussian princess and through his wife the brother-in-law of the Prussian Crown Prince, the situation was peculiarly difficult. He was a colonel in the Prussian army, and was now obliged to go to Berlin to ask for his demission, and to explain that his duty to his country forced him to take up arms against his former comrades. Princess Alice, who was expecting a child very shortly, took it all very much to heart, burst into tears in the middle of a family dinner party, and did not know quite what attitude to adopt towards her sister, the Crown Princess of Prussia. Louis's brother, Henry, who had been in the Prussian army since 1864, remained in the service in spite of all that happened.

The German States were in a condition of absolute panic, if Prince Alexander's reports are to be believed. "To cap all," he says, "cholera has broken out. First at Gersheim and now in Darmstadt. One bankruptcy is following another in every German city; the bricklayers are starving; factories are dismissing their workers; Prussian paper money is no longer accepted. In short, the situation is hopeless *now*—even *before* war has broken out!"

The Tsar and Tsarina were meanwhile still shaken by the

attempted assassination. Thousands upon thousands of messages reached them from all sides congratulating the Tsar on his escape. Anonymous gifts were sent—crucifixes, pictures of saints, prayers of thanksgiving—messages of loyalty and affection from men and women lay piled upon the tables of the imperial palace. The Tsar was touched and yet humble in his acceptance of the messages.

"Men such as he who are pure and lowly in heart", said the Tsarina of her deeply loved husband, "cannot regard this as a triumph. He maintains that he does not deserve it. 'What have I done for them?' he says over and over again, 'that they should love me so much? I have not been able to do anything for them yet.'"

The full gravity of the situation in Germany was not yet recognized in Russia. "Despite the imminent danger", the Tsarina wrote to Prince Alexander of Hesse on May 7th, "I cannot believe that there will really be war. It seems to me so utterly suicidal on the part of Germany." While she was writing the letter the news was telegraphed from Berlin that a certain Karl Cohn, one of the many who were hostile to Bismarck and Prussia, had—though unsuccessfully—fired at the Minister. "We live in fine times!" remarked the Tsarina.

No prospect now remained of maintaining peace. Prince Louis of Hesse, the brother-in-law of the Prussian Crown Princess, had returned from a visit to Berlin where the King had refused to receive him. The Prince, however, had seen a great deal of his brother and sister-in-law. The Crown Princess sent a message by him to Prince Alexander, as he tells in his diary on May 12th, asking him to urge the Tsar once more to impress upon King William even more forcefully the advantages of keeping the peace. Her and her husband's sole hope, she said, lay in this step, because the King set so high a value upon the friendship of the Tsar.

"My nephew Louis has just come back from Berlin," Prince Alexander thereupon wrote to the Tsar on the same day, "where he has been staying incognito, in order to discuss the situation with his brother-in-law, the Crown Prince, and to announce his intention of fighting with our forces against Prussia if war should break out. The Crown Princess sent word to me by Louis that her only hope, which was shared by her husband, lay in the great influence exerted upon the King by the feelings which bind him to you and to Russia. The Crown Princess is convinced that you could induce the

THE TSAR ALEXANDER II AND THE TSARINA MARIE

King—who may still be hesitating—to listen to the peace proposals that he is now rejecting so blindly. You have only to send him one last letter by someone who enjoys your full confidence to open his eyes to the manner in which Bismarck is abusing the trust of his sovereign, and to let him see that the course into which he is so misguidedly allowing himself to be persuaded is raising a barrier between you, and is seriously threatening the bonds of friendship and esteem which have hitherto united you. This is the message which the Crown Princess sent me, without her husband's knowledge, but in the firm persuasion that he would approve of it if he dared so openly to set himself up in opposition to his father's policy. Louis heard, amongst other examples of Herr von Bismarck's want of good faith, the following story from the Crown Princess herself: Bismarck did not inform the King of Austria's honourable proposal[114] on April 26th for simultaneous disarmament, but he put the telegram among a bundle of unimportant papers which he laid on the King's table. In consequence the King knew nothing of the Austrian proposal until he heard the princes discussing it at dinner one day. To the representations of the Crown Prince his father answered: 'Bismarck is too good a Christian to want war!' And it is a fact that Bismarck wrested from him the mobilization order for the whole army by means of a forged telegram announcing the appearance of two Austrian regiments at Troppau. [If not true, this anecdote at least shows the distrust in which Bismarck was held by the Crown Prince and his wife and the Prince of Hesse.] It would take too long to retail to you all the frauds of which the Crown Prince told us. I feel that if you sent an emissary to deliver the letter for which Victoria is hoping, he should point out the dangers of the situation to the King himself, and do so in words which might be stronger than any expressions you could use in the letter itself. Do you not think that Alexander Bariatinsky would be a suitable man for this mission?"

This letter was still on its way when Alexander II wrote again very fully to the King of Prussia, suggesting a congress the aim of which should be the preservation of peace. "I venture to implore you", wrote the Tsar, "to make one last supreme effort to maintain peace."

Meanwhile the small German States had at last set about making preparations. Bavaria began mobilizing on May 11th, and the Grand Duke of Hesse-Darmstadt followed suit. At about the same time Princess Alice, who had given her husband

Louis a letter to take to the King of Prussia, as the father-in-law of her sister, received an answer to it in which King William laid the whole responsibility upon Francis Joseph, just as Vienna accused Prussia.

Prince Alexander transmitted a part of this letter to the Emperor Francis Joseph in writing to him on May 19th. He entered the sense of it, but not the actual words or dates, in his diary on May 13th.

"Austria", run the most important parts of the letter, as passed on to Francis Joseph, "will not permit us to *annex* Schleswig-Holstein. . . . She began on March 14th to pour troops into Bohemia and to threaten our frontiers, while we had not raised a man or a horse above peace strength. So whom do you consider to have given the first provocation? *I know that the Emperor genuinely wishes to keep the peace*; but why does he force me into war by his actions? . . . My honour and that of Prussia do not permit me to suffer such things. . . . My father, my brother, and I have always been suspected of wanting to prey on our fellow-princes in Germany, whereas none of us has ever thought of such a thing. . . . Now we offer the German princes Federal reform and they reply by arming against us! You ask why I mobilized the Rhineland Corps. Why do you not ask, rather, why Bavaria and Württemberg are mobilizing? It would, of course, be simpler for our enemies if we were to deliver ourselves over to them defenceless —for this way will take longer. . . . Why does my nephew Louis want to resign instead of fighting for us against Austria? Of course, if we are forced into war, we shall be ruthless too!"

Princess Alice hastened to show the letter to Prince Alexander and the Minister Dalwigk, who were now convinced that all hope of a possible change on the part of the old King must be abandoned.

At a conference which the Central German States called to consider their future attitude, there were considerable differences of opinion. Baden even spoke of armed neutrality. Prince Alexander thought of resigning from his command of the motley Federal Corps, and wrote to his brother in this sense. The Grand Duke, who preferred not to be troubled about political affairs, received the letter just as he was sitting down to dine on May 16th, and delayed his meal long enough to write in his own hand the following reply:

"This damned business has absolutely spoilt my appetite

for dinner. Is the devil after Dalwigk that he is taking to his
heels too? It is a wretched nuisance that we should be mixed
up with that crew of Swabians. What's to be done now? I can
unfortunately only agree with your decision; much as it pains
and grieves me, not only as head of the family and Grand
Duke, but especially as an old soldier—who has unfortunately
never smelt powder—to have a brave comrade and beloved
brother resign the command of my troops. I do implore
you, my dear fellow, to think over once more whether there
is not some way of counteracting this fool trick of the
damned ink-slingers. Sleep over it once more, and then tell me
what you think to-morrow. Remember our House and our Hesse.
"Greatly troubled in mind and appetite, I remain,
                                      "Your brother
                                              "LOUIS."

To a letter to the Emperor Francis Joseph[115] written on
May 18th telling him of what had happened, Prince Alexander
added a transcript of the portions given above of the King of
Prussia's letter to Princess Alice. He remarked concerning it that
the King of Prussia's letter, which consisted of four large quarto
pages of "lies and complaints of the sad state in which Prussia
found herself owing to Austria's bellicose attitude", proved
how utterly the King had adopted all his Minister's ideas.
Prince Alexander also mentioned that he had helped Dalwigk
and the Princess Alice in the composition of a reply which
would certainly not please the King. Finally, he assured the
Emperor that the troops to the command of which he had been
appointed would undertake nothing that could in any way be
prejudicial to Francis Joseph's interests.

Francis Joseph hoped that the Prince would be able to induce
the Central and Southern States, whose attitude was most
uncertain, to hold to Austria.

At about this time two men, General Louis von Gablenz
and his brother Baron Anthony von Gablenz, determined
to make an eleventh-hour attempt to bring about a reconciliation between Prussia and Austria. The General, who had commanded the Austrian troops at the side of Prussia against
Denmark during the campaign of 1864, knew the working of
the Prussian needle-gun and the organization of the army, and
on comparing them with those on his own side it appeared
to him that it would be wiser to avoid war at present. The two
brothers, who were descended from a Saxon family, determined

to utilize their exceptional position to make a last effort in the cause of peace. Since the General could not very well appear in the matter, Anthony von Gablenz undertook to conduct negotiations. He went to see Mensdorff, the Austrian Foreign Minister, who did not want war, and was given a personal introduction to Berlin. Although Bismarck probably did not take this attempt at mediation very seriously, he felt that out of consideration for his sovereign he should enter into the negotiations, though no doubt with the mental reservation that if, as he expected, they failed, he would be able to hold it up to the King as yet another proof of Austria's desire for war. Gablenz spent May 25th in Vienna, where the Emperor Francis Joseph told him that two months earlier the proposals would certainly have been accepted, despite the fact that according to his suggestions as to the division of the spheres of influence in Germany the lion's share fell to Prussia. Finally, however, Mensdorff as well as Beust at Dresden gave Gablenz to understand that the tension was now so great that no further direct negotiation was possible. According to a letter written by Baron von Werner to Count Mensdorff from Dresden on June 2nd,[116] Gablenz tried vainly to convince Beust of the conciliatory feelings that he alleged to be reigning in Berlin. When Beust said that Austria had decided to bring the whole quarrel before the Federation, Gablenz exclaimed: "There is the *casus belli*."

Meanwhile King William replied to the Tsar's letter of May 14th. The King first of all had the answer drafted by an official in the Foreign Office. The letter then passed through Bismarck's hands, who decided to give it a stronger tone. He chose to do so by means of a postscript, no doubt to let the suggestion of spontaneity make its effect on his own sovereign as well as upon the Tsar. Bismarck had just received news of the failure of Gablenz's mission, of which he had probably never expected anything. He immediately turned the information to account. The postscript is drafted in Bismarck's own hand[117] from the first word to the last, and was apparently taken over quite unaltered by the King in his letter of June 1st. It runs as follows:

"At this moment, just as I was handing my letter to Count Bünting, I received authentic information which I must pass on to you and which unfortunately leaves no further doubt as to the attitude of the Viennese court. The brother of the Austrian General who is in command in Holstein had a little while ago presented to me the plan of a convention with Austria, which was based upon the principle of the reform of the German military system. Baron Gablenz had been provided with a letter of introduction from Count Mensdorff, and is in any case a trustworthy man. Hence I am convinced that he was speaking the truth when he assured me that the broad outlines of the project which he was presenting had been sanctioned, after it had been submitted to the Emperor Francis Joseph. Since I found certain points in it that might have served as the basis for negotiations, I invited Baron Gablenz to return to Vienna and to tell the Emperor that the whole thing seemed to me to indicate a foundation upon which we might build up a joint structure of suggestions to the German princes, who would have to be convened for the purpose. I flattered myself that we had rediscovered the path which would lead to an understanding. To-day Herr von Gablenz returned from Vienna and Dresden to tell me that the Emperor, after assuring him of his best intentions at an audience, had referred him to the Ministers. The answers that he received from them and that he has reported to me are as follows: Count Mensdorff feels that it is too late and that too much mistrust exists on both sides for direct negotiations to be possible. Count Belcredi [then Prime Minister in the strictly Conservative, so called "Three Counts Cabinet"][118] said that the internal difficulties of the Empire peremptorily demanded war for their adjustment; and Count Larisch [Finance Minister in the same Cabinet] declared that the finances of Austria demanded Prussian tribute to the extent of five hundred millions within three months, or else an honest bankruptcy, for which the war might serve as an excuse. Count Esterházy said this for his comfort—that after the first battle negotiations would be carried on with greater prospect of success. In Dresden Herr von Gablenz had Baron Beust's answer: The wine had been tapped and must be drunk. I felt I must tell you all this, my dear nephew, for to my great regret I am now left with practically no hope of seeing my efforts to maintain peace crowned with success. I must ask you to preserve complete discretion upon these details, as Herr von Gablenz has interests in Austria in regard to his brother and other relatives which he must consider."

This postscript of Bismarck's shows his masterly way of altering situations and events to suit his own purposes. Bismarck knew how difficult it was going to be to wrest from his King the decision for war, and he exploited the Gablenz mission to the full, not without accentuating certain of the higher lights. He did so, on the one hand, to bring the King round to the idea of war, and on the other to make it easier for him to tell the Tsar that he was intending to go to war.

The letter, the most important part of which was in the postscript, reached Tsarskoe Selo on June 4th, and impressed the Tsar enormously. He sent for Schweinitz the same evening, read him the letter which Bünting had brought, including—in the strictest confidence—the "interesting" postscript. Alexander II described with the deepest gravity the dangers which threatened all who occupied high positions, and indeed the whole of the present political system, in case of revolution, for which war would certainly be the most fruitful soil. As regards his own attitude, the Tsar said that he would police the frontiers, especially on the Galician side, but would do no more unless the affair spread to the Orient. Then, on June 6th, he wrote an answer to the King, expressed his deep grief at the passing of the last hopes of peace, and repeated his conviction that this disastrous war would only benefit the common enemy of all monarchies—revolution. If, however, it were unavoidable, then he begged that it might be confined within as restricted an area as possible.

The King of Bavaria also directed a last appeal to the King of Prussia from Munich on May 25th:

"A few years ago Your Majesty uttered the inspiring words: 'never to yield a square foot of German soil to the French', and may you always be mindful of them. It seems almost a certainty that a war between Austria and Prussia will mean the loss of the left bank of the Rhine. Keep it for Germany, Your Majesty, it is Germany's fairest domain (and its inhabitants are German in heart and soul), and to regain it Your Majesty took part in the glorious War of Liberation.

I urge this warmly upon the son of *the most German woman* [Queen Louise]. Let Prussia not destroy what she has been most instrumental in building up. When the first Napoleon ceded Hanover to Prussia, he swore vengeance upon Prussia. Waterloo is not yet forgotten. Preserve peace, Your Majesty. With the repetition of this ardent wish,

"I remain
"Your Majesty's most devoted
"Louis II."

This appeal, however, failed equally with the Tsar's efforts owing to the influence of Bismarck.

Prince Alexander was so disgusted and irritated at Prussia's "infamy", as he expressed it, and the vacillations of the smaller German States that he would have preferred to stay quietly at home in Darmstadt and take no further part in the affair. Since he had still received no definite instructions about his command, he sent a sort of ultimatum to the King of Württemberg with the inquiry whether he had decided to mobilize the Eighth Federal Army Corps even if Baden did not join in, or whether it was to be regarded as having been disbanded. He sent this letter for his brother the Grand Duke to see before dispatching it, and asked him to have it delivered. He received the following answer, dated June 12th:

"*Carissime frater!*
Your letter twisting that Swabian ruffian's tail has my fullest approbation, and I am quite ready for one of the officers of the 4th Squadron of the 2nd Regiment of Cavalry to go to Stuttgart as courier—the sooner the better.—Love to you all,
"Your devoted brother,
"LOUIS."

Events began to move quickly. On June 11th Gablenz retired from Holstein under protest and the Prussian, Manteuffel, succeeded him. At the meeting of the Federal Diet on June 14th the Austrian mobilization order was accepted by four Federal Army Corps, though Baden refused to vote. Prussia thereupon declared that the Federation was dissolved owing to unconstitutional voting. The whole of Germany was divided into two vast camps, and eventually Baden also decided, though very unwillingly, hesitatingly, and with reservations, to join the Central and Southern States against Prussia. When the Hessian Parliament voted the supplies for mobilization, Prince Alexander declared that the money was destined for the preservation of the integrity of the land, and no member of his house, which had ruled in Hesse for six hundred years, any more than any other proud, free, simple Hessian, could wish the Grand Duchy to be absorbed into an aggrandized Prussia.

The very next day Hanover, Saxony, and the Electorate of Hesse received the Prussian ultimatum. It was followed immediately by the declaration of war and a Prussian invasion. While requests were already reaching Prince Alexander from

N

Hanover for military support, he was busy taking the preliminary measures for mobilizing the unprepared, badly equipped, heterogeneous contingents from the States forming the Eighth Army Corps. On June 21st war had also been declared on Austria. While the Prussians were entering Hanover and Cassel, deposing and interning the rulers, war also broke out between Austria and Italy. On June 24th the Archduke Albrecht succeeded in defeating the Italian army at Custozza.

Prince Alexander realized that now, on the eve of important events, he must rely upon himself and no longer upon his brother-in-law far away in Russia, from whom he had heard nothing since his last urgent request for intervention. Not until June 30th did he receive a letter from his sister dated from Illinskoe on June 10th (22nd), which explained the Tsar's silence. She also dreaded the dissensions among the small States. "God grant that there may be unity in the decisions and in their execution", she wrote. "That is where I have the greatest fear of failure. I believe Prussia's advantage lies in the fact that it is under the domination of a single will, while there are so many different interests on your side. And I am afraid that they may all pull in different directions. The reason why the Tsar did not answer your letter was because he had already exhausted all the arts of persuasion in trying to reduce the King to reason. Nevertheless he made one more attempt, with Alexander Bariatinsky as his confidential messenger; but Prussia's evil genius, Bismarck, always kept the upper hand." The news that the Tsarina received of the internment of the Elector of Hesse-Cassel at Stettin still further increased her fears for the fate of her nearest relations.

The situation was in truth most critical. Prince Alexander wrote to his sister on June 25th, under the impression of all the alarming news that was pouring in upon him:

"I am standing at the most important cross-roads of my life. All those parts of Germany which have remained true to the Federation are relying on me. Six sovereigns have entrusted me with their troops. The Federation is acting solely upon my instructions. Shall I be able to justify their confidence? Shall I succeed in defeating the Prussians with this hotchpotch of troops, and in reinstating the exiled Princes of Cassel and Hanover?"

This letter was the introduction to a period that was always to be one of the saddest memories of Prince Alexander's adventurous life. The disunion among the individual States continued even after Prussia had declared war, and impeded the preparations as well as the plans of the commander.

Prince Alexander had arranged with Prince Charles, the great-uncle of the young Bavarian King, to unite their two Army Corps, which were known jointly as the West German Federal Army, and proceed against the Prussians who were presumed to be at Cassel or Eisenach, in order to come to the assistance of Hanover which was hemmed in between Eisenach and Gotha.

In reality, however, each State was concerned primarily to protect its own territory, and in consequence the sound main plan was continually being postponed, because preparations were deliberately delayed. Every State wanted to keep its troops in its own country for as long as possible, and dreaded the time when it would be obliged to leave itself exposed, even though it were in order to take action against the common enemy. That was the reason why the Bavarian troops did not join the Austrian army; and why the union which the Bavarians desired between their troops and those of Württemberg, Hesse, and Baden, that is to say, of the Seventh with the Eighth Corps, was so long delayed and was finally carried out only when it was too late. At last, on June 30th, Prince Alexander was ready to take a part of his troops to relieve the hard-pressed Hanoverians. On July 1st he received the news that they had already capitulated to the Prussians on June 29th. The Electorate of Hesse and Cassel had been in Prussian hands since June 1st, and the Elector of Hesse-Cassel had been interned because he would not submit to the Prussian ultimatum and had refused to leave his castle of Wilhelmshöhe without his family treasure, which was worth some forty million talers (about £6,000,000). The prospects were pleasant for the rulers of the remaining States who had refused to submit to Prussia. And the Elector's troops were totally unprepared for war. "They have nothing," Prince Alexander's wife wrote and told the Tsarina, "neither munitions nor horses nor transport. When they went off, it was just as though they were going to a parade, and there was nothing to be done but to send them to the garrison in Mainz until they had been provided with the barest necessaries."

In Austria efforts were made to induce Bavaria to lend her active co-operation, and on June 19th General Count Huyn was sent to Munich to persuade Bavaria to send her troops either to Bohemia or to undertake an offensive in Central Germany. It was obvious that, with such an alternative, local patriotism would be victorious, and that the march on Bohemia would never be so much as contemplated. The germ of the ill-success of the whole campaign was to be found in the wording of a proposed military convention between all the States that were allied against Prussia which was never formally adopted. But its spirit animated all their actions.

"In drawing up the Bavarian Commander-in-Chief's plan of operations", it runs in the handwriting of Baron von Kübeck, given to Prince Alexander at Darmstadt on June 23rd,[119] "care must be taken that operations shall always be in harmony with the local interests of the various States in the allied armies, and that consideration is given to the protection of the commander's own countries as much as to the achievement of the main purpose of the war by the greatest possible concentration of the forces."

Therein lay a contradiction that was bound to cripple anything that was planned subsequently. While Prince Charles and Prince Alexander were getting slowly and carefully to work on June 30th, the Prussian campaign against Austria in Bohemia had already reached a point at which a definite decision was imminent. The Austrians did not realize that they should have attacked the Prussian armies singly as they invaded Bohemia one after another, and thus have beaten them individually. A body of men was sent to meet each one, and in each case it was too weak and was obliged to retire. Thus all the corps were gradually involved, and the whole army's feeling of the certainty of victory was seriously diminished. By July 2nd Prince Alexander had arrived in the neighbourhood of Grünberg to the east of Giessen, and that evening he received a telegram despatched by the Emperor Francis Joseph at 3.55 p.m., which ran: "The Northern army has been forced to retreat from Bohemia without fighting any pitched battle, doubtless owing to checks sustained by individual corps and the efficiency of the Prussian communications. Enemy is not pursuing, so has probably also suffered heavily. Urgently request Your Grand Ducal Highness to take the offensive with the united Federal army *in the direction of Berlin* with all possible speed, thus taking the only possible means of forcing the common enemy to divide his forces and thereby to bring the war to a rapid and successful conclusion. Prince Charles of Bavaria has been informed."

Thus Prince Alexander—who was technically subordinate to Prince Charles of Bavaria—was ordered to advance on Berlin with his weak and motley band of warriors. Vienna was still wrapt in illusions about the military value and the prospects of the campaign conducted by the West and South German States.

This telegram occasioned the greatest astonishment in Alexander of Hesse's headquarters, for only the rosiest reports about events on the Bohemian front had hitherto reached them. In particular, the message of the Emperor's general aide-de-camp telling of the retreat from Bohemia and adding the remark that it would be a good fortnight before it would be possible to proceed to an offensive there, roused the greatest concern.[120] "This shocking news came like a bolt from the blue. . . ." wrote Prince Alexander in his diary. "So all the newspaper reports about successes won by Raming, Gablenz, and Edelsheim were lies. Our situation begins to be very critical. I am trying to link up with the Bavarians, but do not know where they are. Fifty thousand Prussians under Manteuffel and Beyer are encamped at Hersfeld. The line of the Main and Mainz are threatened, and Austria is evacuating Bohemia."

On the morning of July 4th, however, a more reassuring telegram arrived for Prince Alexander from the Emperor. According to this a day's rest had been beneficial, and there was reason to hope that no further retreat would be necessary.

On July 5th an order came in from Prince Charles stating that a union of the two Federal corps north of the Rhön mountains was no longer feasible owing to the Prussian advance. The Bavarians were ordered to retire, while Prince Alexander was to try to get into communication with them and link up. The Prince first made his dispositions and then went to bed. At one o'clock in the morning he was wakened by Colonel von Schönfeld, who had been attached to him from the Austrian General Staff: "I have very sad news to give Your Highness", he said, and handed him a telegram which had just arrived from Count Crenneville. It ran: "The Northern army suffered a great defeat yesterday at Königgrätz. Enormous losses." A commentary which accompanied it from Major-General Baron von Packeny added that the Prussians had lost thirty thousand men and that the Austrian losses were much heavier.

Prince Alexander was absolutely shattered. He had thought

so much of the Austrian army and all his political hopes were built up on the military power of Austria. He must therefore have been particularly hard hit, and the ensuing reaction upon his feelings and his military plans must have been very great.

The news caused Prince Alexander to decide to take his corps back to Frankfurt without waiting for orders. The Baden Division had already marched off in this direction on its own responsibility at the instigation of Prince William of Baden. No notification reached the corps commander. Bavaria was urging that the Prince should march eastwards with his corps as quickly as possible in order to unite with that of Prince Charles of Bavaria, which implied leaving Frankfurt at the mercy of the enemy. The Prince obeyed the command, and thus left the road to Frankfurt clear for the Prussians. On July 16th the Prussian general, von Falkenstein, occupied it, and reported to his King: "All the country north of the Main lies at Your Majesty's feet." When Prince Alexander met the Prince of Bavaria he found him utterly demoralized. "What is the use of our carrying on the war any longer?" he said. "We cannot possibly beat the Prussians now." In St. Petersburg the course of events was followed with anxiety, especially by the Tsarina.

"You can imagine what I feel like," she wrote to Prince Alexander on July 8th (20th); "I may say, what *we* feel like. I can think of nothing but you, what you must be going through, how the immediate future will turn out for you all.

"I cannot tell you how terribly anxious I have been about you. I have never been in such a state of feverish tension since the time of the Crimean War; so much so that to the concern of Hartmann, my physician-in-ordinary, I have got much thinner. He says he hates the Prussians all the more on that account.

"In general, thank goodness, I see no signs of sympathy for them [the Prussians]. N. [icholas, Count] Adlerberg [for a long time military attaché in Berlin] who has just come back from Berlin, says that their arrogance passes all bounds. They talk of taking our Baltic provinces, no less! The people, of course, not the Government. Bismarck is not yet so mad as to attack us directly. On the contrary, he is trying to win us over to his side. But the Tsar was so furious at their revolutionary proclamations, which actually permitted the Polish newspaper at Posen to say that what was good for Bohemia and Hungary was equally good for Poland, that he made the

ambassador tell Bismarck exactly what he thought about it.
What seems to me the coolest thing I have ever heard of is
that Napoleon has actually written to the King of Prussia
warning him of the danger of using revolutionary means,
and telling him that fear of the same danger caused him
to make peace in 1859. So low is the old King fallen! That
really grieves the Tsar very much. Now everyone is wondering
what hope there is for Germany's future. . . . For us, on the
other hand, it is very important not to have Prussia too powerful; and one would think that this was also true for France.
At all events, Napoleon says so in a letter to the Tsar. So why
does he accept their ultimatum?"

In reality, as Prince Alexander some years later heard in
confidence from Shuvaloff, and entered in his diary on May 30,
1870, dramatic events had taken place in St. Petersburg on
July 4th. A telegram had arrived from Napoleon on that day
inquiring whether Russia had decided if necessary to make
an armed intervention in order to paralyse Prussia. A qualified
assent had already been contemplated when a second telegram
arrived an hour later, telling of the great victory at Königgrätz. Thereupon Gortchakoff executed a complete *volte face*,
sent a message of congratulation to the Prussian general, and
the pro-Prussian course was continued, to the great grief of
the Tsarina. True, nobody was pleased. Count Redern was
right when he remarked in a report to his Foreign Office on
July 5th: "A powerful Prussia slipping away from Russian
influence is a thorn in the flesh of every Russian. The Tsarina
is especially hostile to Prussia. The Tsar has a friendly feeling
for the King. . . ."[121]

Meanwhile the Prussians continued to advance in South
Germany. When Prince Alexander met Prince Charles of
Bavaria, he was received with the words: "We are in a bad
way." Then came a telegram from Nikolsburg reporting the
conclusion of an armistice between Prussia and Austria. Now
things began to move quickly. The disunion among the Central
and Southern German States was never more obvious than
at this time. Prussia succeeded in sowing seeds of dissension
among them by totally ignoring Prince Alexander and nego-
tiating separately with the rulers of the States that had formed
his corps. Bavaria also did this on its own account. The
Grand Duke Frederick of Baden had already written to his
father-in-law, King William of Prussia, from Karlsruhe on
July 24th, absolutely throwing up the sponge. "I am writing

to ask you not to cut off us South Germans from the great community of the new Federation that is to be constituted under Prussia's leadership, *without* Austria. . . . My only wish is to serve our common fatherland. . . . I shall endeavour to bring over Baden to Germany in good time, so that we may take our place in the glorious union during the peace negotiations." Arndt's poem, "Germany shall be united", was now, he averred, an expression of the desire of all thoughtful men in the nation. The letter ended with expressions of admiration for the bravery and the achievements of the splendid Prussian army, and with congratulations upon the brilliant results that had attended King William's long efforts at educating the nation up to great feats of arms.[122]

The West German army began to melt away. At last Württemberg, Nassau, and Hesse-Darmstadt also found themselves obliged to agree to an armistice with Prussia. The Prussians had previously occupied as many important cities as possible, such as Würzburg, Nüremberg, Darmstadt, Heidelberg, and Mannheim. This brought the campaign of the Western and Southern German States to an inglorious end. In Frankfurt, which was hostile to them, the Prussians exercised the greatest severity, and among other things imposed a levy of twenty-five million marks (£1,250,000), whereupon the Mayor committed suicide by hanging himself. "Frankfurt", wrote the Tsarina to Prince Alexander on July 19th (31st), "is the summit of Prussian atrocities. It is personal revenge on Bismarck's part, to which the King is lending his support. The Tsar blushes for his uncle. One might think we were back in the Middle Ages, believing that 'might is right' and all that that implies."

On August 6th Prince Charles of Bavaria retired from his post as Commander-in-Chief, and on August 9th Prince Alexander also resigned his command of the Eighth Federal Army Corps and bade farewell to the troops. He then went to Vienna to give the Emperor Francis Joseph a verbal report upon the unfortunate campaign.

On August 18th, the Emperor's birthday, he was received in audience by Francis Joseph. His reception was very gracious, and the unlucky campaign was kindly criticized. The Prince found the Emperor greatly aged on this his thirty-sixth birthday. He referred with indignation to Bavaria's policy and its performance in the field. "I can only be glad", said the Emperor, at the territorial cession, "that Prussia is exacting of Bavaria. They deserve it on our account! The Emperor

Napoleon, too, has betrayed Austria shamefully on more than one occasion, and we have been badly fooled by him again." The Emperor expressed himself as very dissatisfied with General Benedek—his strategy had been incompetent and irresponsible, and he had completely lost his head. The Prince found Vienna and its inhabitants still absolutely shattered by the blow that had fallen upon the monarchy. They were so occupied with their own defeat that they knew practically nothing of that of the West German army, and therefore very naturally regarded it as less serious than their own. It is comprehensible that in these circumstances, and in view of his unpopularity in Hesse, Prince Alexander should wish to be given another Austrian command. The Emperor, however, evaded the question, and Prince Alexander returned to Heiligenberg. Everyone in Hesse-Darmstadt was in fear and trembling, wondering what territorial sacrifices would be demanded by Prussia. It was hoped in both Württemberg and Hesse that, in view of the relationship existing between their dynasties and the Russian imperial house, Bismarck would not make too heavy demands on them. In St. Petersburg, in so far as the Tsarina's letters may be believed—and she was naturally very seriously concerned for the fate of her native land—there was still considerable gloom regarding Prussia's overwhelming victory. "At all events", said the Tsarina in writing to her brother on July 19th (31st), "the Tsar will do his best to insist upon conferences among the neutrals, and will in no case agree to anything that is done without our knowledge and against our will."

But Russia could not assert its authority to the extent hoped by the Tsarina if only because the Tsar had no intention of asserting himself to the extent that would have been necessary to prevent Bismarck from enjoying the fruits of the victorious campaign. Bismarck, again, cleverly spared Russia's susceptibilities, with the result that the Tsarina's mind was soon at rest concerning the fate of Hesse. She recognized this when she wrote: "I believe that the King, and especially Bismarck, wish to spare both Hesse and Württemberg in order not to offend us directly. As regards the other unfortunates, nothing more can be done. Their annexation was, alas! decided upon yesterday."

In August the young King of Bavaria, too, turned to the Tsarina as an aunt who was very fond of him, and begged her on his behalf and that of his country—in a letter which has

recently been published by the Soviet Government—to request
Prussia to reduce the exorbitant territorial demands she had
put forward. The King was afraid at that time that he would
lose a large portion of the Palatinate and Upper Franconia,
as well as the Rhön and Kissingen. The Tsarina replied
that she was afraid she could do nothing. In the end, however,
all that was demanded of Bavaria beyond a large war
indemnity was a slight alteration of her frontiers. The Tsar
now sided warmly with the victors. General von Manteuffel,
who had been sent by King William to Peterhof to explain
what his immediate intentions were, was given a long and
detailed letter,[123] dated July 31st (August 12th), in the introduction to which stood the words: "I, like yourself, regard
Russia and Prussia as natural allies. It is one of my deepest
convictions." The Tsar then deplored the establishment of a
German Parliament, referred to dangers arising out of such an
assembly, which would form the meeting-place for all the
democratic elements, and which no one on earth would be
able to guide as he wished. The letter closed in a friendly
manner with the words: "But you may rest assured that I
shall never be found in the ranks of Prussia's enemies." In a
later letter,[124] written on August 12th (24th), the Tsar expressed
as his dearest wish that Prussia and Russia should remain in
the future what they had been in the past—"old and trusted
allies".

The Tsarina, nevertheless, could not bring herself to like
the new situation. Most of all was she concerned at the reports
which she had from the Russian representative in Darmstadt of
the differences of opinion and the dissensions within the Hessian
princely house. She was given to understand that the younger
generation, led by Princess Alice, was most friendly disposed
towards Prussia, and that her secretary had actually been one
of those who had demanded the annexation of Hesse-Darmstadt
by Prussia. "If I had been in the Grand Duke's place", said the
Tsarina, "I should have sent that man packing!" What made
her most indignant of all was that Prince Henry of Hesse, who
had remained in the Prussian army, had been seen immediately after the occupation of Darmstadt walking about the
streets in Prussian uniform.

"That Henry should have come to Darmstadt at once", was
the Tsarina's opinion in writing to Prince Alexander on
August 6th (18th), "is unbelievably impudent. I could not
refrain from expressing my astonishment to Charles [Prince

Henry's father] that he [Henry] should have remained in *Bismarck's* service. He has not replied. . . . I hope he has not taken it amiss, but I could not help saying it."

Prince Alexander was filled with a deep disgust of all he had been through. He said that he supposed one day children would be told that William of Prussia had been a man who understood the times he lived in and who had brought great and good things to pass; whereas those who were now living and who would then be grandfathers would know that he was only a marionette without shame or principles.

Prince Alexander wrote to his sister on August 23rd and told her that he was sick to death of everything, that he must first take a rest, and would then like to have another appointment in Austria, for he had no desire to assist at the "Borussification of Germany".

Meanwhile, peace had been signed in August. Württemberg, Baden, and Bavaria escaped with little more than war indemnities, while Hesse-Darmstadt had only to cede a small district in the north. Prince Alexander paid a visit to Holland early in September with his family in an attempt to put all his recent unhappy experiences out of his mind. This time really proved the turning-point in his life, though not as he had imagined it. Even he was at last obliged to accept Prussia's predominance in Germany, and to repress—externally at least—as far as lay in him his old ingrained dislike of all that came from there, and especially of Bismarck.

Bismarck's plans had succeeded in every respect. He was victorious all along the line. A great step had been taken towards the unification of Germany under Prussian hegemony. By forcing Austria out of Germany, however, Bismarck subsequently compelled Vienna involuntarily to set the centre of gravity of its foreign policy in the east, so as to find some compensation for its losses in the west. All the Great Powers were striving for territorial and economic gains, and Austria was no exception. In the east, however, Austrian aspirations were bound in time to conflict with those of Russia. Bismarck's genius succeeded in postponing any such conflict, although it threatened often enough, but when the conflict at last burst out in the World War it seemed like a sort of tragic poetic justice that Austria should drag Prussian Germany, which had once driven it out of the west, into the war that had been induced by quarrels with Russia in the east—a war in which all three empires were to perish.

CHAPTER IX

TOWARDS THE UNIFICATION OF GERMANY

THE first task facing Germany was to accustom herself to the changes that had resulted from the war. Peace had just been concluded between Prussia and Hesse, and the Prince felt very ill at ease in his character as a "second-class Hessian Prussian". As things were he would have preferred to shake the dust of his native land off his feet and to re-enter the Austrian service. In Vienna, however, he was regarded only as the brother-in-law of the Tsar, who might in certain eventualities be useful again as a mediator in St. Petersburg.

An invitation came to him at about this time from St. Petersburg for the forthcoming marriage of the Tsarevitch to his late brother's fiancée, Dagmar of Denmark. Schweinitz had advised[125] that a Prussian Prince should be sent to St. Petersburg, because he regarded it as not wise to "leave the field altogether clear for anti-Prussian elements like Danes and Hessians" on such an occasion. Hence it was decided to send the Crown Prince to St. Petersburg.

The Lord Chamberlain of the Russian Court therefore took the precaution of writing to tell Prince Alexander that a Prussian prince would probably be at the ceremony; and that if this was distasteful to him he would be wiser not to come until after the wedding. Prince Alexander replied that he "snapped his fingers at the Prussians". Nevertheless, he realized afresh how strong had been the effect of the Prussian successes upon the Tsar, who was congratulating himself on having maintained a friendly attitude towards Prussia during the war, and on having confined himself to written admonitions beforehand.

Although the Tsar was at times concerned at the great increase in Prussia's power, he was nevertheless determined not to be influenced by his brother-in-law's still very strongly anti-Prussian sentiments. Prince Alexander was furious when on his way through Berlin he saw two hundred and fifty Austrian, Bavarian, and Hanoverian guns displayed on the

Unter den Linden. In St. Petersburg he was received with open arms, every attention was shown him, and he was re-commissioned to the Chevaliers-Gardes regiment in which he had once served. Since he was a keen sportsman, he was invited to the court hunts, which proved to be very unsporting butcheries. In the new park at the palace of Tsarskoe Selo a drive was held at which the unfortunate game was surrounded on all sides and finally forced to pass one particular spot, where the Tsar alone fired no less than a thousand shots.

The wedding took place with unprecedented magnificence. The Prince of Wales and the Crown Prince of Prussia were present, and Prince Alexander took the opportunity to assure the latter that he had no sort of feelings of animosity against him personally.

On his return to Darmstadt he was annoyed to find that in addition to his nephew Henry—the hero of the Prussian war—also Louis and Alice were coming to be more and more in sympathy with Berlin. He was most indignant to hear that they were planning a visit there. "No doubt", he wrote to the Tsarina on January 7, 1867, "Louis is going to apologize to the King for having done his duty as a Hessian prince during the late war. . . ." Alexander hoped to the last that the Grand Duke would forbid the visit, and when he failed to do so wrote furiously in his diary on January 7th: "He cares for nothing but what touches his pocket."

The Tsarina agreed with her brother, and on the subject of the Berlin visit remarked in a letter dated January 5 (17), 1867: "Louis and Alice, with all due respect, are possessed by the devil in their mania for inappropriate visits. These English princesses have certainly inherited their mother's passion for action. Talking of the Queen, Bertie [the Prince of Wales] took no notice of her . . . even on the anniversary of his father's death; what a tender relationship! He was annoyed because she twice refused to allow him to present the Order of the Garter to the Tsar; the Ministers supported his request, but the Queen refused none the less. He has been pouring out his sorrows upon the bosom of Brunnow,[126] who reports that she is absurdly jealous of anything that might bring her son into prominence. . . ."

Criticisms of Prince Alexander also appeared in the news-papers. His attitude of dislike to the situation in general since the recent unfortunate campaign extended to his views regarding the all-pervasive Prussian influence. "The general situation of the country", he wrote to his sister on March 8th, "is as hopeless as it can be, both in a political and a military sense. The latter-day Prussians, as I call them, seem to spring from the ground like mushrooms. They may be divided into two categories, (1) those who were converted by the Battle of Königgrätz, and (2) those who say that they have really always been good Prussians and never cared about Austria, but that they could not swim against the stream! The latter are the more nauseating, to my way of thinking. To the latter-day Prussians must be added the radicals, headed by Louis and Alice, who regard legitimacy and rulers by divine right as outmoded ideas, and can heardly bear to wait for the time when the Grand Duke shall have been mediatized. Three-quarters of the officers' corps has lately joined this party. Finally, there exists in the Grand Duchy the tiny anti-Prussian party which would like to preserve the independence of the State, the grim Jesuits, Blacks, or whatever you like to call them. One section of this party would 'rather think in terms of the French than of the Prussians', which I regard as political blasphemy. These anti-Prussians would be joined by every one of the latter-day Prussians if New Prussia were thoroughly well beaten by France or Austria. As far as I am concerned, I belong to none of these parties. I remain faithful to my principles, and loathe Prussian ways from the bottom of my heart; but I should not like Louis to run his head against the wall and get on to bad terms with Prussia. As things are, there is unfortunately no other course open to the Grand Duchy than to dance to the Prussian piping and to await events."

Prince Alexander did not at all agree with the passive attitude of his then sixty-one-year-old brother the Grand Duke. "Here in Darmstadt", he wrote to the Tsarina on April 24th, "political affairs seem to me to be on their last legs. Louis is utterly ensnared in the toils of Prussia; but he hides his head in the sand so as not to see what is going on. He ratified the military convention with Prussia, after hardly glancing at it; and similarly the offensive and defensive alliance. Doctor Becker, Alice's secretary, is hawking round a mass petition for the entry of the whole country into the Prussian Federation; and Louis [the Grand Duke] has not the courage to do anything against it. He has an ambassador in Berlin who receives instructions from Dalwigk [the Grand Duke's Minister], but only carries out those that are approved by Alice and Vicky, etc., etc. This sort of thing obviously cannot go on for long.

Either Louis must make a determined stand against this secret government or he must abdicate unless he wishes to become simply a Prussian satrap."

Prince Alexander continued to discuss very animatedly the great political questions of the day with his sister.

The Tsarina intuitively perceived the Iron Chancellor's most secret ideas. "Bismarck", she said, "seems to be very sure of his general position as regards the Parliament and Germany; but that does not prevent his dreading even the appearance of an understanding between France and ourselves." The Tsarina was referring to the demands put forward by Napoleon through his ambassador Benedetti at Nikolsburg in 1866, which embodied the cession of certain portions of the Rhineland, including Mainz.

At that time Napoleon was opening the great World Exhibition of 1867, and it was the Tsar's intention to go to Paris and visit it.

Prince Alexander had been hoping, indeed expecting for certain owing to some previous remarks of the Tsar's, that he would be invited to go with him to the World Exhibition. The date, which had been fixed for the beginning of June, was coming very near, and the Prince still waited vainly for a definite invitation. Serious reasons prevented the Tsar's asking his brother-in-law. Since his wife, after having borne him seven children, was now in very delicate health, she was no longer fully capable of fulfilling all her marital duties, and the Tsar, as has been said, had indulged in sundry love-affairs with other women. Up to the present he had never felt more than a passing fancy for anyone. In the course of the year 1866, however, he had lost his heart to a singularly beautiful young girl, a member of the distinguished Dolgoruki family, who were related to the old Russian imperial house. The Tsar had got to know her as a child of ten when he was quartered in the house of her very extravagant father, Prince Michael Dolgoruki, who squandered the whole substance of the family. After his death, Alexander II had had the girl received into the Smolny Institute, where the daughters of the higher aristocracy were educated. She grew up into a young woman gifted with great beauty and more especially with an incomparable charm, and the Tsar, who had always taken an interest in her, now fell seriously in love with her.

In the year 1866 Katherine Dolgoruki was in the eighteenth year of her age. For a whole year she had resisted the Tsar, but at last she gave herself to him in a little summer-house in the park surrounding the palace of Peterhof. The Tsar's figure was still youthful, his manner and appearance elegant, and the expression of his face showed the nobility of his character. Altogether he was a most attractive man. It was therefore not as Tsar that Katherine yielded to him, but she became deeply attached to him for his own sake. Fired with the passion that the evening in the summer-house at Peterhof raised to an ecstasy, he swore to her that if circumstances in any way permitted it, he would make her his wife. During that year the lovers exchanged hundreds upon hundreds of the most ardent love-letters. That first meeting was followed by innumerable others at the Winter Palace, whither those in the Tsar's confidence brought the girl secretly. The Tsarina was not unaware of her husband's liaison, but proudly ignored it as she had done the earlier ones, and thought it would soon come to an end as they had done. This time, however, she was mistaken. The Tsar's attachment could not long remain a secret at the court. For those who live in the public eye to the extent that a Tsar was obliged to do it is impossible to conceal from the rest of the world even the most private matters. And especially not a consuming passion that binds the lovers daily closer, and often betrays them into carelessness. Gossip roused fears in the Dolgoruki family. After several months of happiness, the girl's sister-in-law, who was horrified at the tattle, decided to take the girl with her on a visit to her relatives in Naples. That meant separation; and as usual instead of moderating their passion it only made the flames blaze up the more fiercely. The Tsar revolved in his mind how he might come together again with Katherine Dolgoruki, and finally wrote and told her to be in Paris at the time of his visit to the Exhibition. When the young Princess agreed to this suggestion, the Tsar remembered his arrangement to take his brother-in-law, Prince Alexander, to Paris with him. It would obviously be awkward for him to have in his company his wife's brother, who might only too easily get to know of the liaison. So he simply pretended to have forgotten all about it, and to the Prince's great disappointment the invitation failed to materialize.

On June 1st the Tsar arrived in Paris accompanied by his sons, and after the brilliant entertainments provided for him by Napoleon III, the beautiful Katherine visited him in secret at the Elysée. Both had a terrible shock when the Tsar, who had previously been affronted by the sarcastic shouts of the people, "Long live Poland!", was fired at by a young Pole named Beresowski as he was returning from a review on the Champ de Mars on June 6th. He was only saved by the presence of mind of a court official who rode beside the carriage.

Prince Alexander, disappointed of his visit to Paris, accepted the invitation of the Emperor Francis Joseph to his coronation in Hungary. There he saw the Crown of Saint Stephen set upon the head of the Emperor by the Prince Archbishop together with Count Julius Andrássy, who had been condemned to death in 1850 for his part in the revolution and hanged in effigy, but pardoned in 1857. Andrássy, as Prince Alexander knew, was anti-Russian in feeling, if only because of the Tsar's attitude to his country in 1848.

Meanwhile news came across the ocean that the Emperor Maximilian of Mexico had paid for his dream of empire with death before a firing-squad.

"The ghastly drama in Mexico", wrote Alexander to his sister upon receipt of the terrible news on August 6, 1867, "will, I am sure, have shocked you too. Wrong though the unfortunate Archduke was to enter into Napoleon's hazardous enterprise, he carried through his part heroically to the end. He doomed himself to certain death so as not to desert those who had trusted in him. A good example of the fact that the old proverb 'Blood will tell!' is still true. This saying should be recalled to the King of Prussia, whose baseness knows no bounds. Did you hear that he was not ashamed of making a triumphal entry into Wiesbaden on horseback—on which occasion a wall in one of the streets through which he passed was adorned with the couplet:

> Vivat Wilhelmus Rex!
> If you have any, hide your effects"?

Prince Alexander continued to harbour feelings of resentment against Prussia. On September 17th, for example, when the King came to Frankfurt, the Grand Duke of Hesse-Darmstadt went to meet him and gave a dinner party in his honour. Prince Alexander was not present. On the Prussian side, nevertheless, there was a wish to make friends with the Tsarina's favourite brother. Hence the King of Prussia commissioned Prince Alexander's nephew, Henry of Hesse, who had always remained loyal to Prussia, to greet him cordially

o

and to tell him that the King felt a great desire to be reconciled to any who were still unreconciled to recent events. Prince Alexander none the less could not bring himself to adopt a more friendly attitude towards King William. On the contrary, he embraced this opportunity to indulge in a fresh philippic against Prussia on December 31st, alleging it to be trampling the monarchical principle under foot.

At the court of Hesse-Darmstadt, however, a continually increasing opposition to Prince Alexander's anti-Prussian views was growing up, the chief among his opponents being Louis the heir-presumptive to the throne, and his wife Alice, the sister of the Crown Princess of Prussia. Hence Alexander's ill-will was turned upon this "foreigner", as he called her in a letter to the Tsarina on April 9, 1868, who would barter the country to Prussia and who cherished the incredible illusion that a King of Prussia might prove generous towards Hesse.

Meanwhile Prince Alexander's children were growing up healthy and happy. Princess Marie, the eldest, was already fifteen years old, had just been confirmed, and promised to become a delightful girl, distinguished especially by her serious disposition and charming good sense. The four boys, on the other hand, the eldest of whom, Louis, had reached his fourteenth year, gave their parents some anxiety. They were—as was to be expected of healthy youngsters—full of mischief, refused to attend to their lessons, and, as the diary notes from time to time, were every now and then thrashed by their father because there seemed no other way of dealing with them. On the whole, however, the best hopes might be entertained for their future, for they were all fine specimens, well-grown, and—most important of all—apparently possessed of sound constitutions. Prince Alexander's idea of re-entering the Austrian service was never realized. He was put on the retired list and appointed Honorary Cavalry General. From this time on his relations with the Austrian court began to grow somewhat less intimate. At about that time he became head of a railroad syndicate in Russia, an undertaking that kept him very busy during the next few years, and in which a Prince Serge Dolgoruki was also engaged. The Tsar was, needless to say, not at all pleased that these two should be taking part in railway construction in Russia, and he hesitated to fulfil the various petitions for employment that were addressed to him in this connection, fearing to be accused of nepotism both legitimate and illegitimate. Prince Alexander's eldest son, who wanted to go to sea, was after negotiations with the English royal house, which were carried on through the Princess Alice, accepted by the British Admiralty, not without certain preliminary difficulties. He entered the cadet school, and applied for naturalization in England.

In August 1868 Prince Alexander had another visit from the Tsar and Tsarina at Heiligenberg. Shooting parties and reviews alternated with the still fashionable spiritist séances under the direction of the swindler Hume. The séances took place at Prince Alexander's house, where some of the well-known phenomena called "manifestations" occurred. The table moved, knocks were heard all over the room, an accordion in Hume's hand—he was an accomplished ventriloquist—played "automatically". Prince Alexander wrote the most curious things at the "dictation of the spirits", and finally the table rose completely off the floor and a drop of blood appeared on Hume's hand! Even the Tsar endured this hocus-pocus from nine o'clock in the evenings until eleven-thirty.

The Tsarina took no part in the séances. Her health was causing anxiety again, she was coughing blood and felt very weak. The more the Tsarina's health troubled her, and the more she knew of her husband's infidelities, the more closely did she cling to her brother, the more often was he invited to go and stay with her. The Tsar, too, was glad that she should find distraction, since he did still honour her as his wife and the mother of his six living children. Indeed, the more conscious he grew of his passion for the Princess Dolgoruki the more trouble he took about his wife, looking after her health in every way and treating her with scrupulous courtesy.

Soon after, while the Tsar and Tsarina were again staying at Kissingen to take the waters, King Louis of Bavaria also arrived, and spent a week there, seeing a great deal of them both. The story of the breaking off of his engagement which had set the whole world agog the year before had not yet been forgotten. The details of the King's entering upon and breaking off his engagement to the Princess Sophia of Bavaria, his remark after he had become engaged that he had been too hasty, that marriage was a terrible idea to him, and he would rather jump into a lake,[127] had gone the round of all the courts. When on October 11th the official gazette announced the dissolution of the King's betrothal—the Princess, it may be added, married Duke Ferdinand of Alençon, the nephew of Louis Philippe, and died heroically in a fire which broke

out at a charity bazaar in Paris in 1897—the Tsarina wrote
to her brother on October 17th (29th): "Talking of weddings
reminds me of the King of Bavaria. I give him up, he really
cannot be quite right in the head! I should like to hear what
his mother has to say about it. Some people say he is impotent,
but I don't see what reason there is to suppose so. His grandfather told Mary [Hamilton] in Paris that he [Louis II] thought
you could have children by lying in the same bed with a
woman. I had a letter from him last summer, in which he
spoke so mournfully of his loneliness. In reply I sent him a
warm dissertation upon wedded love. And now this is the
result!" Princess Sophia was the sister of the Empress Elisabeth.

It is not surprising that the Tsarina regarded the King with
some curiosity when she saw him again after this episode.
When she went on from Kissingen to Como, Louis of Bavaria
invited her to visit him on the way at his castle of Berg near
Munich. The entertainment that the King gave for her there
was fairylike, such as could have been conceived by none but
a man of such outstanding artistic gifts as Louis II, with all
his morbid eccentricity, was. The Starnberg Lake was wonderfully illuminated, the park with its glorious flowers and fountains was bathed in a sea of light, and the dinner, which was
arranged on the sweet-scented Isle of Roses, was, according to
the Tsarina, the most romantic that she had ever enjoyed.[128]

When he returned home Prince Alexander came to hear of
a confidential imperial ukase prohibiting all State officials
from taking part in railway undertakings. This could only
be interpreted as a pretty broad hint that any who might wish
to take advantage of their position had better think twice
about it.

Prince Alexander still persisted in his animosity against the
Prussian course in Germany. Most of all was he indignant at
the speeches in favour of the confiscation of the property of
the ruling houses of Hanover and the Electorate of Hesse. He
could not contain his anger when Bismarck spoke at a public
meeting on January 30, 1869, of the "paltry dynastic interests
of King George of Hanover", and said with reference to the
dispossessed regents that "these vicious reptiles must be pursued
to their lairs". The money that was confiscated was pooled to
form a fund for the support of journalists writing in the interest
of the Government, and after this speech was popularly known
as the "reptile fund".

In addition, Prince Alexander was still being much disquieted by persistent rumours of war. "The Prussian nightmare", he wrote to his sister on March 13, 1869, "still oppresses the world and everything in it." Only in military affairs was he obliged to admit that the Prussian influence had been very valuable. "The Hessian troops", he wrote to the Tsar on September 29th of the same year, "have benefited by being united with a large army. Only the Hessian officers are in an awkward position— their King regards them as renegades who are serving two masters at once, and their new fellow-officers look down on them as second-class Prussians."

In St. Petersburg the Tsar continued his liaison with the young Princess Dolgoruki. The Tsarina, who still ignored the affair completely to her brother as well as to the rest of the world, was seriously ill again, and had to go down to her picturesquely situated palace of Livadia in the Crimea on the urgent advice of her doctors. Prince Alexander was given a warm invitation to join her, which he hastened to accept. The Tsar only awaited his arrival before going back again to his beloved, and said to the Prince: "Look after Marie. I count on you to keep her happy and amused." In that excellent climate the Tsarina's health took a turn for the better during the next few weeks, and towards the middle of November she was able to contemplate the return journey in short stages by way of Kieff and Smolensk. At Kieff Prince Alexander and the Tsarina's children, including the Grand Duchess Marie, then aged sixteen, and her lady-in-waiting, the Countess Tolstoi, visited the chief monastery and the catacombs. The visitors were taken about among the underground passages by the seventy-one-year-old Metropolitan of Kieff, who showed them the graves of over two hundred saints who had lived underground here as monks in the early days of Russian Christianity. Prince Alexander received a considerable shock when the venerable Metropolitan suddenly began telling the ladies the most extraordinary stories about one saint who had caused himself to be buried up to the waist in order to escape temptation from women. The old gentleman told them quite blandly that this saint had fallen into the hands of a woman in Hungary who had tried to seduce him. He had, however, resisted her, whereupon the lady had had him castrated. The Countess Tolstoi did not know what to do to prevent the young Grand Duchess Marie hearing these tales, but did not know how to assert her authority against the venerable Metropolitan with his flowing silvery beard.

When they arrived in St. Petersburg Alexander found the Tsar very much prepossessed in favour of the German Emperor. The sentiments of the Emperor Francis Joseph, on the other hand, between whom and his brother-in-law Prince Alexander still hoped to bring about a better state of feeling, remained less friendly. The Tsar was displeased at Francis Joseph's going to the opening of the Suez Canal, where he met Napoleon III, and then on to visit the Sultan at Constantinople. There was every reason for the Tsar to be disquieted, because something detrimental to Russia's Eastern interests might very well emerge from the meetings.

The Tsar's dislike of Austria and strong leaning towards Prussia was expressed openly. On December 8th the centenary of the creation of the Order of St. George—the highest Russian distinction for bravery in the field—was celebrated in St. Petersburg, and King William was invested with the decoration. The anti-Prussian party at court and Prince Alexander tried through the Tsarina at the eleventh hour to prevent his investiture. But on Gortchakoff's advice it took place.

Although Prince Alexander was very angry he was obliged to accept the fact that his political influence upon the Tsar was on the wane. The reason for this was partly that the Tsarina no longer had her husband's ear exclusively.

The Tsarina's letters from the beginning of the year 1870 were full of remarks about anarchists and conspirators planning revolution, about people who "preach the most unbridled socialism and destruction by sword or poison of all who belong to what they consider to be the privileged classes", as she said in a letter to Prince Alexander on January 17th (29th). Thus on February 19th everyone was apprehensively waiting for an armed rising in Moscow, and was greatly relieved when everything remained quiet on that day.

Meanwhile in Darmstadt an event occurred in Prince Alexander's family that pleased them all very much. Marie, the Prince's eldest daughter, who had grown into a delightful girl, had fallen in love with Count Gustavus zu Erbach-Schönberg, and her parents put no difficulties in the way of their engagement. The Tsar and Tsarina promised to make a considerable addition to the girl's dowry. Towards the end of May the Tsar arrived in Ems to take the cure, accompanied, not by the Tsarina, but secretly by the Princess Dolgoruki, which fact he managed to conceal from his brother-in-law. The "quiet, pleasant life" there was spoilt for Prince Alexander

PRINCESS MARIE OF BATTENBERG
(LATER PRINCESS ERBACH-SCHÖNBERG)
1867

by a visit from the King of Prussia, who crashed in "like a careless stick into an ant-heap". This time he was unable to avoid a meeting with the monarch—whom he called the "Berlin usurper"—and Bismarck, although he still considered it "odious" to have anything to do with them. Despite his coldly aloof manner, King William embraced him several times, and took pains to treat the Prince with as much cordiality as possible. Alexander, however, was still unable to forget the past. At a large dinner party the Prince avoided speaking to Bismarck either before or during the meal. A vase of flowers fortunately separated them, although they sat opposite one another. Not until they were having coffee in the garden afterwards did he remark to Bismarck briefly that he had not seen him since the year 1860 at Warsaw.

No wonder that Bismarck, who was very sensitive to any lack of courtesy and who did not forget the attitude of the house of Hesse in 1866, took a deep dislike to Prince Alexander and all his family, though for the time being he was obliged to conceal it owing to their relationship with the Tsar.

Visitors at Ems, however, behaved quite differently. They not only ran after both the royalties, but also after Bismarck. And Prince Alexander was often vexed to see that almost more notice was taken of Bismarck than of his King.

Into the midst of these little troubles burst the news of the candidature of Prince Leopold of Hohenzollern for the Spanish throne. Hardly had it come than war was rumoured on all sides, and on July 15th, Prince Alexander's forty-seventh birthday, it was clearly unavoidable. At the same time the news arrived from every quarter that the whole of South Germany would stand by Prussia. "Napoleon could not have acted more clumsily", Prince Alexander wrote in his diary on July 16, 1870. "He will throw the rest of Germany altogether into the arms of Prussia." The official declaration of war by France which was presented in Berlin on July 19th caused a tremendous sensation in Darmstadt. Opinions were still conflicting, but most people, headed by Princess Alice, were now in favour of Prussia. Princess Alice was beaming with joy, was filled with enthusiasm, prophesied that the King of Prussia would be hailed as German Emperor after a victorious war, and had visions of her sister being the future Empress and the most powerful woman on the continent of Europe. Prince Alexander was determined not to take part in the campaign, but to remain neutral in his character as an

Austrian general. His sister in St. Petersburg was in a terrible state of alarm, fearing to see Darmstadt in French hands. "Where are you going to send your family", she inquired in a letter on July 8th (20th), "if the French occupy the country? Unhappy South Germany, that is always a victim to the ambition of others! The Tsar was greatly troubled at not being able to prevent this preposterous war, which has not even the excuse of German national interests. . . . The thought of our beloved and peaceful Heiligenberg makes the Tsar still more unhappy in picturing the troubles that are likely to fall upon poor Hesse. I certainly have no sympathy with the Prussians, but this time France has put itself absolutely in the wrong, and the defeat of either side will probably mean revolution. God grant that nothing may force us out of our neutrality, if only Austria will stay neutral too. Public sympathy here is with France, because everybody hates Prussia so much. And it would be even more decidedly so if France's attack in this case were not regarded as unjustifiable. As far as I am concerned, I am not in sympathy with either party, but I dread the arrogance of the victor, which ever it may happen to be, and I fear the outbreak of revolution as a result of defeat whether it be in France or Germany."

Almost every letter of the Tsar's or Tsarina's at this time expresses the fear of revolution. Whatever took place, it was probed first and foremost to see whether or not it would advance the cause of revolution; and the acts and resolutions of the court of St. Petersburg were very largely determined by this consideration.

Prince Alexander was about to answer his sister's letter on July 22nd when Major von Vivenot, of the Austrian imperial army, was announced. He had been sent on a secret mission by Beust to study the temper of South Germany regarding the war, and to find out from Prince Alexander whether the Tsar had promised help to the King of Prussia. In the course of the conversation he put forward as his own idea that if Prussia were to suffer a severe defeat Austria would be obliged to abandon its neutrality and to offer King William help in return for the fulfilment of certain conditions that were to be presented to him in the form of an ultimatum. In such a case the following demands would have to be made:

1. The restoration of the *status quo ante* 1866.
2. The repayment of the war indemnity levied on South Germany in 1866.

3. The exile of Bismarck from Germany.
4. The possible cession of Silesia.

Major von Vivenot envisaged the course of events thus: that
in this case Prussia would have to be given six hours to think
it over, and at the end of this time in event of a refusal Austria
would join France with half a million men. Prince Alexander
shook his head, and said he could only partly agree with
Vivenot's views. The Austrian, however, was of opinion that
in case of a Prussian victory the Austrian monarchy would
be lost, and sounded Prince Alexander as to his willingness
to undertake a mission to St. Petersburg to urge Russia to
preserve its neutrality and not to abandon it in favour of active
co-operation with Prussia. Prince Alexander, as he noted in
his diary on July 22nd, replied that he was always ready to
serve his commander-in-chief.

"The second act of the drama of 1866 is about to begin now,"
he wrote to the Tsarina on July 23rd, "when it was least
expected. And the valley of the Rhine is going to become a
battlefield again after fifty-six years. And what a battle! It
will be a battle of races, which will be carried on with the most
terrible grimness, and which I suppose can only end in the
complete subjugation of one or other of the two nations."—"If
King William is victorious", he continued prophetically,
"Prussia will emerge from the war as the *chief power in Europe*
[the italics are Prince Alexander's] and the new German
Empire will be firmly established; by trampling on the bodies
of those of the smaller dynasties which still exist, needless to
say. If Napoleon comes off best, Germany will lose the left
bank of the Rhine, and we shall return to the abominable
conditions that prevailed in the first years of this century."

The declaration of war had also come as a great surprise
to the Tsar. "We, the Tsar and I," wrote Alexander of Hesse,
"were far from having any suspicions during our peaceful
walks at Ems that from these same avenues a month later a
war would emanate that will very probably set the whole of
Europe ablaze."

Prince Alexander ascertained that there was an enthusiasm
equal to that of 1813 throughout Germany and absolute confidence. He himself, however, remained sceptical: "All that
I can do for Prussia is not to wish it to be punished for its
trespasses. I do not like its overlordship—but I should loathe
that of France. . . ." Despite his great hatred of Prussia,

Prince Alexander did in this grave hour become conscious of his German nationality, and it did not need the Prussian victories to make his patriotic feelings triumph over all the bitterness and dislike of former days. Therein was Bismarck's genius manifested—that he was able, by means of war against the traditional enemy from which no German could or would be excluded, to bend even the most stubborn to his will.

Prince Alexander remained a detached but interested observer. A load fell from his heart when the German armies by their first victories carried the war into the enemy's country, and thus preserved Germany and hence also Hesse from a French invasion. He was immensely surprised at the first reports, which showed up the "hyper-prepared" (*archiprêt*) French army in quite a new light, and found it hard to believe that Napoleon could have let himself in for such a war in so unready a state.

The rapidity and greatness of the German successes took Russia by surprise. The Tsarina referred in her letters to her husband's official policy of neutralizing Austria by letting it be understood that if that country were to take part in the war it would have to reckon with Russia. The Russians were anxious to preserve their neutrality, although the enormous increase of power in Prussia was not observed without anxiety. This, however, had only been made possible by the Tsar's having given Prussia what was practically a guarantee to keep Austria quiet, so that King William and Bismarck could enter upon the war with no anxieties about the east or south-east. The Tsar also acted in this sense. On July 11th (23rd) the Austrian Ambassador, Count Chotek, wrote to Beust from St. Petersburg,[129] reporting that the Tsar had said to him: "I wish to keep out of this war entirely; I wish to keep a strict and unarmed neutrality, and shall preserve it so long as none of Russia's direct interests are involved. I should consider the Polish question to be such an interest, and I do not intend to discuss it. The moment Austria adopts an armed and threatening attitude Poland will rise and in consequence I shall be obliged against my will to change my attitude to one of armed neutrality, and to direct my military dispositions against the Austrian frontier. This might lead to a most dangerous and awkward state of affairs. I hope you will convey my urgent request to your Emperor to adopt the same attitude as my own. I warn you against the provocations of the French, who will try to drag you into the war too." It was true, he reported the Tsar to have said further, that Austria still felt a certain rancour against Prussia, even if it was not actually cherishing hopes of revenge. But in the Tsar's opinion it would not be good policy on Austria's part to allow itself to be guided by revengeful feelings. When Francis Joseph sent an evasive answer, and said that he thought in view of the rising danger it was necessary for both empires to make military preparations, the Tsar, as the ambassador reported to Beust on July 28th (August 9th),[130] replied impatiently: "But what danger? If you mobilize or concentrate troops I must do the same. We shall let ourselves in for an exchange of recriminations, and then a chance spark may lead to our relations being seriously disturbed." These were very frank threats to Austria, and they contributed not a little to its decision to wait and see what happened in France before making up its own mind.

The French defeats which now followed soon subdued Austria's military ardour.

When on September 1st the capitulation of Sedan crowned the fabulous successes of the German army within the first month of the war, there was no longer any question of Austrian intervention.

A little while later, on September 14th, Prince Alexander, as he reports in his diary on that date, accepted an invitation from the Crown Princess of Prussia to go to Homburg with his wife and two children. Victoria was, of course, pleased at the great German successes, but she felt extraordinarily sorry for the victims, and was of the opinion that her husband, in spite of the victories, was not much enjoying the war. Otherwise, however, Germany was filled with pride and pleasure in the triumphs which caused the expression, in the Press and in other public manifestations, of the most venturesome hopes, so much so that the other States, including Russia, began to feel a little anxious.

"It appears to me", wrote the Tsarina to her brother on September 3rd (15th), "that in principle the whole of Germany, or at any rate very nearly the whole of it, wants Alsace and Lorraine; but each individual State feels that such an annexation is a very rash undertaking. We know from our experience with Poland what it means when a province is only held by force. I assume that even Bismarck is a little puzzled as to what the solution is to be. I am not particularly interested in the battlefield of Paris, but its bombardment will certainly not increase the repute of German arms. . . . They must be *in extremis* in Paris, for they are knocking at every door, and especially at ours, in the hope of obtaining an official armistice. The Tsar did not want to take the initiative, in order not to risk a rebuff, but Reuss [Henry VII, Prince of Reuss, then Prussian Ambassador in St. Petersburg] was instructed to communicate the application to Bismarck. Actually, Prussia does not dare to put us on a par with the other neutrals whose attitude has at times been doubtful, while ours has contributed powerfully to the successes of the German army."

The atmosphere between Austria and Russia had not been in any way cleared by the war. On the contrary, the Tsar's threatening attitude had mortified Francis Joseph. "Fate appears to be dead against any friendship between Russia and Austria", said Prince Alexander very truly in a letter to the Tsarina written from Heiligenberg on September 20th. "It seems impossible to resolve the discord created by Buol. It would have been a hundred times better if it had come to open war between the two countries in 1854. The fire has gone on smouldering under the ashes ever since that unhappy time."

Now that every day was bringing fresh successes to the German arms in France, Prince Alexander regretted not having taken an active part in the war. What annoyed him most were the "princely amateurs" at the royal headquarters, who were known in the German army as the "Princely Reservoirists" because they lived in the Hôtel des Reservoirs at Versailles, and had all been given the Iron Cross though they had done nothing. Among those who received the decoration was the Duke of Coburg, which angered Prince Alexander particularly. The Tsarina was of the same opinion: "I agree with you", she wrote on January 8 (20), 1871, "that the position of the princes at Versailles, especially of the reigning ones, is lamentable. Have you heard about the answer Bismarck gave to the Duke of Coburg when he complained that so many Iron Crosses had been distributed? 'Yes, but they must be put into two very different categories. The first, consisting of those who have earned them, and the second, of those who have got them on account of their position. You and I both belong to the second category.' Very true, and probably not the rudest answer that princes have had to endure from him."

Prince Alexander was particularly interested in the Tsarina's attitude to the problem of Alsace-Lorraine. He did not altogether agree with her. "That *revenge for Sedan* will altogether take the place of *revenge for Waterlao*", he wrote on September 30, 1870, "is certain. It is therefore essential to make France's next war of aggression—and remember that in a hundred years it has crossed the Rhine twenty-five times—impossible for many years to come. You know that I am no lover of annexations . . . but I believe that Metz and Strassbourg *must* become German again if the result of the heroic efforts to which Germany has been forced by Napoleon III is really to be a guarantee of peace for any length of time."

As a consequence of the French defeats, Belgium was also indulging in some sharp criticism of France and the French. Prince Alexander went over to Brussels in these days, and fell into conversation with an inhabitant of Malines. "They are past all belief, these Frenchmen," was this man's opinion as reported by Prince Alexander to his sister in a letter begun on September 18th (30th), and finished on October 7, 1870, "with their claim to having quite a special kind of national honour, which they will not admit for other nations. They thought it quite natural that as a result of unsuccessful wars—for which they were not even responsible—Denmark in 1864 and Austria in 1859 and 1866 should be obliged to cede parts of their territory. They themselves accepted Nice and Savoy. But to hear them you would say they were *dishonoured* when a similar demand is made of France—which, after all, began this unjust war with the intention of taking possession of German territory along the left bank of the Rhine!" Prince Alexander agreed with every word of this Belgian criticism. But after he had heard it he made no mention of his favourite idea of uniting France and Belgium, and of making the King of the Belgians ruler of both countries in place of the Napoleonic dynasty.

Meanwhile the Germans went from victory to victory. Strassbourg fell, and on October 29th Bazaine capitulated in Metz with something like a hundred and eighty thousand men. Russia now felt it to be unbearable that the restrictions should still be in force that had been imposed in Paris after the Crimean War by this Emperor Napoleon, who had now been so utterly overthrown. On October 31st Russia gave notice that it repudiated those clauses of the Treaty of Paris which curtailed Russian naval power in the Black Sea. The greatest sensation was caused by this news in England and in Austria, which was very much disappointed in the outcome of the Franco-German War. For the first time Andrássy showed the hostility to Russia which had animated him and his country since the Russian intervention at the time of the revolution in 1849. As "interpreter" of the Hungarian nation, he caused Beust to make counter-representations in St. Petersburg. Since, however, as things were, there could be no thought of war against Russia, it was easy for Gortchakoff to return a chilly answer. Prince Alexander, who regarded the manner of this procedure as showing too great a contempt for the other Powers, and especially his beloved Austria, was shocked at Gortchakoff's attitude, and expressed himself very frankly on the subject to his sister. He could not approve of the form of the Russian circular note to the Powers, "for", as he said, "what should we come to if the principle were recognized that anyone who signed a treaty had the right to regard his signature as non-existent if it seemed to him a favourable time to repudiate it?" This was all very well in theory; but since treaties are sometimes imposed forcibly against all justice they are bound to collapse when force can no longer be applied.

Meanwhile, after negotiation with the South German States the foundation had been laid for the constitution of the new Germany and of the empire that was to be proclaimed at Versailles.

"How will Germany develop in its new form?" wrote the Tsarina to her brother on December 5th (17th). "How long will it be before the next revolution? Since 1866 anything is possible! You foretold the Empire when war broke out, but there is too much blood on this imperial crown for it to be enviable, in my opinion. . . . And with all this the war is going on, resistance is growing more stubborn; it may go on until the spring without there being any end to all the wretchedness and misery."

To his censure of the manner of the Russian repudiation of the Paris Treaty the Tsarina replied so spiritedly that it is clear how completely she had become Russian, how, despite his divagations, she shared the opinions of her husband and identified herself with his actions. "I must admit", she wrote, "that I have no scruples regarding the form adopted by us to free ourselves from a clause which was totally incompatible with the dignity and safety of the Empire. Experience has proved that we should never have persuaded Europe to it by kindness, especially England. Every time we have brought the conversation round to this subject we have found only ill-will. We only want one thing, and that is peace. . . . Was it not much more worthy of a great nation to declare frankly that it repudiated a humiliating clause, especially since the Treaty

had been infringed on all sides? Beust, by the way, was unpleasantly surprised, like everyone else, including Bismarck; but
not openly hostile, like Andrássy, who is fulminating against us."

Meanwhile the war continued in France. During the last
days of December the siege of Paris was raised, and on
January 19th a great sortie was repulsed by the Germans.
On the previous day, January 18th, the empire had been
solemnly proclaimed at Versailles. The capitulation of Paris,
the armistice, and the preliminary Peace of Versailles of
February 26, 1871, followed. And on March 7th the German
headquarters removed from Versailles, where they had spent
five months.

Prince Alexander drew the obvious conclusions from the great
events in which he had taken a spectator's part. From the
beginning of the war he had subordinated his hatred of Prussia
to his German patriotism, and could not therefore be accused
of being an opportunist who, after the incredibly brilliant
victories of the Prussians, had gone over to the camp of the
Prussian dynasty, which now occupied a position towering
so far above that of any other in Germany. Once again he set
forth his creed in a letter to his sister written from Darmstadt
on March 12th:

"The war which has now, thank God, come to an end has
meant terrible sacrifices. The results are so astonishingly brilliant, so colossal, that I suppose history can hardly produce
a parallel. But they have certainly been bought too dearly.
The Prussian General Staff was not sufficiently careful of
human life—on that point there is only *one* opinion among all
those who have come back from France. The conditions of
the peace are very hard, but the great majority of Germans
approves and demands them. . . . The only opposition in
Germany to the claim for the restoration of Alsace comes
from the red Republicans, and the very small group of irreconcilable reactionaries, whose motto is 'rather no unified
and powerful Germany than an empire under the King of
Prussia'. You know that for my part I should also have
preferred some other dynasty, and I flatter myself that you
as well as I (and many millions of Germans) feel that 1870
does not altogether give absolution for 1866. But one cannot
strive against the inevitable, and so I freely accept the new
empire, despite its doubtful origin. But I take off my hat above
all to the wonderful German army, to this million heroes, who
sprang from the ground at the call of their sovereign. I bow

before the genius of the Prussian General Staff, which prepared, planned, and guided the whole affair to a successful conclusion, supported by the amazing bravery and loyalty of the troops. I am speechless before the miracles achieved by the other genius [Bismarck], and that a civilian genius, who shuffled the cards in so masterly a manner, who has so resolutely managed since 1859 to force luck to go the way he wished; who has succeeded in deceiving the most cunning ruler of modern times [Napoleon], and who has used him to complete and to crown the work begun by the deception of 1866. But I do not bow before him! What we have just been watching proves that Prussia was fully equipped for the task which it had set itself. But it must be admitted that the means it employed to eliminate its rival [Austria] were in the highest degree contemptible. But now it has been proved that it is worthy in matters political, and more particularly in matters military, to set itself at the head of a great nation that has hitherto not been conscious of its power but is now awakening from its torpor. God grant that this new empire may really be what Napoleon III said—amid universal derision—of his own, *an empire of peace*. But unfortunately it is certain that we shall have an empire that is armed to the teeth and that will be very expensive to maintain."

On this occasion, when the Emperor William, returning from France, came through Frankfurt, Prince Alexander really did attend his reception. "For", said he in his diary on March 14th, "he is, after all, our Sovereign, and I must accept him if I do not wish to become a political exile."

Once again the King received the Tsarina's brother very cordially, and thus the way was gradually made clear for a reconciliation with the Prussian court. Only Bismarck, that good hater, did not forget, and Prince Alexander's family continued to have in him a powerful enemy.

After the dismissal of the Hessian Minister Dalwigk, upon which Bismarck had insisted, Berlin went still further. The Crown Princess Victoria sent for the Hessian Lord Chamberlain, von Capellen, as Alexander of Hesse told the Tsarina in a letter written on April 4th, and informed him that she had ascertained that the Grand Duke had aged very much (he was ten years younger than the Emperor William, and was in his sixty-fifth year), and suggested that Capellen should urgently advise him to adopt his nephew (Louis)—that is to say, Princess Alice's husband—as co-regent. The affair came to Prince Alexander's ears and made him not a little indignant. "These English princesses are impatient", he thought, "and cannot wait their turn to come to power."

All these troubles and experiences were thrust aside at about this time by a happy family reunion. Prince Alexander's only daughter, the Princess Marie, was married to Count Erbach-Schönberg, with whom she had been in love for a long time, and whom, as she herself said, she followed to the altar "delirious with joy". The Tsar and Tsarina behaved in a truly imperial manner; the Tsar gave her a dowry of fifty thousand roubles (nearly £8,000) and a splendid brooch of pearls and diamonds. The Tsarina presented her with a diamond ornament, some magnificent silver, her wedding dress, and some valuable lace.

Since his political views diverged so largely from those of his brother-in-law, and since his affections were fixed on another than the Prince's sister, the Tsar had during the past years written remarkably few letters. On this occasion he sent a cordial letter full of affection for Prince Alexander and his family, but containing not a word upon political matters. The only thing that could be gathered from it was that the Tsarina was not very well again, and that she was planning to go to Ems for the cure. When she came through Berlin on her way thither towards the middle of May, Bismarck took the opportunity to draw the Tsarina's attention to his moderation. He informed her that at Nikolsburg in 1866 King William of Prussia had been determined to annex Bohemia and Bavaria.[131] He said that the King had deposited a document (which has never been discovered) in the Prussian State archives, in which he declared and confirmed by his signature that he had resigned any claim to Bohemia and Bavaria only on account of the opposition of the Crown Prince and Bismarck. Prince Alexander notes this in his diary on June 5, 1871, with three marks of exclamation.

A little while later the Tsar also came to Germany, and Prince Alexander was now asked from quite a new source to act his usual part of intermediary. Queen Victoria planned to marry her son, Alfred, Duke of Edinburgh, to the daughter of the Tsar. Alfred turned to Prince Alexander and asked him to arrange a private meeting for him with the Tsar. Alexander II, however, was not particularly inclined to look favourably upon the suggestion. The political relations between England and Russia were not of the best. All over the East,

P

England was in Russia's way. Britain had, though only as a matter of principle, protested against the repudiation of the Black Sea clause, and there were plenty of sources of friction along the northern frontiers of India and in Afghanistan. Nevertheless the Tsar did not wish to give an abrupt refusal to a direct proposal, and said that everything depended upon his daughter, and the Prince might try to gain her favour; but he could make no promises as yet.

A trenchant change was at that time taking place in Austria's foreign policy. The Prussian victories had baulked Beust's plans, and had also cost him the confidence of the Emperor Francis Joseph, who now put in his place Andrássy, the man who had definitely voted for neutrality in 1870 and 1871 in opposition to Beust. Although the beginning of Andrássy's tenure of office coincided with an apparent *rapprochement* between Austria and the other two empires, which actually led to a sort of Three Emperors Entente in 1872, and to a very highly stipulative Three Emperors Agreement in 1873,[132] these were due rather to Bismarck's work of mediation and reconciliation than to Andrássy's having subdued his hatred of Russia. The power or otherwise of forgetting is as important in political as in private life. Three great statesmen of the time expressed themselves upon this point on the same page of an autograph album belonging to a Count Enzenberg.

"My long life", wrote on March 23, 1870, Guillaume Guizot, the French statesman and historian, whose policy as Prime Minister under Louis Philippe led to the February Revolution of 1848, "has taught me two pieces of wisdom which I have often had occasion to apply—the one is to forgive much, the other is never to forget." Only a fortnight later Thiers wrote underneath: "A little forgetting does not impair the sincerity of the forgiveness." On November 17, 1871, according to an entry in Prince Alexander's diary on November 25th of the same year, Bismarck added the words: "My life has taught me that I have much to forget, but that there is much, too, that others have to forgive me."

The appointment of Andrássy was not looked upon very favourably in Russia owing to his attitude regarding the repudiation of the Paris Treaty. However, it was decided to wait and see what his further demeanour proved to be before condemning him altogether. Domestic cares were at that time occupying the Tsar very seriously. Despite all the outward respect he showed his wife, he fell deeper and deeper in love with Katherine Dolgoruki. He could not tear himself away from her, and took her with him wherever he went. She accompanied him to Tsarskoe Selo, to Peterhof, even to Livadia, the estate in the Crimea, quite regardless of whether the Tsarina happened also to be staying in these palaces. With lacerated feelings, but giving no outward sign, the Tsarina observed his actions while feigning to notice nothing. The Tsar married Katherine's elder sister to his aide-de-camp, Prince Meshchersky, which made it easy to explain that the Princess was staying in the imperial palaces "with her sister".

On May 11, 1872, an event occurred that linked the two lovers even more closely. Katherine became the mother of a son at the Winter Palace, the first child of their love. The Tsarina now realized that this time the Tsar's affection was no mere passing whim, as had always been the case hitherto; but she buried her grief within her own heart. She said no word of the affair to her brother in the letters that were otherwise so intimate, but her repressed sorrow, which is so particularly injurious to tubercular patients, brought about a serious change for the worse in her condition. The Tsar therefore asked Prince Alexander to come to stay with his sister in the Crimea.

The Tsarina was more than usually delighted at her brother's visit, and for the first time they spoke openly to one another of the Tsar's love for Princess Dolgoruki, and of how she had completely ousted a Countess Albedinsky who had previously been the favourite. A lady-in-waiting named Maltzoff, who was jealous of the Princess, kept the Tsarina and her brother very precisely informed. From all he heard, the Prince realized that any intervention would be utterly useless, and that reproaches would only earn him the Tsar's enmity.

The English marriage project now came up for discussion. The Russian Ambassador in London announced that the Queen wished for a speedy decision. Since the Tsarina alleged that not only the Tsar but also her daughter did not care for the idea, and since the Grand Duchess did not contradict this, it was at first decided that the Tsarina should give the suitor a definite refusal. Prince Alexander, however, sought to save the situation, and advised his sister to leave a back door open in case of any change. The Tsarina's answer to Prince Alfred nevertheless sounded very discouraging, and as Prince Alexander noted in his diary on July 10, 1872, ended with the words: "Although the future may not unite us as closely as we hoped at one time, I beg you never to doubt my cordial interest in your welfare."

Through diplomatic channels, however, an answer was sent in accordance with Prince Alexander's suggestion. The Queen was to be told that they did not wish to reject the offer entirely in St. Petersburg, but that a reunion in Italy was pleasurably anticipated.

Prince Alexander went back to Darmstadt after an eight weeks' visit. The Tsarina was really unhappy at his going. She missed him at every turn, and could not bear to see his empty rooms. . . . The more she felt that her husband was slipping away from her the more devotedly she clung to her brother.

Hardly had he returned home before he came in for a storm. This occurred over a sharp letter from Princess Alice's mother, the Queen, who was very indignant at the "quasi-dismissal of Alfred by the Russians", and who blamed Alice as the originator of the idea.

Meanwhile the young Erbach-Schönbergs spent the first year of their married life in the greatest happiness. To their great joy, though it was touch and go for the mother, a fine healthy boy—the present Prince Alexander zu Erbach-Schönberg—was born to them in October 1872. He was called Alexander after his grandfather, and the Empress Marie of Russia was his godmother. At the same time Prince Alexander heard from his sister that her daughter was still considering the English marriage. She had meanwhile reviewed the remaining suitors carefully, and had decided that after all life in England was infinitely preferable to that at a small German court, and moreover that Prince Alfred promised to make in every way an excellent husband. She persuaded her mother to try to reopen negotiations through her brother, though the Tsarina expressed certain scruples owing to the Anglo-Russian antagonism in Asia. Russia had since 1861 been continually advancing towards Central Asia, and was moving its southern frontier ever nearer to Afghanistan and the gates of India. "All this might have some influence upon a project of marriage", she said to Alexander. "What do you think about it? I should add that the Tsar is still *against* Alfred as a *match*. . . . On the other hand, Marie inclines much more to him—and especially his position—than to Stuttgart, Strelitz, or Schwerin; but if you could find me a *charming Prince* who would be prepared to stay in Russia, I should prefer him to any of them."

Prince Alexander answered his sister on December 29, 1872,

that according to what Princess Alice said, Prince Alfred was certainly still free, that he would be quite glad if the occasion presented itself to live in Russia for some length of time, but that the situation was a little awkward because the Crown Princess Victoria had written and told her mother that the Tsar had expressed himself in a derogatory manner about Prince Alfred in Berlin. In consequence the Queen was very angry, and was doing her utmost to find a wife for her son elsewhere. Hence Alfred was in a very difficult position, and must try first and foremost to bring the Queen round to the idea again. The Grand Duchess Marie now importuned her mother to be more friendly towards England, since a Württemberg prince whom her Aunt Olga had introduced did not please her at all. In the spring of 1873, therefore, the Tsarina went to Sorrento as she had planned, after a somewhat stormy discussion with her husband regarding the projected marriage. In the end, however, as the Tsarina wrote and told Prince Alexander from Sorrento on March 20 (April 1), 1873, the Tsar gave way to please his daughter, though not very willingly. "There is so little choice", said the Tsarina. "She didn't like the Prince of Württemberg, and the poor child is frightened about Strelitz because the Prince in question said himself that it was a 'dull little hole'."

In May Prince Alexander followed his sister to Sorrento. She and her brother were given permission to dig up something with their own hands at Pompeii, where at that time excavation had been begun. They were taken to a partially excavated house, and both set to work to open out a room. Since, however, they naturally did not proceed in a very skilful manner, a fine couch with ivory carvings that they found crumbled away as soon as it was exposed to the air. The Tsarina was not offered any keepsake, but she got a sub-prefect to "steal" a little piece of porphyry from a mosaic floor for her. The Grand Duchess Marie meanwhile poured out her heart to her uncle at Sorrento, and confided to him her fear that her parents might still prevent the English marriage. She begged him to be her advocate in the matter, and Alexander promised to do all that lay in his power to promote her desire.

On their way back the Tsarina met her husband at Ems and Heiligenberg, and it was decided to send the Tsarevitch to England to discuss the marriage project with the Prince of Wales. Matters now moved rapidly, and a telegram was sent to Prince Alfred inviting him to Jugenheim.

On July 11, 1873, he arrived by arrangement to lunch with Prince Alexander, where he met the Grand Duchess Marie, who received him with great embarrassment. Since her cousin, Marie Erbach, was also present with her youngest child, the Grand Duchess tried to mask her confusion by playing with the baby. This, however, rather failed of its effect, as the baby had not yet learnt drawing-room manners. Soon, however, difficulties were resolved and the betrothal took place. Nevertheless everything was not quite settled even now. The Tsar was still not altogether pleased about the engagement, and when on July 17th a letter written by Queen Victoria's orders requested that the Tsar should come to England to present his daughter, he exclaimed indignantly, "Silly old fool!" And regarded the demand as so impossible that it was not even worth discussing. Prince Alfred was in a very difficult position. In order to soften down her husband's refusal the Tsarina suggested a meeting with the Queen at Cologne, which she in her turn refused. In fact the Queen ordered her son to take over the command of a frigate immediately. These dissensions were not of very long duration. When Prince Alfred got home he was able to pacify his mother. The Queen, though very unwillingly, waived the matter of the Tsar's visit for the time being. But she returned to the subject of the visit, if only by implication, in a cordial letter that was really maternal where the Grand Duchess was concerned. The young fiancée, all her doubts resolved, wrote a happy letter to her aunt, Prince Alexander's wife, as Prince Alexander wrote and told his sister on November 8, 1873: "I know that you will be glad to know how much I love Alfred, and how happy I am to belong to him. I feel that my love for him is growing daily; I have a feeling of peace and of inexpressible happiness, and a boundless impatience to be altogether his own."

Thereby an affair was brought to a happy conclusion, the failure of which might very well have increased the state of political tension already existing between Russia and England.

Prince Alexander went to St. Petersburg for the wedding, which had been fixed for January 23, 1874. For the entertainment of the princely guests, bear, elk, and wolf hunts were arranged. Prince Alexander shot a bear, but the Tsar asked him if he would mind its being reckoned in the Crown Prince's bag! At a wolf hunt twelve wolves were killed, but Prince Alexander discovered that every one of them had been caught and brought to the hunt from long distances in boxes.

"ALFRED AND MARIE"
July 1873

The Grand Duchess Marie's wedding was celebrated with the greatest magnificence. The bride was given a truly imperial dowry: a million roubles by the State, a million roubles by the Tsar, and six hundred thousand of his savings as well as a pension for life of twenty-five thousand roubles, all of which gave her an annual income of something over thirty-two thousand pounds sterling.

In pursuance of the apparent *rapprochement* between Russia and Austria that was observed during the first years of Count Andrássy's tenure of office—though not he but Bismarck and the Archduke Albrecht were the real promoters of the understanding—a visit of the Emperor Francis Joseph to St. Petersburg was arranged in February 1874. Officially and externally everything was done to prepare a brilliant reception for the Emperor. But within the Russian imperial family the dislike to Francis Joseph persisted. Alexander II was only bowing to the exigencies of policy. His sister Mary declared bluntly: "I shall be polite to the man, but no more." "Unfortunately", remarked Prince Alexander, "the Tsarina is of the same mind, but she expresses herself more cautiously." When the Emperor arrived at the Gatshina Station and greeted the Tsar, he was very much embarrassed. His constraint was not dissipated until the two monarchs were reviewing the guard of honour of the Empress Curassiers. The Emperor Francis Joseph was then also "served" with a bear, but being the splendid shot that he was he really did kill it himself with a single bullet.

The general results of the meeting in St. Petersburg were not nearly as satisfactory as Andrássy's biographer, Wertheimer, has tried to make them appear for Andrássy's benefit. However, St. Petersburg was also anxious for peace. Despite the Grand Duchess Marie's marriage the political antagonism to England persisted, and the sympathies of the Tsar and Tsarina for this country and its ruler had not yet been to any marked degree increased by the new link. Every one of the Tsarina's letters shows the derision with which she regarded English conditions, the court, and the personality of the Queen. She smiled over Prince Bariatinsky, who came back from a short visit to England full of enthusiasm, and explained it by saying that of course he had fallen in love with Lady Dudley, whose beauty had also delighted the Emperor of Austria, and Lady Granville. She much preferred the report of the lady-in-waiting, Marie Wiasemska:

"She, being much more matter of fact," wrote the Tsarina to

her brother on March 26 (April 7), 1874, "quite won the Queen's heart, who confided all sorts of things to her. It is amusing to hear her talk of the etiquette at Windsor, the Queen's fears, the secrecy with which everything is done. She almost died of the tedium there. The English were quite astonished when they heard Marie and Bariatinsky at their first small dinner party talking to their neighbours right and left in their normal voices. They could not understand their not being nervous, for they are oppressed by this feeling the whole time. Marie has discovered that the Queen drinks whisky, sometimes with water but generally without; and that she is afraid of Brown, who treats her like a small child and seems to regard her with a sort of condescension. Once when Marie was given some of this whisky to taste, she made such a face that she is never offered anything but water now. This impudent daughter-in-law avers that her mother-in-law is bored; and as she says anything that happens to come into her head, she makes the Queen laugh and is in high favour. To be quite frank, it is difficult to take such a mother-in-law seriously, and I am sorry on Marie's account. Nevertheless, she impressed our people as being kind-hearted and having delicacy of feeling, and they were touched by it. Between you and me, Marie thinks London hideous, the air there appalling, the English food abominable, the late hours very tiring, the visits to Windsor and Osborne boring beyond belief, but the English themselves less dull than she had expected. It must be added, of course, that the people with whom she has come in contact are some of the most distinguished." Prince Alexander was much interested in all this, since he was now personally concerned in England owing to his son's being a naturalized Englishman, and having just passed his examinations into the navy very well. The Prince's other sons were meanwhile also growing up. Alexander, the second boy, called Sandro, was seventeen, Henry, nicknamed Liko, nearly sixteen. They were fine, well set up lads, and promised to make smart, handsome officers. The same was to be said of the eldest, the young English naval officer, Louis, whom the Tsar had just met on his recent visit to London and had found greatly improved, as he said in a telegram to Prince Alexander, who copied it into his diary on May 24, 1874.

On leaving England the Tsar went back again to Ems for the waters. Alexander joined him there and heard of an unfortunate episode that had occurred in the imperial household. One day some articles of value were found to be missing from the Tsarina's rooms. There appeared to be no question of suspicion falling on any of the servants, and the whole affair was most mysterious. Another time some magnificent diamonds disappeared from the Grand Duchess Constantine's room. She turned to the police and agreed to a fortnight's unobtrusive watch being kept on her household. In the course of this a police officer caught the son of the Grand Duchess opening her jewel case with a pass-key of which his mother knew nothing. The discovery was a terrible shock to the boy's mother, who at first wanted to keep everything dark. But a report had already been sent to the Tsar, and he was determined to have the young man, whom he believed to be a kleptomaniac, declared insane.

In the course of the month of June a family reunion took place on the estate of Heiligenberg that was in the nature of a monarchical congress.

A request reached Prince Alexander from Austria to arrange for a visit of the Archduke Albrecht to Tsarskoe Selo.

The Archduke represented the party that wished for friendship with Russia, and was in this respect more far-seeing than Count Andrássy, the Foreign Minister.[133] The Archduke was in his inmost heart in favour even of taking part in a war if Russia wished to fight Turkey. Andrássy, however, regarded the Archduke's procedure as an interference in his own sphere, and as early as August 1872 had gone direct to the Emperor Francis Joseph to ascertain whether he shared his views or those of the Archduke. At that time the Emperor, with his well-known attitude to Russia—which unfortunately was hardly ever one of really sincere co-operation—decided in favour of his Minister. Now, in 1874, the Emperor did indeed send the Archduke to St. Petersburg, but he had no intention of deviating from Andrássy's general policy. Hence the visit was without effect.

The Archduke gave Prince Alexander a most enthusiastic account of his visit to St. Petersburg, and told him he had found it a great wrench to say good-bye to the Tsar and Tsarina. Undoubtedly the Archduke Albrecht's feelings were much warmer than those of the Emperor Francis Joseph, who never unbent to anyone.

The year 1875 saw a general political uneasiness all over Europe. Rumours of war were unceasingly in the air, for after his performances in 1866 and 1871 Bismarck was suspected of harbouring further bellicose designs. In England it was feared that Bismarck might be planning to annex Holland and Belgium; in France a preventive war was apprehended, which would have occasioned misgivings in Russia too, where Prussian aggrandizement was looked upon with some anxiety. In Germany, where Bismarck was in reality only concerned with the peaceful preservation of what had already been won, it was feared that the French might seek revenge for 1870-71.

"War in sight" was everywhere the cry, and Gortchakoff and the Tsar, who arrived in Berlin on May 10th, issued a circular letter from there claiming the credit for maintaining peace, greatly to Bismarck's wrath.[134] The Tsar thought that Bismarck was very reminiscent of Napoleon III at the height of his fame, and that his moods were equally dangerous. As Prince Alexander recorded in his diary, the Tsar felt that the Emperor William was in a very difficult position as regards his indispensable Chancellor.

Thus in Russia as in England Bismarck was not beloved. Everyone regarded him as the man who had caused the wars of 1866 and 1870, and therefore readily believed him capable of desiring another war. The English royal family was particularly antagonistic to him, because he was always opposed to the Queen's daughter, the Crown Princess. She wrote to her mother on June 5, 1875, giving passionate expression to her views, and saying that while Bismarck's prestige was immense and his power unlimited, he was a person whose ideas were purely medieval. "To me", she adds, "this state is simply *intolerable*, and seems *very dangerous*."[135]

The Crown Prince and the Emperor tried vainly in their letters to the Queen to speak reassuringly and extenuatingly of misunderstandings, and of things said by the Chancellor and his diplomatists that were not intended to be taken altogether seriously. The Queen listened more readily to her daughter and her statesmen who had no love for Bismarck either.

These were the views and tempers prevailing in the great capitals. All over Europe rulers and Ministers regarded one another distrustfully. Nervousness and the fear of future critical developments reigned in the courts and Cabinets of the Great Powers. And this tense situation was in the coming years to be further burdened with the fresh complications that were arising in Eastern and South-Eastern Europe.

CHAPTER X

"THE SICK MAN" OF EUROPE AGAIN

THE agreements made during the past years between the three emperors had not the force of a real alliance. Russia had entered upon them in the hope of thereby gaining a free hand in the East, which should at least enable her to regain the prestige and the territory she had lost in the Balkans through the Crimean War. The Tsar and his chief adviser, Gortchakoff, had constantly had this idea before them since the Peace of Paris. Bismarck had sided with them in order to give himself guarantees against French plans of retaliation, Austria with a view to making good the territory and influence lost in the west by gains in the south-east—an intention which, as was clearly recognized, could only be carried through with the assistance of Russia and not in opposition to it. Thus the Three Emperors Pact was entered upon for purely egoistical reasons by all three States. And the Russian and Austrian spheres of interest lay so close to one another that friction might very easily arise. England stood aside and watched developments in the East with a mistrustful eye.

The Russian hopes of taking revenge for the Crimean War were encouraged by the disorganized condition of Turkey, where economic and political mismanagement was permitted by a degenerate and extravagant Sultan. Among other abuses the Mohammedan landowners oppressed the Christian population of the provinces most barbarously. In the summer of 1875 this led to popular risings in Bosnia and Herzegovina, which gave the Great Powers, and Russia in particular, the not altogether unwelcome pretext of intervening and demanding reforms.

Such a demand had just been dispatched to Turkey in January 1876 when Prince Alexander arrived at the imperial court in St. Petersburg to visit his sister. At the Russian court he was able to see the tension which prevailed between the two opposing parties—the Pan-Slav and the Conservative—regarding Eastern affairs. Otherwise, however, court life pursued its accustomed way. Magnificent balls alternated with bear and elk hunts, and everything revolved about the weal or woe of the individual members of the imperial family. Alfred of Edinburgh and his wife arrived in St. Petersburg early in March. His visit took place for the sake of dispersing certain misunderstandings between the imperial family and their British son-in-law. When the Tsar visited England in 1874 in his yacht, convoyed by Russian battleships, there had been some difficulty about his landing on May 13, 1874, the day of his arrival at Dover. Rumours were circulated of bad seamanship on the part of Russian naval officers.[136] This gossip was repeated to the Tsarina, and it was indicated that her son-in-law had not been altogether innocent in the matter. "Alfred," she wrote to Prince Alexander on October 27, 1875, "has been spreading such insulting rumours about our navy . . . that I am feeling really indignant. There was of course a storm, but Popoff and Tonovareff tell me that it is nonsense to say that there was any danger or that they took the wrong course. The mistake was on the part of the English pilot. They had better say no more, after the [one word illegible] actually ran down a yacht." This was an allusion to the dramatic description in Queen Victoria's diary on August 18, 1875, of a collision between the royal yacht *Victoria and Albert* and a yacht *Mistletoe*, which was sunk in the encounter.

Since the Grand Duchess Marie, Prince Alfred's wife, was expecting a baby, which her husband wished should be born in his own country, she went back to England sooner than she had intended, to the great disappointment of her mother. "The parting", wrote the Tsarina, who was still steeped in the animosity against England that prevailed at the Russian court, "was terrible. Marie felt it nearly as much as she did the first time, and she had great difficulty in growing accustomed to England again, with its dreary, monotonous life and its sleepy climate. She hated the English as soon as she got on to the steamer." The dislike to England and the Queen was shown at every opportunity. When in the spring of 1876 Queen Victoria was preparing to assume the title of Empress of India, it gave rise to a good deal of mockery even in her own country. The Tsarina could not refrain from having her say too. "Shuvaloff", she wrote to Prince Alexander on March 30th, "thinks that this discussion about her title has given the Queen's prestige a blow from which it will not recover. So much the worse for the monarchical principle.

I addressed a letter to her in fear and trembling to-day without putting her new title. But I have not (yet) been officially authorized to do so, though I'm sure she would not have objected to it!"

Meanwhile Queen Victoria's affection for the princely house of Hesse increased. Being intimately allied with it by the marriage of her daughter Alice, she had had the opportunity of learning of Prince Alexander's influence over the Tsar and Tsarina at the time of her son Alfred's marriage. On April 5th, when she visited Darmstadt with her youngest daughter Beatrice, whom Prince Alexander—little knowing that she was one day to be his daughter-in-law—thought nice and fair and chubby but not a beauty, the Queen adopted a somewhat restrained—though perfectly courteous—manner in consequence of the political tension with Russia.

Meanwhile the revolutionary movements in the Turkish provinces, and especially in Bosnia and Herzegovina, were spreading seriously. The Emperor Francis Joseph had undertaken a journey to Dalmatia in the previous year which had had a strongly provocative effect and had contributed to the outbreak of rebellion in the Turkish provinces, in that exaggerated inferences were drawn there from the imperial visit and the reception that had been accorded to Christian Bosnian deputations. The Tsarina certainly went too far when she simply remarked that it was due to the visit of the Emperor of Austria to Dalmatia that rebellion had broken out in Herzegovina. In view of the animosity to the Emperor Francis Joseph which reigned at the Russian court, it was quite natural that all blame should be laid on him. The revolutionary movement was now beginning to spread over Montenegro, Bulgaria, and Serbia; and these peoples were hoping for help from their big Slav brother in the north. The Turks, however, took the most brutal and sanguinary measures against the rebels everywhere.

"The East causes us more and more anxiety", wrote the Tsarina to Prince Alexander on April 9th (21st). "The greatest patience and leniency on the part of Europe only makes the Turks more stubborn. My feelings revolt at the thought of the sanguinary battles that took place during Holy Week. I hope that Turkey's latest infamy in wishing to attack Montenegro will at last awaken Europe to its duty as a Christian Power."

Prince Alexander was seriously alarmed by these letters from his sister. He had grown accustomed to a quiet life again, and described himself as an "old dismantled hulk, embedded in children, deer, and coins".

In Hesse, too, fears of the outbreak of a world war began to be entertained. The Emperor William had been in Wiesbaden early in May 1876, and had spoken to the Princess Alice in a somewhat disquieting manner about "poor Austria, that was once again playing a double game". Alice's impression was that Bismarck's latest plan was to embroil Austria-Hungary with Russia in order then to round off the new German Empire by adding to it Austria's German provinces. Alice and her sister, the German Crown Princess, were convinced at that time that this was Bismarck's private scheme. In actual fact it was precisely the opposite.

Meanwhile the horrors and the unrest in Bulgaria and Salonica had taken on enormous proportions. The Sultan Abdul Aziz had been deposed, and under his melancholic successor three Ministers attempted the forcible regeneration of the Turkish Empire, in pursuance of which they tried to suppress the revolt in Bulgaria with an inhuman ferocity that roused the greatest indignation throughout Europe. Milan of Serbia and Nikita of Montenegro made common cause with the Bosnian insurgents. Milan's armies were led by a Russian general, and innumerable volunteers from the Russian army took part in it.

The Tsar, who had been taking the cure at Ems in June, followed with anxiety events which began to look threatening for Russia, especially in view of the extremely doubtful attitude of England. The Pan-Slav Party and also the Tsarina did their utmost to force the Tsar into war. The only person they were afraid of was Queen Victoria.

"It is hard to say", wrote the Tsarina to Prince Alexander on May 14 (26), 1876, "what England's views are. But they are certainly hostile to us. That makes the Tsar very anxious, on Marie's account too, and does not help the cure."

On visiting the Tsar in Ems, Prince Alexander found him resigned to a universal war. The Tsar tried to turn his relationship with Hesse to account in order to influence Queen Victoria directly. He sent word to her by Alice that Russia neither could nor wished to be on bad terms with England. On the British side, too, despite the Queen's anti-Russian feelings, war was not generally desired. Non-intervention and neutrality were preferred. Nevertheless opinions were sharply divided, and Gladstone and his party carried on a struggle against the russophobe policy of Disraeli and his Tory Cabinet. Politics or no politics, however, love will have its way. The Tsar regarded his love for the Princess Dolgoruki as so universally recognized a fact that he sent for her from Paris— she was expecting her third child—established her in a villa not far from his brother-in-law's estate, where the Tsar was staying on a visit, and rode over daily to see her.

After the German Emperor had paid a visit to Heiligen-berg the Tsar went to meet the Emperor Francis Joseph at Reichstadt, where he arrived on July 8th. A duel of words took place on this occasion between Andrássy and Gortchakoff, the two Ministers for Foreign Affairs; and the two emperors had serious talks which finally ended not in a definite treaty but in a protocol that defined the measures to be taken in the case of Russia's intervention in the Turkish troubles. It was decided that if the Turkish dominions were partitioned, Russia should not be permitted to create a great Slav State in the Balkan Peninsula, but that it should take back Bessarabia and extend further over Turkey in Asia.

Austria was to remain neutral and was to be allowed to annex the greater part of Bosnia and Herzegovina. The result was not altogether to the Tsar's taste. He was obliged, so to speak, to buy permission from Austria-Hungary to be allowed to enter upon the risks of war, and he left Reichstadt with a heart full of bitterness. His relations with the Emperor Francis Joseph were not improved, and the Archduke Albrecht's plans and ideas were completely frustrated by Andrássy. Andrássy was strongly supported by England, in whose eyes anything that promised to create difficulties for Russia was welcome. The Queen and her Ministers were obsessed by the idea of Russia's threat to Constantinople. It seemed to them that if Russia held this city and the Dardanelles, the Suez Canal and the whole of England's intercourse with India might be endangered. Hence they were determined that on no account must Russia be permitted to obtain a foothold there. Brains were racked in London as to what was to be done with Constantinople in the event of the possible collapse of the Ottoman Empire. Leopold of Belgium made the somewhat daring suggestion that the Tsar's son-in-law, Prince Alfred, who formed as it were a connecting-link between the two Great Powers, should be put at the head of a free State consisting of Constantinople and the neighbouring territory. When the Queen suggested this possibility to her son, Alfred was quite horrified and wrote to her from on board H.M.S. *Sultan* at the island of Thasos on July 31st:[137] "I assure you that you frightened me with Leopold of Belgium's proposal. I had no idea, although I had often heard it mentioned, that there was anybody who seriously thought of it. I would sooner end the remainder of my days in China, to such a fearful prospect."

In Russia, Turkey's critical position and its degenerate state were judged much more unfavourably than was justified by actual conditions.

"Turkey", wrote the Tsarina to Prince Alexander from Tsarskoe Selo on August 5th (17th), "is heading for complete disintegration. The Sultan is not mad enough to be deposed, but is too mad to rule. The troops are badly paid and worse fed. All these are so many destructive elements."

"Austria", she continued, "would, I believe, like to annex a part of Bosnia now, and see the remainder organized in as unfavourable a manner as possible for the Slavs, because Austria fears them so much and hates them even more. I regard Bismarck as a sphinx, who is certainly concerned with what is to be gained by fishing in these troubled waters. He is being particularly tender with England and is lurking in Varzin, the old fox. Will he ever come up against anyone who is more cunning than himself?"

Hardly a fortnight after this letter had been written the new Sultan Murad V—who was mentally much weaker than the Tsarina thought—was deposed, and his brother Abdul Hamid II was raised to the throne. The situation, however, was not materially altered by this change of rulers. Success in their efforts against the rebels, and the jealousy between England and Russia, gave the Turkish Government in Constantinople greater confidence.

The Tsar Alexander meanwhile continued to make plans for safeguarding the projected action in the Balkan Peninsula diplomatically. On August 26 (September 7), 1876, he wrote to the Emperor William from Warsaw to say that it might be necessary for him to take up an independent and detached attitude. "I like to think", he said, "that I can count on you as you can always count on me."[138]

Meanwhile British and Russian diplomacy were carrying on a violent struggle. The Pan-Slav Party in Russia began to agitate in earnest and to put serious pressure on Alexander II, who was fundamentally a lover of peace but who also believed the Sick Man of Europe to be so weak that he (the Tsar) might with comparative ease attain his heart's desire—to take vengeance for the Crimean War and to undo its results. Hence he wrote to the Emperor William from Livadia on October 21 (November 2), 1876, to say that he found it impossible to carry on any longer the fruitless labours of diplomacy which had no result but to injure the dignity of the Cabinets[139]:

"I have a right to expect that I shall be given freedom to act even by those who do not wish to co-operate with me." Bismarck added the word "yes" in the margin beside the word "act", and revealed his attitude in the Varzin Memorandum of November 9, 1876, in which he says: "If the Tsar Alexander makes war on Turkey, it will not be such a bad thing for us, and if he is allowed to act without interference, that is to the advantage of the general peace."[140]

It was otherwise in England. There Russia was accused— and the Queen said it in so many words to Lord Beaconsfield[141] on September 28, 1876—of having itself "instigated the in-surrections" in Turkey. The Queen sided passionately against Russia in the Oriental complications, and her Ministers had a hard task to keep within bounds her excitement, which drove her to dangerous lengths. Too many memories remained of the Crimean War from which England had only emerged victorious owing to a series of lucky chances after many reverses. Now it would have been a case of going to war without French help, and Austria—which had been known to be an uncertain quantity since the days of the Crimea—could not have been reckoned on with any certainty.

The situation in the theatre of war meanwhile grew more and more involved. The Serbs suffered reverses, and since this had its repercussions in Russia too, the Pan-Slav Party began by means of manifestos to press the Tsar to act. Alexander II, however, still hoped to win Austria-Hungary over to joint action in the Balkans, which would have been the sole means of expunging all the misunderstandings between the two empires, and of creating a really cordial alliance between them on the basis of the Western Balkans for Austria-Hungary and the Eastern Balkans for Russia. On September 23rd Alexan-der II, by way of a "final effort"—the Tsarina described it to her brother in a letter from Livadia on September 24th, which he entered in his diary on October 4, 1876—sent one of his aides-de-camp, Count Sumarakoff, to Francis Joseph with a holograph letter in which he proposed a joint armed inter-

Q

vention in the Balkans by Austria and Russia. Austria was to invade Bosnia and Russia was to march into Bulgaria. Sumarakoff, however, encountered insuperable resistance on the part of Andrássy. "The Sumarakoff–Elston mission was received in Vienna with almost diabolical mockery," writes Felix Rachfahl.[142] Andrássy drafted a letter from Francis Joseph to the Tsar containing a categorical refusal that destroyed the last opportunity for a complete reconciliation between the two mighty empires. From that time onwards common interests occasionally produced a temporary friendliness. But in reality the deeper-lying hostility remained irreconcilable and ultimately resulted in a war that was disastrous to both empires. But a long time was still to pass before that came to pass. Bismarck, in his *Gedanken und Erinnerungen (Reflections and Reminiscences)*, says very truly : "Mistakes on the part of the Great Powers do not bring their own retribution immediately . . . but they never go unpunished."

Thus the Tsar was obliged to make up his mind to act alone and on his own initiative. An ultimatum to Turkey demanded the cessation of hostilities against the rebels, and by way of lending greater emphasis to the ultimatum a part of the Russian army was mobilized. The Russian court still undervalued the power of Turkey. "The Turkish troops", said the Tsarina in a letter to Prince Alexander from Tsarskoe Selo on November 4 (16), 1876, "will bear the hardships of winter infinitely less easily than ours—that is certain." She was evidently repeating faithfully her husband's views. "They [the Turks] seem to be already demoralized by the cold and by sickness." The Tsarina was convinced that England would declare war on Russia. She received alarming reports from all sides of the temper in England and of the difficult situation in which her son-in-law Alfred found himself.

"Shuvaloff", she reports, "writes that Alfred is regarded in England as being too Russian in sympathy, and that that bad girl Alice says to everyone who will listen that he is steering a dangerously crooked course; that Marie, who has tact enough for two, ought to restrain him if his position is not to be ruined irretrievably, etc.

"Marie tells me that the Queen makes the same complaint about his [Alfred's] having allowed himself to be influenced in Livadia. And the Queen is supposed to be pacifically minded ! Whereas the Prince of Wales [then thirty-five years old] is so aggressive that Shuvaloff avoids as far as possible meeting him."

The Grand Duchess Marie was in a difficult situation. She loved both her husband and her parents, and would have been as happy as possible if she had not feared that an unbridgeable gulf might come to yawn between the two countries, and hence between the reigning families. Every means was still being sought in England to prevent Russia from going to war. A conference of ambassadors of the Great Powers in Constantinople was held. But even this led to no result. The Turks were perfectly well aware of the dissensions between the Great Powers, and therefore refused to take any notice of their warnings. Alexander II did manage to achieve Austria-Hungary's "benevolent neutrality" in case of a war with Turkey by a convention on January 18, 1877.[143]

Extensive preparations were already being made in the Russian army. Six army corps under the Grand Duke Nicholas, the Tsar's brother, were mobilized on the Turko-Rumanian frontier.

While the world in general was anticipating the future with anxiety, the reigning Grand Duke Louis III of Hesse, Prince Alexander's brother, whose health had recently been unsatisfactory, was little concerned with the critical European situation. He was quietly living, as was supposed, with an ex-member of the *corps de ballet* of the Court Theatre in Darmstadt named Helen Appel. It was indeed rumoured that the Grand Duke had married the girl, but until January 3, 1877, Prince Alexander knew nothing officially. On that day, however, the Lord Chamberlain, von Capellen, came to see him and informed him that the Grand Duke had entered upon a formal morganatic marriage with this lady on July 9, 1868, six years after the death of his wife the Grand Duchess Mathilda, and had raised her to the rank of Baroness von Hochstädten. Capellen told Prince Alexander that the Grand Duke had been quite prepared to let her stay on in the ballet until he had pointed out to him that that was impossible. He went on to say that the lady did not wish to emerge from her incognito, that the Grand Duke was very happy with her and that she looked after him with the greatest devotion and self-sacrifice. Later, when Prince Alexander met his brother by the court church, the Grand Duke showed him a photograph of his "Lena" and spoke of her in the warmest and most cordial manner, saying that he had spent nine happy years with her and that he had made arrangements in his will for her financial future. "When I am not here any longer", he said to Prince Alexander, "I hope you will be kind to my little Lena."

Prince Alexander was touched, and said that he felt it was desirable that the truth should be known in Hesse, because the affair had occasioned much gossip. The Grand Duke, however, was of the opinion that if people did not know they were married, at least they must have guessed it long since.

The Grand Duke must have made this communication to his brother with an unconscious presentiment of his impending death. A few months later—early in June—he became seriously ill. He accepted one more invitation to visit Prince Alexander, despite the fact that he could hardly walk. As he was bidding his brother farewell he suddenly said: "My dear Alexander, you might do me a great favour. My dear wife would be so glad to make your acquaintance." Although somewhat taken aback, the Prince agreed, and the next day he went to Seeheim, where he found his brother and his wife in the Grand Duke's study. The Grand Duke tried to rise. His strength failed him, and he sank back weakly in his chair. The Baroness went to meet the Prince, and despite his protests kissed his hand amid truly touching expressions of gratitude for his coming. On the following day the Grand Duke's condition grew worse. The whole family hurried to his sick bed, and thus "compulsorily" made the acquaintance of the Baroness von Hochstädten. Prince Alexander described her to his sister the Tsarina in a letter from Heiligenberg written on June 8, 1877. "She is a fine woman, aged about thirty," he said, "with beautiful eyes and teeth. A real child of the people, simple and loyal, and she has looked after our brother like a nurse for years. But she talks the Darmstadt dialect quite naturally and commonly." She made various remarks in this dialect, "which horrified our good Elisabeth [the widow of Charles of Hesse, the Grand Duke's second brother], who always calls her 'that creature'. Alice, on the other hand, really admired her simple and unassuming devotion, her unpretentiousness which did not even lead her to ape the great ladies. . . . At all events, the persistence with which the poor soul refuses to move from the sick bed and bursts into tears every time the doctors look grave is simply touching. Louis said to her the other day in my presence: 'You are the greatest comfort to me, Lena dear.'" The Grand Duke was beyond human aid, and passed peacefully away on June 13th. The Baroness von Hochstädten could hardly be induced to leave the body, which putrefied with extraordinary rapidity.

Prince Louis—Prince Alexander's nephew and the son of Prince Charles, who had also died only a few months previously—and his wife Alice now ascended the grand ducal throne.

"A new generation is now at the head of affairs," remarked Prince Alexander resignedly in a letter to his sister on June 19, 1877, "and as *senior member of the family* I represent the old days which have gone, and in many respects also ideas which have grown unfamiliar to the young people of the present day and are regarded as *old-fashioned.*"

Meanwhile war had broken out in the East. On April 24, 1877, Russia declared war on Turkey. In conformity with an agreement with Rumania which was seeking some means of throwing off the suzerainty of Turkey, the Russian troops began their march through this country. The dice had fallen, and the European Powers were obliged to accept the fact that Russia was playing a lone hand against Turkey. It was found that nobody, not even England, was feeling sufficiently bellicose to attack Russia immediately, although Queen Victoria, Andrássy, and Lord Beaconsfield watched the progress of events with great anxiety and disapprobation.

In Vienna the Archduke Albrecht, who always advocated friendly relations between Russia and Austria, had been unable to alter the general trend of Andrássy's policy, and lived in continual dread of an armed conflict between the two Powers. He was glad now that at least matters had not gone so far, and wrote to Prince Alexander, as he notes in his diary on April 25th: "Thank Heaven there is no reason to fear any conflict between Russia and Austria, nor even a repetition of the unfortunate policy of 1853–54." His last remark was to be falsified in the event. The antagonism to Russia that had started with the Crimean War revived again with renewed force, and subsequently never fully abated.

The outbreak of war also caused the greatest excitement in the Prince's own family. His son Alexander (Sandro), now in his twentieth year, and a lieutenant in the Hessian Dragoons, was seized with enthusiasm and wished at all costs to join in the campaign by the side of his imperial uncle. Prince Alexander wrote to the Tsarina on May 27th to say that both he and his son wanted to make some acknowledgment for all the kindness that the Russians had shown the family during long years by sending Sandro to fight in Russia's cause. On principle the Emperor William allowed no German officer to take part in the war. But an exception was made in the case of the Tsarina's nephew, since the Tsar made a personal request for him to be given leave.

Alexander II's intention was to join the army about June 1st, so as to be present at the crossing of the Danube. The impending campaign aroused no special anxiety in St. Petersburg. "Here", wrote the Tsarina to her brother on May 9th (21st), "people think that it is hardly worth the Tsar's while to go down to fight the Turks; but I feel that it is better for his nerves to be there than to have the further strain of waiting here, away from the front and continually worrying about news from one telegram to the next." The Tsarina told her brother that it had been definitely decided in St. Petersburg that the campaign was to be conducted with as little loss of life as possible.

The young Prince of Battenberg had meanwhile gone to St. Petersburg, travelling by way of Berlin, where he was "marvellously kindly" received by the Emperor William, who told him to tell the Tsar that he prayed daily that Russia might prove victorious.

He was most cordially received in St. Petersburg, but thought Alexander II looking very ill and very grave. When he gave him the Emperor William's message, the Tsar answered with emotion that he was glad to hear something that he could believe at least from *one* source!

The Prince of Battenberg thought the Tsarina looking very pale and tired. He was "most charmingly" treated by her. It happened that a great cathedral service in honour of the patron saint of the Tsarevitch Alexander was being held on the same day. The court and the imperial family were present, and the Prince was introduced to everybody after the service. "This", he wrote to his father on May 31st, "gives one a very different idea of court life from what one sees in Darmstadt." And in other letters written on June 1st and 12th he says that he did not care for the Tsarevitch. He disliked his long whiskers and his clumsy body; and thought his wife skinny and not particularly good-looking. The Prince was allowed to choose three riding-horses from the imperial stables. "Altogether", Sandro ends his enthusiastic account, "I am so touched by the kindness and graciousness with which I am overwhelmed that every minute I am becoming more Russian even than I was before. . . . Everybody treats me as a member of the family, they call me by my Christian name and kiss me and expect me to do the same."

There were indeed many both within the imperial family and at court who would have preferred to treat him with arrogance on account of his descent. But when everyone saw the Tsar treating him so kindly and as a member of the imperial family they were careful to be equally friendly. The Prince, who was a particularly fine and well-set-up young man, was very popular among the ladies, and found it hard to tear himself away from St. Petersburg on June 3rd in order to join the army in the suite of the Tsar.

"They have just gone. May God watch over them and bring them safely home again", wrote the Tsarina to Prince Alexander on May 22nd (June 3rd). "I hope the Tsar will not be more than six weeks away. That is desirable from every point of view. . . . I hope in any case that this war will not be of long duration and that England will keep quiet. To put it plainly, they are simply *afraid*; and in spite of their practical common sense they think us capable of wanting to hold Constantinople and conquer India for ourselves. But fear is a bad counsellor. After all, things will turn out as God wills. I hope Austria will not desert us altogether as the English Cabinet wants it to do."

Meanwhile the Tsar and Prince Sandro arrived in Bucharest, where the Prince and Princess of Rumania gave them a wonderful reception.

On June 22nd the Russians began the campaign. In the night of June 26th–27th the passage of the main body of the troops over the Danube at Simnitza was begun, and the Prince of Battenberg followed the advance guard across the river in a pontoon. Until the middle of June the Russians advanced rapidly and progressed as far as the foot of the Balkan Mountains, in the course of which they drove the Turks out of half of Bulgaria.

Sandro joined in the advance, and the horrors that he saw daily affected him very deeply. "All the villages", he said in a description of his experiences, "are inhabited by Turks *and* Bulgars. As soon as news of our approach comes, the Bulgars hurl themselves upon the Turks, murder them, plunder and burn everything. One consequence is that the Turks flee betimes and that wherever we come everything is laid waste." This made so great an impression upon the young prince—who had no idea that he would one day become the ruler over these same Bulgars—that in one letter to his brother Louis, written from Trnova on July 8th, the remark escaped him:

"The country is simply magnificent, but the Bulgars are just as fiendish as the Turks!"

Soon afterwards Prince Sandro took part in the attack upon the town of Trnova, the old coronation city of the Tsars of the ancient Bulgarian Empire and the birthplace of the Assenid dynasty. It is for this reason that Sandro's son, Count von Hartenau, who still lives in Vienna, bears the Christian name of Assen. Prince Sandro also took part in a most daring cavalry raid.

"We live amid blood and corpses", wrote the youthful prince, "and see such horrible things that all our officers are disgusted with the war and would much rather go home again."

The rapid successes gained at the outset by the Russian armies very greatly increased England's fear that the Russians would soon be in Constantinople. The Queen especially worked herself up into a state of really passionate agitation. Lord Beaconsfield tells that it was almost literally true to say that she wrote daily and telegraphed hourly on the subject of Eastern affairs.[144] He frequently received long letters from her saying that if Great Britain were to permit the Russians to occupy Constantinople even temporarily, "*England*, as Lord Beaconsfield himself stated . . . *would no longer exist as a Great Power*", and that she "*felt really quite ill* from the strain caused by the *great anxiety* for the honour of our dear country".[145] Lord Derby, the Foreign Secretary, was prepared to do anything except declare war; and so Lord Beaconsfield's advice was taken to regard Russia's occupation of Constantinople as a *casus belli*. A warning to this effect was sent to the Tsar. The Queen's views were shared by her son, the Duke of Edinburgh, who was on board the battleship *Sultan* with the fleet that was lying off the Dardanelles. The Duke did not disguise his fears from Prince Henry VII of Reuss, the German Ambassador in Constantinople. He considered that the policy of the present English Government would drive the country into war by a false view of what constituted British interests. He himself, he continued, was a good patriot, and the English interests came before everything with him, but he could not see how the British interests in India could be threatened if Russia happened to be victorious. The Queen's distrust of the Tsar, however, was insuperable, and there was only one means of preventing her from commencing hostilities against Russia, and that was the influence of the German Emperor.[146]

The Queen again considered "such a division of interests in royal families quite unbearable".[147]

The success which had attended Russia up to the present considerably damped Andrássy's anti-Russian ardour. When Prince Alexander arrived in Vienna early in July in order to announce the accession of the new Grand Duke of Hesse to the Emperor, he found Vienna and the leading personalities there apparently friendly disposed towards Russia and the Russians, as he noted in his diary on July 4th and in a letter to the Tsar written from Vienna on the same date. Francis Joseph congratulated the Tsar on his successes, and Andrássy, who knew very well that every word was reported to St. Petersburg, went so far as to tell Prince Alexander that a complete revulsion had taken place in public opinion and that it would be madness to think of adopting a hostile attitude. The first successful feats of arms on the part of the Russians had done wonders. But this was soon to change as the fortunes of war changed in the course of the year.

Prince Alexander's news greatly pleased the Tsar. He at once sent it on to the Tsarina in St. Petersburg, who wrote to Prince Alexander with satisfaction. "So much the better. We could not have done with treachery on the part of Austria in the difficult situation in which we are at present, what with England always prepared to put a spoke in our wheel!"

In July, however, new men came into power in Constantinople, and the war was at once conducted with far greater energy on the Turkish side. General Osman Pasha, the new commander of the Turkish army on the Danube, succeeded in occupying a strong position at Plevna on the right flank of the main Russian army and in the rear of the Russian forces which had advanced into the Balkans, from whence he repulsed the Russian attack on July 30th with fearful slaughter. The Russian losses were terrible, and Gurko's troops which had advanced across the Balkans were also defeated. The danger became imminent that Osman Pasha would cut off the Russian forces which had advanced so far southwards, and hurl back the main army over the Danube. In the East, too, the Turkish general, Mehemed Ali, was pressing the left flank of the Russians to the south of Rustchuk, so that they appeared to be hemmed in on three sides. Reinforcements could not be sent from Russia as quickly as the situation demanded, and the Tsar was obliged, though much against his will, to call the Rumanian army to his assistance in Bulgaria. In Asia, too, the Russians had not only failed to advance but had actually been forced to retire as far as the old Turkish frontier.

Prince Alexander was seriously concerned for the safety of his son Sandro, who was with Gurko's troops. The change in the situation had immediate political consequences. Austria-Hungary and England suddenly adopted a more arrogant tone. Andrássy said to his son Julius[148] that if the Emperor Francis Joseph were to enter into the war at this juncture hordes of Russian prisoners would soon be passing through Vienna. Nevertheless, Andrássy did not venture to advise the Emperor to declare war upon Russia. He feared lest Russia should recover and take terrible vengeance.

The British Government sent an emissary to the Russian headquarters and repeated its threats. This still further increased the load of care that weighed upon the Tsar, and cost the life of many a brave soldier. For the Tsar, who had by now grown very thin and nervous, was determined at all costs to bring the war to a speedy conclusion. Hence Plevna was attacked time after time during the next few weeks.

Meanwhile Sandro of Battenberg had returned safe and sound to the Russian headquarters, and there described the fierce fighting that Gurko's army had sustained in the southern Balkans. The Tsarina anxiously followed the terrible news and the enormous casualty lists which came in day after day. She thought that English, Polish, and Hungarian officers had been appointed to the Turkish army and that it was thanks to them that the Turks were suddenly fighting so bravely. She was much better able to realize the international reaction of these events in St. Petersburg than was the Tsar in Bulgaria. "We must not indulge in any illusions", she said. "The longer the struggle continues, the more ground we lose politically in favour of our enemies." Prince Alexander was most seriously alarmed. On September 14th he had received a telegram from the Tsar, whose headquarters had been moved to Plevna, saying that the town had not yet been taken and that Sandro was at headquarters in front of the fortress. "The situation of the Russian army", wrote Prince Alexander in his diary on that day, "is terribly critical. Unless Plevna falls soon, a catastrophe is inevitable."

In these anxious days the Emperor William visited Darmstadt and was, as Alexander himself observed, received with "immense enthusiasm". The Prince was by this time completely won over, and his former bitterness altogether overcome by the kindness, the charm, and the indefatigable industry displayed by the Emperor in the discharge of his imperial duties. He felt even more kindly towards the aged monarch when he began to speak with really genuinely deep anxiety of the Russian reverses. He had hardly arrived at the palace before he drew Prince Alexander into the embrasure of a window and poured out his heart to him on the subject. Prince Alexander reported his confidences to the Tsarina on October 7th. The Emperor William said that he could not understand or conceive of the happenings in Bulgaria. The old man spoke with tears in his eyes, and seemed to Prince Alexander to be in every respect sincere.

Prince Alexander's daughter, the Princess Erbach, so bewitched all the guests with her charm that the Emperor impulsively picked up a silver heart which lay on the mantelpiece in one of the rooms, pressed it to his own heart, and then laid it at the feet of the Princess Marie. After a short visit the Emperor bade the Prince farewell with best wishes for the improvement of the situation in the theatre of war. And in fact the redoubled energy with which the campaign was pursued by the Russian army gradually resulted in a turn for the better.

"Plevna is completely blockaded and the town itself is being bombarded. We are all hoping that it may surrender within the next three or four weeks", wrote Sandro on November 3rd from Plevna. He now dared to write rather more openly, because his father had meanwhile gone to visit the Tsarina in St. Petersburg, and he thought that a letter which was conveyed by the Tsar's own messenger would not be censored. To write openly had hitherto been too dangerous, "for", he wrote to his father from Poradim on November 13th, "such hair-raising things happened daily that if I had simply reported the bare facts, everyone would have regarded them as the exaggerations of a pro-Turk. You have no idea (1) of the levity with which the High Command does its work; (2) of the disorder *within* the army and *behind* the army; (3) of the robbery that goes on in the commissariat. The letter would be too long. But if you like I can give you the most extraordinary *proofs* on each individual point. Things are really so bad that it is a mercy we have only the Turks against us—all would have been lost long ago if we had had any other enemy." Sandro reported that the troops, men and officers up to the rank of major, were *splendid*. But from thence upwards they grew weaker and weaker. The famous Gurko, for instance, had already several times done incredible things in the way of sacrificing uselessly and stupidly the lives of the troops under his command.

"Instead of hearing about courts-martial," Sandro continued, "we see nothing but St. George's Crosses and swords of honour! And who is victimized by all this? The Tsar, the idealistic Tsar, whose greatest virtue is his greatest fault. The Russians do not deserve his gentle kindliness! The Grand Duke Nicholas is jealous of his brother [the Grand Duke Michael had commanded the army which had lately made a successful advance in the Caucasus], and so he insists at all costs upon winning a victory. Being unable to do so in the right place, he has sent nearly the whole of the Guards Division to Orhanie and the neighbourhood; and towns are being stormed there by sending 30,000 men against four and a half Turks—congratulations, St. George's Crosses, etc., are raining upon them; and meantime he risks Osman's escaping [from Plevna]. Could anyone be surprised if Osman, who always hears from the Bulgarians what we are doing, takes the opportunity to hurl himself upon the Rumanians—who have terribly little courage—and to get clear away? And who is the victim again? Again the Tsar. The one good thing about this war is that the Russians realize that for the next hundred years they will not be able to undertake the war against Germany which they discuss so calmly. But enough of this vexatious theme. How gladly would I—unlike the Press— write nothing but good of the Russians! It is unfortunately impossible, and no one is sorrier about it than

"Your

"SANDRO."

This exaggerated criticism is no doubt to be ascribed in part to the writer's youth. But there is an undeniable basis of truth. The Prince of Battenberg was not merely an aide-de-camp to the Commander-in-Chief, but was fighting on the most dangerous sectors and saw a great deal of which those who remained at headquarters had no idea. Despite its being sent by the Tsar's personal messenger, however, such written criticism was dangerous. Since the Prince also from time to time gave utterance to similar views in conversation, he made enemies. Moreover, this particular letter quoted chanced to have been written at the very time when the fortunes of war were on the turn. Now came decisive successes in Asia. General

Gurko, too, with the ruthlessness and hardness of which
Prince Sandro accused him, succeeded in repulsing the Turks
at the Shipka Pass. Finally Plevna, a prey to famine and
disease, was unable to hold out any longer. On December 10th
the brave Osman Pasha capitulated with his entire garrison.
When in addition the Turkish defenders of the Shipka Pass
had been forced to yield, the Russians occupied Adrianople
on January 19th, and the way to Constantinople was open to
them. At last Alexander II's anxiety was relieved, and he
joyfully telegraphed to his wife and brother-in-law to tell them
of these brilliant successes. Although the Tsarina was pleased,
her anger against Francis Joseph still raged fiercely. She refused
to admit that Russia had any reason to be grateful to Austria-
Hungary for its attitude during the war. Prince Alexander did
not agree with her, but the Tsarina launched forth into abuse
of the Emperor Francis Joseph and Andrássy. The discussion
became much more violent than Prince Alexander liked.

On December 22nd the Tsar and Prince Alexander of
Battenberg came back to St. Petersburg from the scene of war
amid the most tumultuous rejoicings. Parades and festivities
followed one upon another. The unexpected turn of the tide
in favour of Russia caused great excitement first in England
and later also in Vienna. The Queen wrote letter after letter
to the Earl of Beaconsfield, saying that "England would never
stand (not to speak of her Sovereign) to become *subservient* to
Russia".[149] The Crown Princess of Prussia, whose dislike of
Bismarck had temporarily somewhat abated, also grieved that
it should be Russia and not England which had such great
successes to show in world politics. For, she said, by careful
observation of conditions on the Continent, she had come to be
firmly convinced that England was far ahead of all other
countries in civilization and progress; that it was the only one
which understood the meaning of liberty and really possessed
liberty. And now England seemed to her to have been
humiliated. "*How* I do long", she wrote to her mother on
December 19, 1877, "for *one* good roar of the British lion from
the housetops and for the *thunder* of a British broadside!"[150]
She did not at all agree with the Emperor William. She found
him more Russian than could be described, as she wrote to
Queen Victoria on January 25, 1878.[151] Although nothing was
known of these letters at the court of St. Petersburg, everyone
was perfectly cognisant of the Queen's sentiments, and all the
steps taken by the British Government were attributed to the

influence of the "mad Queen who was hounding them on to war". The ambassador Shuvaloff reported from London that "the old sick woman", as Bismarck called the Queen, was doing more to inflame warlike feelings in England than the whole Eastern question itself. At the last moment the British Government sought an offensive alliance with the Danubian monarchy against Russia. The despatch of the fleet to Constantinople was already under consideration. The Tsar hoped for Germany's mediation in the conflict with Austria-Hungary, and was greatly concerned lest European diplomacy should rob him of the fruits of the success he had at last achieved after so many terrible sacrifices.

On December 9, 1877, the Tsar informed the Emperor Francis Joseph and the German Emperor William of the conditions of peace that he proposed dictating to Turkey at San Stefano. Chief among them were the foundation of an independent State of Bulgaria whose frontiers should touch the Mediterranean, and the reincorporation into Russia of Bessarabia, which had been lost in the Crimean War. The Emperor William was the first to reply on December 13th, saying that he saw nothing at all in the suggested conditions that was incompatible with German interests. Moreover, he offered his friendly co-operation in settling any opposition that might arise from the third ally, Austria, and stated that he counted upon the continuance of the Three Powers Pact.[152]

The Emperor Francis Joseph took much longer to answer. Andrássy advised against the adoption of the conciliatory tone that Bismarck had recommended to his Emperor. With reference to the Tsar's regret that Austria-Hungary had not helped him in the war against Turkey, the Emperor Francis Joseph in his reply on January 8, 1878, observed that he had in previous letters advised against making war on Turkey, and that it would have been better to await the natural process of dissolution in the Turkish Empire. He reminded the Tsar in a manner very galling to him that at the commencement of hostilities he had rejected all idea of territorial acquisition and had alleged the execution of the reforms demanded by the Powers as the sole aim of the war.[153] In an enclosed memorandum the Emperor Francis Joseph, or rather Andrássy, protested against the annexation of Bessarabia, and more especially against the aggrandizement of Bulgaria that implied the existence of that great Slav State which had been one of the things definitely excluded in their agreement. Alexander II was deeply offended by Francis Joseph's answer. He realized anew that the Danubian monarchy had no sympathy with his point of view, and that it was anxious to deprive Russia of the fruits of victory. The Tsar's answer showed his feelings plainly: the complete autonomy of Bulgaria was the only possible solution, temporary occupation was absolutely essential, and Bessarabia was no more than a restoration of territory to its rightful owner.

"I must take this opportunity of reminding you", he wrote to the Emperor Francis Joseph on January 4 (16), 1878,[154] "that the cession of this territory was the work of Count Buol, who evidently overcame your scruples. It was the outcome of a policy that you have abandoned just as I have. But the effects have remained, and I have no doubt that you are anxious to abolish this memory that was incompatible with our friendly relationship. By admitting your freedom temporarily to occupy Bosnia and Herzegovina in the same way as I am occupying Bulgaria, I thought I was leaving the way open for you to transform the temporary occupation into an annexation if you considered it to be necessary for your safety, even after my troops had evacuated Bulgaria."

Bismarck viewed the increasing antagonism between Austria-Hungary and Russia with anxiety. "We must mediate between the other two emperors", he said, "as far as friendly mediation is possible, but we must avoid the danger of taking sides." In deference to Bismarck's wish the Emperor William offered in general terms his services as mediator between his two Eastern allies in a letter to Alexander II, dated January 23, 1878.[155]

This missive was handed to the Tsar on January 26th while he was at the theatre. He had expected something more, and felt it to be non-committal, chilly, and evidently inspired by Bismarck, and was very much disconcerted by it, as Prince Alexander of Hesse reports in his diary on January 26, 1878. Hence Alexander II induced his brother-in-law to return home by way of Berlin and to find out what were the Emperor's intentions.

On his arrival in Berlin the Prince went to see the Emperor, and contrary to the belief of the Crown Princess he found him chilly with regard to Russia and little inclined to put any kind of pressure on the Austro-Hungarian Government. He found the Empress Augusta frankly in favour of Queen Victoria's view that a "firm, a very firm tone" should be taken in regard to Russia. She was continually expressing sympathy for the "unfortunate English and their straightforward, frank Queen", as Prince Alexander notes in his diary on February 1, 1878.

The Prince went to Dresden after leaving Berlin. He had tea with the King and Queen of Saxony, and realized that King Albert was openly anti-Russian. The King, for example, expressed regret that the Turks had not made more of their victory at Plevna at the beginning of September, while the Russian army was so demoralized that the Russian officers went into battle "drunk or weeping". Thus Prince Alexander had nothing good to report to Russia from Germany. Meanwhile an armistice had been concluded at Adrianople on January 31st, to give time for peace negotiations to be carried on. The lack of unanimity in the British Cabinet was shown by its repeated orders and counter-orders to the fleet. There was, however, no really definite desire for war. Prince Alexander was right when he wrote to his sister from Darmstadt on February 12th: "England's part is an unenviable one, and I still think that they will try to avoid war."

On March 3rd a preliminary peace was concluded between Russia and Turkey, of which the main provisions were the independence of Serbia, Rumania, and Montenegro, as well as the foundation of a sovereign principality of Bulgaria with its frontier extending as far as the Mediterranean. This treaty only served to increase the animosity between Russia and England and between Russia and Austria-Hungary. England was so sensitive that a perfectly harmless episode—occasioned, as it happened, by the two sons of Prince Alexander of Hesse, who stood in opposite camps—threatened to turn into a major affair of State. Sandro of Battenberg had hardly arrived in St. Petersburg before he reiterated his wish to rejoin the army in Bulgaria. The headquarters had meanwhile been transferred to San Stefano. When the Prince came to Adrianople the armistice had just been declared. "It has occasioned great joy," he reported to his father on February 3rd, "for the army is sick to death of this war, which has perhaps been the most horrible one to be waged in the whole of this century. Apart from the armies, it has been a struggle between two bitterly hostile races who have done their best to exterminate each other and have outvied each other in cruelties."

In the charming little town of San Stefano, delightfully situated on the shore of the Sea of Marmora, Alexander of Battenberg was quartered in a villa overlooking the sea, and from his desk he had a view of the Isle of Princes, in the harbours of which lay the British fleet, including the battleship *Sultan* on board of which was his brother Louis.

"My heart beats", he wrote in a letter to his parents which was written at various times between February 25th and March 7th, "when I think how close we are together. This morning I rode out with the Grand Duke (who looks after me like a father) up to the heights of San Stefano, and we saw Constantinople before us, with the Aya Sophia, all the minarets, Scutari, etc. Tears filled the Grand Duke's eyes. What a satisfaction it must be for him to be standing at the gates of Constantinople with his army! . . . The Grand Duke gave permission to all foreign officers to go into Constantinople to-day. And to me in particular he said that I might go and see Louis and stay as long as I liked. He would take the responsibility." The young Prince did not need to be told twice. He went to Constantinople and there sought out the German Ambassador, Prince Reuss, who for his part sent word to Prince Louis to tell him of his brother's arrival. While Sandro was having lunch on February 28th the door opened and a British naval officer came in, in whom he was delighted to recognize his brother. Louis invited him to come on board the *Sultan*, where Prince Alfred, the husband of the Grand Duchess Marie and commander of the ship, was awaiting him.

"A small boat", Prince Alexander told his parents, "very soon brought us to the *Sultan*, where I was received by Alfred and the whole ship's company with *extraordinary friendliness*. They all feel more Russian than the Russians, and make no secret of it."

After showing him all over the iron-clad, Prince Alfred took his cousin on to the flagship *Alexandra* and introduced him to Admiral Hornby, who also showed him over his ship. Finally the newest iron-clad in the fleet, the *Temeraire*, was shown him under Alfred's guidance. When the Prince returned to San Stefano he heard the news of the signing of the preliminary peace. His visit to the *Sultan* had taken place at the worst possible moment. England had just determined upon the decisive step of ordering the fleet to Constantinople that resulted in Lord Derby's resignation. Although the order to the fleet was shortly afterwards cancelled, and Lord Derby resumed office again for a short time, the news of Alexander of Battenberg's visit to the fleet made the Queen very angry indeed. Through her daughter, Princess Alice, Sandro heard that she had been beside herself with rage at the Grand Duke

Nicholas's having dared to send a "Russian spy" to the fleet, that he had been positively "fêted" on board, and had been shown over all the men-of-war and even been allowed to see the mechanism of the newly invented torpedo. Queen Victoria was furious with her son Alfred, to whom she ascribed all the blame for this "anti-national" step, and ordered him to be relieved of his command for so long as the *Sultan* lay off Constantinople. Prince Louis was transferred to another ship and sent back home. Princess Alice said, moreover, that it would be impossible for Alfred to show himself in England now, and that her sister Helena had written (as Alexander of Hesse told the Tsarina in a letter on March 20th) to say that she was ashamed of being Alfred's sister! Sandro of Battenberg, the unintentional cause of all the disturbance, was horrified at the consequences of his perfectly innocent visit to his brother. He poured out all his woes to the Tsarina, whose hatred of everything English was thereby increased.

"The poor boy is beside himself", she wrote to Prince Alexander of Hesse on March 31st (April 12th), "that the Queen, crazy old hag, made him the pretext for persecuting Alfred, and more especially Louis. I was so indignant that at first my one idea was that he should leave the English service. But perhaps it would be a rash thing to do if there is really danger of war. But just because the danger threatens, I should be heartily glad for Alfred and Louis both to be out of it, wouldn't you? . . . Marie's telegrams show that they are terribly upset about it in Malta [whither the *Sultan* had meanwhile returned]. . . . She says that if it is a question of treason, Hornby and the captains of the ships of the whole squadron are equally guilty."

The *Sultan* was now transferred to the Channel fleet, and Prince Louis returned overland to England to join his new ship. He and his father Prince Alexander agreed that in the circumstances the only thing he could do was to leave the service unless he could get satisfaction. The Prince asked the Grand Duchess Alice to advise the Queen to this effect. In the meantime the Queen's anger was subsiding. Sandro of Battenberg had declared that no Russian had accompanied him, that he had previously caused inquiries to be made of the fleet, had merely accepted a special invitation, that he was not going to allow anyone to call him a spy, etc. The whole episode was the result of a report sent by Layard, the British Ambassador in Constantinople, who was annoyed that the

meeting should have been arranged not by him but by Prince
Reuss. The Queen caused it to be given out that Louis's
transfer was occasioned by the normal routine and was in no
sense a disciplinary action; and at the representations of the
admiral in command omitted to have the intended reproof
of the Admiralty conveyed to her son Alfred. Thus the episode ended happily. Only the Tsarina Marie bore malice and
indulged in the most violent diatribes against the Queen. In
writing to her brother on April 25th (May 7th) she com-
miserated Sandro for having been "victimized by the old fool",
who had calmed down now that she had indulged her "spleen".
"Marie declares", she continued, "that you only have to give
her a good fright to make her draw in her horns."

At all events the incident served to reveal the tension existing between Russia and England at the time. Nor were things
much better between Austria-Hungary and Russia. Andrássy
sought and obtained a credit of sixty million gulden, and
numbers of people who were averse from any fresh military
experiment after the unfortunate outcome of the previous wars
feared that hostilities might still break out. Hence on February 28th Prince William of Schaumburg-Lippe came on a
secret mission from Vienna to implore Prince Alexander to go
there immediately in order if possible to prevent a breach
between Russia and Austria-Hungary. He averred that the
army was in favour of an understanding, while another section
of opinion led by Andrássy was inciting to war.

About the same time Prince Alexander received a letter from
the Tsarina dated February 20th (March 4th), who suspected
that Russia was to be cheated of the fruits of her victory.
"It has now unfortunately come to be the turn of European
diplomacy, that most terrible of all inventions, in the discussion
of our affairs." The Tsarina was amused at Prince Alexander's
telling her in a letter that the Prince of Wales had asked him
whether it was really true that the Russians were so angry
with the English. "Furious, you should have told him; and
that we hate the English as much as we do the Austrians."

The Queen also expressed herself too violently on the subject
of Russia and the Tsar. She did not know that every word was
immediately repeated to the imperial court. The Tsarina, of
course, commented bitterly to her brother upon each such
attack. "The insulting things that the Queen says in her letters
to Alfred about the Tsar and the Russian people", she wrote
to Prince Alexander on February 27th (March 11th), "are

worthy of a fish-wife. Added to this is her grief that 'our dear Marie' should belong to a nation from whose vocabulary the words truth, justice, and humanity are lacking. Silly old fool. But it is a pity that her son has not got more character."

Prince Alexander was given a hint from St. Petersburg not to go to Vienna for the time being, and at all events not to let it appear that he came as the emissary of the imperial family. Then on March 9th the Archduke Francis Charles, the father of the Emperor Francis Joseph, died. It was an excellent excuse for Prince Alexander to go to Vienna. The following description is based upon the entries in his diary from March 12th to March 25th, and upon one letter from Prince Alexander to the Tsar Alexander II from Vienna on March 6th (18th), and another from Darmstadt on March 19th (31st). On the whole, Prince Alexander found opinion in Austria, including the army, definitely against war with Russia. Only a few of the archdukes were of a different opinion. Thus, for example, the Archduke William annoyed Prince Alexander considerably by saying to him at an informal dinner party that Russia ought to be very grateful to Austria-Hungary for not having taken advantage of her defeat at Plevna to obstruct the Russian army's retirement over the Danube. On the following day, March 17th, Prince Alexander had an audience with the Emperor Francis Joseph, who spent an hour discussing the whole situation with him very frankly. He said that the Tsar's last letter from St. Petersburg had wounded him deeply by its allusion to the events of 1854 which he, Francis Joseph, had thought to be forgotten long ago. Most of all had he been surprised at the expression: "Who evidently overcame your scruples" ("*On avait surpris ta religion alors*"). At first neither Francis nor Andrássy could think what the phrase—which was quite strange to them—could mean. Then it had been explained to them to mean more or less that the Emperor's conscience had been squared in the year 1854. On the 24th the Prince again spent a long time with the Emperor, who told him that it was quite impossible for Austria-Hungary to agree to the Treaty of San Stefano, and also that he was not at all pleased that England was trying to defeat the proposal of a conference and to force Russia into war. When, however, Prince Alexander said that he thought the English felt that they had made fools of themselves, and were therefore anxious at all costs to stage some sort of action, the Emperor replied: "*We* are the ones who have made fools of ourselves!" "Nevertheless", said Prince Alexander, "I am not altogether happy at the idea of a European congress of which world diplomacy speaks, and which is intended to resolve all the differences of opinion that have arisen." His anxiety was increased still further when Lord Derby, who had always promoted the cause of peace, retired, and Lord Salisbury took over the post of Foreign Secretary.

The Tsarina and Shuvaloff were both delighted at a misunderstanding that embarrassed the "English mob". One day a Hyde Park orator was declaiming against the Russians, and the Russian Ambassador, Shuvaloff, happened to be listening to him. He was recognized. Subsequently the crowd thought that they saw him again listening to another of the speakers. He was instantly surrounded by a mob, yelling and shouting, his hat was battered on his head, and he was forced to take refuge in flight. It was, however, Duke Francis of Teck, who was married to Princess Mary Adelaide of Great Britain, and who was the father of the present Queen Mary.

Lord Derby's successor, Salisbury, demanded that the Treaty of San Stefano should be rescinded. All this strengthened Andrássy's position. On the same day that saw Derby's retirement in London, Ignatieff arrived in Vienna bearing a letter from the Tsar, only to discover that the Austro-Hungarian Government was preparing to exploit Russia's present difficulties for their own immediate advantage regardless of their future relations with the Tsarist State. St. Petersburg did not fail to react as might have been expected. "Ignatieff's mission", wrote the Tsarina to Prince Alexander of Hesse on March 31st (April 12th), "has shown one thing most clearly—that Andrássy has discarded all disguise. The man of the sack and cord, the man who was hanged in effigy, has been unmasked in all his cynicism as a man who fills his own sovereign with fear and who would be dismissed by him if he dared to do it."

This letter was brought to Prince Alexander by his son Sandro on his return home. He also had much to tell of the profound resentment with which St. Petersburg regarded the efforts of England and Austria-Hungary to deprive Russia of the fruits of her military victories.

In the year 1878 a series of attempts were made upon the lives of monarchs by members of the Internationale. Among them was the attack upon the Emperor William by a socialist journeyman ironmonger, who fired two revolver-shots at him when he and the Grand Duchess of Baden were driving down the Unter den Linden. "How fortunate", Prince Alexander wrote to his sister on May 14th, deferring to the anti-English feelings of the Tsarina, "that the venerable Emperor escaped. I suppose Vicky's [the Crown Princess'] view was: 'miserable socialist bungler'!"

Then on June 2nd came the second attempt upon the Emperor William's life by a doctor of philosophy named Nobiling, who was a better shot, and wounded the old Emperor seriously. Prince Alexander was greatly affected by this dastardly outrage. "It would be a very serious matter for Russia as well as for Germany", he wrote to his sister, "if the Emperor were to succumb to his wounds at this particular moment. An English empress at the head of German political life would lead to all manner of complications."

Meanwhile there appeared to be signs that the Eastern crisis was approaching some sort of solution. In their heart of hearts neither the Emperor Francis Joseph nor Disraeli wanted war; the former remembered only too clearly the unfortunate end to the campaigns that he had hitherto conducted, and both preferred to extend their realms by any other means than war. England compelled the Turks to cede the island of Cyprus to her; Austria endeavoured to make effective her occupation of Bosnia and Herzegovina. The situation of Russia was such that a new war must appear a highly dangerous undertaking. Hence the foundations for a settlement were laid in preliminary negotiations, and were put into definite form in a congress that met in Berlin from June 13th to July 15th.

Just after the inauguration of this congress, Prince Alexander received a telegram from the Tsar telling him that the Tsarina was once again very ill, and that her condition was regarded as critical. He immediately started for St. Petersburg by way of Berlin. There he found his sister very weak and listless, very worn, and terribly changed. He was only allowed to stay ten minutes and left her, filled with the gravest anxiety.

The Tsar's anxieties—and his conscience on the subject of his relations with the Princess Dolgoruki troubled him more than ever now that the Tsarina was so ill—were still further increased by the news that came to him from the Congress of Berlin. It grew more and more obvious that Andrássy would side with England whatever happened, and that Russia was being driven into a corner by England and Austria-Hungary. The Tsar did indeed say to his wife and brother-in-law that any humiliation of Russia by England must force him into war; but he added immediately that the country had come to an end of its financial resources, and that even the army had dwindled greatly. It was clear, he said, that Beaconsfield was only concerned to show Europe that victorious Russia must yield before the British lion. The Congress of Berlin decided upon the constitution of Bulgaria as an independent sovereign principality, and the question arose as to who should be put at the head of this unstable State. Sandro of Battenberg's name had been mentioned in this connection while the campaign was still on, and Prince Alexander was anxious that his son should be a candidate. But when Prince Alexander suggested him to the Tsar, the Emperor replied that he would never wish him to have so difficult a post. Prince Alexander answered drily: "A youngster can make an attempt at anything!"

The Tsarina grew suddenly and surprisingly better, and on June 28th her brother returned home. Once more he went through Berlin and found the Congress still sitting. He was received in a very friendly manner by the old Emperor, who was sitting in an arm-chair wearing a white dressing-gown and with his head bound up. He stayed with him only a few minutes, and then went on to see Prince Bismarck. He found that the Chancellor had "acquired a paunch and spoke with difficulty amid continual hiccups". At this meeting Bismarck emphasized the fact that he regarded the continuance of the Three Emperors Pact as the sole guarantee for the future, especially against revolution, and then began to speak of the attempted assassinations which had recently also taken place in Russia. A Russian Nihilist, Vera Sassulitch, who had severely wounded General Trepoff, the Governor of St. Petersburg, in revenge for the mishandling of an imprisoned Nihilist student, had, despite her confession of guilt, recently been acquitted by a jury. Bismarck deplored the fact that the Tsar was not more severe with the Nihilists. The judges who had acquitted Vera Sassulitch should have been sent to Siberia immediately, and the twelve jurymen who had agreed to the acquittal should have been hounded out too.

Prince Alexander describes his discussion with Bismarck in his diary under the date June 30, 1878, and also in a letter written from Berlin on July 1st. Concerning the Congress, he said to Bismarck: "I hear praise of Your Excellency's impartiality on all sides. The diplomatists say that you reprove Christians and Turks alike." Bismarck smiled, and replied that it was extremely difficult to preside impartially over such a

Congress, and said among other things: "I have to take into account all interests; I even have to consider the Crown Princess's political views."

On June 30th Prince Alexander dined with Andrássy and Shuvaloff in a restaurant in Berlin, and afterwards all three repaired to a wine-shop, where they discussed the situation quietly. In the course of the evening the Russian brought forward the name of Prince Alexander's son Sandro as candidate for the Bulgarian throne. On the following day the Prince went to see Andrássy, who recommended him to sound Francis Joseph and England on the subject of his son's candidature. He also said that the Emperor Francis Joseph would be quite prepared to get on to friendly terms with Russia again. That sounded like mockery in the middle of a Congress whose deliberations and decisions were inflicting serious damage upon Russia. Life was certainly very difficult for Shuvaloff in Berlin. "I was really sorry for the poor fellow," Prince Alexander wrote to the Tsar on July 1st, "abandoned in the most incredible way by England and exposed to the ill-will of Austria-Hungary; supported to some extent by Bismarck and not at all by Waddington [William Henry Waddington, French Foreign Minister and French representative at the Congress] or Corti [Count Luigi Corti, Italian Foreign Minister and representative of Italy at the Congress]. To help him he only has the illustrious ruin Gortchakoff and that useless creature d'Oubril [Paul d'Oubril, a Russian diplomatist], and in addition he is besieged by the small fry who are all out for their own ends." Prince Alexander left Berlin before the end of the Congress, with the feeling that he had been watching a "party of reckless gamblers at the roulette table".

The Congress of Berlin resulted in a defeat for Russia all along the line. Her only territorial gain was in Asia. Bessarabia was restored to her. South of the Danube, however, everything happened as England and Austria wished. Bulgaria was not made into a large State; on the contrary, the territory inhabited by the Bulgarians was divided, and one—the southern—half was rechristened Eastern Rumelia, remaining a Turkish province, though an autonomous one. Russia was once again excluded from the Balkans and was caught in the mouse-trap of the Black Sea, for the exits by way of the Dardanelles and the Sea of Marmora were still barred to her. Her dream of reaching the Mediterranean had vanished. Andrássy, a very handsome figure, who appeared at the Congress sometimes in the becoming costume of a Hungarian magnate and at other times in the gold-laced uniform of a Hungarian cavalry general, had ably seconded Beaconsfield, the avowed antagonist of Russia. "Andrássy is a handsome aristocrat," he wrote to his Queen with great satisfaction; "I won him over entirely, he supported me on all points. In fact, the Northern Alliance is at an end."

The Hungarian Count did indeed return home with a permit for the occupation of Bosnia and Herzegovina—albeit a wretched substitute for the splendid provinces lost in Italy—but he also bore with him Russia's feeling of hatred and lust for revenge, which had flamed up again more strongly than ever, as they had done after the Crimean War. "The outcome of the Congress", says Rachfahl very truly,[156] "awoke in Russia a burning feeling of disgrace and humiliation. With regard to England this varied in the course of time according to the particular monarch who happened to be on the throne, and also according to the views of different Governments. Time, however, did not change the feelings towards Austria-Hungary which were embodied in the person of the Emperor Francis Joseph, and which grew even more fierce under the successors of Alexander II until the bitter end. The Berlin Congress also marked the beginning of the Russian dislike of Germany, the evil consequences of which could only be kept in check by the brilliant statecraft of Bismarck so long as he was in power. It was felt in Russia that Germany and Bismarck had supported her far too little, and, according to Bismarck, the Tsarina said so to a Prussian representative in the words: "Your friendship is too platonic."

France, who was hoping for revenge, watched developments with covert satisfaction. Bismarck himself was quite alive to the result. He drew the logical conclusion at once. He made up his mind to develop a closer understanding with Austria-Hungary. This in the following year led to the Austro-German Alliance.

CHAPTER XI

DEATH OF THE TSAR AND TSARINA

THE Eastern Question confronted the Tsar with many problems. The anxiety and the worry and the tremendous responsibility that weighed upon him affected his nerves and his general health so seriously that whereas he had left for the scene of war the picture of health, he returned a worn, bowed man with sunken eyes. And as if his burden were not heavy enough there came the unsatisfactory issue of the Berlin Congress. All Russia was grumbling that—except for Bessarabia, which was really only a return of what had formerly been theirs—there was practically nothing to show for the immense expenditure of men and money. In consequence the Tsar's popularity waned. The nervous strain was increased by the double life he was leading between, on the one hand, his wife whom he esteemed and honoured, but no longer loved, and who now lay at death's door, and, on the other, the Princess Dolgoruki whom he had come to love late in life, but perhaps, therefore, all the more ardently. He felt the wrong he was doing the Tsarina all the more strongly since he was chivalrous by nature and was moved by her silent acquiescence in her fate. His love for the young Princess, however, was even stronger, and the inner conflict could not be stilled. The Tsarina, who was now only able to move in a bath-chair, was still making a gallant fight against her illness, and though her handwriting in the letters to her brother was now tremulous, she still took the same interest in politics and her family life, and especially in all that concerned the husband whom she loved so dearly. Nor did she forget her brother and his family. Sandro of Battenberg's candidature for the throne of Bulgaria had once more come into the forefront of public interest. His name was on everyone's lips. Once when Sandro was in St. Moritz undergoing a cure for some gastric trouble, he overheard some Germans at the *table d'hôte* refer to him as an adventurer with nothing to his name, who had only taken part in the Russian campaign for the sake of what he could get out of it. The likelihood of his obtaining the crown, however, became increasingly greater. Prince Alexander heard from Andrássy that Francis Joseph agreed to Sandro's candidature; that, in fact, as Prince Alexander wrote and told the Tsarina on July 31, 1878, he would be very pleased "to see the son of so valued a friend entrusted with the mission of piloting Bulgaria towards a happier future". The Tsarina read this letter to her husband, who said: "Of course, if they decide on him I shall say nothing against it. But in his own and his father's interests I certainly do not covet it for him!"—"You know", the Tsarina added in the letter to her brother in which she told him of this remark, "that I feel the same. I should be wretched to think of one of my sons being in so difficult a position. . . . The election must take place soon; nevertheless a choice that did not suit us would be inadmissible." Austria's favour was no recommendation for the young Prince of Battenberg in St. Petersburg. The Russians were jealously watching Austria-Hungary occupying Bosnia and Herzegovina—an occupation attended by unexpected military difficulties. "The Austrians", was the Tsarina's comment in a letter to her brother on August 3rd (15th), "are meeting with more resistance than they expected. Then they boast of glorious victories, which are really no more than skirmishes with undisciplined bandits. I only hope they will have a thoroughly bad time over the business."

Anxiety regarding foreign affairs retreated before the threatening internal situation in Russia. Agitation was beginning in many of the provinces against the absolutist régime which, despite reforms and the Tsar's benevolent intentions, still oppressed Russia. Sundry reckless desperadoes were banding together and forming organizations and unions, whose political programme was revolution, and whose banners bore resounding devices such as "Land and Property", "The Freedom of the People", etc., which veiled political terrorization of the Government officials and finally of the Tsar himself. An "Executive Committee" led and organized the political terror and issued the necessary orders. The police, including the famous Secret Police, proceeded with increasing severity against the agitators, and every time any of them were arrested those who still remained at liberty dreamt of revenge. Thus on August 16th, two days after a leader of the party popularly called the "Nihilists" had been beheaded, General Mezentsoff, the Chief of the Secret Police, was stabbed in the middle of a populous square. It all happened so quickly that before anyone had had time to realize what had occurred the murderer had vanished and was not to be found. Apart from the loss of Mezentsoff, an able man and absolutely devoted to the imperial family, the escape of the murderer gave the authorities a shock and made them realize the necessity for improving and strengthening the police forces. This was regarded by the other side as a fresh threat and only spurred them on to further efforts.

While the Tsar and Tsarina were living in this condition of latent warfare, Prince Alexander spent his time idyllically in Darmstadt and Ems, where he was taking a cure at the same time as the old Emperor William. His letters seemed to his sister like tidings from an enviable oasis of peace. Everyone in Ems was much interested in the imminent divorce of the Princess Mary of Monaco (*née* Hamilton), who was staying at Baden-Baden with her lover, the "rich young turf-magnate," Count Tassilo Festetics. Despite the fact that for eighteen months past the annulment of her previous marriage had been vainly sought of the Pope, Festetics behaved as if he were already her husband. Both Count Festetics and Prince Frederick of Hesse-Cassel were winning enormous sums in bets on the wonderful Hungarian mare Kincsem, who was just then running her thirty-ninth race. The horse had run for the first time on July 31, 1876, and afterwards easily beat every thoroughbred that ran against her, including the best race-horses in France and England. Kincsem had already run several gruelling races before arriving at Baden-Baden, and also had travelled a long distance by rail. She was obliged immediately to compete against some of the finest horses in the world. Amid the tense excitement of the spectators the first race resulted in a dead-heat between Kincsem and a stallion, Prince Giles I, belonging to Count Henckel. Kincsem's owner, jealous for the mare's reputation for invincibility, proposed a decisive race on the same day. Despite her previous exertions, the splendid mare started once more only an hour after the drawn race. The beautiful dark chestnut with the white star pricked her ears, stretched her tail and in a long, even, tremen-dously swift stride, ran away from all her competitors appa-rently with the greatest of ease. The stallion finished five lengths behind her. After this Kincsem ran another thirteen races, and won every one of them. With an unbeaten record she began her life as a brood-mare. Prince Alexander, who was not as a rule in the least interested in racing, was immensely impressed by this miraculous animal whose achievements for a moment distracted men's minds not only in Baden-Baden but all over the world from their political anxieties.

The Emperor William had just told Alexander that he wished Sandro of Battenberg to be transferred to the Gardes du Corps. Gone was the time when, on November 29, 1865, Alexander of Hesse had written contemptuously of the Prussian Guards to the Tsarina, and had described George von Rudolstadt, who had come to visit him as a "big fool of a fellow, the typical Potsdam Guardsman, with a red face, silly, conceited, and affected, with waved hair and spurs longer than his feet, filled with pity for all the poor devils who do not serve in the Prussian Guards and yet imagine themselves to be soldiers!"

Now he was pleased and proud, but he had more ambitious plans for his son. He inquired of the Tsar in a letter written on September 24, 1878, whether the Bulgarian project were serious or not. But he received no answer. Alexander of Hesse saw the Emperor William in Baden on October 14th, and the Bulgarian plan came up for discussion. The Emperor did not appear particularly surprised, and only asked the Prince if he thought that his son was really capable of filling the position. For his part the Emperor said he would favour the idea if it took concrete shape, but he could do nothing further. "Twelve years ago", said the Emperor, "I refused even as head of the family to say yes or no to Charles Hohenzollern when he wanted to know what he was to do about Rumania. In such a case every man must decide for himself." Meanwhile Alexander of Battenberg had taken up his quarters in his new garrison at Potsdam, where no less than five of the most famous of the Prussian regiments of Guards were stationed. The magnificent white uniform of the Gardes du Corps with its high boots and silver helmet suited the tall, handsome young officer excellently. But he had hardly been in Potsdam for more than a few weeks when his father received from him a not unexpected request for an increased allowance. "Life is so fearfully expensive, and every cabman, every porter, every waiter, and so on, demands an enormous tip simply because one happens to be in the Guards", said Sandro in writing to his father on November 3rd.

At about this time diphtheria broke out in the family of the Grand Duke of Hesse. The Grand Duchess Alice, after nursing her dying child, herself succumbed to the disease on December 14th. The news shocked her mother the Queen profoundly, the more so since the Grand Duchess died on the anniversary of the death of the Prince Consort. "It seems almost incredible and most mysterious!" wrote the Queen in her diary on December 14, 1878. "To me there seems something touching in the union which this brings, their names being for ever united on this day of their birth into a better world."[157]

Although Princess Alice had striven against Prince Alexander's influence all her days, he forgot their antagonism as he stood beside her coffin, and remarked in a letter to his sister on December 19th: "In spite of her faults, Alice was a remarkable, forceful, and clever woman, and it is a thousand pities that everything that she began and planned must now remain unfinished. . . . Louis and his family have become a rudderless ship." The Prince of Wales and one of his brothers had come to Darmstadt for the funeral, but at the Queen's orders, for fear of the diphtheria, they attended all the various ceremonies at a distance. A positive panic reigned. No Prussian or Bavarian prince dared to go near there; and for a time the Hessian capital remained a place that was feared and shunned by all.

Soon, however, life resumed its normal course and the exigencies of politics required that the Powers should define their respective attitudes to the Bulgarian question. The Russian Governor-General of Bulgaria, Prince Dondukoff, would have liked to become ruler of the principality himself, but the Tsar was obliged to veto the idea, knowing very well that Europe would never agree to a Russian. "Everything", wrote the Tsarina to Prince Alexander on December 9 (21), 1878, "that goes on in Bulgaria seems to me so confused, so full of danger threatening for next spring—like our whole position with regard to Turkey—that I am filled with dread and anxiety. The maintenance of the army will ruin us completely; our internal situation, with the total devaluation of the money and the prospect of new taxation which is helping on the underground work of the socialists, is most serious. The burden resting upon the Tsar is almost superhuman."

Russia could not resign herself to the idea of the partition of Bulgaria decided upon by the Congress of Berlin. "Salisbury", wrote the Tsarina to Prince Alexander of Hesse on December 19th (31st), "complained to Shuvaloff that our commissars were supporting the Bulgarians in their desire for union, to which Shuvaloff replied: 'If you cut a nation in two like a sheet of paper, can you suppose that you are doing work that will last?' Salisbury answered: 'All we want is that the Treaty

PRINCESS ALICE

of Berlin shall be carried out. Then we will consider further.'
How does that strike you as logic?"

The Tsarina had become a little more careful in her expressions. She had been warned that her letters to her German relations would be opened and read by the postal authorities. "Since I have heard that Bismarck reads my letters", she wrote to her brother on March 2 (14), 1879, "I am making all those that pass through the post quite colourless."

Meanwhile the Russian revolutionaries continued their activities. Prince Kropotkin, the Governor of Kharkoff, was shot dead in the street, and the Nihilists were preparing feverishly for another attempt upon the Tsar's life.

On March 29, 1879, General Drentelen, Mezentsoff's successor as Chief of the Secret Police, was shot at in his carriage by a Nihilist on horseback. The general was unwounded and the assassin once again escaped. Prince Alexander anxiously observed the continued series of murderous attacks upon highly placed persons. "The whole of Russia", he said, "should rise up as one man against this gang of murderers who are terrorizing the empire." His fears were not unfounded. On April 4th, as the Tsar was taking a short walk near the palace, he suddenly saw a very tall man dressed like a Government official approach him rapidly. When the man was within a few yards of the Tsar, he put his hand into his pocket, pulled out a revolver and fired no less than four shots at the Tsar. Despite his sixty years, Alexander II made a swift and agile dash for safety. Owing to the hastiness of the movements of both men the bullets went wide, and in a moment the assassin was surrounded and hewn down by the sword of a police officer. As he fell he fired a fifth time. The shot passed through the Tsar's cloak and grazed his foot—though he did not notice it until later. He hurried at once to the Tsarina. "You can imagine", she wrote to Prince Alexander on April 11th (23rd), "how I felt. The first thing we did was to thank God on our knees for the wonderful escape. The Tsar is marvellously calm and cheerful. . . . He is fully determined not to flinch before the severest measures. . . . I admit that I feel broken and am longing for rest, which the Tsar needs so badly too. He feels it so irksome never to be able to go out unless he has an escort of Cossacks, to which he has been with difficulty persuaded to agree. May God have mercy upon us."

A statement made by the thirty-year-old assassin, an ex-student named Alexander Solovioff, was subsequently submitted to the Tsar. He said that he and his party considered that the great majority of the people in the country toiled in order that a small minority might enjoy the fruits of this labour and the blessings of civilization that were totally inaccessible to the rest. The document impressed the Tsar very deeply.

While these tragic events occurred in St. Petersburg, the Bulgarian national assembly had met in Tirnova, and on April 29th, after the Tsar, for want of any other suitable candidate, had agreed to Alexander of Battenberg, they unanimously elected the twenty-two-year-old prince as Prince of Bulgaria. Related to the English royal house, a German prince and the son of a general whose Austrian sympathies were well known, a nephew of the Tsar and yet not a Russian, Alexander seemed to be the best fitted to be at the head of the new State that had been born in Berlin, and was regarded so mistrustfully by all the Powers. Salisbury remarked sceptically in a letter to Queen Victoria on January 12, 1879,[158] that no doubt the prince would accept the proffered position, for, "as he was poor and nothing but a lieutenant, he might look upon the principality of Bulgaria as a promotion".

Duke Adolphus of Nassau was voicing the opinion of many when he wrote to Sandro's father from Vienna on May 1st, saying: "I do not know whether I ought to congratulate you or to condole with you, but I rather fear the latter. The young man will be in a position which, even if tenable, will be beset with immense difficulties." The Bulgars at first wished to go and fetch their new ruler from Darmstadt. But despite Prince Alexander of Hesse's protests the Tsar very irritably insisted that Sandro of Battenberg should come to him at Livadia, and that the Bulgarian deputation should meet him there.

Prince Alexander agreed to the long-desired election of his son gladly, but with grave concern for his future. "The poor boy", he wrote in his diary on June 8th, "will have to sacrifice his youth to the arduous task. He seems determined to make the attempt. He will unfortunately be faced with a constitution that is more democratic than any other in the monarchist world. It is an incredibly clumsy piece of work, very democratic in tendency, and full of gaps. In three weeks' time poor Sandro is to take his oath to this constitution, which will make it impossible for him to rule."

Sandro of Battenberg left immediately for Russia. The Bulgarian deputation arrived at the same time and amid great festivities the young man was proclaimed Prince of Bulgaria.

The Tsarina reported that the whole affair had seemed like a family party, during which mistrustful Europe had for the time being been forgotten.

It is noteworthy that the Grand Duke of Hesse actually apologized to his mother-in-law, Queen Victoria, for young Battenberg's going to Russia. "He sets a great value", the Grand Duke wrote to the Queen on May 8th,[159] "on your being informed that he is *not Russian* in heart, and that he is *not* inclined to act as Russia's tool. He is, therefore, rather vexed by the invitation to Livadia, as he sees it is but too natural that people will say he is gone to get his instructions, and as he is altogether likely to be regarded as a Russian vassal. He yielded at length simply to avoid giving offence to the Emperor, and to avoid appearing ungrateful, since he and his family owe so much to the Emperor's kindness."

This communication was not an ordinary matter of courtesy, but really expressed Alexander of Battenberg's inmost feelings, in which the germ of the final issue of the young Prince's Bulgarian adventure lay concealed.

From Livadia the new ruler went on a tour of the European courts, beginning with Vienna and Berlin, where Bismarck bade him farewell at the end of his interview by saying that even if the attempt did not succeed, he "would at all events take away a pleasant recollection".[160]

Sandro next went to London. The Queen received the handsome young Prince and his brother Louis in so friendly a manner that the bad impression left by the so-called espionage affair in Turkey was quite effaced. She promised him her support, urged him not to be too Russian, and wrote most warmly about him to Lord Salisbury and Lord Beaconsfield.[161] Naturally enough her friendliness was looked at askance in Russia. "*A propos*", said the Tsarina in a letter to Prince Alexander on June 7th (19th), "the Queen seems to have been very friendly. It appears that Brown [the Queen's greatly favoured factotum] has deigned to approve of the new Bulgaria. I should have liked to have seen the two boys while they were in her toils!"

Sandro of Battenberg went by sea to Varna, where for the first time he set foot in his new principality. A magnificent reception had been prepared for him and filled him with apprehension in anticipation. As a result of the unaccustomed food in Constantinople, he was suffering from most acute gastric trouble, and in addition a hurricane was blowing, and

S

the waves ran as high as houses. Prince Dondukoff went to meet him, but found him lying in his bunk incapable of uttering a word. After everyone had spent hours waiting for him on shore, the young prince made a supreme effort and entered his new principality pale as a ghost and in danger every moment of fainting. The week's journey round his dominions which followed immediately was, in the circumstances, sheer torture. In Sofia the palace, which looked big enough from the outside, proved to contain very few rooms fit to live in. Five servants were crowded into one room and the kitchen was too small to cater for the requisite number of people. Difficulties arose within the first few days when the Prince appointed a Conservative Ministry. "I could do nothing else", he wrote home. "I am too anxious to prove to Europe and to the country itself that with my advent Bulgaria has become a monarchy . . . and that not only will I not protect Nihilists, but I shall pursue them with fire and sword. Can you believe it when I tell you that in the few days I have been here I have aged by *ten years*? All the scum of Russia has taken refuge here and has tainted the whole country; and the man under whose protection all this gang has collected is Dondukoff. Thanks to Dondukoff's dispensations the Russian system of bribery has actually been sanctioned, and every day I find myself faced with the painful necessity either of agreeing to the *most impudent* demands or of being accused in St. Petersburg of treason and wounding the most sacred feelings of the Bulgars."

Within the first three weeks the Prince had come into conflict with all the Russian officials in Bulgaria, and was obliged to appeal to the Tsar.

"In consequence of all these difficulties", he wrote to his father on July 12th (24th), "the whole country is in a state of great ferment, and petitions reach me daily to save Bulgarian interests."

In consideration of the probability that, as Sandro said, "certain important communications might not be in accordance with the Russian desires", he asked his father to get a special cipher made for his correspondence. The first few months on the throne of Bulgaria nurtured in the young ruler, who was still somewhat too hasty and inexperienced, a violent hatred of all that was Russian. Whenever anything happened he saw the hand of Russia. During the alterations that were being carried out in his palace at Sofia cracks appeared in the building. Sandro wrote home, saying: "The

LOUIS AND ALEXANDER OF BATTENBERG VISITING QUEEN VICTORIA
IN JUNE 1879
Caricature by Prince Louis

disgraceful way in which the few things that the Russians did here were carried out is shown by the fact that in three rooms and in a passage the ceilings *fell in* with a crash like a cannon-shot. Thank goodness nobody was there at the time or they would certainly have been killed.—In consequence a scaffolding has been put up over my bed in case I should be flattened out one night. The ceilings in *all* the rooms have to be taken down now, so that the place is in a horrible mess. . . ."

In the great questions of internal and foreign policy, too, he felt after the first two months that matters could not be worse. "When I took over the government", he said, "I found that, thanks to Dondukoff, Bulgaria was on the worst possible terms with *all* its neighbours." He was even more dissatisfied with internal affairs. He considered that the constitution deprived him of the paramount influence in the government of the principality and complained that he was not allowed to make any alterations in it. He was even prepared to turn to the Tsar Alexander for help, since "the future loomed very black" to his eyes. His Conservative Ministry was being undermined, and in the third month of his reign the Prince was already considering a *coup d'état*. "I would rather fall in a fair fight", he said, "than dig my own grave. I shall be sorry for the Bul-garians, but I shall always have a burning hatred of the rascally Russians who have made things so impossible for me.

"Furthermore, it is so terribly hard to be absolutely depen-dent upon *myself alone*. I trust *nobody*, not even my friends; and you know how foreign that is to my character—how I love to be frank and open! But I have to keep everything to myself, for at every step I am surrounded by spies. At times I feel I shall burst, because I am so longing to talk to somebody and cannot. Just think, the men the Russians left here for me as footmen, lackeys, etc., are *Russian agents*! . . . Every party has its spies in the palace, because each is hoping to get some hold over me and have me at its mercy. Though I am so worried and anxious internally, I have to hide it under an air of great calm and assurance, and always be suave with everyone. Oh, it's simply unbearable!—If only I can carry through the business to a satisfactory conclusion, I shall not mind having borne all this. But someone had the unblushing impudence the other day to tell me that if I would not do it, Prince Waldemar of Denmark certainly would!—My worst enemies are the Russians, and I have to be so desperately careful to save my own skin without injuring the Tsar Alexander."

Prince Alexander of Hesse was filled with anxiety as he read Sandro's first letters from his new country. He was convinced that everything depended on the Tsar and Tsarina's being well-disposed towards him. He was sure of his sister, but her health had recently taken another serious turn for the worse.

Ever since the Congress of Berlin the Tsar had entertained feelings of great resentment against the governments of Austria-Hungary and Germany. More particularly against the former State, whose attitude during the recent war he designated as "equivocal as usual", according to a note made by the Emperor William of a conversation he had with the Tsar on September 4, 1879.[162] A year later things were worse rather than better. Having been informed that German agents in the East had been working against Russia, he was induced to administer to the Emperor William on August 3rd (15th) the famous epistolary snub, in which he not only expressed his views on the Austrians, whom he alleged to have been always systematically hostile to Russia, but also depicted the sad consequences which German policy would have upon the neighbourly relations of the two States, that the Press was already beginning to undermine.[163] The Tsar went on to remind the Emperor of the service rendered by him to Prussia in 1870, and of the German Emperor's saying at the time that he would never forget it. He added prophetically that the consequences of the tension between the two countries could only lead to the downfall of both.

This letter which, without mentioning Bismarck's name, severely attacked his policy, determined the Chancellor finally to decide between Austria and Russia in favour of the former, and to establish a close alliance between Austria-Hungary and Germany. He planned, nevertheless, to remain on such terms with Russia that war should be avoided. A stern struggle ensued between the Chancellor and his imperial master, who could not at first make up his mind to throw overboard the old and tried friendship with Russia. He was the less inclined to do so, because a personal interview with the Tsar at Alexandrovo had confirmed his conviction that to desert Russia—which an alliance with Austria-Hungary would definitely imply—would signify the beginning of the end of the Russian friendship and possibly of immeasurable ill-fortune for both empires. Finally Bismarck had his way. The momentous treaty was concluded on October 7, 1879, with the assistance of Andrássy, who was most anxious to meet

Bismarck half-way, and of the Emperor Francis Joseph who, in Bismarck's words to the Emperor William, "saw no advantage in a closer alliance with Russia".[164] The Emperor William found it very hard to sign the treaty. It was as if he foresaw instinctively the terrible consequences of the breach between the three empires.

Prince Alexander of Hesse, who had all his life been working to bring together Russia and Austria-Hungary, and in whose view the preservation of the Three Emperors Pact was the only guarantee for the welfare of all three realms, was utterly dismayed by the alliance, which, as he wrote in his diary on September 23, 1879, meant the isolation of Russia. Peter Shuvaloff also felt that as a result of the treaty, "whatever happened, the last remains of the Three Emperors Pact had been destroyed". Alexander II's cares were not confined to matters of foreign and internal politics, but he also had his personal troubles. The tuberculosis from which the Tsarina had been suffering since 1872 was running its course slowly, but with deadly certainty. The Tsar watched the gradual fading away of his wife with sorrow in his heart. She had long since accepted the fact that her husband sought other women physically, but that Katherine Dolgoruki should also take her place with the Tsar as a companion was the bitterest grief to her during all that remained of her life. It was terrible to her to have her rival established in the same palace. Nevertheless the Tsarina in this as in all other matters stood by her husband and accepted the insult in silence and with inimitable dignity to the very last moment. A journey to her beloved Heiligenberg and to the milder climate of Cannes made the situation easier for both parties. Meanwhile, however, the conspirators in St. Petersburg were not idle. On June 24th, in the same year, the members of the Executive Committee of the Revolutionary Party held a sort of congress at Voronesh at which the idea of the overthrow of absolutism and the conquest of liberal rights by force of arms and terrorization of the Tsar and his government were discussed. The congress pronounced sentence of death against Alexander II, to be carried out immediately and with any means at their disposal. Despite the fact that the work had to be carried on under the most difficult conditions and in constant fear of arrest—which implied prison, banishment, or death—money was raised and several hundredweights of dynamite were prepared with very primitive means and at the risk of a fatal accident. The Tsar had been staying in the

Crimea with the Princess Dolgoruki and was planning to go back to St. Petersburg. Mines had been laid along the route in three places with the most fiendish ingenuity. One of the plotters, a good-looking young woman richly dressed, went to see a high official on the railway and asked him to give a protégé of hers, whom she described as her footman, a post as signalman on the railway, saying that his wife was suffering from tuberculosis and needed the country air.[165] The request was granted, and thus two dangerous criminals obtained admission to a signal-box not far from Odessa. They at once laid a mine under the railway lines. Fortunately their plan miscarried in consequence of the Tsar's route being changed at the last moment. The imperial train went by way of Kharkoff. Another mine had been laid on this line too. The conspirators were all at their posts as the train passed through, but they had made a mistake in connecting the electrodes and the mine failed to explode. Yet a third attempt had been planned upon Alexander's life at a point where both the imperial train and that carrying the suite must pass. The conspirators did not, however, know which of the two was the Tsar's train and the wrong one was blown up. The two engines and three coaches were thrown off the rails, but by a miracle no one was injured. The signal-box, from which an underground passage had been built to a point underneath the railway lines, was found empty. On the walls hung pictures of saints and portraits of the royal family. The effect upon the Tsar, hunted as he was like a wild beast, and upon the whole of Russia was terrible. In the light of all these events, with their results upon Alexander II's nerves, it is not surprising that the constant complaints which reached St. Petersburg from Sofia were received in none too sympathetic a manner. In consideration, however, of the fact that Sandro was his wife's nephew, the Tsar exercised great patience.

Prince Alexander of Battenberg had meanwhile decided to go personally to St. Petersburg in February, and to demand a new Constitution of the Tsar and the removal of Parentsoff, the Minister for War, as well as absolute powers over the Russians in Bulgaria.

"I pin my hopes", said the Prince in a letter to his father sent from Sofia on December 25, 1879, and covering no less than sixteen pages, "to the Tsar's noble and enlightened mind. But at the same time I am determined not to deviate from my three conditions. I am not discouraged, for I have heard indirectly that the Tsar Alexander is still labouring under an altogether false impression. And nobody could have been through more than I have in the last few months. But the worse the Russians make it for me, the firmer I shall be."

Even before this letter arrived Prince Alexander of Hesse had written to the Tsar in his son's behalf, and had told him that he was convinced that the only hope of salvation for Bulgaria lay in the suspension of the Constitution for several years. At the same time the Tsar also received a letter from Sandro written from Sofia on November 27th, asking for his direct intervention. The Tsar, however, was wholly opposed to any intervention on the part of Russia. He was also opposed to any *coup d'état*, and in a letter written from St. Petersburg on December 16th (28th) he advised Alexander of Bulgaria to find a way out of his difficulties by constitutional means.* He sent a copy of both the letter and the answer to Sandro's father on the same date, adding: "It seems to me much more sensible to keep as far as possible to constitutional paths before deciding on a *coup d'état*, for one may then have a reasonable hope that all the Great Powers will be on our side and in favour of an alteration in the state of affairs in Bulgaria. It is true that the order—or rather disorder—of things in Bulgaria is *not due to me*, but to what was arranged at the *Congress of Berlin*."

The Tsar's advice failed to comfort Prince Alexander, who feared that it would completely discourage his unhappy son. But what was to be done? For the time being no course remained but to wait and see what would happen when Sandro went to St. Petersburg in February.

Meanwhile the Nihilists, despite the miscarriage of their attempts to blow up the Tsar, had not been idle, but were preparing a fresh attempt on his life in St. Petersburg. The Revolutionary Committee was aided in its design by the jealousy of the Lord Chamberlain, Count Adlerberg. He had refused to allow the police any jurisdiction within the Tsar's palaces. In spite of the fact that in December a man had been arrested carrying a detailed plan of the Winter Palace on which the dining-hall was marked with a red dot, and, further, that at about the same time Bismarck had a police report conveyed to the Russian Ambassador according to which part of the Winter Palace was to be blown up on February 17th of the following year, Count Adlerberg permitted unknown labourers to work and actually to live in the palace, although

* See Appendix.

he had a year before disbanded the military labourers' colony on grounds of economy. In this way a carpenter named Stephen Chalturin, a member of the Executive Committee of the Revolutionary Party, had obtained admission to the palace. He made it his business to become friendly with a watchman who lived in the basement, by making love to his daughter. And every day as he came to work he brought dynamite in his tool-box and placed it in that part of the cellar which lay immediately below the room where the Tsar and his family were in the habit of dining. A Finnish Infantry Guard was stationed in an intervening storey, but that in no way disturbed the assassin. By means of his friends at the palace he found out that Prince Alexander of Hesse was to arrive with his two sons on February 17th, and that an informal dinner was to take place at a particular hour.

The day came, but the train was half an hour late. When they arrived at the Winter Palace the Prince and his son Sandro were as always very cordially received by the Tsar. But they thought him much changed and greatly aged. The Tsar proposed taking the Prince to his room at once, but Alexander asked first of all to be allowed to see his sister. Meanwhile the fuse which had been timed exactly for the appointed dinner hour burnt out.

As the Tsar and his guest stepped into the main corridor a fearful explosion was heard which shook the floor under their feet. At the same time everything was suddenly enveloped in a thick cloud of smoke and dust. The gas jets flared high for a moment and then mostly went out. In the indescribable panic which followed, Prince Alexander for a moment lost sight of the Tsar. Someone called out of the darkness to say that a lustre had fallen and thus caused a general explosion. Prince Alexander followed by the Tsarevitch and the Grand Duke Vladimir ran into the Yellow Salon whence the explosion had seemed to come. There the table which had been set for dinner with the most beautiful china and the choicest glass and silver presented a sad spectacle. Broken glass and china littered the floor, all the windows were smashed, a huge hole gaped in the wall and the whole room was filled with dense fumes. Heartrending shrieks were heard from the wounded in the courtyard below. The Tsar dashed instantly to the apartments of the Princess Dolgoruki, whom to his great relief he found safe and unhurt. Then he hurried out again to learn further particulars. As Prince Alexander was about to leave the scene

THE TSAR ALEXANDER II
1878

of desolation he met the Tsar who had just been informed that a large mine had been exploded underneath the main guard-room. Thanks to the fact that the dinner hour had been some-what delayed none of the members of the imperial family had been present in the Yellow Salon, but in the guard-room under-neath seventy men of the Finnish Guards had been blown up with the stone flags on the floor and had then crashed down into the cellars with the wreckage. Eleven men were dead, forty-four wounded, thirty of them seriously. Every one of the windows in the Winter Palace, except those in the Tsarina's room, which faced towards the back, were shattered. The Tsarina, however, had heard nothing of the explosion. She was in a very feeble state and had just fallen into a deep sleep after an injection of morphia. When she woke up she was only told that there had been a slight explosion of gas. In Prince Alexander's bedroom, the only other room in which the windows had not been broken, a table was improvised. It was a gloomy meal and nobody could eat anything. Meanwhile the Prince of Bulgaria and his brother Louis had also arrived, and were with difficulty conducted to the Tsar through the general panic and in the profound darkness that reigned in stairs and corridors. After dinner they all went to the Tsarina, who still knew nothing of the attempted assassination. Prince Alexander thought she seemed just as weak and ill as she had been when he had last seen her at Cannes. The Tsar appeared to have aged ten years in the last few hours. Apart from his fear of assassination, he felt even more deeply a sense of horror that he should be so hated in his country that he could never for a moment be sure of his life. Not until the next day at breakfast was the Tsarina told the truth by her husband about the explosion.

St. Petersburg society and the imperial family speedily re-gained the customary calm. They were getting so used to that sort of outrage that they no longer experienced the same shock and alarm as in former days. From now on, however, any of the conspirators who were arrested were no longer executed secretly and by night, but in the full light of day and in public, as a warning to others.

The whole world was profoundly shocked by this fresh attempt on the Tsar's life. In England anxiety was felt for the lives of Prince Alfred and his wife, who were staying in St. Petersburg, and both were urged to return home. Outwardly court life went on as usual and as though nothing had happened.

Festivities were even held to commemorate the Tsar's silver jubilee. Bell-ringing, cannon-shots, and never-ending hurrahs greeted the Tsar when he stepped onto the balcony. At the theatre in the evening he was cheered to the echo. Although inwardly everyone trembled for him, he drove unmolested through the city in the afternoon, and was everywhere enthusiastically greeted. But on the very next day—March 3rd—a young Polish Jew shot point-blank at Count Loris-Melikoff, who had been empowered with dictatorial police authority, and wounded him slightly. As he was being led away he called out mockingly to Loris-Melikoff: "Unfortunately I did not succeed, but there are plenty more where I come from." Two days later he was executed. It was everywhere observed how many Jews were among the Nihilists. Amid all these agitating events it was impossible for Prince Alexander of Bulgaria to lay his wishes before the Tsar as he had planned. In view of his loneliness in Sofia he began to think about getting married. His mother was anxious to have him engaged to the Princess Helen of Mecklenburg, the daughter of Duke George of Mecklenburg-Strelitz and the Grand Duchess Katherine of Russia. She telegraphed to him daily at St. Petersburg on the subject. But Sandro did not care for the girl: she never had a word to say; he heard the most unfavourable reports of her; the two other children of the marriage were "complete idiots"; and why, he asked in writing to his mother on March 6 (18), 1880, should she be anything else?

He would much rather have married the young Princess Youssupoff, a charming girl and heiress to a large fortune. But her father was very reserved, returned evasive answers, and postponed a decision to a later date without turning him down altogether. Hence this project came to nothing. Meanwhile Sandro's mother, who was anxious regarding the fate of her plan, telegraphed, as Prince Alexander entered in his diary on March 18th: "For Heaven's sake make up your minds. Time is pressing. This is a unique opportunity. Louis's career is nothing compared with such a match. I am burning with anxiety. Reply." Since, however, Sandro's views did not change any more than Prince Youssupoff's attitude, the marriage question was shelved for the time being. Of his political demands the Prince of Bulgaria only obtained the dismissal of the Russian Minister for War in Bulgaria. Russia definitely vetoed the idea of a change in the Constitution.

"In the end", Sandro wrote home, "I left the capital feeling thoroughly exasperated, and I realized that in future I must stand on my own feet, and above all that I should never again ask for advice and comfort in a land that cannot deal with its own difficulties. The Tsar was once again wonderfully kind to me, and I have a feeling for him that nothing can shake. But one cannot avoid a sensation of gloom when one sees the people by whom he is surrounded, and especially those who exert a decisive influence upon the fate of Russia. If I were to analyse my feelings for Russia I should say that I love and honour the Tsar as a god, I love all the imperial family, and *I love Russia*. But I simply hate St. Petersburg and all its creatures in other cities; nor shall I ever ask them for advice again." Sandro, who still thought that he had a good chance of marrying the Princess Youssupoff, felt that he could only do so if she never got to know the society of St. Petersburg, because it was "the most wicked and corrupt in the world, and he was utterly disgusted by it".

Hardly had the Prince returned to Bulgaria than he was faced with innumerable fresh difficulties. The division of the country continued to present the greatest problem. Numbers of people throughout the land were casting longing glances at the part that had been cut off and burdened with the ridiculous newfangled name of Eastern Rumelia.

"I wonder if the damned diplomatists in Berlin have ever guessed what a fine mess they have made of affairs in the Balkan Peninsula?" Sandro wrote to Prince Alexander of Hess on April 25 (May 7), 1880. "I can hardly think so, otherwise hell would be too good for them. My situation is most difficult; there is a general wish to be up and doing, but we are not 'ready'. . . . 'If you will give the signal, we shall all rise as one man', being translated means: 'As soon as you have declared war, I shall become head of the Commissariat and help myself to a few millions . . . .' and so on. (Those who make the most noise in the various countries are the ones who did *not* take part in the last war!)"

Meantime the revolutionary party in Russia became more and more venturesome. Anonymous letters and manifestos descended in showers. For a long time past no one had dared to open packages addressed to the Tsar or anyone in his immediate surroundings in the palace. They were opened at a safe distance amid the greatest precautions by men specially trained for the work, because there was always the fear that explosives might be contained in them.

The Tsarina's health, too, grew increasingly worse. For the past few months she had never left her bed, and her death was daily and hourly expected in the palace. But her strong constitution still fought gamely for life. Owing to the terrible strain on the Tsar's nerves and the false position he was in with regard to his wife, it happened that he sometimes failed for days together to see her. He was living with the Princess Dolgoruki in Tsarskoe Selo, while the Tsarina remained in St. Petersburg. The last few weeks of her life she was barely conscious, and in the night of June 2–3, 1880, she died while no one was with her. Her maid came into the room as usual at seven o'clock in the morning and realized to her horror that life had fled.

The Tsar's telegram, "The soul of our dear Marie is in heaven", came as a terrible shock to Prince Alexander. He instantly set out for St. Petersburg for his sister's funeral, which took place with imperial pomp. The Tsar was deeply moved, although the Tsarina's death removed a heavy load from him in regard to his second family. Countess Marie Vorontsoff, the Princess Dolgoruki's old enemy, did not fail to say spitefully to Prince Alexander that "the Tsar's mistress had stood in the gallery of the palace watching the coffin being carried from the church to the fortress".—"What boundless effrontery!" remarked the Prince in his diary. It was observed that the funeral ceremonial was very much curtailed. While as a general rule the services lasted for a month in the case of a Tsarina, on this occasion everything was over in a week.

Life in St. Petersburg resumed its appointed course. The Tsar, who went in constant fear of his life, was obliged after the death of his wife to make some attempt to secure the future of his illegitimate children. He would rather have waited until the year of mourning for the Tsarina had come to an end. But how could he be sure that he would still be alive in a year's time? He knew that the legitimate children of his first marriage, especially the Tsarevitch, as well as all the rest of the imperial family, were bound to look upon a hasty second marriage with the woman who had been his mistress for years as an affront to them all, and an abominable insult to the memory of the late Tsarina. Nevertheless he regarded the whole matter from a different standpoint. He idolized the Princess and above all the children of their love. The Dolgorukis were a princely Russian family of venerable antiquity; the Tsar Michael, the first of the Romanoffs, had married a Dolgoruki. In view of the anti-German feelings that now reigned at the Russian court it was an immense satisfaction to the Tsar to feel that his illegitimate son was Russian on the mother's side too. Hence he soon made up his mind. About the middle of July, that is a bare six weeks after the Tsarina's death, he decided to marry the Princess Dolgoruki and thus to legitimize her children. The ceremony was to be kept secret from everyone until rather more time had elapsed after the Tsarina's death. On July 18th, Princess Katherine Dolgoruki was married to the Tsar in the presence of only three persons, in a small out-of-the-way room in which only the scantiest preparations had been made, in order to avoid any publicity. At the same time the Tsar also assured the material future of his second family and bestowed the princely name of Yourievsky upon them. For the present this was all that lay in the Tsar's power to do. Future events might still make it possible to raise the Princess formally to the rank of Tsarina.

To keep the marriage secret was a task beset with insuperable difficulties. When the Tsar was planning to go with the Princess to the Crimea, where he was intending his morganatic wife to live in the country house at Yalta that he had given her, while he himself stayed at the palace in Livadia, anonymous letters arrived threatening that she and her children would be murdered on the journey. Thereupon the Tsar decided to take them all in his suite and to let her and the children all live at Livadia with him. The Lord Chamberlain was commanded by the Tsar not to deny the marriage if he were asked, but to refrain from making any official announcement of it.

The Tsar concealed his intention of marrying the Princess Dolgoruki even from Prince Alexander. The Prince continued to remain on terms of the closest friendship with his brother-in-law, and the Tsar now turned to him to ask his intervention in a love-affair of his son's, the Grand Duke Alexis, who wished to marry Elisabeth, the daughter of the Grand Duke of Hesse. Neither she nor the Grand Duke were inclined for the match, since conditions in Russia made living there hardly a desirable prospect. Hence the Grand Duke made various excuses. The refusal that Prince Alexander had perforce to convey to Russia annoyed the Tsar, who had naturally grown particularly sensitive in recent days. Hence he wrote very sharply about it to Prince Alexander.

Prince Alexander had other things on his mind. His daughter, Marie Erbach, had just had another child the birth of which necessitated a serious operation. It was given the names Victor Serge, and Queen Victoria was one of the godparents.

Despite all attempts at secrecy the news of the Tsar's hasty remarriage had reached both Darmstadt and Sofia. Prince Alexander had no words to express his feelings on the subject, but his son found excuses for the Tsar in a letter which he wrote home: "At first the Tsar's remarriage made me very angry. But I calmed down gradually as I considered that the unfortunate man must be the unhappiest creature alive; and that his broken heart would naturally cling to the one person who has never deceived him.—Forgive him, dear Papa. I believe that your sister, who was the kindest person in the world, would bless you for being understanding with the man whom she loved inexpressibly, although she knew that he had been unfaithful."

Prince Sandro was possibly not altogether disinterested in taking such a lenient view of the Tsar's second marriage. He was determined to insist on an alteration of the Constitution and proposed to have the matter settled some time in October. "Now I have realized", he wrote to his father on January 27, 1881, "that a crisis is bound to come, my aim must be to bring it about as soon as possible, and above all *before* I am married. I shall stick to my point and rather perish honourably than humiliate myself to becoming the puppet that dances to the strings pulled by base motives. . . . I still have time on my side. I am young and unmarried, and if chance should go against me, then at all events, as Bismarck said, I shall have had an interesting experience. Once I am married, I am lost. The Bulgars themselves realize that and are urging me to get a wife. Karaveloff told me the other day that on the day I got married the Civil List would be a million, and so on. But I said to him that I could not suppose that he really believed himself that any father would give me his daughter so long as things were in such a state in the country." New marriage projects had recently been in question. A Princess of Weimar, for instance; and it had been hinted that it might be possible for him to win the hand of Victoria, the daughter of the Crown Princess of Germany, who had come to know and to admire the handsome Guards officer in Berlin.

"My trip in the spring", remarked Sandro in regard to a suggestion that he should go the round of the courts with a view to finding a wife, "is to be a holiday. If I happen to meet princesses in the course of it, so much the better; if not, it does not matter, because I will certainly put my affairs in order in the autumn.—I know the Weimar girl; she is old and ugly. It is too early yet to think about the Crown Princess's daughter; at all events to put anything in writing. I shall probably see her in the spring, then I might speak to her about it." The Tsar had also been consulted in the matter of Sandro's marriage projects, but he either forgot to say anything on the subject in his replies, or—which is more likely—he did not wish to be involved in it.

"The only excuse for his absentmindedness", remarked Alexander of Bulgaria, "is that he never knows in the morning whether he will not be dead before night."

The Tsar was also occupied in securing his new wife's position in the imperial family circle. The children of the late Tsarina adopted a very uncompromising attitude. The Tsarevitch and his wife could not but put a good face on it. But none of them could reconcile themselves to the new marriage in their inmost hearts. They regarded it as an appalling disgrace in the eyes of the whole world; and were, finally, not a little anxious regarding the male members of the second family, who had more Russian blood in their veins than they themselves. This circumstance was to prove more than a little conducive to the Tsarevitch's showing himself much more friendly disposed to the Pan-Slav movement than his father had done. A letter of the Grand Duchess Marie (*née* Princess of Mecklenburgh), the wife of Vladimir, the Tsar's younger son, writing to her uncle, Prince Alexander of Hesse, reveals very clearly the feelings of the whole family. She waited for a long time for an opportunity to send him this letter by German hands, for she regarded the Russian couriers as too unreliable. "This marriage of the Tsar's," she wrote, "six weeks after the death of our dear Tsarina, is hard enough to bear in itself. But that this woman, who for fourteen years has occupied such a very invidious position, should be introduced to us as a member of the family surrounded by her three children is more painful than I can find words to express. She appears at the family dinners large or small, and also in the private chapel before the whole court. We are forced to receive her and to visit her. The Tsar goes on visits with her in a closed carriage, though not yet in a sleigh. Since her influence is very great, things go a step farther every day, so that one cannot see where it will all end. Since the Princess is very uneducated, and has neither tact nor intellect, you can imagine the kind of life she leads us. Every feeling, every sacred memory, is trodden under foot, we are spared nothing. The Tsar has commanded us as his subjects to be friendly with his wife; if not he would force us to it. You can imagine the internal conflict that agitates us all, and the perpetual struggle between feelings, duty, and external pressure."

Hatred and revulsion against this woman whom none of them wanted to accept find expression in every word written by the Grand Duchess. "The new wife", she continues, "is nearly always ill-humoured, treats her husband very badly and without the least consideration, and he takes it all smiling. I have hardly ever heard her speak a kind word; she has something unpleasant to say of everybody, and since he believes everything she says, she is doing incalculable harm. . . . Things occur which I cannot bring my pen to set down. They would pain your fraternal feelings too greatly. My heart is so full that I cannot find the right words to give you an idea of the complete overthrow of everything that one had hitherto thought to know as rules of conduct. I often feel that things *cannot* go on for long in *this* way, that the Tsar's eyes must at length be opened to the worthlessness of the creature who seems to have him bound as in a spell, to make him deaf and blind. Up to the present he is utterly and blissfully happy, looks very well, and years younger."

The Grand Duchess's last words show that she was not altogether just in her very severe criticism. She contradicts herself, because she did not take the trouble to imagine herself in the position of the Tsar, who was being hunted like a wild beast and who had for the past fifteen years been bound to a wife who was suffering from an incurable disease. The Tsar found his sister Olga, the Queen of Württemberg, much more understanding. True she did not live at the Russian court, and did not, therefore, experience the awkwardness of the situation. The Tsar had written her a long letter as early as October 20, 1880, telling her everything: "I should certainly not", he said, "have married again before the end of the year's mourning if the times in which we live had not been so critical, and if I had not every day to run the risk that a fresh attack would successfully put a sudden end to my life. I am concerned, therefore, to secure as soon as possible the future of the being who has lived only for me during the past fourteen years, as well as of the three children which she has borne me. Despite her youth, Princess Katherine Dolgoruki preferred to forgo all

OLGA NICHOLAEVNA, QUEEN OF WÜRTTEMBERG

the pleasures and amusements of society, which generally mean so much to young people of her age, in order to devote her whole life to surrounding me with love and care. She therefore has every right to my affection, my esteem, and my gratitude. She has literally never seen anyone except her only sister, and never mixed herself up in anything, in spite of many temptations to do so. Indeed people have had the impertinence to use her name without her knowledge or permission. She lived for me alone, and devoted all her time to bringing up our children, who have hitherto been an unadulterated joy to us . . . I can assure the family that Katherine completely understands her position as a morganatic wife, and will never make claims which do not *correspond with my wishes as head of the family and as sovereign.* I only hope that other members of the family will remember this and not force me to remind them of it."[166]

The Grand Duchess Olga replied most cordially that if the Princess made the Tsar happy she was entitled to the gratitude of the whole family. Eventually Alexander II also decided to tell his brother-in-law of his marriage. The Tsar referred briefly to the postponed betrothal of his son and to the hostility of Queen Victoria, expressed the hope that Sandro would be able to maintain his honourable post in spite of the intrigues by which he was surrounded, and deplored the internal crisis in Russia.

"The fire of revolution", he wrote, "continues to smoulder under the ashes, as we have daily opportunities of realizing. I can never go out without an escort, which gets terribly on my nerves. . . ." Then he referred to his marriage. "When I ask my conscience, it appears to me that in my situation every decent man would have acted as I have done. My wife already knows you through me, and knows that in you I have a faithful friend, whose friendship has never wavered for forty years. Hence she has learnt to value you at your true worth, and loves you without having had the opportunity of making your acquaintance. I am taking the liberty of commending her to you and also to Julia, and I hope that for my sake you will give her some degree of your friendship. Regarding my feelings for you, you know that they will never change, and that in me you will always find your old friend and affectionate brother Alexander."

Prince Alexander received this letter with mixed feelings. There was nothing for him to do, however, but to acquiesce.

T

Only too soon were events to prove how right the Tsar had been to set his house in order betimes. The revolutionaries did not stay their activities. They had already made six attempts upon the Tsar's life and had paid for these with the hanging of no less than twenty-one persons. They were determined not to abandon their aim. The blood of those who had paid the penalty seemed to lay a sacred duty upon them, and hence a series of the most various plans for attack was concocted. One idea was to lay an underground mine beneath Little Sadovaya Street, along which the Tsar was in the habit of driving. For this purpose the revolutionaries rented a small shop where they set up a dairy business. The business was only a pretext. While cheese and butter were being sold upstairs, they were busily at work below digging a tunnel. The only difficulty was what to do with the earth that was dug out. Finally it was put into large butter kegs that were stacked in the cellar and at the back of the shop. A police officer once came to investigate the place in the guise of a sanitary inspector. He observed the dampness of the kegs and inquired the reason for it. "I spilt some cream at Easter-time", answered one of the conspirators. The police officer did not inquire further and discovery was avoided. The tunnel was not finished and the mine not laid when the news came that the Tsar would probably be driving down Little Sadovaya Street on Sunday, March 13th. The conspirators worked feverishly during the last hours that remained to them. In addition to the mine, they spent fifteen hours during the night of March 12th to 13th manufacturing bombs with immense difficulty. These were finished at precisely eight o'clock on the morning of the fateful day. The conspirators knew that they were threatened by almost certain death, either by their own bombs or else by arrest and execution. But their fanaticism was greater than their fear—they envisaged themselves as the saviours and liberators of Russia. Their faith raised them above all fears, and spurred them on to perilous deeds. They were still not quite sure how or where the attacks upon the Tsar were to be carried out. The Tsar himself spent the last few days of his life in the closest intimacy with his second family. Sometimes he felt so happy that he was quite frightened, for he feared that it could not possibly last. The continued oppression of the menace to his life caused him repeatedly to tell his eight-year-old son George and his seven-year-old daughter Olga, while stroking the hair of little Katherine, a baby of two, how they were to behave when their father should no longer be with them. The Tsar's was fundamentally a noble nature, though possibly lacking in resoluteness. He sympathized with his people. But he was continually prevented by circumstances and by those surrounding him from carrying out his humanitarian ideals. On that fateful March 13th he had just drawn up a form of Constitutional Government for Russia which he embodied in a memorandum that he gave to Count Loris-Melikoff shortly before leaving for his last drive.

His good intention was destined to remain unfulfilled. After arranging to meet his wife at a certain time to go for a walk, the Tsar drove to see the changing of the guard at the St. Michael Cavalry barracks. The Tsar did not drive down Sadovaya Street. The revolutionaries, therefore, abandoned their tunnel and the mine, and decided to make their attempt on his life as he came back, when he would probably drive along beside the Katherine Canal. Men with bombs were posted at four separate places. If one failed, another was to step into the breach; the Tsar was at all costs to be killed this time. It is interesting to note that after the Tsar's failure to appear on Sadovaya Street it was a woman named Perovskaya who realized the situation, and with lightning rapidity reorganized the affair.

Meanwhile the Tsar watched the changing of the guard in the immense square at the St. Michael Cavalry barracks. After this he paid a short visit to his cousin the Grand Duchess Katherine before returning to the Winter Palace. The Tsar was driving in a sledge drawn by two splendid white horses, and closely escorted by six Cossacks. Police officers and aides-de-camp followed in two more sledges. At this time—about 2.15 in the afternoon—the quay along the Katherine Canal was practically empty. Only an occasional soldier or policeman was to be seen, a young man with long hair, who was leaning against the railing, carrying a little parcel wrapped in newspaper, and a boy aged about fourteen coming along the quay with an empty basket. As soon as the imperial sleigh passed the man with the newspaper parcel, he raised his hand and hurled the package at the Tsar. A fearful explosion followed. Everyone was smothered in clouds of snow and smoke out of which came the heartrending cries of the wounded. Two Cossacks with their horses, whose sides had been torn open, were rolling on the ground, staining the snow with their blood. Beside them lay the little boy with the basket. The Tsar's sleigh was very little damaged, the windows were broken and the Tsar himself saved as by a miracle. The coachman had been told that if anything of the kind were to occur he was to whip up his horses and drive back to the palace with all possible speed. He was about to do so, but the Tsar ordered him to stay and, as he was preparing to disobey, Alexander II seized the reigns and brought the horses to a standstill. He sprang out and was about to go over to help the wounded Cossacks.

At that moment another man who had meanwhile come up with his hands hidden under his cloak threw down a white object at the Tsar's very feet. It was the Nihilist Grinevitsky, who had seen that his companion Rissakoff's bomb had failed to do its work. The second bomb was better aimed. It tore the Tsar's legs below the knee, blood poured from the hideous gashes, wounds gaped in his right side and his face and the right hand was torn to pieces. His cloak and cap were in tatters. The assassin too lay bathed in his own blood. The Tsar's suite seem to have behaved with singular clumsiness and stupidity and to have lost their heads entirely. At last they went over to the prostrate Tsar and were concerned above all to take him away instead of first bandaging his wounds. In a faint voice the Tsar said: "Quicker . . . home, take me to the palace . . . die . . . there."[167] The Tsar was now hastily lifted into his sleigh, the cushions of which were soon dyed scarlet with his blood, and driven at a furious gallop back to the Winter Palace. Cossacks bore the Tsar, whose wounds were still open and unbound, through several apartments to his own bedroom. A long trail of blood marked the way to the bed. There was still another delay at a door that would not open. The Tsar's blood poured in streams while the door was burst open.

Meanwhile the Princess Yourievsky was waiting unsuspectingly in her hat and coat ready to go out with her husband, who was usually so punctual. She began to grow a little uneasy when it came to be twenty minutes past the appointed time. At that moment a servant dashed into her room pale with terror, gasping out the words: "His Majesty the Tsar is ill." Filled with horror the Princess snatched up a bottle of oxygen which she had prepared for such an occasion and hurried across to her husband's bedroom. She was appalled to see the consequences of the incredible remissness with which the transport of the Tsar had been carried out. Having been carried into the palace with no bandages on and without a stretcher, he had suffered a fearful loss of blood, and now lay pale as death, unconscious, and barely breathing.

"It is I, it is I, my beloved, don't you hear me?" sobbed the Princess, and knelt at the head of the bed, dabbing her husband's forehead with ether and holding the bottle of oxygen to his nose. The doctor came up to her: "Be brave, Princess; we shall have to amputate the feet. May we?"

"Yes, yes; do anything, only save him."

But it was too late. The wounds were too terrible. The priest gave him the last unction. The Tsar never recovered consciousness. At thirty-five minutes past three he was dead.

On the evening of March 13th Wagner's *Flying Dutchman* was being performed at the Opera House in Darmstadt. In the course of the second Act the door of Prince Alexander of Hesse's box was flung open and his daughter Marie Erbach appeared with an unopened telegram from St. Petersburg. Prince Alexander seized it, read it, grew deadly pale, and handed it to his wife. "A fresh and irreparable misfortune has befallen us", it ran. "Papa has been assassinated and is dead. Vladimir." Trembling with horror, Prince Alexander and his wife left the Opera and went to tell the terrible news to the Grand Duke. It took a long time before Prince Alexander and his family realized what this death meant to them all. The Tsarina had faded away, and now eight months later her husband had followed her into the grave.

The whole of Europe was appalled at the Tsar's assassination, though the numerous unsuccessful attempts that had previously been made upon his life should have in some sense prepared the public for it. While the world was filled with horror and indignation, the revolutionaries were delighted and enthusiastic. They felt that now all the imprisonments and banishments, all the executions, had been avenged. Reaction had been stabbed to the heart. In reality nothing whatever had been accomplished. A new Tsar came to the throne. His first act was to withdraw and cancel the Constitution that had been drawn up and signed by his father. A few weeks later came the day of reckoning for the revolutionaries. The murderers of the Tsar went to the scaffold. At their head walked their ringleader Sophia Lvovna Porovskaya. It was revealed at the trial that she came of a very distinguished family, and that her father had actually been Governor of St. Petersburg for a time under the murdered Tsar. It was for the first time realized how far social disintegration had gone, and that Nihilists were drawn even from the privileged classes.

Prince Alexander of Hesse immediately left for St. Petersburg to attend the Tsar's funeral. He broke down utterly as he stood beside the frightfully mutilated body of the Tsar whose face was concealed beneath a covering, and whose right hand was invisible. In the coffin lay the glorious brown hair of his sister's rival. She had cut it off as a sign of her overwhelming grief and despair. In horror he gazed upon the bloodstained tatters that remained of the Tsar's cloak and uniform, of his trousers and boots, and the red marks along the floor of the superb apartments through which the wounded man had been carried to his deathbed. Then the Prince drove to the place where the murder had taken place, and where a temporary chapel had been erected at which masses were read for the soul of the departed, in the presence of thousands upon thousands who wept and mourned their late ruler upon their knees. More clearly than ever did the Prince realize the incredible extremes of the Russian soul. Bathed in tears, the thirty-six-year-old Alexander III followed the coffin of his father and predecessor. He could not but ask himself whether he would not one day encounter the same fate.

CHAPTER XII

BULGARIA

As Prince Alexander of Hesse watched the landscape slipping past the windows of the railway carriage on his way home from St. Petersburg, he must have wondered how the change of rulers in Russia would affect the relations between the European Great Powers, and also what difference it would make to the relations of his own family with that of the new Tsar. He knew and had already had proof in various small ways that the warm affection which, despite the misunderstandings of the last few years, Alexander II felt for Germany and its imperial family was not shared by his son. The new Tsar did not like the Germans and hated having German blood in his veins on his mother's side. A story was current that the Tsarevitch·had been in the habit of imposing a fine on anyone who spoke German at his soirées. As a daughter of the King of Denmark, whose land had suffered so much at the hands of Bismarck, Alexander III's wife, Dagmar, was no more inclined than was her husband to foster a love of Prussia and Germany. These antipathies did not at the outset appear in the conduct of foreign affairs. During the last years of the late Tsar's reign and with his sudden death Alexander III had passed through too hard a school not to realize that in the present internal situation of Russia no military adventures could be embarked upon. During the Russo-Turkish War he had seen only too clearly how for a time the fate of Russia hung in the balance. Moreover, a war against Germany and Austria-Hungary was a very different proposition from one against Turkey. In addition, the Tsar had seen how strong the Nihilist movement had become after the war. Alexander III went in fear of his life and withdrew to Gatshina, where precautions to ensure his safety could most easily be taken. He was determined to maintain his autocracy uncurtailed and put an end to all ideas of Constitutional Government. Officially he proposed to keep the peace with all the Powers. Unofficially, however, he allowed the Pan-Slav movement to carry on its work unhampered, and indeed encouraged it by his sympathy. The cautious foreign policy which the Tsar desired for the time being to see pursued found its right exponent in Giers, who was not at once appointed Foreign Minister, but who in reality had controlled foreign policy for a long time past.

Since Bismarck and especially the Emperor William I were anxious that Russia and Germany and Austria-Hungary should enter into a close relationship,[168] the so-called "Three Emperors Agreement" was signed on June 18, 1881. It was a very artificial union. The conflicting interests, especially of Russia and Austria-Hungary, were not in any way resolved by it—only the settlement was postponed to a later date. This postponement of the day of reckoning suited Bismarck's plans and he pursued that policy all his life, which made it possible to safeguard Prussia and Germany against Russia even more certainly later by the "Reinsurance Treaty". Hence the relations between the three empires evolved along these lines in the immediate future. It had always been Prince Alexander's great aim in life to help to keep them on good terms with one another. Now he felt otherwise. The new Tsar excluded the Prince altogether from international affairs; he was told nothing; he no longer had the Tsarina's letters to keep him informed; and the direct consequence was that Prince Alexander also lost his political significance at the Viennese court, since it had always rested solely upon his close relationship with the Russian court.

On the other hand, the Prince of Bulgaria now came into the limelight. Unfortunately, however, not in a manner calculated to improve his father's relations with Russia. The Tsar and the young Prince had never been particularly friendly, but it is not in accordance with facts to say that Alexander III never behaved towards Sandro with anything but dislike and hostility. It is true that the Tsar lacked his father's warmth of feeling, but at first he manifested towards the Prince of Bulgaria a certain kindliness not far removed from friendship. Prince Alexander of Battenberg, of whose feelings for Russia no doubt was now possible, made mistakes in his behaviour to his imperial cousin. He forgot that he must treat the Autocrat of all the Russias not merely as a somewhat older cousin but also as the ruler of a mighty realm. He did not observe the customary formalities in his correspondence with the Tsar, and thus immediately brought about a personal rift. As in the course of time Alexander III realized with increasing certainty that Prince Alexander was in no sense merely the executive organ of the Tsar's will in Bulgaria, but was on the contrary in many ways working against Russian influence, friction sprang up between them, which finally led to dislike and hostility. The youthful impetuousness shown by the Prince in the early days

was not a little to blame for it. St. Petersburg cast a mistrustful
eye upon the wide powers which Sandro induced a newly
elected and complaisant Sobranie to give him by a sort of
coup d'état on July 13, 1881, and also upon his marriage projects.
It is true that nobody in St. Petersburg as yet knew that the
Crown Princess of Germany had hinted to Prince Alexander
of Hesse when he had last stayed in Berlin that she would
be glad to see her daughter Victoria married to his son;
but it was supposed that an Austrian marriage was contemplated.

For a moment, indeed, the Vienna Government did contemplate such a possibility, which would have resulted in
bringing the young ruler of Bulgaria under Austrian influence. Baron Alexander Biegeleben, a friend of Prince Alexander of Hesse, came to see him at the request of Prince
Charles of Ysenburg-Birstein, to offer him an Archduchess
for his son Sandro. The lady in question was the Archduchess
Maria Antonia, the eldest daughter of the late Archduke
Ferdinand of Tuscany. She had been born in 1858, and her
widowed mother had asked Prince Ysenburg to undertake the
mission. Prince Alexander replied that he felt that nothing
could be more flattering, and telegraphed to his son immediately. Sandro's reply, as entered in his father's diary on
November 27, 1881, was: "Must see photograph before
deciding. Fear effect in Russia. Otherwise very flattering.
Cannot remember having seen her since Dresden."

In a subsequent letter written to his father from Sofia on December 1st (13th), Sandro expressed himself even more plainly:
"As regards the Archduchess, I must admit that it would be
by far the best alliance as there is no Russian princess. But
hatred of Austria is so violent here that I fear it will be impossible. Hatred of Germany—which after all never did
Bulgaria any harm—is almost strong enough to undermine my
position, and this is as nothing compared with their hatred of
Austria. It is one of the hardest things to bear in a foreign
land—to hear one's own country maligned. It absolutely
demoralizes one.—At present the tendency in St. Petersburg
is more than ever hostile to Austria. The Tsar himself is blind
in his hatred. . . . He sent me a code telegram the other day:
'After all the loving care of which my father and I have given
proof to Your Highness and Bulgaria, I fail to understand that
Your Highness did not find it possible to prevent the conduct
of affairs falling into the hands of a party *hostile to Russia*.' "

"In the Tsar's present mood anything might happen", added the Prince.

This letter gave Prince Alexander of Hesse food for thought. He observed with anxiety the growing tension between his son and the Tsar: Sandro was paying too little regard to Alexander III's wishes and had appointed a Minister who did not please him. Thereupon he received a telegram saying that the Tsar regretted that the Prince of Bulgaria had elected to enter upon a path on which he could no longer support him. At the same time the Russian Minister in Sofia announced that he had requested to be transferred "as he no longer cared to be a witness to the Prince's *Austrian* policy". This proved once again that no treaties or understandings could diminish the lasting—indeed increasing—antagonism between Russia and Austria-Hungary. Ever since the accession of Francis Joseph, Vienna had become increasingly Russophobe. Indeed, Metternich had embarked on this anti-Russian policy during the last years of what must be called his reign. The Tsar Nicholas had positively courted Austria. Alexander II had done his best until the very last to re-establish good relations, although Austria's attitude during the Crimean War had left an enduring feeling of burning resentment in his heart. Nevertheless he was obliged to realize that Austria-Hungary did not wish to be friendly, but indeed was continually placing obstacles in Russia's path in the Balkans. During the Russo-Turkish War and at the Congress of Berlin Andrássy gave added offence by his hostile attitude. Throughout the last years of his life Alexander II had come to realize that no real reconciliation or community of Austro-Hungarian and Russian interests was possible, unless the Danubian monarchy completely reversed its policy.

Alexander II died. But the Emperor Francis Joseph went on living and reigning. The new Tsar was restrained from embarking on any fresh military undertakings by the critical internal situation of Russia and the necessity for reorganizing his army. While hitherto the lion's share of the blame for the deterioration in Austro-Russian relations must be laid at the door of the Vienna Government, Russia from now on became the aggressor, persistently disregarded Austria-Hungary's interests, and whatever the latter subsequently did she invariably found Russia barring her way, just as she herself had previously barred Russia's. Old sins were bringing their punishment. And all the efforts of Andrássy's successors and even of the Emperor, whom increasing years made more pacific, were destined to remain fruitless. The catastrophe, however, did not work up to a rapid climax; it was postponed for decades. At that time the antagonism found expression in the person of Prince Alexander of Bulgaria, who was too young to cope with so delicate a political situation. He was tossed back and forth by the conflict of interests of the various Great Powers and the corresponding parties in Bulgaria. Added to this was the fact that he felt more closely akin to the German Powers. "It is my misfortune", he wrote to his father, "that the Russian diplomats distrust me personally purely on account of racial hatred, and are always accusing me of being swayed by *Austrian* motives."

An intolerable situation had already developed in Bulgaria. A Russian Colonel named Timmler, who was at the head of the Bulgarian Ministry for War, had the presumption at an official dinner when someone proposed the Prince's health ostentatiously to push away his glass and at the same time to stare at Prince Alexander insolently and challengingly. After dinner the Prince informed the Colonel that unless he were beyond the frontiers within forty-eight hours he would be brought up before a court-martial. By way of reply, Timmler laughed in his face and said: "To be turned out by you, my dear sir, is the best of recommendations in Russia,"[169] Thereupon Prince Alexander demanded of the Tsar by telegram that Timmler should be suspended from his rank for a year. The Tsar acceded to his demand. The year had hardly passed, however, before the Colonel was promoted to the influential post of Assistant to the Chief of the Russian General Staff. A more obvious slap in the face for Prince Alexander could hardly have been imagined. The Prince was now obliged to make up his mind once again to go to St. Petersburg in person to lay his complaints before the Tsar and try to find a solution for his difficulties.

Meanwhile Giers, who was moderate and pacifically minded, had been officially appointed Foreign Minister in Russia. On the other hand the Pan-Slavist agitator, Count Ignatieff, was Minister of the Interior. The Russian general, Skobeleff, alarmed Europe by making after-dinner speeches in which he expressed his deep sympathy for the Southern Slavs whom he alleged to be oppressed by Austria-Hungary, and uttered the wish that Russia and France should unite to settle Balkan problems.

When Prince Alexander of Bulgaria arrived in St. Petersburg he was amazed at the precautionary measures that had everywhere been taken. The Anitshkoff Palace, which was surrounded by a deep moat to prevent mines being laid, looked like a fortress in expectation of a siege. Day and night it was patrolled by Cossacks. Anyone who wanted to enter had to pass the scrutiny of crowds of officers and sentries. Even in the part of the grounds that was reserved for the Tsar, grenadiers were stationed everywhere, as well as members of the so-called "Sacred Drushina", whose primary duty was to guard the Tsar's life. Prince Alexander's welcome was not of the warmest. Nor did the prospect of his marriage with Helen of Mecklenburgh appear very promising. Everyone taunted him with being anti-Russian. On May 15, 1882, as recorded in Alexander of Hesse's diary, Sandro telegraphed to his father from St. Petersburg: "Since my arrival the most disgraceful rumours have been going about the town concerning me and my doings in Bulgaria. The Tsar no longer exists, Giers is more cowardly, and the military party hostile to me is stronger than ever. I can find nobody to be Minister for War in Sofia, and am wasting precious time in awkward explanations. Even the Grand Duchess Katherine is beginning to hesitate and refuses to make any definite decision. She distrusts the situation in Bulgaria and wants me to wait. The Press slanders me and finds willing listeners, and nobody believes what I say, because I speak as an interested party. I cannot get away until I have found Ministers. St. Petersburg is a dreadful place. No Tsar, no royal family, no government, nothing! Not a single theatre. I live here as I do in Sofia, and am melancholy and dispirited." Prince Alexander tried to comfort his son, who continued to complain that the Russian military party hated him as a German. But he could not alter the facts. In the marriage project with Helen of Mecklenburgh Sandro was given a rebuff, which was due not only to politics but also to the personal feelings of the Princess in question. Vanovsky, the Minister for War, whom the Prince of Bulgaria asked for help in his troubles, only replied: "I can do nothing at all so long as ignorant Grand Dukes fill all the highest posts." The Lord Chamberlain omitted even the most ordinary courtesies. In the end, however, the Prince was offered two Russian generals, Kaulbars and Soboleff, as Ministers for War and the Interior. The Prince's views regarding conditions in St. Petersburg were also coloured by the meagre result of his visit. He went from there straight to his home and told his father how hopeless things were in

Russia; that the Tsar was an absolute cipher, felt that nobody would obey him, and was even at times quite apathetic about it. Sandro was to experience in his own person that this opinion was not in accordance with facts. At all events, he was so pessimistic that he advised his father at once to transfer any capital he had in Russia. His opinion was not based solely on the fact that he had repeatedly seen General Skobeleff in St. Petersburg and heard him boast of his alleged successful efforts to persuade the Tsar into war with Austria-Hungary and Germany. "My friend Gallifet will support us", Skobeleff would say on such occasions. It is no wonder that, when news of this description was filtering through, Austria-Hungary and Germany not only made a closer alliance but extended it to include Italy—which was then on bad terms with France—to form the Three Power Pact on May 20, 1882.

Sandro decided to make one last attempt to work with the Russians, and if that failed he determined that he would consider Bulgarian interests only. In making this decision he was over-estimating the means at his disposal, and believed that he could be independent. The future was soon to prove him wrong. In order to improve his relations with his neighbours he arranged a meeting with Milan of Serbia and also with Charles of Rumania. King Charles was a little dubious regarding the somewhat tempestuous domestic policy of his young colleague. "Charles", wrote Sandro to his father from Rustchuk on October 14 (26), 1882, "is by conviction and character unenterprising, and is thus an opponent of my policy. . . . Both he and she [Carmen Sylva] were rather chilly, and I was obliged to summon up all my energies to break the ice. After forty-eight hours I had succeeded perfectly . . . and we finally parted the firmest friends . . . so that Elisabeth was inclined to weep when we said farewell, Charles crept about my room in a melancholy fashion, and each of the four young ladies-in-waiting sent me a *billet-doux* requesting me to say good-bye to them in their several rooms so that it might be done without witnesses. And so I did—amid kisses, sobs, and embraces, each one believing herself to have been the favoured one.—To turn from this picture of Rumanian customs to more serious matters, I must tell you that I discussed the subject of my marriage fully with the Queen. I particularly asked her about Hilda von N. She advised me strongly against it, saying what is perfectly true, that it is better to have no wife than one who is a fool. She says H. [elen] has even less sense than her brother, though

he is stupid enough for anything."—On his return to Sofia,
Sandro met King Milan of Serbia, who shared his dislike of the
Russians. It was the more necessary to come to an understanding with him, as he wrote to his father on January 21,
1883, since "Bulgars and Serbs, alas, are hereditary enemies,
and five centuries of Turkish rule have done nothing to mini-
mize the old hostility". Milan falsely denied having any
Austrian leanings, and affirmed that his attitude was due
solely to his conviction that war between Russia and the
German Powers was inevitable; that it would be suicidal to
side with Russia, as it would be "beaten hollow" in this war.
On the other hand, owing to their common Slav ancestry, it
would be a crime to fight against Russia. Hence they must
remain neutral. This conversation between the two Balkan
Princes shows only too clearly how the relations of the three
"allied empires" were really regarded by the Balkans and the
rest of the world.

Prince Alexander of Bulgaria's interviews roused mistrust in
St. Petersburg where an anti-Russian character was ascribed
to them. The new Russian Ministers and the Bulgarians were
within a very short time "like cats and dogs". Nevertheless no
news had been heard from St. Petersburg for a long time. The
Prince drew somewhat too hasty conclusions from this. "I hear
nothing of the Tsar now", he reported. "We do not write to
one another and he does not interfere in our affairs, for which
I am very thankful."

Prince Alexander of Hesse did his utmost to help his son. He
had just been invited to go to Moscow for the coronation that
was planned for the following May, and which had been
hitherto postponed for fear of assassination. Even this invitation
had not come spontaneously. Hence the Prince tried to get in
touch with the royal families of Austria-Hungary and Germany
in order to put in a good word for his son. In April 1883 the
beautiful Empress Elisabeth was staying in Baden-Baden to
take the cure, and her visit seemed to afford Alexander a good
opportunity. Hence he tried to obtain an audience with her,
but days and weeks passed without his receiving an invitation.
Bulgaria, the Prince of Hesse, and all the rulers of the world
were a matter of complete indifference to the Empress Elisabeth. Baron Nopcsa, who supervised the Empress's travelling
arrangements, was obliged at length to tell the Prince that he
was really at his wits' end. He himself hardly ever saw Her
Majesty, because from eleven o'clock in the morning until

eight o'clock at night she went out riding or scrambling about in the mountains. She never took dinner, and therefore did not invite guests. Prince Alexander, however, did not desist and was finally received. He met the Empress, whom, on account of her "dieting and excessive physical training", he thought "impossibly slender", and tried to talk to her. Elisabeth replied to his questions by careless monosyllables. Hardly had her visitor made a move towards the door than she dismissed him abruptly and hurried away. The attempt ended as a complete failure.

Soon afterwards the Prince went to Wiesbaden where the Emperor William was staying and asked him to help his son. The Emperor replied that the Tsar was much displeased at Sandro's attitude, and did not pursue the matter any further.

Meanwhile the day fixed for the coronation in Moscow approached. Prince Alexander and his son prepared to attend the ceremony. It was to be celebrated with tremendous pomp to show an admiring populace that though the base designs of the Nihilists might bring about the death of a Tsar, they could not touch the power and magnificence of the ruling house. Despite the fact that the police declared expressly that they could not undertake the responsibility if the coronation procession with the whole imperial family and the foreign princes from all over the world were to pass through the streets of Moscow, the programme was carried through without the smallest regard for the possibility of any disturbance. Prince Alexander was lodged in the Kremlin. The princes all rode in a magnificent procession from Petrovski, which lay outside the city to the Kremlin. In front came the Tsar on a splendid milk-white Cossack stallion, immediately behind him his brother-in-law Alfred of Edinburgh. Then the Tsarevitch and Prince Alexander of Hesse. The Tsar's hand trembled slightly as he saluted the cheering masses thronging the streets on both sides. He expected any moment that a bomb might be thrown. When a lady immediately behind the lines of troops dropped her umbrella in her excitement at the very moment the Tsar passed, many a man in the suite started. The Tsar grew deadly pale, but remained calm and for a moment gazed very gravely at the woman who looked as if she wished she could have sunk into the ground. Behind the Tsar's procession came golden coaches drawn by eight horses and containing the Tsarina and the Grand Duchesses. Sixty thousand soldiers formed a double spalier all along the route; the front row facing the procession, the back row facing the watching crowds. The procession lasted a good hour and a half, and was a great strain on the Tsar's nerves. But everything went off quietly.

While Alexander of Bulgaria was staying in Moscow, the Russian generals who were acting as regents in Bulgaria behaved as they liked. They completely undermined the Prince's reputation, and even spoke openly of Prince Waldemar of Denmark as a candidate for the Bulgarian throne. Sandro did his best to come to an understanding with the Tsar and with Giers, but without success. On the contrary, the breach now became more marked. The Prince refused the Alexander Nevski Order with diamonds which was offered him, because he wanted the St. Andrew's Order. The question of a dowry of a million roubles in the event of the Prince's marriage was discussed. But during the coronation further news came in from the Russian representatives in Bulgaria which was highly prejudicial to the Prince and which still further poisoned the atmosphere. His father was also made to feel it. At the Court Ball on May 28th he was only introduced to ladies of lesser degree, and he and his son were then sent home, dripping with perspiration, while the immediate members of the family went to supper with the Tsarina. "I'll be damned", said Prince Alexander of Hesse, "if anyone ever sees me in Russia again on any ceremonial occasion." And in fact it was the last time that he was ever to set foot on Russian soil.

On June 3, 1883, the anniversary of his beloved sister's death, Prince Alexander sadly compared his present position with what it had been then. He was obliged to see his son ask repeatedly and vainly for an audience with the Tsar, until at length to the Tsar's wrath he forced his way in unbidden to his presence. Father and son quitted St. Petersburg with very bitter feelings. The Tsar, however, had come to the conclusion from what had happened while the Prince of Bulgaria was in Moscow that those who represented him as the covert enemy of Russia were right. He was filled with burning anger. He regarded himself as deceived and betrayed, and Russian influence in Bulgaria threatened by the Prince's ingratitude. He demanded that Sandro should submit altogether to the wishes of the Russian generals who were his Ministers. While a letter dated June 22nd still referred to him as his "dear Cousin", and ended with "sincere and cordial greetings", one of July 27th addresses the Prince as "Your Highness", and omits the "cordial" from the signature. The lack of cordial feelings was reciprocal, and induced Prince Alexander to request his father, in a letter written from Sofia on August 13th (25th), not to take any more steps on his behalf with the Tsar, whom he regarded as a "poor specimen of a man of honour".

No further attempt was made to disguise the hostility to the Prince of Bulgaria. He had realized that a Russian marriage was impossible. On his way home he met the Crown Princess of Germany, who had for several years past secretly cherished the plan of marrying her second daughter Victoria—a slender and elegant, though not actually pretty, girl—to the young Prince of Bulgaria, who had greatly taken her fancy. She had soon realized that the old Emperor, and more especially Bismarck, would oppose the marriage on political grounds. Berlin was very well informed regarding the relations between Prince Alexander and the Tsar, and was bound to realize that the marriage of a Prince who was in such disfavour in Russia to the daughter of the Crown Princess of Germany might be interpreted as an act unfriendly to the Tsar. The Prince and Princess did, as a matter of fact, come to a sort of understanding at that time in Berlin. In view of the prevailing circumstances it was kept so secret that Sandro did not even tell his father about it.

Meanwhile Louis, Prince Alexander of Hesse's eldest son, was betrothed to his cousin Victoria, the daughter of the Grand Duke of Hesse and grand-daughter of Queen Victoria. Thus once again Prince Alexander's family came into closer relationship with the British royal family, which despite Gladstone's pro-Russian policy was not on friendly terms with the Tsar. At the same time negotiations were carried on for the betrothal of Ella, another daughter of the Grand Duke of Hesse, to the Grand Duke Serge in place of the late heir-apparent Alexis. These negotiations were rather hanging fire owing to the fact that the Princess was apparently in love with someone else. Serge, however, was resolved upon this marriage and once more came to Heiligenberg in September, where he met the Princess again. When on this occasion the conversation turned on Bulgaria, Serge said that he had hitherto always defended Sandro, but that he could no longer support him because Sandro had not been straightforward with the Tsar. The whole imperial family, he said, was dismayed at the complete change in Sandro's attitude, and at the extraordinary manner in which he had permitted himself to behave all the time he was in Moscow.

U

At about the same time, on September 23rd, Count Hatzfeld, the German Secretary of State for Foreign Affairs, came to see Prince Alexander of Hesse, who talked to him about Bulgaria too. The Count was as frigid as he could be, displayed little sympathy with the young Prince of Bulgaria, and said that Bismarck thought that he had committed some serious faults. He added that Germany could do nothing to support Alexander of Bulgaria as it was most anxious not to quarrel with Russia. The Emperor Francis Joseph's tone was very different when the Prince went to Vienna at his invitation on September 26th. The Emperor once again manifested his hostility to Russia. Prince Alexander notes in his diary on September 26th that he spoke in the most friendly way about Sandro, who, he considered, should be given "credit for having without any help from the other Powers chosen the right means to combat the clumsy brutality of the Russians". Meanwhile an open breach with the two Russian generals in Bulgaria had occurred. The Prince dismissed them despite the Tsar's ultimatum. Then on October 1st (13th), he sought to make the situation clear to the Tsar in a fifteen-page memorandum recapitulating the whole woeful history, and added to the document the words: "The present situation must not and cannot continue. Despite all that has happened, despite all the insults that your agents have inflicted upon us, I stretch out my hand to you, Sire. Bid your people to consider my views, to come to an agreement with me . . . for no matter what anyone may say, I love Russia with my whole heart; and, no matter what anyone may say to contradict it, I have a feeling of deep friendship for Your Majesty's august person and for the whole of the imperial family." These final assurances did not accord with the true facts, nor did they carry any conviction in St. Petersburg. Indeed they did harm rather than good, for the Tsar regarded them simply as hypocrisy. Sandro reckoned his own position too highly and undervalued the power and influence of Russia. Only such mistaken ideas could cause him to send the following telegram to his father on September 23rd, which is copied into the diary on the same date: "I am supported so widely by the Bulgarians that Russia will have to come down a peg." And two days later: "Tsar Alexander has not replied to my telegrams. All Bulgarians are on my side. Tsar will have to give way. Shall avoid open breach, but feel frightfully insulted." Sandro ascribed all this to the actions of the generals, "who absolutely turned the country topsy-turvy".—"I have sent prayers and warnings thousands of times," he wrote to his father on October 3rd (15th), "but in vain. The Tsar with his limited mentality believes that I do not know the country; and the reason why he is now so furious is that he is feeling guilty." That, however, was not altogether true. The Tsar was particularly annoyed that the Austro-Hungarian railway had received the Prince's sanction to extend its lines into Bulgaria, while the Russian had failed to do so. The Prince was proud of this railway, which he was convinced would confer prosperity upon Bulgaria. But while he was gathering in a meed of praise from Austria-Hungary for "firmness and fairness", he was putting the final touch to the quarrel with Russia. Nevertheless he went still further, and aspired to do away with Russia's influence over the Bulgarian army, which was under the sole control of Russian officers from the Minister of War downwards. This was a fresh ground for a brisk and acrimonious exchange of notes with Alexander III. The Prince wrote to his father saying that while he would do all he could to avoid an open breach, he would make it clear to Russia that he might be led by kindness but would not be driven by insolence; and therefore he had sent a letter to the Tsar which merely noted without criticizing all Russia's base actions. The Prince's efforts towards independence and the wish of Bulgaria to be ruled by Bulgarians was altogether comprehensible and obviously the ideal to be striven for. But he had taken over the crown of Bulgaria on precisely the opposite terms and had not the forces at his command to realize his desire in the face of Russia's opposition. England and Austria-Hungary were disposed to be friendly, but if matters grew serious these Powers would stop at platonic good will or regrets. Even those who seemed to be his best friends did not wish for his sake to be drawn into a war of which they could not foresee the outcome, and Bismarck on no account whatsoever.

Meanwhile the Tsar Alexander was planning to bestow upon Prince Alexander of Hesse the Order of St. Andrew with diamonds on the occasion of his completing fifty years as an officer in the Russian army, in order to prove to the world that though he might be angry with the son that did not affect the esteem in which he held his uncle, the young man's father. In thanking the Tsar, Prince Alexander took the opportunity to put in a good word for his son. "I implore you, Sasha," he wrote on October 7 (19), 1883, "by the friendship which unites us and of which you have afforded me so many proofs, to hold out the hand of forgiveness to a young man who has had so many severe trials to sustain. He will always be faithful to you and to Russia; I am as sure of him as I am of myself."[170] Nobody believed the assurances of the father any more than they did those of the son. Again they were regarded simply as insincerity, for Russia was now on the defensive in Bulgaria. The Tsar answered his uncle's letter, and did not hesitate to refer to his extreme dissatisfaction with Sandro. Meanwhile the Russian representative in Sofia forbade a certain officer, who was well-disposed to the Prince, to take over the Ministry for War. When the Prince protested, the Russian representative said laughing and in a sarcastic tone: "Leave things alone. I have full power to bring about a breach. And it is not we who need fear anything if that happens."

Alexander replied: "God is my witness that it is not I who wish for a breach; but if Russia insists, I shall not flinch from it."

Soon afterwards three Russian officers who were loyal to the Prince, among them the nominee for the Ministry, were ordered to leave Sofia within forty-eight hours. This was of course a terrible insult to the Prince, and did not improve the situation. "The Tsar's impossible and boorish conduct", wrote Sandro to his father on October 20th (November 1st), "needs no further comment. . . . A deep gulf now yawns between the Tsar and myself, and I suppose it will never be bridged. Hatred and contempt are the feelings which animate this crowned fool, who is too cowardly to live in St. Petersburg, hides at Gatshina, imagines that he can impress his people by stirring up revolution among his neighbours, and permits the newspapers to drag the names of his nearest relations in the mud." Amid the worst possible auspices Baron Kaulbars, the Tsar's aide-de-camp, on November 11th brought the letter acknowledging Prince Alexander's telegram and letter of October 1st (13th).

"I do not propose to answer it at present", wrote the Tsar. "I regard it as absolutely essential not to be too hasty about anything in such an important matter. . . . I note your assurances of loyalty. Your Highness will doubtless not question my good will. I am giving you a further proof thereof by sending you . . . my personal aide-de-camp to settle the position of Russian officers in the Bulgarian service, which has been affected by recent events."

The Tsar did not consider that the time had yet come to put a final end to the political existence of the Prince of

Bulgaria. It seemed not impossible that if he used force European complications might ensue which he wished at all costs to avoid. Queen Victoria was very much on Sandro's side, and Austria-Hungary and Turkey also appeared to be supporting him. Hence it was not an altogether simple matter to get rid of Alexander of Bulgaria, although Bismarckian Germany would not stir a finger to help him.

The Tsar's wrath did not abate. The Prince of Bulgaria did his best gradually to bring the army under his own control and to oust the Russian officers. "From the Bulgarians", he wrote to his father on February 16 (28), 1884, "I am threatened by no danger—danger threatens solely from the side of Russia, and that only so long as the army is in their hands." He therefore induced the National Assembly to pass a resolution dismissing all Russian subalterns and also forty-eight Russian company commanders. The effect upon Russia may be imagined. Sandro himself realized it. "This will mean a struggle with Russia," he had remarked to his father in a letter on January 9, 1884, "but it has this great advantage for me— that I shall be supported by three hundred and fifty Bulgarian officers whom I shall win over to my side by this means. . . . The first step was the hardest. I don't think Russia will dare to behave to me in such an impudent and insolent way again." In this he was profoundly mistaken. Prince Alexander of Hesse warned his son and exhorted him to be more careful and to try to improve his relations with the Tsar, for among decent people it was the custom to keep politics out of social life. That was just what the Tsar had not done, replied Sandro. And he went on over-optimistically: "The Tsar will soon give way, for at this moment an agitation is going on in St. Petersburg in my favour."

Prince Alexander of Bulgaria observed carefully the Tsar's relations with Germany, which seemed to be improving during the early part of the year 1884. "Russia's swinging over towards Germany," he remarked, "after all that has happened during the past years, reminds me of a married couple getting a divorce. Just when they are about to sign the deed of divorcement their eyes meet and they remember all the good times they have had together. Instead of signing, they fall into one another's arms shedding tears of joy. It won't last long; they will hate each other all the more in the end." This remark was made with reference to the negotiations then taking place for the extension of the Three Emperors Pact.

Von Schweinitz, the German Ambassador in St. Petersburg, who saw a great deal of Alexander III as he had done of his predecessor, sent a dispatch to Bismarck dated March 9, 1884, telling how he had heard the Tsar speak of the renewal of the Pact which would "assure peace and order to *both* States". Before Schweinitz could interject that surely *three* States were in question, the Tsar remarked that he was not including Austria-Hungary, because there were so many points upon which the interests of that country and of Russia diverged. The Tsar expressed the earnest desire that even the negotiations as far as they had gone should be kept secret, because the knowledge that an agreement had been made with Austria-Hungary would rouse much discontent in his realm. Nevertheless the Three Emperors Pact of June 18, 1881, was extended for a further three years on March 27, 1884. But the accompanying circumstances filled Bismarck with serious misgivings as to whether in case any great strain were put upon it the Pact would fulfil its purpose. Prince Alexander of Hesse knew nothing of all these secret proceedings. He was now altogether excluded from political affairs; his rôle as mediator was played out.

Meanwhile Darmstadt was preparing for the marriage of Prince Louis of Battenberg to Princess Victoria of Hesse. Queen Victoria and the Prince of Wales with his wife, the Grand Duke Serge, the betrothed of the Princess Elisabeth, and the Prince of Bulgaria, all came to attend the ceremony. The projected festivities which were to be on a grand scale were, however, somewhat marred by a wholly unexpected episode. On April 21, 1884, the Grand Duke Serge came and broke it to Prince Alexander that his nephew, the Grand Duke Louis IV of Hesse, was about to marry Frau Kolémin, a divorcée, by birth a Countess Hutten-Czapski, at the very moment when Queen Victoria, his first wife's mother, had arrived in Darmstadt. The story was perfectly true. The Grand Duke had shortly before admitted to his daughter that he had promised to marry the lady and that he was determined to do so.

"Terrible prospect!" wrote Prince Alexander in his diary, full of dismay. "Louis seems to have lost his head completely, and believes that the bad reputation his flame bears all over Europe is an invention. Julia is quite beside herself, and so am I." The Queen had no idea of it, and for the present no one dared tell her.

Princess Victoria's wedding took place on April 30th, amid the greatest anxiety of all those who were privy to the Grand Duke's own plan of marriage. Victoria herself looked pale, thin, and ill, and the Grand Duke was in an indescribable state of nerves and agitation. At length the Queen heard through the Prince of Wales of the sword of Damocles that hung over the family. The heirs to the English and German thrones declared indignantly that they would break off all relations with Louis if he married Frau Kolémin. On the following morning the Queen asked Prince Alexander to come and see her. She received him with the words: "The situation seems to be even more serious than we thought. There appear to be rumours that Louis is already married." She asked him to find out how much truth there was in the report. Prince Alexander discovered that the Grand Duke had in fact contracted the civil marriage on the day of his daughter's wedding. He at once reported this to the Queen, who was furiously indignant. "Dear Cousin," she wrote to Prince Alexander on May 2, 1884, "I can only say that I am beside myself—I am utterly crushed, for I loved Louis as my own son, and he was very near to me. To do *this*, at *this* moment, *on the day* that his dear daughter married your dear son, when we were all gathered together here, is simply beyond all expression. I cannot understand Louis. For the next few days . . . nothing must be done publicly, steps must not be taken until after we have all gone. Meanwhile, however, I do beg you to do all you can to collect proofs of this woman's badness, and if possible also to discover whether the marriage is legal.—Poor Louis. *How* unhappy he will be, and how he will repent of this!"

The Queen was absolutely determined that the marriage with the woman whom her rigid principles of morality led her to condemn unheard as "horrible and abominable" should be annulled. The Prince of Wales immediately made the most intensive efforts to this end. He undertook to obtain Frau Kolémin's signature to the following document: "I admit that I agreed too hastily to the act of the civil marriage on April 30, 1887, and promise on my word of honour to retract it and to regard it as null and void." After a stormy interview that lasted for two hours the lady demanded to see the Grand Duke before she would sign anything. They met and there was another lengthy interview. When she came back to the Prince of Wales she told him flatly that in no circumstances would she give up the Grand Duke. On the following day she had

an attack of hysterics and threatened to do away with herself.
She was with difficulty prevented from making the attempt.
Subsequently the matter came up before the courts of justice,
and after much discussion the marriage was eventually dissolved by mutual consent. The Queen, however, had left
Darmstadt in high displeasure, and only the happiness of the
newly married couple induced her gradually to become
reconciled again with the Grand Duke.

At the time of the wedding, Sandro of Bulgaria confided to
his father that he had in the previous year secretly engaged
himself to the Princess Victoria of Prussia with the knowledge
of her mother, but against the wish of the Emperor. The
Empress Augusta was furious when the idea was suggested to
her and induced the Emperor to write a note to the Crown
Prince saying that "so long as he lived no princess of his house
should marry a Battenberg." Furthermore, the Russian Government, in order to prevent the Prince of Bulgaria's marriage,
caused it to be officially "insinuated" through the embassies
in Berlin, Vienna, and Rome that he was loaded with debt
and consorted quite openly with ladies of doubtful reputation
in his palace in Sofia. When the Prince came to Berlin,
William I expressed his surprise[171] that he should have come
there at all, since Wiesbaden had been the place suggested by
the Emperor for the meeting. He remonstrated with Prince
Alexander among other things for not adopting a proper tone
in his letters to the Tsar. The Prince replied that in all official
documents he had kept to the prescribed forms, which was
more than could be said of the Tsar. In private letters he had
written as one cousin to another, though without ever being
discourteous. "Cousin, cousin!" replied the monarch, as
Prince Alexander told his father in a letter dated April 20
(May 2), 1885. "An emperor is an emperor. My own son signs
himself 'your most obedient servant' when he writes to me."
Finally the Emperor advised him to settle his quarrel with
Russia. Bismarck was still more outspoken and said plainly:
"We want peace with Russia and shall drop anyone who
stands in the way of it." He continued that the Prince could
only maintain his position in Bulgaria—in which Germany
was not interested—under Russian protection. There was no
future for him there; and as regards marriage, for as long as he
was Chancellor no Prussian princess should go to Bulgaria.
Bismarck feared that if this marriage were to take place there
would be serious difficulties with Russia. And, as he said, "not

all the Hesses and Battenbergs in the world were worth that",
especially since they had always opposed his policy most
strenuously, and, he considered, had only made their peace
with Prussian Germany out of motives of expediency and under
the pressure of dire necessity after the year 1870. There were
quarrels within the imperial family. The old Emperor re-
proached his son most violently for allowing Sandro to come to
Berlin—which had really been the Crown Princess's doing—
and forbade Sandro to see the Princess Victoria again. Since,
contrary to the usual custom in Berlin at the visit of the head
of a foreign State, the Emperor did not give a dinner party for
the Prince of Bulgaria, the Crown Prince invited him with
all the Ministers, etc., but with no ladies present. The Crown
Princess secretly gave Sandro a locket containing her daughter's
portrait and hair. Her plan was warmly supported by the Queen
and all the English royal family. It was hoped by this means
to keep alive Sandro's anti-Russian feelings, and that gratitude
to his mother-in-law would bring him more into sympathy
with England. Hence the Prince of Wales, who happened to
be staying in Berlin with his sister, undertook on his own
responsibility to arrange a private meeting for the couple at
Potsdam, which passed off dramatically amid protestations of
love, and tears over the enormous difficulties that confronted
them.

The marriage project did not remain a secret and was soon
being bandied about throughout Berlin society. Prince William
and Prince Henry, the brothers of the Princess Victoria, were
definitely opposed to it. They did not regard Sandro as of
suitable rank. Prince William, moreover, was opposed to it
because his mother was so anxious to bring it about. In his
opinion—as Count Alfred Waldersee says in his Memoirs—
she had never become a Prussian, but had always remained
an Englishwoman, and directly worked to further English
interests against Prussian and German. What Waldersee calls
Prince William's "innately Prussian feelings" revolted against
the marriage, and the opposition between mother and son
went to such lengths that Waldersee wrote in his diary on
June 10th of that year that if the marriage came off Prince
William would break with his parents altogether.[172] The
Crown Prince was soon entirely on the side of his wife and
daughter. To Waldersee he said: "It is surely our duty to
uphold the interests of German princes, and thus to support
the Prince of Bulgaria." The long-standing conflict between the

Emperor, Bismarck, and Prince William, on the one side, who at that time were still of one mind in political matters and were anxious at all costs to be friendly with Russia, and the Crown Prince and Princess on the other side, whose leanings were all towards England, found its strongest expression in their attitudes towards the Prince of Bulgaria. For it was in that country —Bulgaria—which lay so near to Constantinople that the interests of Russia and England came into serious collision.

On this point Prince William was in full accord with Bismarck, whose English policy was largely determined by the colonial crisis, and who was therefore in violent opposition to that country and to its attempts to influence the German Government through the Crown Princess. Ever since November 1883 Bismarck had felt that a positive "family conspiracy" had been formed in London for the purpose of putting Germany in a cleft stick over this marriage by supporting Prince Alexander of Bulgaria and embroiling Germany with Russia. According to General von Schweinitz[173] the Chancellor did not conceal his views from the Crown Prince. He was determined to deprive Prince Alexander of his wife or of his principality or of both. He saw the hand of England in everything. Hence Bismarck's relations with the Crown Prince's family became so strained that the former did all he could to get someone appointed to the Crown Prince's household who would act skilfully as an intermediary. For this purpose Bismarck selected Count Radolin-Radolinsky, who had hitherto been in the diplomatic service, and who, apart from his possession of private means and a great social position, was also, in the Chancellor's opinion, a man of excellent moral character. Radolinsky became the Crown Prince's Lord Chamberlain, and actually Bismarck's confidential agent.[174] Thenceforward Radolinsky formed the connecting link in the political intercourse between the Crown Prince and Princess and the Chancellor. The more he came to know the Crown Prince and his family, however, the more did he sympathize with the two young lovers. He came especially under the influence of the Crown Princess, and he soon came to disapprove of the Chancellor's anti-Battenberg attitude, just as he did of that "Russomania" of von Schweinitz, the German Ambassador in St. Petersburg, which was directed towards the same end.

Bismarck made the most of the fact that Prince William shared his views in the Battenberg question. He sent him to St. Peters-

burg "to put the Tsar's mind at rest about Bulgaria" as well as
to make it quite clear to him that Germany was not in the
least interested in Prince Alexander, and that neither the
Emperor nor the Imperial Chancellor would dream of forward-
ing his aspirations. Prince William wrote to his grandfather on
May 19, 1884,[175] saying that the Tsar had discussed the matter
quite frankly and openly, and seemed pleased at the attitude
taken up by the Emperor and the Chancellor towards the
Prince of Bulgaria. William went so far as to say to the Tsar
expressly "that of course there could never be any question
of marriage, and that Germany cared nothing at all about the
Prince and his country". At all events not enough to make the
Emperor William permit the friendly relations subsisting
between himself and the Tsar to be disturbed by the Bulgarian.
This remark evidently greatly eased the Tsar's mind. He
seemed literally to breathe more freely. In the tones of a deeply
disappointed friend he described how utterly he had been
mistaken in the Prince of Bulgaria. That he had been quite
pleasant and reasonable to begin with, but that later he had
shown other sides of his character and had at length behaved
to him in such a manner that the situation became quite
untenable. He said that the Prince not only made things very
awkward for the Russian Government but was also ungrateful,
spent a great deal of money, and had been detected in untruth-
fulness. "He won't stay there much longer", added the Tsar,
to which Prince William: "Perhaps that would not be such
a terrible misfortune." Whereupon the Tsar beamed with
pleasure, was doubly affable to Prince William, and used the
familiar form of address to him. Giers expressed himself
delightedly to Herbert Bismarck, who was at that time
Councillor of Embassy at St. Petersburg: "You should have
heard the Tsar talking about your young Prince, and about
what he said to him concerning the Prince of Bulgaria!"[176]
Prince William, however, regarded his success as a tribute to
his own personality, and Herbert Bismarck still further confirmed him in his high opinion of himself by reporting to his
father the Chancellor on May 22, 1884: "It is a great triumph
for Prince William. In two days he reached a point to which
six months of our diplomacy failed to bring the Tsar."[177]

This episode brought about a considerable improvement
in the relations between Germany and Russia. Those with
Austria-Hungary remained markedly cool. "You know", said
Giers to Herbert Bismarck, "that we don't really care about

them. . . . The Tsar does not like the Austrians. We make terms with them purely on political grounds." These feelings were reciprocal. Count Kálnoky, who had been Austro-Hungarian Foreign Minister since November 1881, was not disposed, though a moderate man, to desert Prince Alexander for Russia's sake and to show himself so unfriendly to Bulgaria as Germany did. Prince Reuss's dispatch from Vienna on June 19, 1884, on the subject bears some most interesting marginal notes of Bismarck's. Against the remark that the Prince of Bulgaria was now very depressed, since the German Government had also dropped him, Bismarck wrote: "Yes. He is the skeleton at the feast; and he is trying to climb by marriage."[178] When the Prince continued with a plea that the Prince of Bulgaria should not be entirely abandoned, notwithstanding the fact that he was by no means a paragon, Bismarck commented: "Why on earth not?" And beside the word "paragon" he wrote quite unjustly: "Hooligan!"— "Prince Alexander", Bismarck wrote to Reuss on June 23, 1884, "appears to me in the light of a climber and a disturber of the peace, whose efforts to make a marriage, which Queen Victoria favours, are a political threat to *us*, so long as he remains Prince of Bulgaria. Once he goes back into private life, his marriage is no longer a political question but a purely family affair. But even then I should be sorry to see a fresh door for political intrigues opening in our royal house. Our State interests have suffered much from such influences ever since the year 1840."[179]

Thus Bismarck's attitude to Prince Alexander was mercilessly cold and matter of fact. The young Prince had meanwhile returned to Sofia feeling very sad and cast down. The results of his journey had been awaited with tensest interest in Bulgaria, and everyone was greatly disappointed at the news of the failure of his marriage project. The wildest rumours were going about Sofia on the subject. "While I was in Darmstadt", Sandro wrote to his father from Sofia on May 31 (June 12), 1884, "the Agence Havas telegraphed to Sofia saying that I had proposed for the hand of the Princess Victoria, but that the Emperor had refused. This telegram went from hand to hand and for a whole week was the sole subject of conversation in Bulgaria. —Three days after my visit to Berlin a rumour was spread through Sofia by the Russian Consulate that the Agence Havas's story was true, that the Emperor had refused my proposal because he held a very low opinion of me, and because he and Bismarck had both recommended me to abdicate. At first the Bulgars would not believe it. Their Oriental vanity will not let them believe that anyone could refuse me—they think that any princess would be delighted to come and rule over them. But since I returned unbetrothed, the Russians have produced the following story: that I was incapable of marrying, that I suffered from venereal disease, further—amongst other things—that the Bulgarians must surely have observed that in all the five years that I have been here I have never had a woman—the reason being that I did not care about women because I had 'Turkish' tastes, and that the reason why the Tsar had recalled Polsikoff and Messoloff [the Prince's Russian aides-de-camp] was because they prevented my marrying!—In addition is the fact that in Bulgaria every man who becomes independent gets married at once, and anyone who does not is regarded as dishonourable and immoral."

Sandro was naturally furious at these baseless accusations. Russia seemed at last to have found the likeliest means of making the Bulgarian people turn against the Prince to whom they had hitherto clung in the feeling that he was more on their side than on that of the foreigners.

"I simply cannot tell you", he continued, "how much I suffer under these conditions. I am powerless in such a struggle carried on with such weapons. My name has been besmirched in Bulgaria and in all Europe. Would it not be more dignified to make one's exit while it can be done with honour, instead of waiting until one is thrown out, sullied and dishonoured? Dear papa, as things are, I believe it would be a good plan if you were to write to the Tsar and tell him quite frankly that I cannot stay in Bulgaria unless I get married. Tell him that I turned down the marriage with the Archduchess Maria Antonia only at Russia's categorical demand; and that I cannot marry Vicky for the same reason. And no other possibility has presented itself.

"Possibly when the Tsar sees that the matter is urgent he will say that he has nothing against Vicky, and then all may yet be well. If not, at least I can still clear out. I should regard departure in the light of a blessed relief—to go on living in such appalling conditions is utterly unthinkable. . . . I have had nothing but painful disappointments and bitter experiences. The cleft between the Tsar and myself cannot be bridged. I *hate* the Tsar and shall never be able to forget what he has done to me. . . .

"I am absolutely crushed and am suffering more than I can say under the burden of my present life. Why, oh why, did God permit the death of the late Tsar? With him went my sole support."

Prince Alexander was very much grieved at the receipt of this letter which showed so much discouragement. But he knew his mercurial son, and knew that he was very much at the mercy of the mood of the moment. If Sandro was to be judged correctly, not every one of his moods must be taken literally, for often a telegram full of the rosiest hopes would follow a fortnight later to show that he was once more taking too optimistic a view of life. Prince Alexander decided for the moment to do nothing, but made up his mind to be very reserved in his behaviour to the Russian royal family.

The wedding of the Grand Duke Serge and the Princess Elisabeth of Hesse took place at St. Petersburg in June. On this account Prince Alexander of Hesse did not attend it. The marriage was to come to a horrible end in the future. It would have been better for the Princess Elisabeth to have followed her first instinct, which was to refuse to marry into Russia where so many political murders had taken place. Fate overtook them late but terribly. The Grand Duke Serge was assassinated in the year 1905; the Grand Duchess sought out the murderer in prison and asked him why he had robbed her of her husband in such a brutal manner. Little did she guess then that in the year 1918 the Bolsheviks would bring her to an even more frightful end.[180]

Bismarck's distrust of the whole Hesse-Battenberg connection and their "subterranean English plans and intrigues" was given further nourishment by another betrothal. On July 25th Prince Alexander's third son, Henry, informed his father that he had every hope of becoming the husband of Princess Beatrice of England, Queen Victoria's youngest daughter. The Princess had fallen in love with the Prince while she was on a visit to Darmstadt. To begin with, however, the Queen would not hear of any engagement, and thought that it was no more than a passing fancy on her daughter's part. But the Princess fretted terribly, grew thin and pale, would eat nothing, and crept about looking the picture of misery. Then her mother abandoned her opposition. Prince Louis of Battenberg joyfully wrote home announcing the happy turn of events, and his father entered the letter in his diar yon June 30, 1884: "The Crown Princess [of Prussia] has no idea, nor will she be told until it is made public. [Prince Alexander put two large question marks beside this remark.] She will be very pleased, and I am sure that the Crown Prince will soon come round. The rest of the Berlin lot can go to blazes for all I care."

When Sandro heard of the latest engagement in his family, he wrote to his father from Sofia on August 4 (16), 1884, and said: "Liko's [Henry's] engagement is of incalculable value, and I congratulate you with all my heart. How the youngster managed to make Beatrice fall in love with him is a puzzle to me; for it must be admitted that Liko is not on a level with her intellectually. Of course, I noticed in the spring that they were making eyes at one another, but I did not take it seriously, as I should never have thought that the Queen would agree. . . . How strange the fate of our family is! I wonder how it will all end." Sandro for his part reported that he had, through the Crown Princess, received a ring and a letter from her daughter which appeared to promise a happy ending despite obstacles. "Louis wrote and told me", continued Sandro, "that the Crown Princess had said to him recently that I had better abdicate and marry Vicky. I telegraphed to Louis at once that I would do so with the greatest possible pleasure if I could have Vicky. If Liko marries Beatrice, the Emperor will give way too. . . . I feel that Vicky will stick to me. I hear from Berlin that people who are in close touch with the Emperor are already beginning to look dubious and to say that Vicky will get her way after all.—So if the Crown Princess of her own initiative suggests my abdicating, this seems the happiest possible means for me to get out of this wretched Bulgaria with a whole skin. I am most curious to hear what Louis will answer. . . . I cannot remain so miserably lonely for years on end— there is *nobody* left to me now. If you could see into my heart you would be horrified. Serge writes to me from St. Petersburg that everything will be all right again. Do you really believe that I could ever be on good terms again with the Tsar? There are things in life that make too deep a wound for it ever to heal. You simply have no idea what a fearful hatred I have for the Tsar and for his government. You will never have the slightest idea of what I have suffered and borne in these last five years. . . . And this Tsar with whom I was always absolutely frank, who knew everything, this—cur, how did he behave! The very memory of it makes me sick. . . . Can you mention a single prince who ever had such a slap in the face before the whole army, before the whole country, before Europe, as was

given to me when my aides-de-camp were hounded out? . . .
I should never have believed that any human heart could be
so terribly, so immeasurably embittered. And that idiot Serge
calls it 'a fit of bad temper'; it is pathetic. I suppose you will
say to me: 'How illogical—he says he hates the Russians and
yet he accepts money from them!' I feel that myself. And if I
ever realized what it is like to have a high position and no
money, I realize it now."

Sandro protested that he felt the "abominable humiliation"
as a frightful indignity, and all he wanted was never again in
all his life to be obliged to shake hands with a Russian, nor to
have anything more to do with their loathsome country.

This letter considerably spoilt Prince Alexander of Hesse's
pleasure in his son Henry's engagement. He was vexed that
Sandro should be dallying with the idea of abdicating, and
wrote testily to his eldest son Louis expressing annoyance at
his "brainless way of deciding Sandro's fate behind his father's
back". In December the engagement of Henry of Battenberg
and Princess Beatrice was officially announced. The young
man was delighted with the friendly reception accorded him
in England, and with the simplicity and naturalness of court
life and of the royal family.

"You can't think", he wrote home from Kent House on
December 25, 1884, "what a pleasant difference there is
between the people of the court here and those in Germany.
Everybody is so natural and unaffected that one feels at home
at once." The Queen wrote to the father of her latest son-in-
law with real cordiality from Osborne on December 31, 1884:
"You know that I found it very hard to give my consent to
this, for Beatrice has been *everything* to me during these last sad
years, and I had hoped that she would never marry. However,
since Liko is prepared to live here with her, and since it was her
dearest wish, and Liko was so *very* much attached, I yielded, and
am glad to receive another dear son. . . . You know my dear
Beatrice, and *anyone* who *knows* her—I must say it openly—*must*
love her. Such a good daughter can only make a good wife."
In Berlin, however, the news was received with very different
feelings. Above all, it increased Bismarck's fear that the
English royal family would gain a fresh means of influencing
German policy. The Emperor, too, was thoroughly displeased.
It is true that he himself acknowledged that the Battenbergs
were handsome fellows. Once when he was at a dinner party
at the British Embassy at which Henry of Battenberg was

present, he suddenly said to the young man: "Stop your ears a minute!" and then turned to the other guests and remarked: "I've never seen a handsomer family than these Battenbergs." However, the effects of their manly beauty were beginning to be distinctly troublesome to him. Queen Victoria regarded the telegraphic replies from Berlin to the announcement of the engagement of Princess Beatrice as positively rude, and therefore had not a good word to say for her Prussian relatives. According to an entry in Prince Alexander's diary on January 10, 1885, the Empress Augusta said amongst other things, in a letter to the Queen, that she had heard that Henry of Battenberg was an insignificant little man, she did not know him, and did not care to have acquaintances of that sort. Even if the letter was not really worded quite so strongly, it is at all events true that in Berlin, where Prince Alexander of Battenberg's proposals had been refused, the marriage of his brother to a member of the English royal house was not popular.

After this fresh matrimonial episode Bismarck worked harder than ever to frustrate Prince Alexander's marriage to Princess Victoria of Prussia. He accused the Crown Princess to her husband and to the Emperor of having allowed her daughter to become secretly engaged to the Prince of Bulgaria, and both called her to account on the subject. Sandro heard the news with great anxiety. "My brain reels when I contemplate my future," he wrote home on February 22, 1885; "God knows how it will all end. I have already done too much harm in my life. Things have always ended badly for anyone who loved me. I should feel like a criminal if I started on any fresh marriage project. Until Vicky marries I am not free.
                    "Your sorely tried
                              "SANDRO."

The German Crown Princess was more than ever determined to carry her point regarding her daughter's marriage. And once again, as she and her daughter had done in their affectionate letters to him at the previous Christmas, she exhorted Sandro to patience.

The relations of the three empires seemed to outward appearances to have become more friendly as a result of the meeting of their rulers at Skiernevice from September 15–17, 1884. Nevertheless the encounter had in reality only demonstrated once again that although it seemed to be easier to maintain the recent better relations between Germany and

x

Russia, the Tsar's deep distrust of Austria-Hungary remained unabated. Their antagonism was insurmountable, though for the moment it was disguised under mutual demonstrations of friendliness. Once again Prince Alexander of Bulgaria was the sacrifice offered up to the better understanding between Russia and Germany. On March 18, 1885, the Emperor William wrote to the Prince demanding that he should give a written undertaking to renounce all claims to his granddaughter, and informing him that his first duty was to keep on good terms with the Tsar.[181] It is noteworthy that a copy of this letter was sent to Russia in order that Bismarck's intentions might be the more certain of realization. The messenger who bore the Emperor's letter had also been instructed to tell the Prince of Bulgaria that the best denial of the marriage rumours would be a speedy marriage to somebody with plenty of money.[182] It was against the traditions of the House of Hohenzollern that a Prince should live in Berlin exclusively in the rôle of a son-in-law as was possible in England. If he sent a definite promise to relinquish all claims, the Emperor William would undertake to be an intermediary between St. Petersburg and Sofia. In any case the Prince must be prepared to submit unconditionally to Russia, to be no more than the Russian Governor of Bulgaria, to have no independent policy, and simply to obey the Tsar. The Emperor did not, however, see any other reason why he should abdicate.—If he did not write and give up the Princess Victoria, he must be prepared for a definitely hostile attitude on the part of Germany. This message shattered the Prince. He was now, as he said himself, in a terrible position; and was furious at Russia's apparently being too cowardly to do anything itself and hiding behind the old Emperor. Must he simply sacrifice his conviction that Bulgaria could only be happy if she were freed from Russian influence, and send a flat rejection to the Princess, who loved him and who had clung to him most unselfishly? Bismarck was more Russian than the Tsar, and to one mighty foe was now added a second almost mightier. Of what use to Sandro was the obvious sympathy of England, which was at the moment on particularly bad terms with Russia again over Afghanistan? He was obliged to submit. In a long reply on April 26th, 1885,[183] he gave the required renunciation and also stated in ambiguous words his proposed political attitude to Russia, which he described as the "fulfilment of an order". The letter had been composed with the help of his father, who, in view of the numerous ties which now bound him to England, dreaded the apparently inevitable war between Russia and England. Nevertheless he did his best to pacify his son, who had again telegraphed to him, as Prince Alexander entered in his diary on April 1, 1885, asking him to help him to extricate himself from Bulgaria with dignity. Berlin, however, remained suspicious. And Bismarck especially was quite alive to the fact that the letter did not imply a full and unconditional renunciation. In his attitude to this matter he was in accord with Prince William of Prussia, the son of the Crown Prince Frederick, who, in open opposition to his mother, never missed an opportunity of emphasizing his dislike of the Battenbergs.

Meanwhile Henry of Battenberg's marriage, which was so sourly looked upon in Berlin, was fixed for July. Prince Alexander of Hesse went to London and was most cordially received. The Queen addressed him in the familiar second person singular, which embarrassed him considerably in conversation. The wedding had been planned to take place with the greatest pomp and magnificence chiefly in order to disguise the fact that the Prince was not of equal rank with his bride. At the wedding breakfast ten pipers in the picturesque uniform of a Highland regiment marched round the table on which was an immense wedding-cake. Wonderful illuminations in the park at Osborne and on the ships at sea closed the day, which had greatly affected the Queen, whose emotions were always easily roused. "A happier-looking couple can seldom have knelt before the altar", she said. Although this was now the ninth child and the fifth daughter whom she had seen married, she had never been so deeply moved as on this occasion. The wedding festivities had been practically ignored by Germany, though the Crown Prince and Princess of course were warmly interested from afar. The presence of the Prince of Bulgaria at the wedding considerably annoyed Russia. Anglo-Russian relations were strained and the Tsar wondered what new plot was being hatched against him.

Thus the waves of international politics rose and fell and were mirrored in the family relationships of the rulers of Europe.

CHAPTER XIII

BULGARIA—*continued*

THE personal relations of Alexander III and the Emperor Francis Joseph were frigid. Nevertheless, since both, and especially the latter, were anxious to avoid war and Bismarck was urging them to come to an agreement, the two imperial couples met at Kremsier on August 25 and 26, 1885.

Soon afterwards Prince Alexander of Bulgaria, who had been invited to the army manœuvres at Pilsen, came to Austria. The Tsar had not said a great deal about Sandro at Kremsier, but had merely spoken regretfully of the situation which, he intimated, was *entirely* the Prince's fault. None the less Kálnoky did not regard a reconciliation as altogether out of the range of political possibilities. The Prince visited Giers, the Russian Foreign Minister who happened to be staying at Franzensbad, in order to point out to him that the continual undermining of his authority in Bulgaria was a two-edged sword that must harm Russia as much as himself. "You must decide once and for all", he said to Giers. "If you want me to get out, say so frankly—I should be more than glad to return the crown of thorns that I received from Russia into her own hands. But if you wish me to remain, then make an honourable peace with me. . . ." As far as his own imperial master was concerned, Giers would rather have bidden the young man abdicate, but he had also to think of the other Powers, and so he asked the Prince what solution he had to suggest.

Prince Alexander replied : "Eastern Rumelia might be united with Bulgaria and the whole principality be ruled over by a Governor approved by Europe." Giers replied that that seemed quite a sound idea, that he would report it verbatim to the Tsar, and that he would suggest to him to forget the past and to be reconciled with Alexander. "Your marriage project", he added, "irritated the Tsar very much, and I was obliged to state in Berlin that Russia would not agree to it. If you could make up your mind to marry one of the daughters of the Prince of Montenegro, everything would be in order again at once."

The Prince was pleased with the result of the interview, and thought for a moment that possibly a reconciliation might really take place, especially since, as he said to his father in a letter from Vienna, dated September 2, 1885, Russia had quarrelled with all parties in Bulgaria and was, "if the truth were known, at her wits' end".

When Prince Alexander returned to Bulgaria he received an unexpected telegram at Varna on September 18th, saying that the Eastern Rumelians had risen and had everywhere proclaimed a union with Northern Bulgaria under Alexander as Prince of the united country. Without asking advice of any of the Powers, the Prince at once decided to put himself at the head of the movement, which he knew to be the fulfilment of the heart's desire of every Bulgarian. He telegraphed to his father at 4.45 p.m. on the same day to say that for good or ill he was going to Philippopolis. His father replied on September 19th: "Am utterly appalled. Cannot think that this is the right moment. God keep you."[184]

Actually all that was happening was what Russia had demanded at San Stefano, and which had been prevented at the Congress of Berlin chiefly by England and Austria-Hungary. Hence Russia should have been delighted. But the situation had been radically altered since then. A man was ruling over Bulgaria who showed every sign of acting on his own initiative irrespective of Russia's orders, and who had only too often affronted the Tsar by his tactless, careless, and impulsive ways. The increase of such a man's power in the Balkans, which the Tsar had always regarded as his own particular domain, could not be looked upon with favour in Russia.

A complete change had taken place in the policy of the Great Powers. Because Prince Alexander of Battenberg was at the head of them, Russia would have nothing to do with the Bulgarians and commanded all Russian officers to resign instantly from the Bulgarian army.

In June a Conservative Government under Lord Salisbury had succeeded to Gladstone's which was too russophil to please the country. Salisbury at first thought that the union of Bulgaria and Eastern Rumelia was a preconcerted affair between Bulgaria and Russia. But when he learnt the Tsar's attitude he realized his mistake, and the warm sympathy of the Queen for Prince Alexander did the rest.

"At the time of the Berlin Congress," wrote Queen Victoria to the Marquis of Salisbury on September 25, 1885,[185] "Bulgaria and the Prince himself even, were considered very Russian, and Lord Beaconsfield thought, doubtless, it was more prudent to divide Bulgaria and Rumelia. But for the last two years, nearly, the Prince has shown that he is only anxious to get rid of the Russian influences. . . ." Hence, she concludes: "that the more powerful the principalities and kingdoms of the Balkan were, the stronger would be the buffer against Russian aggression of Turkey . . . ".

Thus English policy too had changed. As a result Bismarck, in pursuance of his Russian policy, abandoned Prince Alexander even more openly, which made the Queen and also of course the Crown Princess in Berlin most indignant. Just before Prince Alexander had originally gone to Bulgaria, he had given the Queen a slightly exaggerated account of his interview with Bismarck. The Chancellor, he said, had positively forced him to take the Bulgarian princely throne, had shut the door behind him, saying: "You do not leave this room till you have promised that you will go to Bulgaria."

Now she remembered the Prince's story, and was naturally indignant at Bismarck's deserting him, as she wrote to Lord Salisbury from Balmoral on October 6, 1885.[186] Meanwhile the German Crown Prince had been completely won over to Prince Alexander's side by his wife, and wrote to his mother-in-law to say how much he admired Sandro's ready and assured bearing. According to information from Henry of Battenberg, which Prince Alexander of Hesse entered in his diary on October 31, 1885, the Crown Prince went on to say that he did not see that Sandro could have acted any differently, that he hoped he would be successful and prove to be the regenerator of his people.

Prince Alexander of Hesse did all he could to help his son. He wrote to the Queen; he wrote to Austria. From the former he received the definite assurance that the Prince should be preserved from deposition, from the latter only half promises. The Queen would have liked to do a great deal more if her Ministers had let her have her way. "Mama is quite wretched," wrote Prince Henry of Battenberg to his father from Balmoral on October 16, 1885, "not to be able to do more to help Sandro. At all events England is the one Power that really honestly wishes him well." The situation was extraordinarily critical. The neighbouring rulers, especially Serbia, were jealous of Bulgaria's increased power. They were even more disturbed than Turkey, who suffered most, since it was one of her provinces that had seceded.

Austria-Hungary favoured King Milan, because it regarded Serbia as coming within its sphere of influence, and Kálnoky, despite all Prince Alexander's assurances, persisted in believing that in Bulgaria Russian influence was the strongest. Hence when King Milan planned to declare war on his high-handed neighbour, who had dared by a stroke of the pen practically to double the size of his dominions, Austria-Hungary accompanied Serbia's undertaking with the best of good wishes. They thought that King Milan would soon defeat the Prince of Bulgaria and his leaderless troops. According to a marginal note made on a dispatch on September 10, 1885,[187] Bismarck too was convinced that Prince Alexander would be brought to his senses by Serbia, and a Bulgarian victory was the last thing he expected. In the same way Russia allowed King Milan to do as he pleased and regarded him as a tool by the aid of which the tiresome Prince of Bulgaria might be removed cheaply and efficaciously without any action on Russia's part. When that had been done the Serbian campaign was to be brought to a close. Prince Alexander had immediately filled the vacant posts in his army with his own subjects. When Serbia's declaration of war arrived in Sofia on November 14th, the troops from Eastern Rumelia were already advancing with the greatest alacrity.

"I am not afraid of war," he wrote from Philippopolis on November 1st (13th), (he erroneously headed the letter Sofia), "because I am not afraid of death. I am ready to die and shall be glad if by this means I can at one and the same time get rid of my hated position in Sofia and be of use to the Bulgarian people, for my memory will give them no peace until they possess their whole fatherland." As he was closing this letter between two and three o'clock in the morning of November 14th, the declaration of war was handed to him. "God help me," he added in a hasty postscript; "I shall do my duty. Shame, eternal shame upon this fratricidal war!"

Meanwhile the Tsar had realized that the recall of the Russian officers had been merely a case of beating the air. They were all too rapidly replaced by Bulgars, and it was also reported to the monarch that the Prince had expressed himself as delighted with the measure. Then the Tsar's personal dislike broke out in full force. On November 5, 1885, he announced in an order of the day that Prince Alexander's name was to be erased from the Russian army list. The Queen was highly indignant at this step, and with the greatest secrecy sent word to Sandro by Prince Henry of Battenberg adjuring him not to give in, as Prince Alexander of Hesse notes in his diary on November 8, 1885. "The Queen", wrote Prince Henry to his father from Balmoral on November 7th, "is of opinion that you should write as uncle to nephew expressing your disgust at his conduct; saying that you would not have mixed yourself up in any political affair, but since this is a purely personal matter you felt that you could not do otherwise." Prince Alexander did not act upon the suggestion. In his opinion the only way of meeting the latest Russian infamy was with silent contempt. He merely asked Giers for an explanation. Then came a letter from the Tsar to his uncle dated from Gatshina on November 10th (22), 1885 :*

"My dear Uncle,—I have been obliged to resort to a measure with regard to Sandro that has cost me a good deal. I have done my best for him for the sake of the memory of my dear parents, and . . . have been grieved to see him succumb to influences that led him to behave as the avowed enemy of Russia. . . . I was obliged to censure an undertaking carried on without my consent, by revolutionary means that were bound to set the East ablaze and jeopardize the future of Bulgaria. Events have proved me to be only too right. The country is at war with the neighbours who should be its allies. The results of this act of folly are that the land is invaded, the capital threatened by the enemy, and the people ruined for years to come."

When the Tsar wrote this letter he had evidently not yet heard of the defeat of the Serbs at Slivnica in the fighting from November 19th–21st. Hardly had the letter been sent before the news arrived which was contrary to all the Tsar's expectations, and which roused great surprise as well as considerable admiration of the young Prince of Bulgaria throughout Europe. The Serbs retired in confusion, Sandro crossed the Serbian frontier and pushed far into the interior of the country. King Milan turned for help to his suzerain in Vienna, and Francis Joseph did in fact decide to put a spoke in the victor's wheel.

Meanwhile Prince Alexander of Hesse was doing his best from Darmstadt to support his son. He was delighted at the success, but saw it all endangered by Austria-Hungary's attitude. He appealed to Henry at Windsor to find out whether it would not be possible for the Powers to take any steps, by

* See Appendix.

which he meant in particular England. Henry answered that he was moving heaven and earth, and that the Queen had also sent a strong telegram to Salisbury. Prince Alexander also applied direct to Kálnoky, from whom he heard of the intention of Austria to intervene.

The following telegram was thereupon despatched by Prince Alexander of Hesse to Slivnica on November 25th:[188] "I implore you to agree to an armistice as soon as you are on Serbian soil without proceeding further into the country." Hardly had it been sent off before Prince Alexander received a congratulatory telegram from Queen Victoria:[189] "My warmest, most cordial congratulations upon Sandro's victories. You must be very proud."

As a consequence the Tsar received a most uncompromising reply from his uncle, written from Darmstadt on November 29th:*

"My dear Nephew,—Thank you for writing to me. You owed me an explanation, for which I have up to the present waited in vain. The extraordinary action in which you have seen fit to indulge at my son's expense has deeply wounded and offended me. You accuse him of having behaved to the Russian officers in the Bulgarian service in such a manner that you felt obliged to dismiss him from the army as if he were a criminal. Permit me to inquire upon what this accusation is based. Even supposing that the Prince were guilty, it would have been your duty as a sovereign to tell him of what he was accused, to appeal to his honour, to give him the chance of vindicating himself, to await his reply, and then to condemn him if he had deserved it. It appears to me that even a *Russian subject* might in a similar case have claimed to be heard first. In your own interests you should not have acted so hastily. All Europe is crying out against your arbitrary procedure. Your dear father did my son the honour to give him the rank of General in the Russian army, to appoint him chief of a battalion with whom he was among the first to cross the Danube in the cause of Russia. He decorated him with the Cross of St. George, won on the field of battle—and at a stroke of the pen you have undone it all. . . . That you should declare Alexander, and *him alone*, to be responsible for this 'act of folly', the aim of which was hostile to Russia, is a grave injustice. . . . Monsieur de Giers knows very well that the revolution came as a complete surprise to Alexander, and that unless he had cravenly deserted

* See Appendix.

his country he could not have acted otherwise than he did. I *should have done the same in his place. . . .* As your mother's brother I felt obliged to speak quite frankly to you. It depends entirely on you to give me the opportunity to get back again on to the good terms on which we used to be. I sincerely hope that it may come to be so."

This letter was a bitter pill for an Autocrat of All the Russias to swallow. Prince Alexander's feelings had run away with him, and now not only had the Tsar and the Prince of Bulgaria quarrelled beyond redemption, but also the uncle and the nephew. Sandro was glad that his father had really spoken his mind at last. "Your letter to the Tsar is so forcible", he remarked in his next letter to his father on February 11, 1886, "that I hardly think he will have shown it to anyone or even preserved it. I don't suppose it will do much good, but it is a satisfaction to think that the thick-headed, narrow-minded oaf should for once have been told the truth." The satisfaction, however, was to cost them both dear.

Meanwhile the Prince of Bulgaria's triumphal march had been brought to an end by the intervention of Austria-Hungary, and an armistice had been demanded. The fact that Austria-Hungary should be assuming the decisive rôle did not please the Russians despite their antipathy to Prince Alexander of Bulgaria. Events in the Balkan theatre of war began to be a matter of serious concern in the relations of the three empires, especially in Vienna and St. Petersburg, and to rouse in Bismarck anxiety that Austro-Hungarian policy might possibly involve Germany in a breach with Russia. This was by no means what he wanted. Hence he began to preach moderation on all sides; the more so since Sandro's successful campaign evoked the greatest enthusiasm among many Germans, which again disturbed Bismarck's pro-Russian friends. The greatest interest, of course, was taken in these events at the court of the Crown Prince in Berlin.

Mother and daughter followed the news from Bulgaria with feverish excitement. At the first news of the outbreak of war, the Crown Princess had, as she said herself, "nearly gone up to the ceiling with astonishment, dismay, and alarm".[190] Neither she nor her daughter could eat or sleep. Victoria was wildly proud of her lover and only regretted that she could not run away in men's clothing to take part in the war at Sandro's side. Whatever he did was regarded by both as brave, resolute, self-sacrificing, and brilliant. They hoped that now a united

Bulgaria would arise in the shape of a kingdom[191] and then the marriage question would very easily be settled. Both were heart and soul on the Bulgarian side, and had so far persuaded the Crown Prince that he too was altogether of his wife's opinion. Everything that happened was viewed from the standpoint of its effect upon the marriage.

The Prince was given as much help as possible from England, and information that might be useful to him was continually being sent through the Queen's son-in-law, Henry of Battenberg, to his father. It was realized in London that in the highest circles in Berlin there were two parties—the one consisting of the Emperor and Empress, Prince William and Herr von Bismarck, against the "revolutionary" Sandro; and the other—consisting of the Crown Princess, her daughter and her husband, for him.

Meanwhile Prince Alexander of Battenberg had sent his father the first detailed account of the campaign in a letter from Pirot in Serbia, dated November 24 (December 6), 1885. He told him how he had lived in a sort of ecstasy and terrible excitement ever since the day war had been declared. He inspired the troops by telling them that unless they stood firm their land was lost. "While I was outwardly calm and collected", he said, "I was seething with fear inwardly. I knew that the fate of Sofia and of my crown hung in the balance." The feeling of elation that overcame him when the victory was his, when his troops crossed the frontier with bands playing and flags flying, was indescribable. It was hard, of course, that the victory could not be exploited, but not much more was to be gained in any case. "I thank God on my knees", he continued, "that we have got through so well. I was filled with terror to such a degree that if it had been prolonged for another fortnight I should have gone off my head; for despite the bravery of the officers and men which was beyond all praise, my situation was indescribably difficult with none but young and inexperienced officers. I was continually afraid lest one of them should do something foolish that would ruin everything. I was everywhere at once, in front, behind, right, and left. But one man alone cannot do everything. Still, all's well that ends well. But I am thankful that it is over. All that fortnight I never *once* washed and never *once* took my boots off, so that I have got chilblains and a bad cold on my chest. But otherwise I am well." Now came the much more difficult diplomatic battle that must be fought to settle definitely the union of Eastern

Rumelia with Bulgaria. It was not an easy matter in view of the Tsar's attitude. Prince Alexander of Hesse showed that he realized this by coming down off the high horse that he had ridden after hearing of his son's victory. He even felt it to be advisable to recommend his son to take some steps to try to improve his relations with the Tsar.

Sandro answered resignedly from Pirot on December 9, 1885, that if it would please his father he would do so, but that for his part he wanted to have nothing to do with the Tsar, since the good will of such a "stupid, dishonourable, false, disgusting creature" could at best only be temporary.[192]

Prince Alexander of Bulgaria thereupon issued an army order attributing the victory of the Bulgarian army to some extent to their Russian instructors, and then asked whether he might come to St. Petersburg to discuss matters with the Tsar. Alexander III, however, replied on December 24th that he did not yet regard the time as favourable for a personal interview.[193]

The attitude of Queen Victoria was very different. She had followed the ups and downs of the war with ardent sympathy. Now that things appeared to be gradually settling down she gave vent to her feelings.

"Dear Sandro," ran her letter dated from Osborne on December 26th,[194] "I must follow the impulse of my heart and tell you how *warm* and fervent my sympathy and my prayers have been for you. My admiration for your heroic conduct that was at the same time so dignified and moderate is *great*. But we have all endured sad hours full of anxiety on your behalf since September 17th and the outbreak of war. . . . I will not enter into political affairs in this letter, which is only intended to express my personal feelings for you, and to wish you both a happy new year and continued prosperity." The Queen also expressed her warmest interest in a letter to his parents, the text of which Prince Alexander of Hesse entered in his diary on December 24, 1885: "God has graciously preserved your heroic son. Your hearts are I am sure filled with gratitude, and I must say that mine is too."

Politics were expressed in broad outlines in the personal feelings of the rulers: in England the antagonism to Russia, and in Russia hatred and jealousy of Austria-Hungary. The Tsar could not get over the fact that Austria-Hungary had intervened in his sphere of interest in the Balkans, and declared that he had been betrayed. The Three Emperors Entente, and

thus Giers' policy, received a considerable shock. In Berlin the
anxiety lest Austria-Hungary should quarrel with Russia over
the Balkan question was so great that the outbreak of a great
European war was feared. If the matter had rested with
Andrássy, who advised—though not from a responsible
position—that the opportunity should be used to dislodge
Russia from the Balkans altogether, war would have broken
out then and there. But Kálnoky and the Emperor were not
inclined for so catastrophal a policy. They feared a clash if
only because they knew that Bismarck would not join in a war
in which Austria-Hungary was the aggressor. Hence Vienna
moderated its policy.

Once again the threatened conflict was averted. But the
tension remained. This time it was no longer Russia who
sought Austria-Hungary's friendship as in the days of Nicholas I
and at times under Alexander II.

Austria-Hungary remained a very problematical friend and
the Tsar a bitter foe. Nor was the heartfelt sympathy of
England of very much help to the Prince of Bulgaria.
Salisbury's Ministry fell in 1886, and Gladstone, who displayed
little sympathy with the Prince's affairs, came back to power.

What was happening in Berlin can be seen clearly from
the contrast between two letters, which Prince Alexander of
Bulgaria received from the Emperor and from the Crown
Prince. He had written to the Emperor to congratulate him on
completing twenty-five years of his reign on January 2, 1886.
The Emperor's thanks for his good wishes were formal and
curt, and contained some strong words of admonition: "Your
Highness will be in a position", he wrote on January 24,[195] "to
assist effectively towards the fulfilment of your wishes that I
may be unbowed by sorrow in my old age, if Your Highness will
do your utmost to preserve the peace in your country and upon
your frontiers, and to prevent the peace of Europe being
endangered from there by actions which jeopardize the treaties
upon which that peace rests." Not a word was said about the
Prince's military success, and the effect was correspondingly
damping. He thought that what the Emperor said was unbelievably inconsiderate, indeed "positively shameful". "His
answer", he wrote to his father on February 11th, "is so infamous that I have sworn never . . . to write another line to
him."

The Empress Augusta seconded her husband in every way.
Once when Lady Mary Hamilton began to speak of the

Prince of Bulgaria, she answered: "Don't mention that person to me." The lady protested: "But you must have admired his bravery!" To which the Empress replied: "Oh yes, of course. But revolutionaries are always brave." Someone told the story to Prince Alexander of Hesse, who entered it in his diary on June 10, 1886.

Quite different was the tone of a letter from the Crown Prince which arrived from Berlin dated February 6th:[196]

"It has been a great pleasure, both to the Crown Princess and to myself, to watch the manly courage, the endurance, and the discernment which you, and you alone, displayed in a situation which appeared impossible, thereby winning for your country a valuable extension of territory, and for your own person the respect, I may say the admiration, of your contemporaries. . . .

"To witness such actions in a fellow-countryman, who received his military training in the German army, must fill everyone except those who wilfully distort facts with the sincerest pleasure. May you now enjoy undisturbed peace, and succeed in using and securing what you have won both on the field of battle and by a wise handling of existing circumstances. . . . Frederick William."

The difference in the views of the two camps at the German court could not be better shown. Sandro was delighted at the Crown Prince's charming note, which he designated as the "balm on the wound inflicted by his father's abominable letter", in a telegram to Prince Alexander of Hesse from Philippopolis on February 27th.[197]

The Crown Princess's enthusiasm for the Prince knew no bounds. "My admiration for him", she wrote to her mother, "increases every day. As a patriot, a soldier, and a statesman he has shown an energy, patience, perseverance, modesty, and moderation such as one has rarely seen and which one can only find in the perfect gentleman. . . . He and his cause indeed deserve sympathy and support from all well-minded people, and it is only the wilfully prejudiced who can find anything to blame in his conduct."

Meanwhile Prince Alexander had agreed to the compromise that established a personal union of Bulgaria with Eastern Rumelia and relegated himself to the position of a Governor-General with a five years' tenure of office. England supported the Prince, but Russia did everything possible to make things difficult for him. Sandro was of opinion that he had merely made a formal concession, but had "saved the principle against the whole of Europe", which view future events did in fact confirm. He hoped that Russia would "swallow" its wrath and comfort itself with hopes of success in the next war. Sandro was very pleased to hear of Queen Victoria's congratulatory letter to his father, but was somewhat sceptical at her further remarking that Germany was now on England's side, and that in Lord Rosebery she had a very able and energetic young Foreign Secretary. He did not share Queen Victoria's opinion that Rosebery would follow so closely in Lord Salisbury's footsteps. Actually British policy now accorded Prince Alexander very slight support, in spite of the Queen's feelings.

His cousin the Grand Duke of Hesse had only the most unsatisfactory account to give of a visit he had paid to St. Petersburg. The Tsar had told him, so Prince Alexander of Hesse notes in his diary on March 22nd, that Sandro was an anti-Russian revolutionary, who had alone been responsible for the rising in Philippopolis, and had then told lies to Giers at Franzensbad in order to put Russia in the wrong. There was no hint of any hope of reconciliation. He had found this confirmed also during the negotiations which preceded the very loose union of the two countries, which was proclaimed on April 6, 1886.

The Bulgarians were horrified and dismayed to find that their great sacrifice of men and money had again resulted in no more than a provisional settlement.

Prince Alexander of Hesse now began to be seriously alarmed for the life of his son. Threatening letters came in from every side, and at Burgas he discovered a plot that was being organized by one of the regular Russian officers to ambush the Prince and his suite in a forest.

Furthermore the German newspapers on June 24th published the information—alleged to be from Berlin—that the Prince of Bulgaria had been struck off the Prussian active army list to please Russia.

In reality Bismarck had opposed the suggestion of the Crown Prince and Princess that Alexander of Battenberg, who already held the rank of Major-General in the German army, should be advanced in rank, alleging that the Tsar's feelings must be considered. That he had been struck off the list as had happened in Russia was pure invention. The Crown Prince and his wife at once determined to explain the real state of affairs to various prominent persons, in order that Prince Alexander's reputation might not suffer. Amongst others, the Crown Princess addressed herself to the Grand Duke of Hesse-Darmstadt.

"You will see from the enclosed paper", she wrote to him on June 25th,[198] "that some piece of mischief or tactlessness has again been staged. . . . The fact of his not being given a rise in rank has disappointed us very much and we cannot understand it. But it is not intended in any way as an insult, and to take it as such would only do harm to Sandro and annoy and exasperate Prince Bismarck, which would really be a great mistake just now."

Nevertheless Prince Alexander of Bulgaria, though he still hoped in his inmost heart that he might one day win over Bismarck to his side, took this as a serious affront, and held the Chancellor responsible for it. "It is he", he wrote to his father on July 9th (21st), "who wrote and induced the Emperor to pass me over. It is a matter that is unimportant in itself, but which is a public slap in the face, and which will cause a howl of triumph among my enemies."

Bismarck now set himself systematically to exclude from public affairs all those who were at all friendly disposed to Alexander of Battenberg. The Crown Prince himself was given proof in his own person of the extent to which the Chancellor held the old Emperor in his control, when he found that once again his son William was to be sent as imperial envoy to the Tsar instead of himself. Bismarck wished him to go, because he knew that the Crown Prince would not in speaking to the Tsar refer to Alexander of Battenberg as the Chancellor wished in the interests of his policy, while Prince William, whose dislike of Prince Alexander was always obvious, would certainly do so. In vain did the Crown Prince direct an urgent memorandum to Bismarck on August 12th to prevent his son being sent, saying that he was too immature, and had not the experience necessary to form an opinion on political questions.[199]

Bismarck did not give way. He insisted that Prince William should go to St. Petersburg, and as usual the old Emperor fell in with his Chancellor's wishes. The Crown Prince and his wife were furious. The Crown Princess especially flew into a passion which did not pass before she had let fall some violent remarks about her son William whom she considered "as blind and green, wrong-headed and violent on politics as can be".[200] It was a difficult situation for Prince William, and he indicated to his grandfather that it was awkward for him that his father should be passed over. The Emperor replied that Bismarck

was absolutely opposed to the Crown Prince's being sent, as
he was Anti-Russian, pro-English, and friendly with Alexander
of Battenberg whom the Tsar hated. Then he sent the Prince
to the Chancellor. When William again pointed out to Bismarck
that his father was bound to feel that his own son had intrigued
against him, the Chancellor cut short all objections with the
remark that the Emperor had commanded, and it was the
Prince's duty to obey.[201]

Alexander of Hesse followed the kaleidoscopic change of
the political situation with tense interest. On August 22nd,
when the Prince came home from an evening party, his wife
rushed to meet him crying: "Sandro is a prisoner!" She was
carrying a special edition of the *Frankfurter Zeitung*, according
to which the Prince had been kidnapped and deposed, and a
new Government had been formed in Bulgaria. The news
corresponded to the facts. During the night of August 20th
to 21st, the Prince had been taken prisoner as the result of
a plot hatched by Russia, had been rushed on to a steamer
under threats of his life, and taken downstream, while a pro-
Russian Government was formed by the rebels in Sofia.

The brief and quite indefinite news of the Prince's arrest
that was telegraphed throughout the world caused the greatest
dismay and alarm not only to the Prince's father but also at
the Crown Prince's court in Berlin and to Queen Victoria at
Balmoral. In the greatest anxiety Prince Alexander telegraphed
at once to all the Foreign Offices, but could get no certain news
of Sandro's fate.

King Charles of Rumania replied from Castell Pelesh on
August 24th: "Despite all efforts we have failed to get into
communication with Sandro. . . . Connection with Sofia
interrupted. We are filled with anxiety at the unexpected event
and send you our deepest sympathy. Charles."[202]

Then came the first cheering news. Prince Henry telegraphed
to his father from Balmoral on August 24th: "News just
received that a counter-demonstration has occurred in Sofia
and Alexander re-elected Prince."[203]

Further good news followed soon. A telegram came from
King Charles in Bucharest on the evening of August 24th:
"Boat arrived at Reni at six o'clock to-night. . . . Revolutionary Government overthrown in Sofia. The whole country is
for Sandro. God keep him. . . ."[204]

In England, where the good news did not arrive so early, the
Queen was, in her own words, horrified. She regarded the whole

Y

incident as the work of "these Russian fiends". She already had
visions of the outbreak of a European war, and exhorted her
Ministers to take a very firm stand, since one of the bravest and
wisest rulers in Europe had been lost, and one who was moreover
a firm friend to England. Her sympathy for the "dear, brave,
and so cruelly used" Prince, for the "heroic, noble young
sovereign of Bulgaria" was the more intense owing to the
Queen's intimate relationship to his family.[205] The Queen
regarded Russia's "monstrous" behaviour and that of its
"barbarous, Asiatic, tyrannical Emperor"[206] as "without
parallel in modern history".[207] Prince Louis of Battenberg,
together with his wife who insisted on accompanying him,
instantly set off for the Continent to look for his brother, and
if possible to give him moral and material support.

At the same time the British Ambassador in St. Petersburg
was instructed to make strong representations. This, however,
only had the result of still further increasing the Tsar's hatred
of Prince Alexander, if that were possible.

Anxiously did Prince Alexander's father await news of his
son. At length, during the afternoon of August 25th, the first
tidings came from the Prince himself:[208]

"Have to-day been delivered prisoner to the Russian police
at Reni. Was released at the order of St. Petersburg, and am
going by way of . . . Lemberg to Breslau, from where I will
send further news. . . . I am absolutely shattered by the fearful
anguish I have suffered."

Prince Alexander of Hesse immediately instructed his son
Louis to go to Breslau and to enlighten Sandro, who knew
nothing about events in Sofia, where the new Government had
been overthrown and his return was impatiently looked for.

At eleven o'clock on the evening of August 26th a courier
arrived in Darmstadt on a most secret mission ostensibly from
the Crown Princess, but in reality sent by Radolinsky. This was
a certain Professor Langenbuch, a physician who was altogether devoted to the service of the Crown Prince and Princess.
This man had been sent to Sofia by the Berlin Red Cross in
1885, at the time of the Serbian war, and had spent the winter
of 1886 there. Prince Alexander of Bulgaria liked him, took
him on a journey with him, and wished him to remain as his
personal physician. The professor, however, refused to do so.
He was a man no longer in his first youth, and the Prince
described him as a very clever and entertaining individual,
who was not only a famous doctor but also a delightful com-

companion, which, as he said to his parents in a letter dated
May 16, 1886, one greatly appreciated in a place like Sofia.

Dr. Langenbuch brought the news that Prince Dolgoruki
would start for Sofia on August 27th as the Tsar's Commissar
in order to take over the reins of government. The Crown
Princess urged Prince Alexander of Battenberg to go back to
Bulgaria immediately so as to anticipate Dolgoruki. Langenbuch reported further that the old Emperor had said to
Bismarck: "If the Prince of Bulgaria comes here, I shall no
longer refuse him my grand-daughter Victoria. It is causing
too much misery." And that Bismarck had replied: "Perhaps
you are right." Prince Alexander was delighted to hear this,
and made a note of the conversation in his diary on August
26th, though it is now known, of course, that the story certainly
cannot have been true. Prince Alexander felt that the mysterious
envoy behaved in a somewhat unceremonious manner, but
decided in view of this story that he was a pleasant enough
fellow, who had "found his way into the Crown Princess's good
graces (duplicated by Radolinsky)" owing to his relations with
the Prince of Bulgaria during the war.

This mission of Langenbuch's was the second time that the
Crown Princess intervened directly in Bulgarian affairs. Her
action was obviously taken independently of all responsible
authorities, and her emissary Langenbuch rather overshot the
mark in his zeal to serve the Crown Princess.

When in addition to this envoy a very urgent message came
from Henry of Battenberg, sent off at 9.10 p.m. on August 26th
from Balmoral, to say that it was most necessary for Sandro
to return with all speed if he would avoid disaster,[209] Prince
Alexander of Hesse roused the post office officials during that
night and made them dispatch a telegram from him to Duke
William of Württemberg, the General in Command at Lemberg:
"Please be so kind as to urge my son in my name to return
immediately to Sofia on account of very important and
authoritative information (through Dr. Langenbuch). Please
add that Dr. L. came to see us."[210]

Queen Victoria also telegraphed direct to Prince Louis to
tell him to urge his brother as emphatically as he could to
return with all possible speed for the sake of the peace of
Europe. The Queen informed the Earl of Iddesleigh, the
Foreign Secretary, of her action in a letter dated August 27,
1886, and added: "And we must stand by him."[211]

When Prince Alexander of Bulgaria arrived in Lemberg he

found in addition to all the telegrams an invitation from the Duke of Württemberg to spend the evening of August 27th with him.

While he was with the Duke, Prince Alexander was still quite undecided about his future plans, as Count Zaleski, the Governor of Galicia, wrote from Lemberg, to Count Kálnoky on August 28th.[212] During the evening he received a telegram in cipher from Balmoral, which bore the signature "Grand-mama", which he rightly presumed to have come from Queen Victoria, but which he was unable to decode. On the following morning, August 28th, when Prince Louis of Battenberg arrived in Lemberg, his first act was to telegraph to Balmoral to say that the Queen's telegram had arrived, but that it could not be deciphered as they had no key, and to request that a veiled statement of the contents should be wired. Thereupon the following telegram arrived from Balmoral without any signature, as was again reported by Count Zaleski to his chief in Vienna: "Sense of telegram, urge immediate return in view of real temper of the people."

Stimulated by this news, and by the information given him by Louis of Battenberg, who had also brought considerable monetary supplies, Prince Alexander realized that, though there was every reason for him to fear for his life, his honour as a sovereign and as a soldier demanded that he should not yield to a mob of paid conspirators, but should go back to Sofia since the people and the army were urging his return, triumphant over Russia's base trickery.

On the morning of August 28th he had definitely made up his mind, and telegraphed to his father: "I am going to Bulgaria, where I arrive to-morrow morning. May God help me."[213]

It was too much to expect of the young Prince. His nerves were strained almost to breaking-point, and when he arrived at Rustchuk on August 29th everyone noticed how ill and weary he looked. Nor did his appearance improve despite his pleasure in the tremendous enthusiasm with which he was everywhere received. To crown all, the astute Russian Consul at Rustchuk succeeded in making the Prince believe that more than two-thirds of the people and of the Bulgarian officers had taken part in the plot. Then he did his best to persuade him that salvation lay with Russia alone and induced him to send a conciliatory telegram to the Tsar on September 2nd, ending with the unfortunately chosen words that since Russia had

ALEXANDER III AS TSAREVITCH, WITH HIS WIFE AND SON

given him his crown, he was ready to return it into the hands of the Tsar.

This telegram came at exactly the right moment for Alexander III. He had watched the Prince's return to Bulgaria with disgust and fury. Now he was able to say unequivocally that he did not agree to it, that he foresaw dire consequences, and that the Prince must know by now what it was his duty to do. In addition, this confidential correspondence was published in the official Gazette.

The reply had been sent off on the Tsar's own initiative and implied the end of the Prince's position in Bulgaria. Even Prince Alexander of Hesse now gave up his son for lost. "Poor Sandro," he remarked in his diary on September 2, 1886, "how could he think that any impulse of nobility was still to be hoped for from this stupid, malicious, and revengeful despot. Sandro's telegram was a great political mistake, which will put him in the wrong with his supporters in Bulgaria, and will spur on his enemies to fresh plots against him. All that remains now is for him to retire as soon as possible and with what dignity he can muster."

His attempt at reconciliation with Russia had been brutally repulsed. On the same day that Prince Alexander made his ceremonial entry into Sofia, amid the jubilations of the populace, he heard of the publication of the telegrams by the Tsar. Indignant at this further "slap in the face", the Prince poured out his troubles to his father, who thereupon urged him to abdicate. "Tsar's reply", telegraphed Prince Alexander of Hesse on September 4, 1886, "and publication abominable. Only choice left you is between fresh Russian conspiracies and voluntary abdication."[214]

On the previous day he had been informed by letter—again via Langenbuch—that in a *certain* quarter, meaning the Crown Prince's court, it was desired that Prince Alexander should send a timely request to the imperial Chancellor to apply to the Tsar that his son's supporters in Bulgaria should in case of the Prince's abdication be given good terms.

This was done. Bismarck replied to this telegram in the most forthcoming manner,* and it was obvious from his friendliness how glad the Chancellor was that Alexander of Battenberg was soon to vanish from the political scene.

When Sandro arrived in Sofia, he had already made up his mind to abdicate. He did not need the stimulus of the absence

* See Appendix.

of the German and Russian representatives at his entry, nor
the request which immediately reached him from both not to
execute the conspirators.

Prince Alexander of Hesse now declared himself to be
satisfied that his son should abdicate voluntarily and with
honour. Queen Victoria agreed to the decision much less
readily. On receipt of the first news from the English representative in Sofia she urged the Prince very stringently to
remain, but after receiving a letter from him she modified her
opinion. Alexander of Bulgaria wrote on September 6th[215] to
say that almost three-fourths of the officers had been involved
in the plot and that the whole machinery of government in
Bulgaria was in the most hopeless state of confusion. All that
remained to him was to abdicate of his own free will, guarding
his honour, or to remain amid bloodshed with no hope of
success, and with the choice of either being murdered or being
driven away by Russian bayonets.

The murder argument made the greatest impression on the
Queen. She realized that her responsibility might become a
terrible one if she persuaded him to remain any longer. Hence
she also agreed to the inevitable, though with a heavy heart.
She felt not merely that she was accepting a personal insult,
but that it was a political triumph of Russia over England.

On September 9, 1886, Prince Alexander left Bulgaria and
returned home.

While large numbers of people in Germany took Prince
Alexander's part, Bismarck remained hostile. Prince Alexander
of Hesse notes in his diary on September 10th that on the day
before Sandro left Sofia, Bismarck sent a telegram to inform him
that if he should return to Germany the Emperor would not
be able to receive him, as the Opposition Press in Germany was
showing immoderate antagonism to the Emperor's party and
its language was too excitatory. This telegram filled the Prince's
father with fury, and he refers to it in his diary as a baseness
unworthy of a great statesman.

Prince Alexander of Battenberg left the land where he had
the mighty of Tsar of Russia as his enemy only to find that
when he got home another hostile Tsar was waiting for him
whose name was Bismarck. The scene of action changed, but
the relentless struggle continued.

Bismarck's attitude was one of complete antagonism to
Prince Alexander of Battenberg. The Chancellor knew very
well that he still had a passionate opponent in the Crown

Princess, who represented the English tendency in German foreign policy, and that the project of his marriage with Princess Victoria had still not been dropped.[216] He saw in it an interference with his own foreign policy, a sphere in which he guarded his independence and autocratic position most jealously. He hated and persecuted anyone who cut across his path, not disdaining to use the most ruthless measures. The Chancellor had very carefully observed personally and by means of spies the state of feeling in the Crown Prince's household during this critical time, and knew exactly the excitement and painful tension with which the ups and downs in Bulgaria had been followed. He also knew that the Crown Princess and her daughter after striving and hoping for years were all the more determined not to give up the Prince in his time of misfortune; and this determined his future attitude to Alexander of Battenberg even after his return to private life.

If the Tsar believed that he was at the end of his difficulties in Bulgaria with the removal of the Prince, he was to find himself sorely mistaken. The sentiments of nationalism and liberty that Prince Alexander had encouraged during the time he was on the throne also manifested themselves after he had been turned out, in resistance to Russian oppression and manifestations in favour of the recall of Prince Alexander.

"The Tsar", wrote the future imperial Chancellor Bernhard von Bülow to Bismarck from St. Petersburg on November 15, 1886, "feels that he has been made a hopeless laughing-stock in Bulgaria. He is furious, because even now that his arch-enemy of Battenberg has been turned out, things are still going altogether contrary to his expectation and wishes."

The Tsar was especially displeased with Austria-Hungary, which was coming increasingly into conflict with Russia. Count Andrássy had once again raised his voice and had on November 13th spoken in the Delegations, with obvious reference to Russia, of the unnatural grouping of the Three Emperors Pact. Even Kálnoky, who despite his antipathy to Russia was in agreement with his Emperor and opposed to Andrássy in advocating the cause of peace, indicated on the same occasion how different Austria-Hungary's attitude must have been if Russia had actively intervened in Bulgarian affairs. Therein was implied a threat for the future. General Tcherevin had given telling expression to the Tsar's feelings on August 10th of that year when he said to Bülow, then German chargé d'affaires, who reported it to Bismarck:[217]

"Austria is a swindler. Let us come to an agreement between ourselves, without Austria. If you like, at its expense." Although Bismarck was absolutely determined not to allow himself to be driven to war with Russia by Austria-Hungary, and caused this to be emphasized in Vienna repeatedly, the Tsar considered none the less that Germany gave in too easily to the Danubian monarchy. The result of the Bulgarian crisis on the Russian side was an increasingly deadly and unjust antagonism to Austria-Hungary. It went to such lengths that Count Paul Shuvaloff, the Russian Ambassador in Berlin, broke out into maledictions of Austria-Hungary and suggested—under the influence of a certain amount of drink, it is true—that Germany should have done with Austria-Hungary and should concentrate on a permanent alliance with Russia. It was absolutely necessary, he continued, that Germany and Russia should leave that Empire to vanish from the map of Europe. Germany should annex Austria-Hungary's German provinces, and nothing could then separate the two remaining empires. "So let us have a shot at Austria . . ." said the ambassador.[218]

The Tsar was not yet quite prepared to abandon Germany. For owing to its constitution and its attitude to the Nihilists and Anarchists, of whom he was naturally very much afraid, the Tsar was still so distrustful of France—the only great European republic of the day—that he would for the present not entertain the idea of any treaty. Thus the way was prepared for a temporary secret understanding between Russia and Germany in the following year.

Alexander of Hesse took no more part in these events in international politics. The antagonism between Austria-Hungary and Russia was no longer mitigated by his services as go-between. The events in Bulgaria had deepened and perpetuated the breach. Alexander of Hesse and his son, as well as his other children, were in spite of their close relationship with the Russian royal family looked upon with utter disfavour in St. Petersburg. The tragedy was that this was true also of Berlin. Lady Mary Hamilton, Prince Alexander's old friend, who met the Emperor William at Baden in October, wrote to Prince Alexander on October 10, 1886, and explained the situation to him fully.

"The Emperor", she wrote, "was . . . with me several times. He appeared to be very much prejudiced in favour of the Tsar of Russia. He is anxious at all costs to preserve *peace*, and that is the reason why he has kept so tremendously *neutral*.

He is quite mistaken, but he said several times: 'At all events we three empires are very *united*, and shall never have to endure another war.' The poor old Emperor has grown very weak. He is deaf and he rambles a little. His great fad is 'peace at all costs'. But Bismarck is the executive power and the Emperor's will depends on his. It must have made you very sad to see how little support your son found among the Powers. But of course charity begins at home, and they are all afraid of the great might of Russia, who is getting her own way in everything now. . . . It is unbelievable that everyone should let her do as she likes in this manner without making any move to oppose it."

Nevertheless the accomplished fact was now unalterable. The Bulgarian question brought an unrest and nervousness into international politics that was still further increased in the following years.

CHAPTER XIV

DECLINE AND FALL

SADLY Prince Alexander of Hesse and his family sat together for an hour after their dinner on New Year's Eve, 1887. The last day of the year had brought yet another "Prussian box on the ear" for the ex-ruler of Bulgaria. He was now put down in the army lists simply as His Serene Highness Prince Alexander of Battenberg, attached to two regiments. So all his higher titles had been taken from him. The Grand Duke of Hesse received a depressed letter from the Crown Prince of Prussia, who had done his level best to prevent this fresh blow. His efforts, however, were unavailing against a telegram from Bismarck to the Emperor.

Sadly Prince Alexander closed his diary for this year with a question to Fate as to what lay in the future of his unfortunate son Sandro. He had been thrust from his throne by the Tsar, and on his return home deprived of all his dignities by the Emperor at Bismarck's instigation, and left without means of any description. It was very hard. He was suffering for Prince Alexander of Hesse's former anti-Prussian and anti-Bismarck views and attitude. Bismarck never forgot anything, and he was the best hater of his day.

If the interests of Germany could be combined with procedure against a family that he disliked in any case, there was not much hope for that family. The only comfort was that information came from Count Radolinsky to Prince Alexander of Battenberg that he was continually kept in mind—possibly almost more by the Crown Princess than by her daughter— so that a happier future might make up for his present sufferings.

To Prince Alexander of Hesse's great surprise a telegram arrived from the Tsar and his wife wishing them a happy new year. In the circumstances it could only be regarded as sarcasm. The Tsar, however, was in a conciliatory mood now that his aim had been achieved with the fall of Alexander of Battenberg. If Alexander had gone back to Bulgaria as a large party in the country wanted him to do, the Tsar would have been deeply wounded in his self-esteem—an injury that very few people can bear, and a Tsar and an autocrat least of all. Every step taken by the Russian Government in the succeeding years proves the essential correctness of this surmise.

It was shown most clearly in a course entered upon by the two brothers Paul and Peter Shuvaloff, the one as ambassador and the other as envoy extraordinary in Berlin. On January 6th they went to see Herbert Bismarck, then Foreign Secretary, and informed him that the Tsar was in a continual state of anxiety lest the Prince of Battenberg should attempt some fresh move. In case of his return to Bulgaria the Tsar would ruthlessly occupy the country, for the honour of Russia would demand it. The two brothers Shuvaloff wished to find out whether the Tsar might address a letter to the Emperor William requesting that in his capacity as Commander-in-Chief of the German army he would give Prince Alexander of Battenberg definite orders to drop any plans he might have thought of making for a return to Sofia.

Bismarck never missed an opportunity of dealing Sandro a blow. He therefore wrote the following marginal note upon Herbert's report: "I consider . . . the idea of a letter from the Tsar to our Emperor as a useful means of producing a reply from our side that shall indicate the distinction between *us* and all the Battenberg gang!"

In consequence an indication was given to St. Petersburg that if the Tsar were to write the letter it would be answered as he desired.

A few days later, on January 10, 1887, Count Peter Shuvaloff also paid a visit to the Crown Prince Frederick. The supple diplomat's tone was quite different in this case, and especially in the matter of the Battenberg question. In the course of the interview the Count told the Crown Prince that he had been instructed to discover what truth there was in the story of the alleged plan of Alexander of Battenberg to return to Bulgaria, and that he had found it to be merely an idle tale.

To the Crown Prince's question why the Tsar troubled about such reports which were proved to be untrue, Shuvaloff replied that it was not easy to approach the Tsar, as he spent the greater part of the year in the country, generally saw nobody except his own servants, and received even his Ministers as seldom as possible.

Peter Shuvaloff emphasized, moreover, that Prince Alexander had repeatedly mortified the Tsar's personal dignity and self-esteem, had insisted too much upon his own position as a sovereign, and had thereby at last brought things to such a pass that the Tsar had conceived a boundless hatred for him. The Tsar, he proceeded, continually gave expression to his sentiments in the strongest language. He had pressed for the Prince's deposition by every possible means. But when at last it had been achieved, the Tsar had admitted to Shuvaloff that he could think of no suitable person to succeed him. The prospects of various possible candidates were discussed by Shuvaloff and deemed unsatisfactory.

Although it did not altogether accord with the truth, Count Shuvaloff, in order to please the Crown Prince, expressed his disapprobation at Prince Alexander's being deprived of his higher titles in Germany, and remarked, as it were in passing, that Giers's private opinion was that the restoration of Prince Alexander would still be the best solution. The Crown Prince asked Shuvaloff to remind the Tsar that while he was still Tsarevitch they had together settled the principles of a peaceful understanding between Germany and Russia, and that for his part the Crown Prince still adhered to them, and would always do so. The Count took his leave with friendly grace, and with the vague phrase that the Tsar had every confidence in the Crown Prince. But Frederick attached an exaggerated significance to it.

Immediately after this conversation had taken place the Crown Prince wrote it down and sent the manuscript to his mother-in-law, Queen Victoria.[219] The Queen could not reconcile herself to the idea that Alexander of Battenberg, who was "a really remarkable and distinguished as well as excellent young Prince", should be "lost to the world", as she wrote to Lord Salisbury on December 22, 1886.[220] She was pleased with everything that appeared to be favourable to Prince Alexander. And when she received the unexpected report of the Crown Prince's interview with Shuvaloff, she too accepted it at its face value, and made her daughter Beatrice send a copy to Alexander of Battenberg at once, and on January 19, 1887, wrote a memorandum entirely in her own hand regarding the interview which she then sent to her daughter the Crown Princess.* She regarded the remark about Giers's "private opinion" as most promising.

* See Appendix.

There was no need for the Tsar to like or to meet Prince Alexander; he need only allow him to work independently. It would be best of all if the Crown Prince would himself act as intermediary in the affair.

Meanwhile the Tsar had written to the Emperor William[221] on January 4 (16), 1887, the letter which had been the subject of Count Shuvaloff's mission. He emphasized in it that notwithstanding all the base plots that had been concocted in order to provoke him and force him to act, he had hitherto dealt pacifically with the Bulgarian problem. If the Prince were to return, he would be forced to take more decisive action and to allow the opponents of peace to triumph. Hence he requested the monarch as paramount Lord of the German Empire to prevent any such attempt on Prince Alexander's part. The first answer that the Tsar received was an indirect one. It was Bismarck's great speech before the Reichstag on January 11, 1887, which was so prophetic of the World War and its consequences. In it he emphasized once again Germany's complete indifference to the question of who ruled in Bulgaria, and what became of the country. He closed his speech with the famous words that the historic trial by battle between France and Germany might yet be revived, and that if the French were victorious they would be cruel and intemperate victors and would bleed Germany white. This implied that the most important task was to ensure that Russia did not help France to gain such a victory, and that compared with such an aim, Prince Alexander, Bulgaria, and any other contingencies were no more than a speck of dust.

A move towards Russia on the part of Germany implied in the existing state of world politics a corresponding withdrawal from England. The Crown Prince had meanwhile discovered from various sources in Berlin that it had been Shuvaloff who had prepared the way for the Tsar's letter without having said a word to him (the Crown Prince) about it at their meeting. He also discovered that Shuvaloff had spoken very differently about Prince Alexander of Battenberg to other people than he had done to him.

He unbosomed himself indignantly to his mother-in-law on the subject in a letter written on January 22, 1887.* "The observations of Count Peter Shuvaloff in his interview with me, of which I recently sent you a note, are the complete antithesis of anything that one is accustomed to hear from a

* See Appendix.

man of his views. Hence it would appear that he was playing the part of *agent provocateur* in order to find out my intentions by misleading me as to his own sentiments regarding Prince A.[lexander]. Shuvaloff, however, must have been disappointed, for I merely confirmed what the Tsar has known for a long time, while the Count has exposed himself badly and given proof of his insincerity. He parades his dislike of Prince A. before the Russians, for he expressed himself as quite delighted at the Embassy when he heard that the Prince had been passed over for military advancement by us, whereas when he spoke to me he inexplicably censured the Prussians for depriving him of his title as sovereign. If Shuvaloff ascribes to Giers the sentiment that 'in his private opinion the best means of settling the Bulgarian crisis would be to restore Prince A.', it can only be supposed that he does so in order to undermine still further Giers's position."

"The Russians are masters of intrigue", concluded the Crown Prince; "they will stop at nothing to gain their ends. *Just as they once plotted against the life of Prince A., so they will now plot against the liberty of Bulgaria. And if ever circumstances took Prince A. back there, it could only be if Russia were conquered and the Prince were to assume the royal crown of Bulgaria against their will.*"

Queen Victoria was very much vexed at this fresh piece of information, and instructed her son-in-law, Prince Henry of Battenberg, to write to Prince Alexander's father about it. "She is very much disappointed at the result of her efforts," wrote Prince Henry from Osborne on January 25, 1887, "as she had assumed that Shuvaloff was speaking the truth at his interview with the Crown Prince. It is clear, however, from a further letter from the Crown Prince that Shuvaloff said exactly the opposite in Russophil circles in Berlin. The Queen is anxious that Sandro should be apprised of this discovery, perhaps by yourself."[222]

This was done at once, and Prince Alexander's only comment was that he was surprised that Russian duplicity was so little recognized in England that they could still be deceived by a man like Shuvaloff. If the Queen and the Crown Prince had seen the Emperor William's reply to the Tsar's letter written on January 30, 1887, which played upon the Russian monarch's weaknesses with particularly masterly psychological insight, they would have been convinced of the utter hopelessness of trying to achieve anything for their Battenberg protégé within the lifetime of the aged Emperor. The Emperor had assured the Tsar that he shared his opinion that the return of Prince Alexander to Sofia was impossible; that he could not have foreseen that the Prince would prove to be ungrateful to Russia; that he had, in spite of the "ramifications and relations of his mother's family in Poland", given him a post in the army because he believed that he was thereby honouring a relative and friend of the Russian royal house. A second time did the letter—by Bismarck's inspiration—make clever allusion to the Poles whom Alexander III regarded with so much suspicion by referring to ovations which he said had been given to Prince Alexander at Lemberg after his abduction.[223]

This was a period of great mistrust among the Cabinets of Europe. Each one thought the others planning war, and the greatest nervousness prevailed in political and diplomatic circles. Therein lay the roots of Bismarck's desire for closer ties with the third member of the Triple Alliance—Italy. Italy had been making overtures to England, and on February 1st Count Luigi Corti, the Italian Ambassador in London, had made Lord Salisbury an offer of alliance.[224] It was taken up in a friendly manner, and led to an agreement about the Mediterranean question, but not to a definite treaty. This made Italy all the more anxious to enter into the second Triple Alliance of February 20, 1887, concluded at the instigation of Germany.

The opposition between the Crown Prince and Princess and Bismarck's adherents also made itself felt in the attitude taken up by the British Government. It was difficult for the Queen and Salisbury to believe that Bismarck was not cherishing military ambitions, in view of the chauvinistic manifestations of the French poet and Germanophobe Déroulède and of General Boulanger, the Minister for War, when the Crown Prince of Germany was writing to the Queen as if war with France were an understood thing, as Prince Henry of Battenberg said in a letter to his father from Osborne on January 25, 1887. The Tsar's fears of Alexander's return were not altogether unfounded. The Crown Prince's circle in Berlin was seriously considering it, and it is certain that Queen Victoria would have been pleased if it had happened. To crown all, the unhappy Prince, who was still left in uncertainty both politically and on account of his marriage, caught typhus towards the end of February 1887, and was very seriously ill. Even that was not allowed to pass in Berlin. On the Crown

Princess's instructions, Dr. Langenbuch wrote and told the father of the ex-Prince of Bulgaria that in official—that is to say hostile—circles it was believed that the illness was merely simulated in order to mask a possible sudden disappearance connected with a return to Bulgaria. The typhus, however, passed comparatively quickly, and in three weeks' time the young man was well again.

Suddenly and quite unexpectedly Dr. Langenbuch appeared in Darmstadt on March 25th, as Prince Alexander of Hesse noted in his diary on March 26th, and visited the ex-Prince of Bulgaria.

Langenbuch affirmed that he was not permitted to say who had sent him, nor to state definitely that he had come from Bismarck. However, he let it be inferred that he had come by the Crown Princess's desire, and she obviously wished that it should appear that the Chancellor was in agreement with her.[225]

The Professor handed Prince Alexander of Battenberg a memorandum from the pen of Count Radolinsky, as well as copies of dispatches from the German Ambassadors in London and Paris. The memorandum was to the effect that the moment had come for the Prince to return to Bulgaria; that a treaty had recently been concluded between Germany, Austria-Hungary, and Italy which guaranteed the mutual integrity of these countries, and—which was not exactly true—that definitely declared the entry of Russian troops into Bulgaria to be a *casus belli*. It went on to state that so long as Salisbury remained at the head of affairs England would join the alliance, and that even Turkey was not disinclined to recognize an independent kingdom of Bulgaria. In conclusion the memorandum recommended that Prince Alexander of Battenberg should go to Orsova as soon as possible, so as to be at hand when the National Assembly proclaimed the country's independence. Prince Alexander was exceedingly surprised, but somewhat suspicious. He prepared two documents, one for the Regents of Bulgaria, in which he informed them of Langenbuch's communication, and told them that they might carry on the Government quietly, as there was no further danger of a Russian occupation. Then he announced the conditions on which he would return to Bulgaria. Namely, that before he started for Sofia, Germany, Austria-Hungary, Italy, England, and Turkey must recognize an independent united kingdom of Bulgaria with himself as king on its proclamation by the Bulgarian National Assembly.

Langenbuch returned to Berlin with an exact copy of this document for Radolinsky, and then proceeded to Vienna, where he met Stoiloff, the secret envoy of the Bulgarian Regency, and encouraged him to proceed to the re-election of Prince Alexander.[226] The Prince's conditions were very reasonable, and he had every reason to insist on them. Bismarck had just opened one of the meetings of the Cabinet with a groan over the "never-ending Battenberg fuss"; and with reference to the marriage project had complained that it was really too much to be obliged to worry about all these "confounded love-affairs".[227]

The Chancellor also raged against the Crown Princess and her sister, the Princess Christian of Schleswig-Holstein (Princess Helena, daughter of Queen Victoria), whom he alleged to have persuaded the heir to the Austrian throne to take back Prince Alexander to Bulgaria and to set him up as regent there even against Russia's will.[228]

The Langenbuch affair gave Prince Alexander and his father much food for thought, the more so since no further move followed. Was it likely, they asked themselves, that Bismarck really had anything to do with the matter, and that he was suddenly venturing upon a move that was utterly contrary to what his whole policy had been up to the present? If that were the case, it could only be on account of the international situation, which perhaps made Bismarck feel that it would be advisable to divert Russia's attention to the Balkans again. It was quite certain that Bismarck was not actuated by concern for the interests of the Battenberg family.

No reply came to Prince Alexander of Battenberg's statement of his terms.

He made up his mind that if ever another agent were to come, no matter at whose instigation, he would speak his mind without circumlocution. And, in fact, it was not long before Langenbuch appeared again, as noted by Prince Alexander of Hesse in his diary on April 5, 1887, once more to urge Sandro to go back to Bulgaria. To the question as to who had sent him, he again gave an evasive reply, but intimated that if *he* spoke with the Prince it was as though Bismarck were doing so. Thereupon Prince Alexander exclaimed furiously: "I'll ask you to come and see me if I get the typhus again. But if Prince Bismarck wishes to negotiate with me about politics, he can either give you identification papers from the

z

Foreign Office or else communicate with me through the Prussian Minister in Darmstadt." He then dismissed him.[229]

The Prince was staying with his sister, Marie Erbach, at Schloss König, in the Odenwald. He came back to his hosts pale and distraught after this interview, and said: "I've sent *him* home with a flea in his ear. I'm not going to be Bismarck's tool any longer. If he wants to reopen the Balkan question, he can find someone else to do his dirty work."[230]

Meanwhile the Bulgarians had begun to negotiate with Prince Ferdinand of Coburg, who had given indications that he would be willing to accept the thorny crown. Many Bulgarians, however, would still have preferred to have Prince Alexander back again. Towards the middle of April they redoubled their pleas for his return. As Prince Alexander of Hesse noted in his diary on April 17, 1887, Radolinsky, in the name of an "anonymous group of well-wishers", sent more and more pressing appeals through Dr. Langenbuch to the Prince to return to Bulgaria, but did not say who these well-wishers were. The German Crown Prince and the Emperor Francis Joseph, on the other hand, still advised him to wait. The Bulgarian Minister, Stoiloff, wrote from Vienna daily: "Now or never!"

Prince Alexander of Battenberg became really ill in consequence of all this agitation. He wanted to wait and see; to wait and see what happened about his going back, but also to wait and see what happened about his marriage.

Meanwhile Bismarck did not rest, but did all he could finally to put an end to the marriage project. Radolinsky was now working on the Crown Prince's side. One day, however, Bismarck sent for him[231] and explained that "though the Princess Victoria of Prussia and Prince Alexander had become secretly engaged with the permission of her parents, the engagement had already dragged on into the third year with no prospects of its ever coming to anything owing to the refusal of the Emperor to agree to it, and it was therefore desirable for both parties that it should come to an end". Considerations of delicacy, however, prevented any of those closely involved from taking the initiative in dissòlving the bond. It could only be done through the intervention of some third person. So now he, the Chancellor, proposed to intervene as *deus ex machina*. And he suggested that Radolinsky's "social position, pleasant and attractive manner, and diplomatic training made him the most suitable intermediary. He therefore proposed to send him to Prince Alexander with instructions to explain matters to him, to point out the delicacy of the situation in which the Princess Victoria and her parents were placed, and to urge him—though without importunity—in the interests of the Crown Prince and his family to extricate them from this awkward position". The Chancellor's most cogent argument consisted in his pointing out that the continuance of the secret engagement made it impossible for the Princess to enter upon any other matrimonial alliance; and that therefore to persist in this unpopular marriage project might involve the Crown Princess, who bore the chief responsibility for it, in the most unpleasant material consequences, including disinheritance and so forth, which were indeed already being seriously considered by His Majesty.

Radolinsky undoubtedly informed the Crown Prince and his family of his mission. And it is probable that in order to avoid conflict with the Chancellor it was decided that it should be carried out, and that Prince Alexander of Battenberg should be induced to give the Princess her freedom as a matter of form, which would in no sense prevent the engagement from being resumed at a more favourable season.

Hence the Count came secretly to Niederlahnstein, near Darmstadt, and telegraphed to Prince Alexander that he wished to speak to him there incognito on the evening of May 14th. The Prince put in a very unwilling appearance, and listened to Radolinsky's compromise between the Crown Princess's wishes and Bismarck's. He agreed to the suggestion, and wrote a letter couched in general terms. The substance of the letter was, that in order to contradict certain rumours which had come to his knowledge, he declared that his present circumstances did not permit him to be a suitor for the hand of Victoria of Prussia, and that the Princess was absolutely free. Then Radolinsky again urged the Prince to return to Bulgaria, and told him various stories, some of which Alexander simply did not believe. Amongst others, as Prince Alexander of Hesse entered in his diary on May 15, 1887, that Bismarck had threatened in the Prince of Wales's hearing to lock up the Crown Princess in Castle Benrath on the Rhine.

Count Radolinsky conveyed the letter to Prince Bismarck, who received it eagerly and perused it with satisfaction. His remark was: "I think more of the fellow for this letter." Radolinsky said that he reminded him of "a lion eating a sheep".

The Crown Prince and his family, nevertheless, had no intention of relinquishing the marriage, although they were not altogether pleased to find that the ex-Prince of Bulgaria seemed no longer to be so passionately eager and to be lacking in energy in the pursuit of his quest.

At the beginning of the year a new and terrible anxiety had arisen that temporarily pushed the Battenberg marriage question into the background.

In January 1887 the Crown Prince, who was then fifty-six years old, had suddenly grown very hoarse, and on March 6th a small growth was discovered in his throat, which naturally gave rise to some concern. When, on March 22nd, the Crown Prince made a speech in honour of the Emperor William's ninetieth birthday, his hoarseness was very pronounced, and everyone noticed it with anxiety. Since the trouble did not improve, the doctors began to suspect cancer, and the Berlin surgeon, Professor Bergmann, was already planning to perform the delicate operation of removing half the larynx—which it is essential to do at once—on May 21st. The greatest caution had to be observed in performing so severe an operation upon a future Emperor, and Bismarck refused to allow it to be carried out without the consent of the patient and of his father.[232] The Chancellor at the same time ordered all the most prominent throat specialists in Germany to be convened, and they all expressed themselves in favour of the operation. Bismarck, however, further advised Professor Bergmann to summon the best-known specialists from abroad, to which Bergmann agreed. In accordance with this order, and not by the Crown Princess's desire, a famous British throat specialist, Sir Morell Mackenzie, arrived in Berlin on May 20th, the day before that fixed for the performance of the operation. He declared that the Crown Prince was not suffering from laryngeal cancer, that the dangerous operation was therefore not necessary, and that a change of air would restore him to health.

The delirious joy of his wife, who loved and honoured him beyond everything, was indescribable. She could not and would not believe that her adored husband, with his splendid physique, the prototype of manly strength and beauty, could be suffering from so insidious, so fatal a disease, at the very moment when he stood on the steps of the throne, for by all human calculations the old Emperor could hardly be expected to live much longer. Hence, filled with hope, she accompanied her husband to the Isle of Wight, and thence to San Remo.

Nevertheless, contrary to Sir Morell Mackenzie's expectation, the disease steadily gained ground.

The fact that the Crown Prince was temporarily shut out of public life and away from Berlin was a relief to Bismarck politically. He knew very well that the Crown Princess had won over her husband to favour Alexander of Battenberg's marriage with their daughter. The Chancellor, on the other hand, was preparing to sacrifice the ex-Prince of Bulgaria to the Tsar in order to win Russia back to friendship with Germany. A fierce struggle was in progress in Russia between two great parties to obtain control over the Tsar. On the one hand were the followers of Katkoff, who were Francophil and Pan-Slav, and were not only antagonistic to Austria-Hungary but also to Germany. On the other were certain members of the imperial house, notably the Grand Duke Vladimir, who were well-disposed towards Germany on account of their family connections there.

Tradition and the bonds of relationship with Germany were still too strong to allow Alexander III to break the peace that had now subsisted between Russia and Prussia—recently extended to include all Germany—for over one hundred and twenty years. Apart from anything else, he always had before his eyes the memory of the many attempts made upon his father's life shortly after the last war. Moreover, hostility to Austria-Hungary had become too great to allow of even a formal renewal of the former treaties. Thus the conditions for the conclusion of the so-called Reinsurance Treaty on June 18, 1887, between Russia and Germany arose, as it were, spontaneously. In it Bismarck purchased security against France by fulfilling the Tsar's dearest wish for a free hand in regard to the Eastern portion of the Balkan Peninsula, including Constantinople and the Straits, and by promising in no circumstances to permit the restoration of Alexander of Battenberg. It was this last point in particular that caused Bismarck to keep the Reinsurance Treaty—which was also kept secret from Austria-Hungary—a secret even from the German Crown Prince. Indeed, the serious illness from which Frederick was suffering made it possible that Bismarck might never, even if he became Emperor, have to tell him of the existence of the Treaty. His days were already numbered.

Prince Alexander of Hesse also knew nothing of the Reinsurance Treaty, and was still hoping privately that the marriage of his son to Princess Victoria might be celebrated when the Crown Prince ascended the throne. His illness caused Prince Alexander the greatest concern. In view of Prince William's hostile attitude he was bound to realize that the fate of his house was sealed if Frederick died. The Bulgarians, in their desire at least indirectly to get back their former ruler, sent Alexander of Hesse a telegram asking whether he— the father of that former ruler—would accept the position of Prince of Bulgaria. When he asked his son's opinion of this curious offer, he received the laconic reply: "God preserve you from it!" Prince Alexander said, "Amen!" and declined it.

"This is the third crown that I have refused", he remarked in his diary on June 18–21, 1887: "the Greek in 1863, the Rumanian in 1865, and the Bulgarian in 1887." Actually none of them had been formally offered to him.

Prince Alexander of Battenberg's experiences were still too fresh in his mind to permit of his seriously considering a return. "In my opinion", he remarked in a letter to his parents from Kissingen on June 21, 1887, "one ought to thank God for having got out of this Bulgarian business with a whole skin. It is blasphemy to keep on hankering after Bulgaria."

His opinion was hardly shared by his father, who would have given a great deal to see his son once more on the throne of Bulgaria. Since both father and son refused definitely to accept the throne, Prince Ferdinand of Coburg was unanimously elected Prince of Bulgaria on July 7th. As a consequence of the ill-treatment meted out to his family in Germany, Prince Alexander of Hesse now turned his attention to England, whence his son Henry was sending him very gratifying accounts. Alexander of Battenberg visited Prince Henry at Balmoral in the autumn of 1887, and wrote home to his parents on October 21st delighted at his brother's happiness with Beatrice, whom he described as a perfect "treasure of love and kindness and intelligence".

No sooner had he returned from England than he heard from the hereditary Prince of Meiningen that the Emperor feared lest the Crown Prince should leave directions for Victoria's marriage to Sandro in his will.

Meanwhile the health of the Crown Prince who was now staying in San Remo grew gravely worse, and although the Crown Princess simply refused to admit it, it was clear that his life was despaired of. Prince William, who was the next heir to the throne, was already making preparations for his succession. He was also staying at San Remo, and frequently came

into serious conflict with his mother. Nevertheless Prince
William realized more clearly than did his mother the true
nature of his father's illness. He therefore urged that an
operation should be performed immediately. The Crown
Princess was in an agony of suspense regarding her husband's
health, and was at times inclined to be unjust even to people
whose intentions were good, although she herself was swayed
only by the purest and most humane motives in her fear for
her husband and the future of the Empire. What would
happen if her husband were to die? In her opinion it would
be a "blessing if the reign of the all-powerful Bismarck were
not to last for ever", and if fresh impulses and ideas and a
new spirit were to enter into the government of Germany.
She had no confidence at all in her own son. Under him, she
was convinced, a régime would begin that was far removed
from the liberal views of her husband, who desired the well-
being of all his subjects, and who would foster friendship with
England. Bismarck, she believed, would also remain in office
if her son came to the throne.

Meanwhile the Emperor William demanded through the
intermediary of the Hereditary Prince of Meiningen that
Alexander of Battenberg should once more solemnly renounce
Victoria's hand. Obediently Sandro wrote once more to the
Crown Princess to say that he loved the Princess truly and
faithfully, but that circumstances forced him to request her
to dispose of her daughter's hand without any regard to
himself.[233]

The Crown Princess laid the letter aside. She was not the
woman to give up anything that she earnestly desired. The
Emperor William could have no more than a short span of
life before him. Then her husband, even if he were seriously
ill, would be Emperor, and it would be possible to settle the
question of the marriage. Her hopes had taken on a new
lease of life, for Sir Morell Mackenzie still refused to admit his
mistake. As late as December 27, 1887, he telegraphed to
Queen Victoria, as Prince Alexander notes in his diary on that
day: "The new growth in the Crown Prince's larynx has
vanished. Hence cancer is out of the question." He allowed
the Queen to continue in this belief until January 30th,
although in the meantime the right side of the Crown Prince's
larynx was also attacked. On February 9th the long-postponed
operation had to be performed. The unhappy Prince's larynx
was at length removed and was replaced by a canula amid

keen differences of opinion between the doctors in charge
of the case. He could now no longer speak, and had to write
down anything he wanted to say on slips of paper. The Crown
Princess nursed her unfortunate husband with selfless devotion,
and racked with the most terrible anxiety. Once when Prince
Alexander thought of applying directly to the Emperor
William to settle their outstanding differences, his son in
England dissuaded him from it. "My remark", he wrote on
January 30, 1888, "was inspired by very sure information,
according to which Bismarck's hatred of our family is such that
so long as he holds the Emperor in leading-strings you and your
sons must be considered as outcasts. Any letter of yours to the
Emperor *must* be handed over by Albedyll [the Emperor's aide-
de-camp] to Bismarck, father or son. You would thus merely
provide both of them with an opportunity to give vent to their
base feelings against us."

On February 6th Bismarck, in his great speech on foreign
policy, made another attack on Alexander of Battenberg in
saying that he was contrary to all expectation opposing the
legitimate influence of Russia in Bulgaria. His further remark
was to become famous—that Bulgaria was certainly not an
object of sufficient importance to cause the whole of Europe
from Moscow to the Pyrenees and from the North Sea to
Palermo to plunge into a war in which nobody would be
certain at the end what they had been fighting about.

On the morning of March 9th, within twelve days of his
ninety-first birthday, the Emperor William I died peacefully.
His last words were concerned with his anxiety lest the Tsar
should forget his promise to preserve peace. The Emperor
was dead and his successor lay seriously ill. None the less he
immediately left the sunny climate of San Remo to return
to the cold and inclement atmosphere of Berlin—an emperor
with an heroic frame, but with a canula in his throat, an
emperor who could not speak, but a man who was nevertheless
inspired by a sense of his mission and who cherished a thousand
plans for making his empire and his people happy according
to his own ideas. At his side he had a wife filled with tremendous energy, great will-power, and holding strongly pronounced
views. Her dynamic personality swayed her husband by its
sheer force. These two personalities stood in the strongest
opposition to the actual ruler of the country, Prince Bismarck,
and also to their own son, the new Crown Prince. In these
circumstances, and notwithstanding the new Emperor's illness,

a struggle for power was inevitable, and no one could tell what its outcome would be if the Emperor lived. Fateful questions of foreign policy were bound up with the question of whether the new régime would last for any length of time.

On the day after the old Emperor's death, Bismarck sent for Doctor Bergmann and ask him how long the new Emperor would live. The doctor replied that he could not survive the summer of 1888. His reign was regarded by everybody as nothing more than a short and tragic interlude. No one realized it better than the new Empress Victoria, who summed up the whole situation in the words: "I believe that we are generally regarded as no more than shadows flitting by, soon to be replaced by the substance of William's form."

As the funeral cortège passed beneath the windows in which stood the new Emperor, who was too ill to take part in the ceremonies, he was overcome by his feelings and almost collapsed. For decades he had been preparing for the moment when he should ascend the throne, had studied his prerogatives, and formed his plans. And now that the time had come his physique failed him.

Among the crowd of princes following the hearse was Prince Alexander of Hesse. He had come unaccompanied by his son. The new Empress had sent him a message which resolved itself into the words "Not yet". The very fact of the father's presence was nevertheless an outward testimony to the existence of a new government in Berlin. He was received most cordially by the Emperor and Empress, but found the Dowager Empress cold and distant. When the Prince bent to kiss her hand she made a movement as if to withdraw it, at the same time muttering some unintelligible words, which caused the Prince to make an acid remark in his diary on March 15th concerning the "old mummy". At the dinner which followed, and at which ninety-eight persons were present, Prince Alexander, who had been a healthy man all his life, suddenly had an attack of severe pain in his abdomen and back. It passed off again quickly, and he was able to go through with the rest of the ceremonies. On March 17th visits of condolence were paid to the new Emperor and Empress. It was a painful moment when the monarch, after making vain efforts to stand, at length fell back into a chair, and gave his hand to each person in silence but with the kindest and most friendly expression on his face. Overcome with emotion Prince Alexander embraced the Emperor, who scribbled a few cordial words on his writing-block. The Empress was waiting in the adjoining room with her daughter Victoria. She received Alexander with the greatest cordiality. Although nothing was said of the question in all their minds, the warmth of the greeting showed their feelings.

On March 19th and 20th the Prince was once again seized with pains in the abdominal regions, and was obliged to consult a doctor, who at once ordered him to return home for rest and treatment. Treatment was easy enough, but rest was another matter. It seemed an impossibility in the trying time that lay before him and his son Sandro.

One of the first matters that the new Emperor, and more especially the Empress, intended to settle now that they had come to power was the long-postponed marriage of their daughter Victoria. The Empress Frederick proposed to celebrate it without delay, although even her mother, Queen Victoria, urged her not to be too hasty and first to come to an understanding about it with her son William. The Empress disregarded the warning and suggested to Prince Alexander of Battenberg to ask the Emperor for a post in the army. He acted on her suggestion. An answer was returned to the ex-Prince of Bulgaria from the Emperor Frederick, written in his own hand and inviting him to come to Berlin on April 2nd. The reply added that he might confidently leave to the Emperor the matter of his appointment in the army.

At the same time the Emperor instructed the chief of the military cabinet to consider the question of the bestowal of an army command upon Prince Alexander of Battenberg, but first to inform the Chancellor of it. Then the storm burst.

Bismarck immediately set in motion all the forces within the imperial family and the army that were hostile to the project. Especially did this affect Prince William, now the Crown Prince, who straightway discussed with the Chancellor the steps that must be taken in the matter. The Crown Prince telegraphed to his brother Henry, who was staying in Darmstadt in order to see the Princess Irene of Hesse, and to the Grand Duke, asking them to lodge an immediate protest with Bismarck against the insult to the memory of the late Emperor that was being planned. Bismarck also said to the Emperor's uncle, the Grand Duke of Baden, who was staying in Berlin, that he was indifferent to the Emperor's permitting a mésalliance for the Princess Victoria. On the other hand he enter-

tained the strongest possible objection to anyone with a past
like Prince Alexander of Battenberg's being treated with
marked distinction by the Emperor. It would be as if the Tsar
appointed General Boulanger as Governor-General in Warsaw,
and would imply a breach with the whole of the Chancellor's
foreign policy. "He could not destroy all that he had spent
years in creating—it was too much to expect him to bring
discredit upon himself before all the rest of the world. The whole
affair was an *English intrigue in high politics*, which had been
brewing for a long time, and was intended to thrust him aside,
and to substitute for the pacific German policy one which was
anti-Russian and served English interests—that is to say, a
policy which would lead to a European war, at which England
of course would simply stand and look on."[234]

Meanwhile the Grand Duke of Baden wrote a warning letter
to his sister-in-law the Empress Frederick, and then went
direct to the Emperor, with whom he did not touch on the
Battenberg question itself, but remarked that he had found
Bismarck in a state of great irritation and occupied with
thoughts of retirement. And he exhorted the Emperor on no
account to allow his indispensable Chancellor to go.[235]

The old antagonism dating from the days of 1866, which
the Baden family felt for Prince Alexander, flamed up again.
Bismarck himself asked to speak to the Emperor. The Empress
Frederick felt desperate as she saw the overwhelming effect
produced even by the suggestion of a possible military appointment for Alexander of Battenberg. The consequence was a
long and, as Prince Alexander of Hesse said, "quite mad" letter
from the Empress to his son. She evolved the wildest plans.
The Prince was to be secretly married and then leave Berlin
again. Her sons and the Dowager Empress Augusta would of
course be furious, but would finally submit when confronted
with an accomplished fact. She added that there were certainly
great obstacles to Sandro's receiving a military post. Albedyll,
Waldersee, and Bismarck were against it; her daughter would
be quite satisfied if he went into the Austro-Hungarian army.
These were very different prospects from those that Prince
Alexander and his son had hoped for after the last invitation.

Meanwhile Bismarck had been to see the Emperor Frederick
on March 31st, and had protested violently against Prince
Alexander of Battenberg's engagement or his being given any
appointment. He said that if these projects were realized all
that he had achieved with the Tsar would be lost. He would in

that case be obliged to resign. The Emperor, who had been forced to listen to this tirade with a high temperature and a bad headache, and immediately after one of the numerous painful dressings of his throat, was between two fires. On the one side was his wife who was pursuing her aim passionately with her whole soul and the utmost energy, and his daughter who was really in love. On the other was Bismarck who attributed an importance to the whole affair that the Emperor could not altogether grasp. He was bound to think it grossly exaggerated, for he knew nothing of the Reinsurance Treaty which Bismarck had concealed from his new master. However, impressed by the threat of his resignation and the urgent warnings of the Chancellor, who had worked so well for the Empire and for his father, the sorely tried man decided to telegraph to Alexander of Battenberg and tell him to postpone his visit. Bismarck was instructed to submit a memorandum on the subject and to discuss the matter with the Empress.

She and her daughter heard of this new and unfavourable turn of events with absolute despair. The Empress, however, did not relinquish the struggle. On the evening of the same day she sent Count Radolinsky to the Chancellor. The Court Chamberlain found Bismarck tired and depressed, but in a state of great agitation. He repeated over and over again that the Emperor must choose between him and the Prince of Battenberg. The Empress wrote to Sandro that same evening to tell him that her daughter Vicky was wretched, and that she had been counting so definitely on being publicly betrothed to him at last on Easter Monday.

Meanwhile on April 3rd Bismarck submitted the report that had been demanded by the Emperor Frederick.[236] In it he stated that Alexander of Battenberg had through his past actions achieved a position of European importance, the significance of which lay in the fact that he had quarrelled with his Russian relatives while he was in Bulgaria, and had thus incurred the enmity of his imperial cousin in St. Petersburg. The focus of the policy of the German Empire, however, lay in Russia, or rather in the Tsar, who could determine at will whether a country with one hundred million inhabitants should be Germany's friend or foe. There was every chance of Russia's making an alliance with France; and a war against these two countries, even if it resulted in victory, would be one of the greatest calamities that could befall the German people. "Austria's support", wrote Bismarck prophetically, "upon which we reckon is not as strong as it might be, and in certain eventualities, if a change in the distribution of votes and in the government were to take place in Italy, might be considerably decreased by a reversal of Italian policy, so that we should be driven to rely upon ourselves almost exclusively in case of an attack by both neighbours. Whether we are in danger of war with both at the same time lies once again in the sole decision of the Tsar, who represents the Russians." It would be, he concluded, an arbitrary destruction of the relations between Germany and her autocratic neighbour and would mean a complete inversion of the principles hitherto adopted in German policy.

There was no mention of England in this memorandum. Since, however, the Chancellor felt that his complete disregard of that country must be obvious to everyone, and especially to the Emperor Frederick, he sent in a supplementary memorandum on the following day. He pointed out that the nation as well as the Tsar would be bound to assume that it was not solely German interests, but also English influences that had brought about this unexpected change in German policy. It would obviously be of considerable value to the policy of Great Britain to create difficulties between Russia and Germany. Bismarck said not a word about the engagements which he had undertaken regarding Alexander of Battenberg in the name of the German Empire in his Reinsurance Treaty with Russia. He merely pointed out that it was particularly characteristic of the sensitiveness of the Tsar Alexander III in the Battenberg question that there had been some hesitation as to whether the Tsarevitch should be sent to attend the Emperor William's funeral owing to rumours having got about St. Petersburg that the ex-Prince of Bulgaria was expected to be present.

Bismarck desired his private memoranda to be supported by some communication from St. Petersburg. Hence on April 4, 1888, he telegraphed to Schweinitz[237]: "His Majesty the Emperor informed me on March 31st that Prince Alexander of Battenberg was expected on a visit to Charlottenburg on April 2nd. The visit was postponed telegraphically at my request, whether permanently prevented I do not know. I have requested to be allowed to resign in case it should occur. Kindly send me telegraphic report whether you and Monsieur de Giers share my opinion that if this visit takes place—*which I believe to have been instigated by the Queen of England*—Russia will view it as a proof of anti-Russian feeling and an alteration in the policy we have hitherto pursued. Public opinion here in Germany would be similarly affected."

Upon receipt of this telegram from Bismarck, Schweinitz went immediately to the Russian Foreign Minister. But the Tsar proved to be quite indifferent as to whom Sandro married so long as he did not go back to Bulgaria. Hence he sent word that although he would be sorry if Sandro visited Berlin, he would nevertheless never doubt that neither the Emperor Frederick nor the Chancellor would alter their friendly policy towards Russia and would remain true to their agreement not to allow Prince Alexander to regain his Bulgarian throne. Schweinitz added a few more words to this message, but they lacked the firmness that the Chancellor wished. His expressions were much too lukewarm for Bismarck, who had hoped for much stronger support from St. Petersburg in his struggle with Alexander of Battenburg. In this episode Bismarck showed himself more papal than the Pope and more prejudiced than the Russian Tsar against the ex-Prince of Bulgaria. His attitude proves clearly that in the Battenberg affair Bismarck was not only taking thought for the preservation of the relationship between Germany and Russia that he was always talking about, but also for his struggle against that English influence which he feared in the house of the new German Emperor and son-in-law of Queen Victoria.

In his disappointment Bismarck telegraphed angrily to Schweinitz on April 8th[238] that the St. Petersburg Cabinet appeared for the present "not to have the courage of its convictions", and he considered that "dealings with it are made much more difficult by the vagueness and reserve of Monsieur de Giers. In consideration of the incalculable reaction upon our relations with Russia that may result if the Prince worms his way into our court, I had expected that Monsieur de Giers would have put me in a position to show forcibly the dangers of the Anglo-Battenberg intrigues. The consequence will now be that, although I believe myself to be acting in the sense approved by His Majesty the Emperor and to be advocating his real wishes, I shall not be able to oppose successfully Her Majesty the Empress's plans, of which you are aware, because *I cannot be more Russian than the Russian Government.* I had assumed that I should find that support from Monsieur de Giers which Count Shuvaloff's tone appeared to promise when he was here, against the realization under English influence of an anti-Russian and anti-pacific change in our policy. . . . If I have been mistaken in this", protested the Chancellor, "*I lose all foundation for my standpoint the basis of which is the anger of the Tsar,* not merely against the Prince of Battenberg, but against the conduct of German policy according to the views of the Queen of England. If the support of Russia fails me either because the Cabinet in St. Petersburg has not the courage of its convictions, or because it is carrying on some subtle game with me personally, the victory of English policy will be complete here, and that will necessitate my own retirement. I should regret this all the more because I am convinced that His Majesty, whom to serve is my sole desire, privately shares my opinion, and even regards my threat of resignation as a support for his views as against those of the Empress. If, however, *the Russian Cabinet supports me only in a lukewarm manner, or with reservations, over this affair, then the ladies and England will emerge victorious from the conflict. . . .*"

In this case Bismarck feared that the "impudent climber", as he called Alexander of Battenberg, would gain influence over the imperial family and exploit it politically. Russia was not giving him effective support, but that did not matter. Bismarck hated Alexander of Battenberg. He interfered with his political arrangements and therefore he would fight him to the death. The Emperor Frederick was a dying man, his reign could not last much longer. Hence it was only necessary to gain time, to postpone a decision. The Crown Prince was of one mind with him. Once the Emperor was dead all would be well. Prince William in collaboration with Bismarck had just written a very sharp letter to Prince Alexander of Battenberg[239] saying that he was absolutely opposed to his marriage with Princess Victoria, and that he would regard anyone who contributed towards its realization "as the enemy of his house and of his fatherland for all time". Thus the Chancellor was sure of support from the future Emperor.

The ex-Prince of Bulgaria received this letter from the Crown Prince at the same time as letters from the Empress and her daughter referring to an imminent wedding. The Empress, in fact, enclosed a letter from the Grand Duke of Hesse, written on March 31st, in which to her indignation he had also implored her to abandon this marriage in view of the consequences. The effect of these contradictory letters upon the unfortunate young man may be imagined. He hardly knew what answer to send to the Crown Prince.

Meanwhile Bismarck had had another audience with his

sick Emperor on April 5th, and inquired whether Frederick
had read his memorandum. The Emperor nodded, but gave
no definite indication of opinion.

As Prince Bismarck left the Emperor's presence the Empress
met him and entreated him most vehemently not to ruin her
daughter's happiness in life. Bismarck avoided any further
discussion of the question for the moment. Nevertheless he
realized that he must act speedily if he intended to have his
way.

Once again the Grand Duke of Baden was called upon to
help. Bismarck and the Crown Prince induced him to send his
Minister, Baron Marschall von Bieberstein, to Darmstadt to
seek once more to induce the ruler of Hesse to use his influence
in his capacity as head of his house.

The Grand Duke received Marschall at once, told him that
Prince Alexander was deeply wounded by the Crown Prince's
letter, and had decided to submit it to the Emperor Frederick
on account of its insulting tone. There had been no idea of any
engagement; they had merely been corresponding about his
entering the army. The Prince did not want the engagement.
He knew too well how bitterly it was opposed by the heir to the
throne and his brother Prince Henry. Obviously, however,
if he were to meet the ladies and a "family scene" were to
develop, he could not say no.[240]

Marschall now adduced all Bismarck's familiar counter-
arguments, and the Grand Duke agreed to see Prince Alexander
and to suggest to him to write a letter of renunciation to the
Emperor Frederick too.

With great irritation Alexander of Battenberg replied:
"What does all this mean? I cannot write and refuse something
that has not been offered to me. Frederick III has never said a
word to me about it."

The Grand Duke of Hesse meanwhile agreed that if necessary he would himself write a letter of renunciation to the
Emperor Frederick in the name of Alexander of Battenberg.
Bismarck, however, continued to vent his fury: "He was
cashiered by the Tsar with ignominy. If he is honoured by
Germany, it is a slap in the face of Russia. If this English
policy is adopted by our royal house there is no more room for
me here. Alexander of Battenberg is an adventurer who is
much run after by women . . ."[241] and so-forth. Of the
relative indifference of Russia to the Battenberg marriage
Bismarck said nothing.

To the Grand Duke of Hesse's letter to the Emperor, Alexander of Battenberg added one of his own stating that he had done nothing to occasion the Crown Prince's attack on him. To be frank, he continued, he failed to see how such a marriage could be interpreted as a threat to Russia. He would, nevertheless, sincerely regret to be the cause of the resignation of the great Chancellor. At the same time he wrote to the Empress saying that he did not wish either to be regarded by the German people as the man who had caused the fall of Bismarck or to be decried as one who was in the pay of England and had destroyed the German Empire.[242]

Here was another letter of renunciation following on the many that had preceded it. At all events Bismarck had achieved what he wanted: the postponement of the marriage. On April 10th the interview between the Empress and the Chancellor desired by the Emperor Frederick took place. Bismarck steadily pursued his plan of postponing the marriage for the time being on account of the Emperor's fatal illness. He was noticeably accommodating, hinted that at some later date he might not be disinclined to return to a discussion of the idea, and went so far as to mention that it would be necessary expressly to renounce Bulgaria to have a private wedding, and so forth.

In great satisfaction the Empress once more sent letters to Alexander of Battenberg by the hand of Dr. Langenbuch. The Emperor wrote to say that he was obliged to ask him to give up his visit to Berlin, but the Empress added that she had come to an agreement with Bismarck. In May the Emperor was to visit Homburg, and there the Empress wished to celebrate her daughter's marriage privately. She said that Bismarck had among other things suggested that the marriage should be concluded without his knowledge. He would then tender his resignation, which the Emperor was nevertheless under no obligation to accept. The Empress went so far as to request Sandro not to say anything about the matter even to his own parents. She said that Bismarck had promised the Tsar of Russia that Alexander of Battenberg should never hold any post in the army. Moreover, the Crown Prince had stated definitely that once he came to the throne he would neither recognize Alexander as his brother-in-law nor give him any appointment in the army.

During his interview with the Empress the Chancellor also laid emphasis upon the fact that the Prussian Minister at

Darmstadt, Thielemann, had reported that the ex-Prince of
Bulgaria was telling everybody that he was not in the least in
love with the Princess Victoria any longer. Bismarck showed
the Empress the dispatch. Whereupon she replied: "Diplomats
are often more wily than well-informed."

Dr. Langenbuch, who brought the letters, finally advised
Prince Alexander, as his father noted in his diary on April 12,
1888: "You had better accept the marriage in this form. Otherwise you will achieve nothing at all."

The Empress Frederick regarded Bismarck's new attitude as
an advance, perhaps not a very great one, but still one that
admitted of a faint hope. In reality she had no more reason to
be satisfied with Bismarck than before. He was allowing time
to work for him, but his hatred remained unchanged, and
among his intimates he gave full vent to it.[243] It had been
repeated to Bismarck that the Empress Frederick had said
that after all it would not be such a misfortune if he were to
resign.[244] This raised his anger to boiling-point.

The other side did not give way either. The Empress induced
her husband to declare in drafting his Will on April 12th that
in case of his death he laid it as a filial duty upon his son to see
that his sister was married to Alexander of Battenberg.

The sufferings of the unfortunate Emperor had increased in
severity. On the day the Will was made he had been almost
suffocated by the forcing of a larger canula into his throat.
The Empress was desperate at what she called the "doctor's
brutality". Then she spoke of the wedding again, and that
perhaps it might take place at Homburg in May. If the Emperor
were to die, she hoped for a private wedding in England,
which of course would be synonymous with the banishment of
the couple from the Kingdom of Prussia.

The Empress continued to keep up an unremitting correspondence with Alexander of Battenberg, and was now
expecting a visit from her mother, Queen Victoria, who,
despite advice to the contrary, had made up her mind to go to
Berlin and find out for herself the true state of affairs.

The Queen had been told that Bismarck had had "one of his
fits of rage" early in April. She was annoyed at the way her
daughter was being treated, as well as at the "abominable
behaviour" of Prince William, when the question of the marriage had broken over them "like a storm, indeed a regular
blizzard". She considered that a purely family matter was
quite unnecessarily being turned into an affair of State. Rumour

said, as Colonel Leopold Swaine (the British military attaché in Berlin) wrote and told the Prince of Wales on April 13, 1888, that in view of the imminent death of the Emperor almost everyone was "behaving in a way as if the last spark of honour and faithful duty had gone—they are all trimming their sails". It was said, moreover, that Prince Alexander was by no means anxious himself for the marriage. With his departure from Bulgaria had gone the political reason for it, and he was now carrying on a love-affair with "a member of the histrionic art".[245]

The Queen determined to be very careful and to advise her daughter also to be circumspect. But, as she wired to Lord Salisbury in cipher on April 13, 1888,[246] she found Bismarck's "tyranny" quite "unbearable", and made up her mind that she must investigate the rights of the case for herself. The Chancellor was unexpectedly pleasant when the Queen received him in Berlin. The prospect of victory induced something like a desire for reconciliation to spring up in his bosom. This conciliatory spirit manifested itself on one occasion when he happened to be sitting opposite to Queen Victoria and her daughter at dinner, and "ardently did his best to be amiable and agreeable". At dessert, for instance, he "selected a large bonbon with a photograph of the Empress, and, after calling Her Majesty's attention to it in some graceful words, unbuttoned his coat and placed it next his heart".[247] He probably knew nothing at that time of the contents of the Emperor's Will.

Prince Alexander of Hesse, whose health had continued indifferent, watched the struggle with real anxiety and apprehension. As things were, it was impossible to visualize a happy solution for his son, although he was now as always engaged in trying to smooth the way for him. For this reason he decided once again to visit the Emperor Francis Joseph in Vienna, and find out how things were in that quarter. At their meeting the Emperor deplored "the incomprehensible way in which the imperial Chancellor grovelled to the Russians".

The feelings of animosity towards Russia which Francis Joseph had never been able to overcome all his life, and which were now more justified in view of Alexander III's attitude to Austria-Hungary, thus received renewed expression. "I tell all Prussians", said the Emperor as Prince Alexander of Hesse noted in his diary on May 12, 1888, "I am convinced that a little more firmness would achieve better results in Russia than the continual fear with which they are treated."

Prince Alexander convinced himself that the attitude of the Emperor and of all the upper classes was still very unfriendly towards Russia, and that the imminent danger of war between Austria-Hungary and Russia at the end of the year 1887 and the beginning of 1888 had left ineradicable traces. He himself had always done his utmost to promote good relations between Austria-Hungary and Russia so long as he had had influence through his brother-in-law, the Tsar Alexander II. But he now realized vividly to what an extent the relations between the two courts had changed for the worse since the accession of Alexander III. While in earlier days it had been the Emperor Francis Joseph who had often contributed towards the estrangement of the two empires, it was now the Tsar's fault that matters continued to go from bad to worse. While Prince Alexander did not overestimate the part he had formerly played, he could not help recognizing the plain fact that since his elimination from public life matters had not changed for the better.

On his return to Heiligenberg Prince Alexander found very bad news awaiting him from Berlin, coming not from the Empress but from another source.

The Emperor suffered terribly during the first two weeks in June. His distress was intensified by the conflict between the doctors, whose orders and prescriptions were often contradictory. It was heartrending to see how the Empress hovered between hope and fear during these terrible days. She still clung to the least glimmer of hope, although she was bound to begin to lose faith. "I feel like a wreck," she wrote to her mother on June 13, 1888, two days before the Emperor's death, "a sinking ship, so wounded and sore and struck down, so sore of heart, as if I were bleeding from a thousand wounds."[248] And a moment later, if she happened to see that her husband's colour was a little better, or that he smiled, her mood would change to one of the most resolute optimism. On June 13th she wrote to Alexander of Hesse: "My beloved Emperor asks me to tell you that he has given his consent to the betrothal of our daughter Victoria to your son Alexander. He has made the declaration now because, though he is inspired and filled with the hope of getting better, he does not wish to leave his child in a state of uncertainty while he is so seriously ill. If God spares us the dear life of our darling and our protector, we can decide upon the time and manner in which the contract shall be fulfilled. The Emperor has laid it upon our son, the Crown

Prince, as a duty if he should soon succeed his father on the throne to see that his desire and command are carried out. We expect it of his sense of duty and his filial piety; but we do *not* wish to press him, so as not to make more difficult his transition from the attitude he has previously taken to this affair to that required by his father. Hence silence is at present imperative. The Emperor is very, very ill, but does *not* suffer either pain or discomfort, and is *absolutely* clear in his mind, quiet and contented."

The last words were not strictly in accordance with the facts, but the Empress wanted to make credible that which she so passionately hoped for, and to represent her husband's condition if possible as less grave than it really was. Even Sir Morell Mackenzie now realized that there was no more hope. "The Emperor is sinking", he telegraphed to his Queen on June 14th.

By the time the Empress's letter arrived at Darmstadt the Emperor was dead. At a quarter past eleven on the morning of June 15th he passed away quietly and painlessly.

Prince William was now the Emperor. The Empress Frederick was utterly broken. "Oh, my husband, my darling, my Fritz!" she wrote to her mother on June 15th, "so good, so kind, so tender, brave, patient, and noble, so cruelly tried, taken from the nation, the wife, and daughters that did so need him. His mild, just rule was not to be."[249]

When Prince Alexander came to answer the letter which had been addressed to him while the Emperor was still living, he was obliged at the same time to add his sympathy. "I was much touched", he wrote on June 17th, "to hear the message which our beloved Emperor gave you for me during the last hours of his life. Overjoyed as I was by the consent of her father to the marriage of dear Victoria with the man of her choice to whom she has clung to faithfully, the cruel loss which has since stricken us seems doubly heavy to bear. What is to happen *now*? Will the young Emperor be able to make up his mind to carry out his father's wish, after having already expressed himself so roughly and ungraciously to my son"?[250] Prince Alexander realized that he must now bury his last hopes. A completely new course was entered upon in Berlin, in conformity with the character of the new Emperor. The Empress Frederick was immediately excluded from affairs. Indeed she felt as if she and her suite had been put under arrest. When she asked to speak to Bismarck, he excused himself on the score of pressure of work. Finally she positively "fled" to her little estate near Bornstedt. In words of passionate grief she wrote to her mother lamenting that she must now forgo the joy of helping her husband to raise their beloved Germany to strength and greatness not by the sword but by everything in which justice, culture, progress, freedom were immanent. She emphasized also that her husband had always been the faithful friend and ally of England, and that it had always been his steadfast aim to bring the two countries as close to one another as possible. Now all that was over, and she had to suffer the harsh blows that rained upon her from all sides. Nevertheless she would not even now abandon the idea of the marriage and of her daughter's happiness. Had she not the Will that from beyond the grave commanded her son as a filial duty to see that the marriage took place?

Bismarck's star appeared to be once more in the ascendant. He believed himself to have reasons for thinking that the new ruler would follow him blindly, and the venerable Chancellor was filled with emotion as he bowed his knee before the young Emperor and kissed his hand at the imposing opening of the Reichstag on June 25th, which was attended by all the German princes. Shortly afterwards Friedberg, the Minister for Justice, placed the testamentary disposition of the late Emperor regarding his daughter's marriage in William II's hands. The new Emperor was very disagreeably surprised by it. The glib Minister, however, added immediately that the document was legally worthless. The late Emperor had signed it only at the instigation of his wife and at a time when he was no longer in full possession of his faculties.

William seized upon this interpretation, did not accept the Will, and told the King of Saxony that he would never agree to the marriage. He added that the King might inform the other princes of his decision. Then he wrote another letter to the ex-Prince of Bulgaria demanding that he should make a solemn renunciation of the hand of the Princess Victoria to him as Emperor.

Prince Alexander of Battenberg answered that he could not reply to the letter before he had seen the text of the Emperor Frederick's Will. William II received this letter in the presence of his brother Henry and said with great annoyance that he refused to have a fresh postponement or to write another letter. He would have his intentions communicated verbally.

Thereupon Thielemann the Prussian Minister in Darmstadt

came to see Alexander of Battenberg at ten o'clock on the morning of July 3rd, and stated that the Emperor had nothing to add to his letter of June 17th. Once more Alexander of Hesse wrote to the Emperor and said that at his orders his son had now definitely broken off his engagement with the Princess Victoria, and he would now like to know whether his son might hope for some post in the army.

It is surprising that the Prince should have made the request, since he might have known the answer. In fact, he wonders sceptically in his diary: "Will the rude and heartless young Emperor answer?"

The only thing that could for a moment make him forget all his sorrows was hunting—a sport to which he remained faithful all his life. But the next thing that happened was something that the sixty-five-year-old Prince, the brother-in-law of the Tsar Alexander II, had never expected. His letter to William II was returned unopened on July 9th. Soon afterwards the Prussian Minister came and announced that his imperial master could not give the Prince of Battenberg any position in the army, and that it was improbable that the Emperor Francis Joseph would find any use for him in the Austro-Hungarian army.

Prince Alexander was utterly shattered: "So the Emperor wants to drive my son back to Bulgaria by force. Now I understand why my letter was kept in Berlin for two days, and perhaps read before it was closed up again by some means that I do not understand, and returned to me. Obviously it was for the sake of gaining time to cut off every chance for the Prince in Vienna too." Thielemann protested. Prince Alexander rose: "I will tell you one thing more. And that is, that in all my long years of intercourse with mighty sovereigns I have never met with such lack of courtesy and consideration as I do now. At all events my first letter to the Emperor William will also be the last." The Prince went to the door and opened it: "If Your Excellency has nothing further to say to me, I will wish you good day." It was with mixed feelings that the Minister left the Prince. Shortly afterwards he informed the ex-Prince of Bulgaria that the Emperor would not oppose his entering the Austrian army, and that it depended only upon the Tsar's making no objection.

A final end was thus put to the Battenberg plans. In acting in this manner the Emperor William was ignoring the wishes expressed in his father's Will, which had appealed to his "filial duty", and inflicting fresh sorrow on his mother. Doubtless he believed himself to be obliged to do so for the sake of Germany's welfare. The Bismarck family supported the young Emperor most vigorously. This is clearly shown in a very private and "quite confidential" audience that Herbert Bismarck had with the Tsar.[251]

After Herbert Bismarck had made the shrewd observation that the three emperors had much more to lose from revolution than they could ever win from each other, the conversation turned upon the Empress Frederick and her relations with her son, the present Emperor. Herbert Bismarck said that she felt altogether as an Englishwoman, and that the fault was all hers. He recalled that the Emperor had once remarked when he was to have intervened with his mother: "I realize that whatever I do will be in vain. We stand on different bases. My mother is always an Englishwoman and I am a Prussian. How could we ever feel alike?"

The Tsar replied that he had for a long time suspected that the Emperor Frederick was no more than a tool in the hands of his wife, but the manner in which the new Emperor had put a speedy and forcible stop to the Battenberg affair had certainly impressed him very favourably. The Tsar was also pleased when Herbert Bismarck added that the young Emperor was sick of the unsolicited tutelage of Queen Victoria, and had said so to London in terms which would ensure that it was not attempted again in the future.

On his return from St. Petersburg, Herbert Bismarck was given a high Order with Diamonds. But the Bismarck Press had much difficulty in bringing back into the approved way of thinking a large section of the German people who had followed the affair with very pronounced sympathies for the Empress Frederick and the young couple.

Prince Alexander's health was very much impaired by his recent worries. It was discovered that he was suffering from abdominal cancer. His condition was rendered more serious by the fact that the position of the growth made an operation very difficult and dangerous. In September and October of the year 1888 his own personal affairs for the first time take precedence in his diary of the events occurring in the world at large. Nevertheless he kept his diary most accurately up to the last days of his life. On December 8, 1888, he said: "I suffer badly from hiccups."

A few days later the illness had taken a surprisingly rapid hold on one who had been so thoroughly healthy all his life. He died on December 12, 1888. Prince Alexander did not live to see his son enter the Austrian army and marry an actress; nor to see the Princess Victoria find domestic happiness two years later with Prince Adolf of Schaumburg-Lippe, and to fall into the hands of a Russian adventurer after her husband's death. And neither did he—fortunately for himself—live to see the relations between the three empires growing steadily worse year after year, nor to see the cancellation of the Reinsurance Treaty between Russia and Germany during Alexander III's lifetime, and, after the Tsar's having overcome his antipathy to Republican France, the coming into being of the alliance between France and Russia that Bismarck had so dreaded. He did not live to see the breach between Bismarck and the young Emperor. If he had grown uncertain of Russia, Bismarck's master hand would have readjusted matters in good time, as he had done in 1879. He might even have adopted the policy of an English alliance favoured by the Emperor Frederick.

The personal factor also played its part. The rulers of England and Russia—and in the latter country a weak character had ascended the throne with Nicholas II—did not like William II personally. Germany's relations with England, especially under Edward VII, did not improve, and the Tsar was only too easily swayed by men like Isvolsky and Sasonoff, who were completely under the domination of France. The increasing hatred of Austria was eventually also extended to its ally Germany, and altogether blinded the rulers of Russia to the fact that they were being used as a tool by France in her revenge against Germany. The tragic end was the downfall of all three empires in the World War, owing to their disunion, and that triumph of revolution which Herbert Bismarck had once prophetically feared.

Could it have been otherwise?—Possibly. But only if the fatal tumour had not appeared in the Emperor Frederick's throat, and he had had time to guide the destinies of the German Empire for several decades with the help of his able and energetic wife. Who can say? Possibly an alliance with England that stands on so much higher a level of civilization would have enabled Germany to weather the storm after that with Russia collapsed. Unfortunately the successors to Bismarck and the old Emperor deepened the antagonism to Russia and England until it turned to hatred.

After the crushing of Germany between the upper and nether millstones of the Great Entente during the World War, despite the heroic and almost superhuman achievements of her soldiers, the words of the Empress Frederick written on June 8, 1888,[252] a week before her husband's death, cannot be read without emotion:

"If Fritz goes, I do not the least care what becomes of me. I do not want these people's love and I scorn their hatred. Fritz and I shall be more than avenged some day by the course events will take when these people come into power. . . ."

APPENDIX

VALEGGIO, *July* 9/10.

[Presented at Verona at 3 a.m. on July 10, 1859]

I beg Your Highness to tell His Majesty the Emperor that I shall be happy to come to Villafranca on Monday at nine o'clock, and shall look forward with pleasure to meeting him there.

With the renewed expression of my highest esteem,

NAPOLÉON.

Note handed by Napoleon III on July 9, 1859, to Prince Alexander of Hesse as envoy bearing the flag of truce:

Italian confederation of all Italian sovereigns.
Union of Lombardy and Piedmont.
Venice under an Archduke.

Letter from the Tsar Alexander II to Prince Alexander of Hesse

HOPSAL, *July* 19 (31), 1859.

I am very happy, my dear and excellent friend, to be able at length to fulfil the promise I made to you in my last letter. Here is the Cross of St. George, 3rd Class, which you have so worthily earned by your noble and heroic conduct during the grievous war which has now fortunately come to an end, though in a manner so unexpected. I beg you to accept it as a token of affection from our army, which is proud to have your name upon its lists, and in which you have left so happy a memory of yourself and so many friends who will be yours for life, among whom I hope you will consider me to be one of the foremost. I need not say that these are no mere idle phrases, for which I have no love, but that I am speaking the simple truth.

You know that by the new statutes of the Order you keep the fourth class Cross, and I am glad to think that in that way the memory of my father who had such an appreciation of your noble conduct during the expedition to Andi and Dargo will be mingled with that of myself.

On our arrival here at Hopsal we heard that you had got safely back home again. I can imagine how tremendously pleased they must have been to see you again after all the dangers you have passed through and wherein the might of God has so evidently protected you. As regards the peace which has concluded this war that I was unfortunately not able to prevent, I agree with you that it is far from satisfying the various interests concerned, and that Italy—for the sake of whose so-called independence the whole affair was undertaken—has come off worst of all. The generally accepted assertion that the three Great Powers, Russia among them, had proposed conditions of peace agreed to among themselves and which were less advantageous than those offered by France *is a scandal*, at all events as far as we are concerned, *for we knew absolutely nothing about it*. We have made a protest on the subject, following the example of Prussia. Prussia is now—and in my opinion most unjustly—being made the object of all manner of accusations by the rest of Germany in general and Austria in particular. Its position was very difficult, and I admit that there might have been greater steadiness in the conduct of its policy. None the less I do feel that it has rendered a real service to Europe at large by preventing the war from becoming general, which would inevitably have brought about the collapse of our whole social order; for then revolution, which was at Nap.'s heels, and before which he seems himself to have flinched, would have had no further bar, and must have broken out everywhere.

I have no illusions, I may say, about this lame peace that has just been concluded in a manner so unexpected by everyone. I regard the future as more than ever pregnant with trouble, and my confidence in our friend Nap. is seriously shaken. It remains to be seen what this strange but fortunate individual will think of next to occupy the ardent imagination of the French. I can quite understand how disagreeable you must have found your mission to him; and I also realize as a soldier how this unexpected peace must have come as a cruel disappointment to the brave Austrian army, whose one desire was to have its revenge, and for which, I repeat, I have kept all my old affection. And now, amen to politics.

We have been here at Hopsal since the 16th (28th) with the children, whom, thank God, we found all well. We are enjoying perfect quiet here, but unfortunately the weather is more like autumn than summer, after May and June having been perfectly glorious. We found a great many people here, including Julia's sister, Mme Stockelberg, whom I told that we were sending this courier and who intends to enclose a letter. Tell Louis that a company of the fourth Reserve Battalion of his regiment will be mounting guard for us while we are here.

I have nothing more to add except to tell you of our great desire to see you here again soon—if possible in time for Nixa's coming-of-age, that is to say, about September 8th (20th). It would make us very happy if you could come.

Now good-bye, my dear and excellent friend, or rather I will close with the hope of seeing you again soon, and with my most cordial love. Remember me to all the family and especially to Julia. I know how tremendously pleased she must have been to see you again. May God keep you happy and watch over all that are dear to us.

Your ever-devoted friend and brother,

ALEXANDER.

Letter from Prince Alexander of Hesse to Tsar Alexander II

[At the head stands the following note in the Tsar's own handwriting: "This letter is most interesting and shows once again what knaves we have to deal with. Send it back to me when you have read it."]

HEILIGENBERG, *May* 18, 1863.

My dear and well-beloved brother,

I feel it to be my duty to send you a line to tell you about two political conversations that I had in London and Paris (unsought by myself) with the English Ministers and with the Emperor Napoleon. I am, of course, not going to presume to tell you whether there is anything new in them, but my satisfaction in having put in a word for you and for the rights of Russia in Poland is too great for me to resist the temptation to tell you about it.

Our little niece Victoria Elisabeth was baptized at Windsor on April 14th (26th), and after the ceremony the Queen introduced various notabilities to me, amongst them her notorious Prime Minister, Lord Palmerston. The cunning old rascal first spoke to me upon the burning question of the day and produced the most inconceivable ideas on the subject of Poland. My very frank replies appeared to surprise him, and on the following day he wrote a note to the Queen to say that he wished Lord John Russell to make my acquaintance, and that he would send him to Windsor that evening to hear my opinion on Polish affairs. The Queen told me at the same time that "I should be doing her a great service if I endeavoured to pacify her Ministers and to commend coolness to them". I promised to do my best, but added that I dared not flatter myself that I should succeed in correcting the political ideas of two such seasoned statesmen. Lord [John] Russell did in fact come to see me, and we had a very long talk, of which this is the gist: *In his opinion it was absolutely essential for England to do something for the Poles.* He hoped that the Russian Cabinet would prove conciliatory, and feared that the Emperor of the French might have decided upon war even if he were obliged to enter upon it all by himself. In other words, it was a naïve admission that the English Cabinet had not quite made up its mind what it really did want you to do for the Poles.

Upon being pressed by me to explain himself more clearly on this point, Lord [John] Russell *finally spoke of a kingdom of Poland enjoying complete autonomy* under a *prince of the Russian imperial family*, with a national parliament, and a guarantee from the other Powers that neither the old Polish provinces in Russia, nor Galicia, nor Posen should ever aspire to form a part of the new kingdom. Since Lord [John] Russell himself spoke of this idea in the very vaguest terms, I felt that I might allow myself to call it *most dangerously Utopian*. I told him that none of the reasonable Poles saw any salvation for their party save in union with Russia, so long as that country would renounce its efforts to russify them. Since, however, the European revolutionaries had transferred their headquarters from Italy to Poland, and since France and England were encouraging the conspirators, it was very natural that the Poles should have begun to dream of a restoration of the great Polish Empire of olden times, which would nowadays be even more impossible than it was then. "Unless you are seeking a pretext for a renewal of hostilities with Russia, it should be easy for you to put a check on the Emperor Napoleon's ambitious plans; for I am very sure that he is never dreaming of the enterprise which you are attributing to him [to land 40,000 men by Riga, and make a demonstration on the Rhine by way of paralysing Prussia and the rest of Germany]. If you wish to do something of lasting worth for the Poles, you should begin by advising the insurgents to accept the amnesty offered by the Tsar A., and dispel their illusion that you are envisaging the same vast empire at which the most inflammatory spirits among the Poles insist upon aiming. You may force Russia into war by demanding impossibilities, but do not flatter yourself that you will have the Russian democrats on your side. As the first shot is fired, patriotism will awake in Russia, internal dissensions will be forgotten, and the Russians will arise as one man at the call of their emperor to repel the foreign invasion." I concluded by telling Lord John that the Austrian Cabinet was counting upon the English Ministers to ensure its not being driven beyond the limits of diplomatic action; that if Palmerston and Napoleon were mad enough to plunge Europe into a war—which could not this time remain localized as it did in 1859—that then only would Austria ask herself on whose side she was, *not being able a second time to remain neutral between Russia and the Western Powers*; and that England would be deceiving herself if she reckoned too surely upon a favourable decision on the part of the Vienna Cabinet.

When I got to Paris, where I was meeting my wife, I found that in spite of all my efforts to remain incognito the Emperor had heard of my arrival. So I allowed Prince Metternich to arrange a visit for me with the great man in the forenoon (morning dress), although after his ignoble trickery in 1859 I had promised myself never to meet him again save on the field of battle. What decided me was the hope that I might carry on the pacific rôle that I had begun in London—that I might be able, so to speak, to talk openly and freely in your name. The Emperor received me in the most friendly manner, and spoke to me for over an hour about the political situation. His unconstraint and frankness were so well assumed that I congratulated myself mentally upon its not being my first meeting with His Majesty—for he would infallibly have taken me in. As I was only speaking in my own name, I had plenty of elbow-room. Hence I permitted myself to express my opinion without the least disguise. When Napoleon asked me what the English Ministers thought of the Russian Cabinet's answer to the notes of the three Powers, I replied: "Prince Gortchakoff's note was exactly what they had expected, Sire, but they are afraid of being drawn into a war by Your Majesty which might prove disastrous for the whole of Europe." "Oh, these English! You have no idea how difficult my relations with them are. When we advised the Poles to trust to the generous intentions of the Tsar Alexander, the English forced us into war, offered us the left bank of the Rhine, suggested all manner of absurdities. And now that enthusiasm for the Polish cause has gained adherents in France and public opinion forces me to intervene on behalf of the Poles with Russia, the English accuse us of wanting war and complain that we are dragging them into it against their will! It is certainly not I who wish to draw the sword on Russia. My personal liking for the Tsar Alexander and the numerous interests which we have in common with Russia would make me regret very sorely the need for such a measure. But unfortunately Russia has allowed the favourable moment to pass for doing anything that would finally satisfy the Poles. At the time of our interview at Stuttgart I permitted myself to draw the Emperor Alexander's attention to the discontent of the Poles and to the necessity for providing a timely remedy. I fear the Tsar took my advice in bad part. Nevertheless it was dictated solely by a sincere care for his interests."

I said much the same thing to the Emperor Napoleon as I did to Palmerston and Russell, preaching *moderation above all things*, and, I must own, making the most of their mutual suspicion. "I do not know how far Your Majesty's confidence in Lord Palmerston's policy goes (Syria, Mexico!!), but it appeared to me that he would not be sorry to see Your Majesty engaged alone in a war against Russia and the German Confederation; reserving to himself the privilege of deciding on his own actions according to the issue of the war." When I expressed my astonishment at not having found any clear idea in London as to what they wanted the Russian Cabinet to do for the Poles, the Emperor admitted ingenuously that he was in exactly the same case. When I pressed him, he came out again with the theory of the independent Kingdom of Poland in much the same terms as Lord J. Russell had done, but even more vaguely. To which I replied: "The guarantee of the Great Powers did not help King Otto, and if this new Kingdom of Poland were to come into being, we should probably have a repetition of what took place in Italy. Your Majesty will remember that the stipulations of Villafranca said nothing at all about a Kingdom of Italy, which nevertheless was constituted in spite of the treaties and under the very noses of the Great Powers. In the same way an independent Kingdom of Poland would attract, or at all events would certainly do its level best to attract, to itself all the other provinces of the same nationality."

Referring to the fine speech of Craint-plomb [*Prince Napoleon*], the Emperor expressed himself in the strongest terms on the subject of this unqualifiable outburst on the part of his cousin. Which did not, I am convinced, prevent his having heartily approved the speech in question. Finally the Emperor assured me that he cherished the constant hope that his efforts would result in conferences at which we might all discuss things with one another without any fear that peace would be endangered. God grant that it may be so. What chiefly struck me in my conversations with these great people was the wrong ideas they have about Poland. The first chance comer from the Czas at Cracow knows as much about it as the men who determine the fate of England and France. The Emperor Napoleon, for example, could not get over his surprise when I told him that the majority of the civil servants in the Kingdom of Poland have been natives for a long time past. "Oh, indeed! Then I think it is a great pity that the Russian Government has not made more of this fact of which I was entirely ignorant. Altogether, I could wish that they had used a little more showmanship, if I may so express myself, in regard to Europe. The title of Viceroy, for instance, given to the Grand Duke Constantine would have made a better impression."

But I see that I am abusing your patience shamefully, and I really wonder whether you will have troubled to read to the end.

Unfortunately it is too late to send a letter to Marie by the same sure messenger, but please give her my fondest love. I will write to her in a day or two and tell her a few non-political details about my recent journey.

Julia sends you her affectionate homage, and so good-bye, my dear and well-beloved brother.

May God keep you. With best love,

Your faithful and devoted friend,

ALEXANDER.

Letter from the Tsar Alexander II to Prince Alexander of Hesse

TSARSKOE SELO, *June* 12 (24), 1863.

Having been awaiting an opportunity to send you a letter by a safe means, I have not been able until to-day to thank you myself, my dear and excellent friend, for your kind and interesting letter of May 6th (18th). Everything that you did and said was admirable. Your words were true and well considered, and you spoke like a faithful friend, who is as careful of our dignity as of our interests. I am cordially grateful to you for it; for I hardly know which causes me greater surprise—the ignorance of foreigners in regard to everything concerning Poland, or the heedlessness with which they raise questions of which they understand nothing whatever.

If truth has not lost all its force, your words must have impressed them, especially your opinion as to the probable policy of Austria. That is your own personal view, and I hope it may prove to be justified, for the crux of the present situation lies in Vienna. But I confess that I find it difficult to understand the policy they have pursued up to the present. I do not doubt that their chiefest desire is to preserve peace, and to prevent any crisis arising that would endanger the Conservative interests of Europe.

I realize that a Government must seek to guarantee itself in difficult times by prudent measures; but there are occasions when the danger is aggravated or even actually created by trying to compromise with it.

I leave it to the Emperor Francis Joseph to determine whether the present situation is not of this kind. It is easy to estimate the progress that has been made in the past ten years to the detriment of the Conservative Powers by the party which is working towards the disintegration of Europe. The present state of affairs can only be compared with that prevailing at the beginning of the century between 1804 and 1813. It is high time we stopped ourselves from slipping further down this slope, the direction of which no longer leaves any room for doubt. I was also very glad indeed to have the assurance of the Emperor Francis Joseph regarding the identity of his interests with ours in the Polish question. That is also my conviction, and I am delighted to find that he shares it. At all events, whatever may happen—whether it be thought better to provoke the crisis or merely to face it if it should burst upon us—a frank understanding appears to me to be essential. Uncertainty, friction, and doubt paralyse everything. These are the principal weapons of the party which seeks the dissolution of Europe. As far as I am concerned, you will have guessed what I have decided—I shall wait for the new proposals to be made to me, and I shall receive them in the same spirit of conciliation which caused me not to refuse to discuss with the Powers a question that I might very well have considered to be a purely domestic concern.

2 B

In recognizing a European side to the question, I am in no sense admitting any interference in the affairs of my country.

If any proposals of this kind should be put to me, my attitude is a very definite one: they would touch the honour of Russia, and I shall never compromise with that. You know how tremendously fiercely patriotism expresses itself here. My duty is plain. I am ready for anything—for conciliation if it is possible, for resistance if it is necessary. But I repeat, whatever may come, my chief desire is to have some light upon the reciprocal intentions and interests. Whatever may be the facts revealed by it, anything seems better to me than the dangerous obscurity that conceals traps and makes it impossible to distinguish good from bad.

It is essential that each one should know where he is walking and how far he is prepared to go. There is no problem which offers a more favourable opportunity than the present one for an agreement among the Powers directly concerned. The way is indicated by historical precedent. The treaties which put an end to the independent existence of Poland were signed by these three Courts; between them were concluded the negotiations in 1815 which determined the fate of the Duchy of Warsaw. Their interests in it are direct, immediate, and similar. An agreement between them would be the best guarantee of that universal peace in the name of which the other Powers justify their intervention.

If a discussion must take place, I would only agree to its being conducted privately between my Cabinet and the representatives of the various Great Powers accredited to St. Petersburg. In this form it might lead to the agreement with Austria and Prussia that I consider desirable. For my part, I should enter upon it with the best intentions, and should depend upon the other members of the conference doing likewise.

I am being absolutely frank with you, my dear Alexander, and I know that in giving you my whole confidence I am giving it to one who is both loyal and well-disposed. In any case, you may assure the Emperor Francis Joseph that I should be delighted to find myself of one mind with him in the appreciation of our common interests.

Since consulting Seanroni, who set our minds at rest regarding dear Marie's condition, her health has improved visibly, thank God, and she is planning to go down to the Crimea in a fortnight or three weeks' time, accompanied by her faithful Janten. If business does not prevent me, I hope to join her in August and to take a little holiday at our beloved Livadia.

Nixa left us yesterday for a long tour in the interior of Russia, which is to end up in the Crimea.

My best wishes to Julia and your dear children. And my love to yourself.

Your devoted and affectionate brother and friend,
ALEXANDER.

I enclose two of our new cards for you and Julia.

Letter from the Emperor Francis Joseph to Prince Alexander of Hesse

LAXENBURG, *July* 14, 1863.

Dear Cousin,

I must preface my cordial thanks for your letter of June 30th and the enclosure of that from the Tsar Alexander by asking your pardon for not replying until now. Pressure of business and the amount of time I have to spend in moving about between Vienna, the camp at Bruck, and Reichenau must be my excuse.

I regretted the more not seeing you in Kissingen as I had been looking forward with certainty to having that pleasure. You should know from experience that you never come amiss to my wife and myself, but that we are always glad to see you. You must not allow your modesty to get the better of you in this respect!

According to your wish, I was told by Count Apponyi and Prince Metternich of your interviews with the English Ministers and with the Emperor Napoleon, and I am happy to assure you that I agree on all points with what you said. Moreover, it appears to me a matter of course that you felt it to be your duty as a friend to inform your brother-in-law the Tsar Alexander of your discussions with the leaders of the policy of the Western Powers.

I need hardly say that I read the Tsar's reply which you sent me with all the interest evoked by my personal feelings for the Tsar Alexander and the importance of the questions touched on. The Tsar's letter states that the revolutionary party has won ever-increasing success during the last ten years, and that the obscurity and mistrust which govern all relationships are the chief breeding-ground for the strength of this party. These are matters of serious fact; and if I were to enter into the causes of the present evils I should feel obliged in my turn to state that if the Conservative principles had not been so lightly sacrificed upon many occasions, neither would so many dynasties have been dethroned, nor would so pernicious an instability have entered into the relations between the Powers.

I believe, nevertheless, that we must make up our minds to face the present situation; and I find it difficult to think of any peaceful way out of it, unless Russia is prepared to make great concessions. Anyone, therefore, who wishes the Tsar Alexander well should advise him very seriously to agree while there is yet time to the stated conditions, which touch neither Russia's title to her Polish possessions nor her honour, and thus to preserve his realm from devastating wars and Europe from incalculable upheavals.

Please convey my most respectful homage to the Princess and my cordial greetings to the Grand Duke.

I remain

Your most devoted cousin and friend,

FRANCIS JOSEPH.

Letter from the Tsar Alexander II to Prince Alexander of Bulgaria

DATED FROM ST. PETERSBURG, *December* 16 (28), 1879.

I heard with profound regret of the internal difficulties of which you spoke in your letter of November 27th, and of which the details were reported to me by Colonel Shepeleff.

It seems to me that great circumspection is called for. It must not be forgotten that the existing Constitution of Bulgaria was prepared according to the decrees of the Treaty of Berlin, by the representatives of the nation, to whom complete liberty of decision was expressly reserved by my orders. The Constitution has been recognized by all the Powers, as it emerged from their deliberations. Direct intervention on my part to abolish it and to grant a new one would expose me to the accusation of exercising illegal intervention in the affairs of the Principality. Hence it is not desirable to proceed by this means to remedy the difficulties that experience has shown to exist. On the other hand, a *coup d'état* effected by your authority in order to abolish the Constitution would furnish the pretext for an agitation dangerous to yourself and to the country.

Hence I think, as I wrote to you from Livadia, that some means of modifying an order of things that has led to so unhappy a state of affairs must be sought in legitimate channels and with the greatest possible discretion. As a beginning, it seems to me that you might order the election of a new Chamber according to the prescribed forms.

In the interval you might bring your personal influence to bear upon leading people in all the parties so as to induce in them a sounder appreciation of their duties and of the interests of the country.

If, as I hope and believe, the great majority of the nation is sinning chiefly through ignorance and inexperience, if the people have only been led astray by the influence of certain leaders, their minds can be worked upon, they can be made to understand the consequences of the path which they are being tempted to follow, and can be brought back to reason. Your Ministers, other right-thinking persons, and those of your functionaries who are invested with your confidence can usefully second you in this task and influence the electors, being careful, however, to avoid any illegitimate procedure, which might later furnish a pretext for the attacks of the evilly intentioned.

If in this propaganda for reason and for the public weal the authority of my name, my advice, and the sentiments of gratitude of the Bulgarian people to Russia can be of any assistance to you, you have full discretion to make use of them.

My sympathy for the Bulgarian nation and the self-sacrifice of my brave soldiers redeemed them from an abyss of misery and oppression. I have confided its destinies into its own hands. If on the morrow after this work that has been so laborious and that has cost so dear, the Bulgarians show themselves incapable of sustaining the liberty with which they have been endowed, if they reveal anarchical tendencies that render them unfit to form a normal social organism, they will ruin themselves irretrievably in the opinion of civilized Europe; they will justify the reproaches that have been levelled at them of lacking the qualities whereby the political vitality of a nation may be recognized; they will nullify our good intentions, alienate our sympathies, and oblige us willy-nilly to saddle them with the responsibility for their actions.

This is what is essential for them to know, and what you may tell them in my name.

If the Parliament that results from the new elections thus prepared for proves to be animated by a better spirit and provides a Government majority, you can try to proceed with them along constitutional lines and to arrive legally at a revision of those articles of the original pact which experience has proved to be unworkable.

If things turn out otherwise, you will, after this fair attempt which will attest in the eyes of Europe your wish to respect the laws, be justified in having recourse to stronger measures. You can dissolve the Chamber once the impossibility of governing with it has been proved, then appeal to the country by convoking a general meeting, at which you can propose a new constitution revised with the necessary maturity and in accordance with the experience that has been acquired.

It is not in the least my intention to insist upon your following this course. It may be that you will consider a fresh electoral effort to be useless or even detrimental in the present state of feeling, and that you will prefer to have immediate recourse to the extreme measure of the convocation of a general assembly. I leave you to judge of that for yourself. But I think that if the procedure which I have suggested is possible, it will be more judicious, and will give more time for reflection and persuasion. It is hardly necessary for me to tell you again that my best wishes are with you in this crisis that you are about to face, and that all the moral assistance which is at my disposal, whether in my own name or through my agents, is yours in place of a direct and avowed intervention, which would be damaging rather than helpful. I was sorry for the importance which was given to the matter of your title. In my opinion, your personal position and the great prestige which you have acquired in Europe should put you above such incidents. If the Bulgarian nation lets a few radical leaders lower its own dignity in the person of the Prince whom it has elected, it is doing wrong to nobody but itself, and there is reason to hope that sooner or later it will realize that.

Take a lofty view of the task which you have undertaken. Carry it out with the firmness and the perseverance which it demands, but at the same time with a feeling of indulgence for the unfortunate nation which was crushed by long oppression, and which has never had the chance of learning how to rule itself. The present fever must be allowed to die down and the necessary means to allay it must be used. Given time, everything will settle itself, and the conservative elements which are present in an agricultural people, though sorely tried, are industrious and resistant, and will come to the fore again in the end.

At all events, my most affectionate sympathy is with you in your work. You will gain the esteem of Europe, and, as I like to think, the gratitude of the nation to whose welfare you are devoting yourself. . . .

Letter from the Tsar Alexander III to Prince Alexander of Hesse

GATSHINA, *November* 10 (22), 1885.

My dear Uncle,

I have been obliged to resort to a measure with regard to Sandro that has cost me a good deal. I have done my best for him for the sake of the memory of my dear parents. I have been grieved to see the forces that have estranged him from us, and to see him succumb to the hostile influences that have led him to behave as the avowed enemy of Russia. I do not wish to pass judgment on the motives of his conduct. His memories and his feelings should have prevented his behaving so. I have been obliged to censure an undertaking carried out without my consent, by revolutionary means that were bound to set the East ablaze and to jeopardize the future of Bulgaria. Events have proved me to be only too right. The country is at war with the neighbours who should be its allies. The results of this act of folly are that the land is invaded, the capital threatened by the enemy, and the people ruined for years to come. There you have the consequences of this senseless freak. I foresaw them, but anything I could have done would only have aggravated the situation and endangered the peace of Europe. For the sake of our family connections I should have liked to spare him the results of the serious incidents he so rashly stirred up. But the manner in which he comported himself both in words and deeds towards the Russian officers in the service of Bulgaria has imposed upon me a duty towards my army. I have been obliged to fulfil it, but I have done so with the most profound regret. I hope you will realize the painful necessity with which I was confronted, and that it will not alter our relations.

I send you my best love, my dear uncle, and beg you to believe that my feelings for you are always the same.

Your affectionate
NEPHEW.

Letter from Prince Alexander of Hesse to the Tsar Alexander III

DARMSTADT, *November* 29, 1885.

My dear Nephew,

Thank you for writing to me. You owed me an explanation, for which I have up to the present waited in vain. The extraordinary action, which is unprecedented in any other European country, in which you have allowed yourself to indulge at my son's expense, has deeply wounded and offended me. You accuse him of having behaved in word and deed to the Russian officers in the Bulgarian service in such a manner that you felt obliged to dismiss him from the army as if he were a criminal. Permit me to inquire upon what this accusation is founded? Even supposing that the Prince were guilty, it would have been your duty as a sovereign to tell him of what he was accused, to appeal to his honour, to give him the chance of vindicating himself, to await his reply, and then to condemn him if he had deserved it. It appears to me that even a *Russian subject* might in a similar case have claimed to be heard first. In your own interests you should not have acted so hastily—all Europe is crying out against your arbitrary procedure. Your dear father did my son the honour to give him the rank of General in the Russian army, to appoint him chief of the battalion with whom he was among the first to cross the Danube in the cause of Russia. He decorated him with the Cross of St. George, won on the field of battle—and at a stroke of the pen you have undone it all. You have branded the Prince of Bulgaria with the seal of infamy before the whole of Russia, the whole Russian army, without having so much as tried to hold an inquiry into this unhappy affair. As soon as my son gets back from the front, I shall tell him what you say in your letter, and I shall require him to tell me the *truth* about the accusations which are made against him. I will inform you of his reply immediately. Upon learning of your decree through the newspapers, Alexander wired to me to ask what your reason could be for this unheard-of measure. I replied: "I know no more than you." Those are the only words we have exchanged upon this deplorable affair, but I am very sure that my son is incapable of having affronted brave officers, whom he would be much more inclined to commiserate and to regret. I cannot enter into details of all the other accusations that are contained in your letter; that would lead us too far afield. But that you should declare Alexander, and *him alone*, to be responsible for this "act of folly", the aim of which was hostile to Russia, is a grave injustice. I trust that M. de Giers has told you as he promised how conciliatory and frank my son was at the interview at Franzensbad. Alexander wrote and told me how pleased he was with the interview; they parted on such good terms that my son was already in hopes of a reconciliation between him and yourself. M. de Giers knows very well that the revolution came as a complete surprise to Alexander, and that unless he had cravenly deserted his country he could not have acted otherwise. *I should have done the same in his place,* and many other people have said so too. My son has never for a day ceased to bless the hallowed memory of your dear father, his benefactor and that of Bulgaria. As your mother's brother I felt obliged to speak quite frankly to you. It depends entirely upon you to give me the opportunity to get back again on to the good terms on which we used to be. I sincerely hope that it may come to be so.

Your affectionate uncle,

A.

Letter from Queen Victoria to the German Crown Princess

Osborne, *January* 19, 1887

I think Fritz's conversation with Count Pierre Schouwaloff [Schuvaloff] most interesting and cannot help believing that something might be made out of it.

(1) The Czar admits that he has been deceived as to the feelings of the Bulgarians.

(2) That no Prince can be found, and the Czar cares little for it.

(3) That some temporary arrangement should be made like what I think I told you of—some governor who the Powers would place there. (This is Sandro's own recommendation, and we are trying to urge it as the only way for the present to keep peace and to avoid a new Prince.)

(4) Giers says the best thing would be to restore Sandro!

Now in answer to the first: If the Czar saw that he was misinformed and that the people love their Prince—why not say so and let them have him? The Czar is not obliged to *love* him, or to see him, but merely to behave *fairly* and honestly to him, not to allow undermining intrigues—and to try and be on friendly terms, which I am sure Sandro himself would wish to be. And not to interfere with his independence. Someone could surely be found who could act as *mediator* in this proposal. Why not Fritz?

The two other points (2 and 4) all resolve themselves with the first, viz. no Prince can be found, and Giers thinks it best to replace Sandro.

The third point, however, "a temporary arrangement", ought to precede this and all efforts ought to be directed to obtain this. I feel convinced that this might yet be brought about, and I am sure no one could help more than dear Fritz himself. We believe Austria would agree to the temporary arrangement.

V.R.I.

It is absolutely necessary that there should first be a temporary arrangement which might last a year or so.

Telegram from Prince Bismarck to Prince Alexander of Hesse

BERLIN, *September* 3 (1886). 9.54 p.m.

I am prepared to act in the sense of the wishes graciously communicated to me; and am glad to have already had an opportunity to begin in a conversation to-day, the tone of which gives me reason to hope for success.

Letter from the German Crown Prince to Queen Victoria

BERLIN, *January* 22, 1887.

The observations of Count Peter Shuvaloff in his interview with me, of which I recently sent you a note, are the complete antithesis of anything one is accustomed to hear from a man of his views. Hence it would appear that he was playing the part of *agent provocateur*, in order to find out my intentions by misleading me as to his own sentiments regarding Prince A[lexander]. Shuvaloff, however, must have been disappointed, for I only confirmed what the Tsar has known for a long time past, while the Count has exposed himself badly and given proof of his insincerity. He parades his dislike of Prince A. before the Russians, for he expressed himself as quite delighted at the Embassy when he heard that the Prince had been passed over for military advancement by us, whereas when he spoke to me he inexplicably censured the Prussians for depriving him of his title as sovereign. If Shuvaloff ascribes to Giers the sentiment that "in his private opinion the best means of settling the Bulgarian crisis would be to restore Prince A.", it can only be supposed that he does so in order still further to undermine Giers's position. Shuvaloff said that if his advice were asked, he would recommend that a new Council of Regents should be established composed of men of all parties, and that this should remain in power until further notice. If the man were sincere there would be much to be said for him, and he would be a proof that the Russians are moderating their demands. Nevertheless a Council of Regents of this description would be impossible, at all events for a length of time. No coalition composed of such heterogeneous elements has ever been able to maintain itself; and in the present case the natural consequence would be that the pro-Russian members of the Regency would in a very short time gain the upper hand, and would probably oust the rest by intrigues and by all manner of ignoble practices. If the Russians adopt this plan, and also seek to make the Sultan agree to it—and he is actually already beginning to work along these lines—it will be done solely in the Russian interests. They hope by this means to regain their former influence in Bulgaria without saddling themselves with the odium of occupying the country. Russia is afraid of what the Austrians might do if she went into Bulgaria; it would inevitably lead to a conflict, of which she cannot foresee the end. A procedure such as that referred to above would achieve the same result without giving the Austrians any excuse for making an armed protest against injury to their interests. That the Russians do not like the idea of burning their fingers over Bulgaria is shown by what happened in Constantinople. The Russian Ambassador there said that if there were any serious move towards restoring Prince A. in Sofia, Turkey would have to intervene in Bulgaria to prevent it! So Russia was calling for help upon that very Turkey which it had recently pushed out of Bulgaria as the oppressor of its Slav brethren! Obviously the Russians liked the idea of Turkey's pulling the chestnuts out of the fire for them. Russia will never agree to the re-election of Prince A. . . . Even if a temporary agreement were to be reached and the Russians were apparently to declare themselves satisfied with a minimum of their requirements, the situation would in a very short time be made untenable again by intrigues. And the Russians are masters of intrigue; they will stop at nothing to gain their ends. *Just as they once plotted against the life of Prince A., so they will now plot against the liberty of Bulgaria. And if ever circumstances took Prince A. back there, it could only be if Russia were conquered and the Prince were to assume the royal crown of Bulgaria against their will.* Not until he has the upper hand will he be able to assert himself there and defy Russia. Unfortunately the office of mediator is a thankless one in so confused a situation and could lead to no profitable result.

NOTES

The alternative dates that are given in some instances are owing to the difference between the Russian calendar (old style) and that in use in the rest of Europe—a matter of twelve days.

The diary of Prince Alexander of Hesse, and all letters written to him, as well as those to and from the Tsarina Marie, are, unless otherwise stated, preserved in the archives of the Erbach-Schönberg family.

1. The history of Prince Alexander of Hesse's youth is derived mainly from the journal kept by his tutor, Captain Frey, from December 19, 1829, to August 27, 1840. There are fourteen volumes of it, as well as appendices. It lies in the Erbach Archives.
2. Of Prince Alexander's two elder living brothers, the first, born June 9, 1806, later became the Grand Duke Louis III. The second, Charles, was born on April 23, 1809. The title "By Rhine" was assumed in 1816, when the territories of the various principalities were redistributed, and the Grand Duchy was assigned a small piece of land on either side of the Rhine in compensation for some that had been taken away.
3. Count Woyna to Prince Metternich. St. Petersburg, November 24 (December 6), 1841. Vienna State Archives.
4. Duke Max of Leuchtenberg was the son of the daughter of the King of Bavaria and Napoleon I's stepson, Eugène de Beauharnais, whom the King created Duke of Leuchtenberg.
5. Vienna State Archives.
6. Count Woyna to Prince Metternich. February 23 (March 7), 1842. Vienna State Archives.
7. Vienna State Archives.
8. Tsar Nicholas I to Emperor Ferdinand. July 5, 1842. Vienna State Archives.
9. The stories of the Tsar Nicholas's many attempts to find a husband for his daughter Olga are taken from the Tsar's own incredibly frank statements to Count Ficquelmont, who in return reported the imperial confidences to Prince Metternich. October 3, 1843. Vienna State Archives.
10. June 2, 1840. Vienna State Archives.
11. According to the Tsar's story to Count Ficquelmont. Ficquelmont to Metternich. Vienna, October 3, 1843. Vienna State Archives.
12. Ficquelmont to Metternich. July 21, 1840. Vienna State Archives.
13. Count Colloredo to Metternich. August 5, 1843. Vienna State Archives.
14. Metternich to Ficquelmont. September 13, 1843. Vienna State Archives.

15. Metternich to Ficquelmont. September 16, 1843. Vienna State Archives.
16. Cf. Viktor Bibl, *Der Zerfall Oesterreichs*, Vienna, 1922, Vol. I, pp. 215 *et seq.*
17. Metternich to Ficquelmont. Vienna, September 13, 1843. Vienna State Archives.
18. Archduke Louis to Metternich. February 22, 1844. Vienna State Archives. From information given by Count Orloff to the Archduke.
19. Warsaw, September 23, 1843 (two dispatches), and October 3, 1843 (four dispatches). Vienna State Archives.
20. Metternich's instructions to Count Lützow in Rome. March 3, 1844. Vienna State Archives.
21. January 20, 1844. Vienna State Archives.
22. January 21, 1844. Vienna State Archives.
23. Pressburg, February 21, 1844. Vienna State Archives.
24. Vienna State Archives.
25. February 17, 1844. Vienna State Archives.
26. Archduke Louis to Metternich. February 22, 1844. Vienna State Archives.
27. These "expositions" were voluminous documents, which showed clearly that Metternich did not wish the marriage to take place, wherefore he was raising every possible complication and difficulty. Vienna State Archives.
28. Archduke Louis to Metternich. February 22, 1844. Vienna State Archives.
29. March 7, 1844. Vienna State Archives.
30. Count Lützow to Metternich. March 23, 1844. Vienna State Archives.
31. Count Colloredo to Metternich. April 13, 1845. Vienna State Archives.
32. Fort Gersel-Aull, July 21 (August 2), 1845. Hesse Archives.
33. Cardinal Lambruschini to Nuncio Alfieri. Rome, February 4, 1845. Vienna State Archives.
34. Count Lützow to Metternich. June 29, 1845. Vienna State Archives.
35. Cf. also Colloredo to Metternich. Private letter, St. Petersburg, March 3, 1846. Vienna State Archives.
36. Metternich on his wife's interview with the Tsar on December 31, 1845. See appendix to his dispatch to Lützow in Rome, January 3, 1846. Vienna State Archives.
37. Count Esterházy to Metternich. January 16 (28) and January 22 (February 3), 1846. Vienna State Archives.
38. Count Colloredo to Prince Metternich. St. Petersburg, March 3, 1846. Vienna State Archives.
39. Archduke Louis to Metternich. March 13, 1846.
40. May be gathered from a private letter from Metternich to Colloredo. January 18, 1847. Vienna State Archives.
41. Colloredo to Metternich. May 17 (29), 1847. Vienna State Archives.
42. August 28, 1847. Vienna State Archives.
43. Count Franz Thun to Ficquelmont. March 24 (April 5), 1848. Vienna State Archives.
44. Baron von Lebzeltern to the Vienna State Chancellery, March 9 (21), 1848.
45. Thun to Ficquelmont. March 24 (April 5), 1848. Vienna State Archives.

46. Frederick, Burgrave, and Count zu Dohna-Schlobitten, Prussian General, 1784–1859. Entered the Russian service in 1812 and helped to conclude the Convention of Taurage. Returned to the Prussian service in 1815. Married Scharnhorst's daughter. Retired in 1854 with the rank of Field-Marshal.
47. Vienna State Archives.
48. December 22, 1848 (January 3, 1849). Vienna State Archives.
49. Draft, Olmütz, May 1, 1849. Vienna State Archives.
50. April 28 (May 10), 1849. Vienna State Archives.
51. In this part, and only here, numerous erasures have been made in the diary, and occasionally whole pages have been cut out. The changes have been made in the handwriting of the Princess Marie Erbach—the eldest daughter of Prince Alexander—and of the Countess Julia Hauke, later his wife.
52. Vienna State Archives. Cf. also Joseph Redlich, *Kaiser Franz Joseph von Oesterreich*, Berlin, 1928, pp. 124 *et seq.*
53. Vienna State Archives. Cf. also Redlich, *op. cit.*, p. 152.
54. Count Mensdorff to Count Buol. July 21 (August 2), 1852. Vienna State Archives.
55. Tsar Nicholas to Emperor Francis Joseph. January 13, 1853. Vienna State Archives.
56. Draft, June 16, 1853. Vienna State Archives.
57. November 14 (26), 1853. Vienna State Archives.
58. Vienna State Archives.
59. Vienna State Archives.
60. Vienna State Archives.
61. April 13, 1854. Erbach Archives.
62. Tsarskoe Selo, May 12 (24), 1854. Erbach Archives.
63. Peterhof, July 10 (22), 1854. Erbach Archives.
64. Tsarskoe Selo, September 11 (23), 1854. Erbach Archives.
65. December 20, 1854 (January 1, 1855). Erbach Archives.
66. Cf. Martin Mandt, *Ein deutscher Arzt am Hofe Kaiser Nikolaus I von Russland*, Munich, 1923, pp. 37 *et seq.*
67. cf. C. de Cardonne, *Alexandre II*, Paris, 1883.
68. St. Petersburg, March 5 (17), 1855. Vienna State Archives.
69. Cf. Dr. Franz Schnürer, *Briefe Kaiser Franz Josephs an seine Mutter, 1838–1872*, Munich, 1930, p. 232.
70. Schnürer, *op. cit.*, p. 179.
71. Schnürer, *op. cit.*, p. 259.
72. Verona, February 6, 1857. Erbach Archives.
73. Cf. E. von Glaise-Horstenau, *Franz Joseph's Weggefährte*, Vienna, 1930.
74. Schnürer, *op. cit.*, p. 264.
75. Erbach Archives.
76. Only Prince Alexander's notes upon the meetings have been used here. For further details, cf. Roux, *Alexandre II, Gortchakoff et Napoléon III*, Paris, 1913, pp. 211 *et seq.*
77. Alexander of Hesse to Baron von Drachenfels in Vienna. Milan, February 14, 1858. Erbach Archives.
78. Cf. Ernesto Artom, *L'opera politica del senatore E.A. nel risorgimento italiano*, Bologna, 1906, p. 359.
79. cf. Egon Corti, *Die Trockene Trunkenheit, Ursprung, Kampf und Triumph des Rauchens*, pp. 268 *et seq.*

80. Cf. the three publications of the Austrian General Staff. Also Konrad Molinski, *Dissertationen, Gyulai's Verhalten bei der Eröffnung des lombardischen Krieges, 1859*, Berlin, 1917.
81. June 11, 1859. Bismarck's collected works, Vol. III, p. 52 (German edition).
82. Schnürer, *op. cit.*, p. 214.
83. The correspondence of Napoleon III with the Emperor Francis Joseph is in the Vienna State Archives, and was published by Senator Francesco Salato for the first time in the *Nuova Antologia*, Vol. CCXXXII, Series VI, 16 dicembre, p. 289.
84. Vienna State Archives.
85. The original note, undated, is preserved in the Erbach Archives.
86. Published in Alfredo Comandini, *Il Principe Napoleone nel risorgimento italiano*, Milan, 1922, pp. 281 *et seq.*
87. The description of the quarrel between Cavour and the King of Piedmont is based upon the information of Isaac Artom and Carlo Arrivabene, as well as upon that of the *Daily News* correspondent. It is not to be taken as incontestable, since the notes of those who actually took part in the interview have not hitherto been available for publication. Cf. also Cilibrizzi, *Storia d'Italia*, Vol. I, p. 248. And Alfredo Panzini, *Il 18 da Plombières a Villafranca*, pp. 364 *et seq.*
88. Ludwig Kossuth, *Meine Schriften aus der Emigration*, Pressburg, Leipzig, 1880, Vol. I, pp. 518 *et seq.*
89. Cf. Engel-Jánosi, *Graf Rechberg*, Berlin, Munich, 1927, pp. 57 *et seq.*
90. Cf. Engel-Jánosi, *op. cit.*, p. 55, where a story is told of the Prince Regent of Prussia (afterwards William I) saying to the painter Gudin that he only wanted peace and had no intention of coming to Austria's assistance.
91. Tsarskoe Selo, May 6 (18), 1860. Erbach Archives.
92. Peterhof, July 12 (24), 1860. Erbach Archives.
93. Schnürer, *op. cit.*, p. 294.
94. Louis of Hesse, 1837–92. Grand Duke from 1877 on. His mother was Princess Elisabeth of Prussia. Grand Duke Louis III was childless.
95. On February 13, 1861, the King and Queen of Naples-Sicily surrendered at the fort of Gaeta, the news of which was received with horror at the Conservative courts as a new revolutionary success.
96. Prince Alfred, second son of Queen Victoria, 1844–1900. Duke of, Saxe-Coburg Gotha from 1893 until his death.
97. Cf. Engel-Jánosi, *op. cit.*, pp. 102 *et seq.*
98. The Tsarevitch Nicholas, born September, 20, 1843, died April 24, 1865.
99. Cf. Gottfried von Boehm, *Ludwig II, König von Bayern*, Berlin, 1922, p. 378.
100. Copies of these telegrams are preserved in the Vienna State Archives. Most are also published in Bismarck's collected works.
101. A son of the Princess Marie, daughter of the Elector of Hesse, and Prince William of Hesse-Philippstal-Barchfeld.
102. Berlin Foreign Office Archives.
103. Berlin Foreign Office Archives.
104. Berlin Foreign Office Archives.
105. March 29, 1866. Berlin Foreign Office Archives.
106. Berlin Foreign Office Archives.
107. April 17(?), 1866. Berlin Foreign Office Archives.

108. Vienna, April 7, 1866. From the copy enclosed by the Tsar Alexander II in his letter to King William on April 21, 1866. Berlin Foreign Office Archives.

109. Report of General von Schweinitz to Bismarck, April 21, 1866. Berlin Foreign Office Archives.

110. Berlin Foreign Office Archives.

111. King William of Prussia to Tsar Alexander II, April 26, 1866. These sentences in Bismarck's own handwriting. Berlin Foreign Office Archives.

112. Baron Henry von Gagern, 1799–1880. Avowedly Pan-German sympathies from 1862 onwards. Hessian Minister in Vienna, 1864–72. His brother Maximilian was at the same time chief of a department in the Austrian Foreign Office.

113. Copy among the papers of Alexander of Hesse. Erbach Archives.

114. Cf. Friedjung, *Der Kampf um die Vorherrschaft in Deutschland, 1859–1866*, Vol. II, p. 212.

115. Darmstadt, May 18, 1866 (despatched May 19th). Draft in the Erbach Archives.

116. Vienna State Archives.

117. Berlin Foreign Office Archives.

118. Three Counts Cabinet: Belcredi, Larisch, Mensdorff.

119. Erbach Archives.

120. Lieutenant-General Count Huyn, repeating a dispatch from Count Crenneville to Meiningen, July 2, 1866, 7.30 p.m. Erbach Archives.

121. Berlin Foreign Office Archives.

122. Berlin Foreign Office Archives.

123. Tsar Alexander II to King William of Prussia. Peterhof, July 31 (August 12), 1866. Berlin Foreign Office Archives.

124. Berlin Foreign Office Archives.

125. Private letter from General von Schweinitz to von Thile. Tsarskoe Selo, October 17, 1866. Berlin Foreign Office Archives.

126. Count Philip von Brunnow, 1797–1875. Russian diplomatist of German extraction. At that time ambassador in London.

127. Cf. Boehm, *op. cit.*, p. 369.

128. Cf. Boehm, *op. cit.*, p. 380.

129. Vienna State Archives.

130. Count Chotek to Beust. July 28 (August 9), 1870. Vienna State Archives.

131. Cf. Bismarck, *Gedanken und Erinnerungen*, popular edition, Vol. II, p. 57. Bismarck refers to the King's wishes, which according to this were not so far-reaching. See also the King's marginal note upon Bismarck's report of July 24, 1866, in his collected works, No. 498, in which the King complains that he is obliged to renounce indemnities and territorial gain in order not to endanger the main object.

132. Cf. *Die grosse Politik*, Vol. I, p. 206.

133. Wertheimer, *Julius Andrássy*, Vol. II, p. 69, says that the Archduke Albrecht was an excellent soldier, but that as a politician he was carried away by ideas—such as friendship with Russia as a safeguard for the future—which would not have conduced to the greatness of Austria, for which he genuinely wished. Wertheimer was to live to see his own words falsified by the facts, and all three empires perish for want of unity in the World War.

134. Cf. Bismarck, *Gedanken und Erinnerungen*, Chap. XXVI, under the title "Intrigues".
135. Cf. Monypeny and Buckle, *Life of Disraeli*, Vol. V, Chap. XI, and Ponsonby, *Letters of the Empress Frederick*.
136. Cf. *Letters of Queen Victoria*.
137. Cf. *Letters of Queen Victoria*.
138. Cf. *Die grosse Politik*, Vol. II, p. 44.
139. Cf. *Die grosse Politik*, Vol. II, p. 85.
140. Cf. *Die grosse Politik*, Vol. II, p. 87.
141. *Letters of Queen Victoria*.
142. Felix Rachfahl, *Deutschland und die Weltpolitik, 1871–1914*, Stuttgart, 1923, Vol. I, p. 118.
143. See *Die grosse Politik*, Vol. II, pp. 111 *et seq.*, for the text of this convention and that of the supplementary one.
144. Cf. *Letters of Queen Victoria*, July 15, 1877.
145. Cf. *Letters of Queen Victoria*, July 15, 1877.
146. Prince Henry VII of Reuss to Bismarck. Bujukdere, July 10, 1877. *Die grosse Politik*, Vol. II, p. 158.
147. Queen Victoria to the Crown Prince of Prussia, July 20, 1877.
148. Count Julius Andrássy, junior. Cf. *Diplomatie und Weltkrieg*, Berlin, 1920, p. 19.
149. Cf. *Letters of Queen Victoria*, especially one on December 1877.
150. Cf. *Letters of the Empress Frederick*, also in *Letters of Queen Victoria*.
151. *Letters of the Empress Frederick*.
152. Berlin Foreign Office Archives.
153. From the copy sent to Berlin. Berlin Foreign Office Archives.
154. Vienna State Archives.
155. Berlin Foreign Office Archives.
156. Rachfahl, *op. cit.*, p. 250.
157. *Letters of Queen Victoria*.
158. *Letters of Queen Victoria*.
159. *Letters of Queen Victoria*.
160. *Letters of Queen Victoria*. Entry in her diary on June 8, 1879.
161. *Letters of Queen Victoria*. Letter to Salisbury, June 10, and to Beaconsfield, June 26, 1879.
162. *Die grosse Politik*, Vol. III, p. 63.
163. *Die grosse Politik*, Vol. II, p. 14.
164. Prince Bismarck to the Emperor William. September 5, 1879. Berlin Foreign Office Archives.
165. Cf. Vera Figner, *Das Attentat auf den Zaren*. Berlin, 1926, pp. 32 *et seq.*
166. From a copy of the letter enclosed in the one written to Prince Alexander of Hesse on January 20 (February 1), 1881. Erbach Archives.
167. Cf. Victor Laferté, *Alexandre II. Détails sur sa vie intime et sa mort*, 1882.
168. William I to Francis Joseph. January 16, 1881. *Die grosse Politik*, Vol. III, p. 161.
169. Prince Alexander of Bulgaria to Prince Alexander of Hesse. Sofia, January 28 (February 9), 1882. Erbach Archives.
170. Copy in the Hartenau Archives.
171. Cf. Egon Corti, *Alexander of Battenberg*. Vienna, 1920, pp. 163 *et seq.*
172. Cf. *Denkwürdigkeiten des Generalfeldmarschalls Alfred, Grafen von Waldersee*, Vol. I, pp. 240, 241.

173. Cf. *Denkwürdigkeiten des Botschafters General von Schweinitz*, Berlin, 1927, Vol. II, pp. 271 *et seq.*
174. Biegeleben to Kálnoky. London, July 21, 1887. From personal information given by Radolinsky. Vienna State Archives.
175. Emperor William II, *My Early Life, 1859–1888.*
176. *Die grosse Politik*, Vol. III, p. 341.
177. Berlin Foreign Office Archives.
178. *Die grosse Politik*, Vol. III, pp. 342 *et seq.*
179. *Die grosse Politik*, Vol. III, p. 345.
180. Cf. Nicholas Sokoloff, *Enquête judiciaire sur l'assassinat de la famille impériale russe*, Paris, 1924.
181. Cf. Corti, *op. cit.*, pp. 181 *et seq.*, where a facsimile of the letter is given.
182. Alexander of Battenberg to Alexander of Hesse. Copy in the handwriting of Henry of Battenberg. No date. Hartenau Archives.
183. cf. Corti, *op. cit.*, p. 183.
184. Hartenau Archives.
185. *Letters of Queen Victoria.*
186. *Letters of Queen Victoria.*
187. *Die grosse Politik*, Vol. V, p. 21.
188. Copy in the Hartenau Archives.
189. Copy in the Hartenau Archives.
190. Corti, *op. cit.*, pp. 210 *et seq.*
191. *Letters of the Empress Frederick.* Crown Princess Victoria to Lady Ponsonby. December 5, 1885.
192. Copy in the Hartenau Archives.
193. Corti, *op. cit.*, p. 239.
194. Copy in the Hartenau Archives.
195. Copy in the Hartenau Archives.
196. Copy in the Hartenau Archives.
197. Copy in the Hartenau Archives.
198. Copy in the Hartenau Archives.
199. *Die grosse Politik*, Vol. V, p. 55.
200. *Letters of the Empress Frederick.* Crown Princess Victoria to Queen Victoria. August 11, 1886.
201. Cf. William II, *My Early Life.*
202. Copy in the Hartenau Archives.
203. Copy in the Hartenau Archives.
204. Copy in the Hartenau Archives.
205. *Letters of Queen Victoria.*
206. Corti, *op. cit.*, p. 226. Letter from Queen Victoria on September 4, 1886.
207. *Letters of Queen Victoria.* The Queen to Lord Salisbury. August 25, 1886.
208. Copy in the Hartenau Archives.
209. Copy in the Hartenau Archives.
210. Copy in the Hartenau Archives.
211. *Letters of Queen Victoria.*
212. Vienna State Archives.
213. Copy in the Hartenau Archives.
214. Copy in the Hartenau Archives.
215. *Letters of Queen Victoria.*
216. Cf. *Die grosse Politik.* Private report of Bismarck's. September 30, 1886.
217. *Die grosse Politik*, Vol. V, p. 53.
218. *Die grosse Politik*, Vol. V, p. 66.

219. Copy in the Hartenau Archives.
220. *Letters of Queen Victoria.*
221. *Die grosse Politik*, Vol. V, p. 164.
222. Copy in the Hartenau Archives.
223. *Die grosse Politik*, Vol. V, p. 165.
224. *Letters of Queen Victoria.* Cf. also Dr. Alfred Francis Pribram, *Die politischen Geheimverträge Oesterreich-Ungarns, 1879–1914*, Vienna, 1920, pp. 37 *et seq.*
225. Heinz von Truetzschler, *Bismarck und die Kriegsgefahr des Jahres 1887*, pp. 91 *et seq.* The actual facts of Langenbuch's mission have frequently been called in question. Hence they have been very carefully verified by the present author, who has been greatly helped in his work by the diary of Prince Alexander of Hesse, and the private papers of Prince Henry of Battenberg. It is nowhere stated that Dr. Langenbuch's mission was inspired solely by the Crown Princess, and had nothing to do with Bismarck. But it seems very possible, indeed probable. If this is so, then the conclusions drawn by Prince Alexander of Battenberg himself, and thus also by the present author in his book, *Alexander von Battenberg*, are wrong, and the "straight line" of Bismarck's policy is restored. The fact of Langenbuch's visit, however, and of all that was said in the course of it, remains entirely true. The Crown Princess appears to have instructed Langenbuch not to mention her as the instigator of the visit, but—without actually saying so—to allow it to be understood that it had been Bismarck's wish. Alexander of Battenberg and all his family believed this to be the case. (See the letter of the Prince's secretary to K. Stoiloff, written from Darmstadt on April 11, 1887.)
226. Cf. Corti, *op. cit.*, p. 300.
227. Lucius von Ballhausen, *Bismarckerinnerungen*, Stuttgart, 1920, p. 375.
228. Ballhausen, *op. cit.*, p. 377.
229. Cf. Corti, *op. cit.*, p. 295, where, owing to an error on the part of the Prince's secretary, Menges, the words are said to have been spoken on the occasion of Langenbuch's first visit.
230. Princess Marie zu Erbach-Schönhausen, *Aus stiller und bewegter Zeit*, Vol. I, p. 158.
231. Radolinsky to Biegeleben. Reported in Biegeleben's dispatch to Kálnoky of July 21, 1887. Vienna State Archives. Prince Alexander's diary says nothing about the renunciation of the marriage. Sandro seems only to have told him about the interview in very general terms.
232. Bismarck, *Gedanken und Erinnerungen*, Chap. XXXIII.
233. Cf. Corti, *op. cit.*, p. 315.
234. Gagliardi, *Bismarck's Entlassung*, Tübingen, 1927, pp. 263 *et seq.* From documents in Karlsruhe.
235. Gagliardi, *op. cit.*, p. 264.
236. *Die grosse Politik*, Vol. V, p. 282.
237. *Die grosse Politik*, Vol. VI, p. 281.
238. *Die grosse Politik*, Vol. VI, p. 291.
239. Corti, *op. cit.*, p. 328.
240. Gagliardi, *op. cit.*, p. 269.
241. Gagliardi, *op. cit.*, p. 270.
242. Corti, *op. cit.*, p. 330.
243. Gagliardi, *op. cit.*, p. 262. *Gespräche*, Vol. II, p. 611.

244. *Denkwürdigkeiten des Fürsten Chlodwig zu Hohenlohe-Schillingsfürst*, Vol. II, p. 435.
245. *Letters of the Empress Frederick.*
246. *Letters of the Empress Frederick.*
247. Sir Edward Malet to Lord Salisbury. April 28, 1888. *Letters of the Empress Frederick.*
248. *Letters of the Empress Frederick.*
249. *Letters of the Empress Frederick.*
250. Copy in the Hartenau Archives.
251. Dispatch from Herbert Bismarck. July 25, 1888. *Die grosse Politik*, Vol. VI, pp. 326 *et seq.*
252. *Letters of the Empress Frederick.*

INDEX